Adventures in Phenomenology

“Self & Bandon” photograph by Nathan Wirth; courtesy of Nathan Wirth.

Adventures in Phenomenology

Gaston Bachelard

Edited by

Eileen Rizo-Patron

with

Edward S. Casey and Jason M. Wirth

SUNY PRESS

SUNY series in Contemporary French Thought

David Pettigrew and François Raffoul, editors

Published by State University of New York Press, Albany

Printed in the United States of America

For information, contact State University of New York Press, Albany, NY
www.sunypress.edu

Production, Diane Ganeles
Marketing, Kate R. Seburyamo

Library of Congress Cataloging-in-Publication Data

Names: Rizo-Patron, Eileen, editor. | Casey, Edward S., 1939– editor. | Wirth, Jason M., 1963– editor.
Title: Adventures in phenomenology : Gaston Bachelard / edited by Eileen Rizo-Patron with Edward S. Casey and Jason M. Wirth.
Description: Albany, NY : State University of New York, 2017. | Series: SUNY series in contemporary French thought | Includes bibliographical references and index.
Identifiers: LCCN 2016040640 (print) | LCCN 2016042265 (ebook) | ISBN 9781438466057 (hardcover : alk. paper) | ISBN 9781438466064 (pbk. : alk. paper) | ISBN 9781438466071 (ebook)
Subjects: LCSH: Bachelard, Gaston, 1884–1962.
Classification: LCC B2430.B254 A38 2017 (print) | LCC B2430.B254 (ebook) | DDC 194—dc23
LC record available at https://lccn.loc.gov/2016040640

10 9 8 7 6 5 4 3 2 1

Contents

Part 2
Adventures in Methodology

Part 3
Adventures in Language

Part 4
Adventures in Alterity

Preface

Edward S. Casey, Eileen Rizo-Patron,
and Jason M. Wirth

> In this work we are engaging new arguments . . . in order to respond to our properly philosophical function. Our attempt is to reach the zone where the mind thinks hesitatingly, where it risks itself outside of its own experience, and lays itself open to controversy.
>
> —Bachelard, *The Philosophy of No*

Like Schelling before him and Deleuze and Guattari after him, Gaston Bachelard made major philosophical contributions to the advancement of science and the arts and to our ongoing inquiry into their wellsprings. Committed only to the school of constant learning and critical adventure, he remained an autonomous thinker who forged his own way—a way that has captivated generations of readers who find his apposite and eloquent words immensely attractive, indeed irresistible. He did this by consistently submitting his manner of thinking and writing to the precise matter at hand. His nimble and incisive approach yielded striking insights into questions of time, imagination, language, otherness, and negation in ways that continue to have momentous repercussions.

In addition to being a mathematician and laboratory-trained scientist whose influential work in the philosophy of science is still being absorbed, Bachelard was one of the most innovative thinkers of the experience of poetic creativity. His approaches to literature and the arts by way of the material elements and reverie awakened long-buried modes of thinking that have inspired literary critics, poets, and artists alike. Alternating between the expansive-contractive movements of artistic imagination and scientific conceptualization throughout his career, Bachelard refused all static systems, considering his work unfinished and indeed unfinishable—an open invitation to his students and readers to continue down pathways that he helped to stake out.

It is our contention as editors of this volume that Bachelard's extraordinary body of work, unduly neglected by the English-language reception of continental philosophy in recent decades, exhibits a capacity to speak to the full complexity and wider reaches of human thinking. The chapters in this volume are, thus, all intended as exercises at the cutting edge of Bachelard's phenomenological adventures.

November 2015

Acknowledgments

The editors wish to express their gratitude to all the publishers and individuals who gave kind permission to reprint previously published work in revised form in this volume.

Chapter 1: Edward S. Casey, "The Difference an Instant Makes: Bachelard's Brilliant Breakthrough" is an updated, adapted, and revised version of an essay first published in *Philosophy Today* 47 (SPEP Supplement 2003): 118–23. Reproduced with permission.

Chapter 2: Jean-François Perraudin, "Bachelard's Non-Bergsonism," is a revised and updated translation of his article "Un Bachelard Non-Bergsonien," originally published in *Gaston Bachelard: Du rêveur ironiste au pédagogue inspiré*, ed. Jean Libis (Dijon: Centre Regional de Documentation-Pédagogique, 1984), 61–76. Also published in English translation by Eileen Rizo-Patron with the title "A Non-Bergsonian Bachelard," in *Continental Philosophy Review* 41 (2008): 463–79. Permission granted by Jean Libis to publish the translated text in this volume. Revised version reproduced with permission of Springer Publishing.

Chapter 3: Richard Kearney, "Vertical Time: Bachelard's Epiphanic Instant," is a revised and updated version of the essay "Bachelard and the Epiphanic Instant," published in *Philosophy Today* 52 (SPEP Supplement 2008) 38–45.

Chapter 6: Anton Vydra, "Bachelard vis-à-vis Phenomenology," is a corrected and updated version of "Gaston Bachelard and His Reactions to Phenomenology," initially published online by Springer Science and Business Media (Dordrecht, February 4, 2014), then printed in *Continental Philosophy Review* 47 (March 2014): 45–58. Revised version published with permission of Springer.

Chapter 7: Eileen Rizo-Patron, "Bachelard's Hermeneutics: Between Psychoanalysis and Phenomenology," appeared in an earlier form as "*Regressus ad Uterum*: Bachelard's Alchemical Hermeneutic," in *Philosophy Today*

52 (SPEP Supplement 2008): 21–30. The current version includes a new commentary on Bachelard's *Lautréamont*, among other significant changes.

Chapter 9: David L. Miller, "Gaston Bachelard and Henry Corbin: On Adjectival Consciousness," was presented in quite different form at the Dallas Institute of Humanities and Culture's "Conference on Gaston Bachelard," organized by Dr. Joanne H. Stroud, December 4, 1983. A portion of this material, adapted for an entirely different context, was published in *Apophatic Bodies*, ed. Christopher Boesel and Catherine Keller (New York: Fordham University Press, 2009).

Chapter 10: Roch C. Smith, "Bachelard's Logosphere and Derrida's Logocentrism: A Distinction with a *Différance*," is an updated and modified version for English language readers of a piece which appeared with the title "Bachelard's Logosphere and Derrida's Logocentrism: Is There a *Différance*?" in *French Forum* 10 (1985): 225–34. Reproduced with permission of University of Nebraska Press.

Chapter 12: Eileen Rizo-Patron, "Sounding the Living Logos: Bachelard and Gadamer," appeared in a former version entitled "Awakening the Inner Ear," in *Translation and Literary Studies: Homage to Marilyn Gaddis Rose*, ed. Marella Feltrin Morris, María Constanza Guzmán, and Deborah Folaron (Manchester: St. Jerome, 2012), 54–67. Revision published with permission of Taylor & Francis Group.

Chapter 13: Edward K. Kaplan, "Reverie and Reverence: Bachelard's Encounter with Buber," is an updated version of an essay published in *International Studies in Philosophy* 35, no. 1 (2003): 75–88, under the title "Imagination and Ethics: Gaston Bachelard and Martin Buber." The revised essay is printed with the permission of George Leaman, director, Philosophy Documentation Center, Charlottesville, Virginia.

Chapter 14: Edward S. Casey, "Missing Land: Between Heidegger and Bachelard," is an updated version of a lecture delivered in 2002 at the Bachelard Conference of the Dallas Institute of Humanities and Culture, in Dallas, Texas, on the occasion of the publication of Kenneth Haltman's English translation of Bachelard's *Earth and Reveries of Will*.

Chapter 16: Madeleine Préclaire, "Bachelard's Open Solitude," is an updated version of chapter 10 of her book *Une Poétique de l'homme* (Montréal: Bellarmin, 1971; © Éditions Bellarmin); permission granted by Éditions Fides, April 28, 2014. Eileen Rizo-Patron translated the essay into English for use in this volume, with thanks to Madeleine Préclaire for her handwritten approval of the revisions, as well as to Dr. Bart Kasowski, Collège Jean-de-Brébeuf, Montreal, for his helpful review.

Appendix A, a newly revised translation of Bachelard's preface to Martin Buber's *I and Thou*, was first published by Edward K. Kaplan in *International Studies in Philosophy* 35, no. 1 (2003): 89–94. It is reprinted here by permission of George Leaman, director, Philosophy Documentation Center. Bachelard's original "Préface" appeared in French in Martin Buber's *Je et Tu*, translated from German by Geneviève Bianquis (Paris: Aubier Montaigne, 1938), 7–15. All references to Bachelard's preface to Buber cite the revised version printed in this volume.

Appendix B, a testimony on Bachelard by Georges Gusdorf, is an excerpt entitled "Rétractation 1983," in *Mythe et métaphysique: Introduction à la philosophie* (1953; Paris: Champs/Flammarion, 1984), 304–6, which is in the public domain and available online: http://classiques.uqac.ca/contemporains/gusdorf_georges/mythe_et_metaphysique/mythe_et_metaphysique.html. Gusdorf's text later appeared under the title "Témoignage" in *L'Association des Amis de Gaston Bachelard Bulletin* 9 (2007): 80–82. Excerpt translated into English by Eileen Rizo-Patron with the permission of Jean Libis, AAGB Bulletin director, and reproduced with permission of Éditions CNRS, July 11, 2016.

Finally, we would like to express our deep gratitude to Lissa McCullough, for her expert guidance and editorial advice in the preparation of this volume, as well as to our long-time Bachelard colleagues and friends: Edward K. Kaplan, Richard Kearney, Mary McAllester Jones, David L. Miller, Roch C. Smith, and Joanne Stroud. The spirit of their work and fellowship touches this volume in many ways. At the State University of New York Press, we are especially grateful to Andrew Kenyon, our acquisitions editor, whose faith in the present volume was a welcome encouragement. His contributions to the presence of the continental philosophical voice are deeply appreciated. Our thanks also go to our production editor, Diane Ganeles, for her marvelous efficiency and patience in the final stages of this publication.

Sigla

Texts by Gaston Bachelard

References to texts by Bachelard are identified throughout this volume by acronyms followed by page numbers (for example, PS 9, RA 15). Full publication details are provided in the bibliography. In the case of texts not available in English, the acronyms abbreviate the French editions. Where a comparison between English translation and French original is warranted, page numbers for both editions are cited, separated by a slash (for example, WD 16/24). Any modification of a published translation is noted as "trans. modified." The year of original publication in French for each text is indicated below. All references to Bachelard's preface to Martin Buber's *I and Thou* cite the revised version printed in this volume as appendix A.

AD *Air and Dreams,* trans. Edith Farrell and Frederick Farrell.
L'Airet les songes (1943)

ARPC *L'Activité rationaliste de la physique contemporaine* (1951)

DD *The Dialectic of Duration*, trans. Mary McAllester Jones
La Dialectique de la durée (1936)

É *Études* (1970)

ERR *Earth and Reveries of Repose*, trans. Mary McAllester Jones
La Terre et les rêveries du repos (1948)

ERW *Earth and Reveries of Will*, trans. Kenneth Haltman
La Terre et les rêveries de la volonté (1947)

FC *The Flame of a Candle,* trans. Joni Caldwell
La Flamme d'une chandelle (1961)

FPF	*Fragments of a Poetics of Fire,* trans. Kenneth Haltman *Fragments d'une poétique du feu* (1988)
FSM	*The Formation of the Scientific Spirit,* trans. Mary McAllester Jones *La Formation de l'esprit scientifique* (1938)
IA	*Les Intuitions atomistiques* (1933)
II	*Intuition of the Instant*, trans. Eileen Rizo-Patron. *L'Intuition de l'instant: Essai sur la Siloë de Gaston Roupnel* (1932)
L	*Lautréamont*, trans. Robert Scott Duprée *Lautréamont* (1939)
MR	*Le Matérialisme rationnel* (1953)
NM	"Noumenon and Microphysics" (1970), trans. Bernard Roy, *Philosophical Forum* 37 (2006): 75–84; originally published in *Études,* 11–24
NSS	*The New Scientific Spirit*, trans. Arthur Goldhammer *Le Nouvel esprit scientifique* (1934)
P	Preface to Martin Buber's *I and Thou,* trans. Edward K. Kaplan Préface à *Je et Tu* de Martin Buber (1938)
PCCM	*Le Pluralisme cohérent de la chimie moderne* (1932)
PF	*The Psychoanalysis of Fire*, trans. Alan C. M. Ross *La Psychanalyse du feu* (1938)
PN	*The Philosophy of No*, trans. G. C. Waterston *La Philosophie du non* (1940)
PR	*The Poetics of Reverie,* trans. Daniel Russell *La Poétique de la rêverie* (1960)
PS	*The Poetics of Space*, trans. Maria Jolas (1st ed.) *La Poétique de l'espace* (1957)
RA	*Le Rationalisme appliqué* (1949)
RD	*The Right to Dream*, trans. J. A. Underwood *Le Droit de rêver* (1970)
WD	*Water and Dreams*, trans. Edith Farrell *L'Eauet les rêves* (1942)

Introduction: Bachelard's Living Philosophical Legacy

EILEEN RIZO-PATRON

The aim of this collection on the French philosopher Gaston Bachelard (1884–1962) is to pursue four major paths of inquiry in his work—time, methodology, language, alterity—which call to be explored at greater depth in the English language, while tracing specific ways in which his phenomenological adventures[1] contributed to the advancement of twentieth-century culture, and may further contribute in the twenty-first. With that in mind, this volume gathers recently written critical studies together with a few updated studies by established Bachelard scholars—pieces which, taken conjointly, are designed to stimulate discussion on potentials of Bachelardian thought in the fields of ontology, hermeneutics, aesthetics, ethics, psychology, science, the arts, and religion, as well as interdisciplinary fields in cultural, political, and environmental studies. By bringing Bachelard's work into close proximity and dialogue with the work of contemporary thinkers—including several who came after him—we thus intend to highlight the relevance and fecundity of Bachelard's insights vis-à-vis philosophical questions currently being debated in continental philosophy. Such a critical reopening of Bachelard's oeuvre is both timely and necessary at this historical juncture, considering the partial eclipse that Bachelard's oeuvre underwent during the heady rise of postmodernism after his death, and given the impasse that has persisted in the relation between the sciences and the humanities at the turn of the new millennium—challenges that may be more productively tackled if illumined by Bachelard's farsighted perspectives.

Overview of an Unusual Philosophical Trajectory

In the late 1920s and early 1930s, Bachelard began an epistemological exploration of the revolutionary character of the scientific spirit spurred by twentieth-century discoveries in relativity and quantum theory from the perspective of the historical and critical rationalism then being advanced by his professor and mentor Léon Brunschvicg (1869–1944).[2] As the theoretical subtlety and applications of his thinking evolved through the 1930s, Bachelard's reflections increasingly focused on the transformative powers of imagination. It is often assumed that this shift in focus from the productions of reason to the imagination (and its ensuing alternation) occurred suddenly while writing *The Psychoanalysis of Fire* (1938),[3] yet the first glimmers of Bachelard's fascination with poetic intuition can be detected as early as the *Intuition of the Instant* (1932),[4] a meditation on the nature and enigmas of time prompted by his reading of Gaston Roupnel's philosophical drama *Siloë* (1927).

During the period that followed, and throughout the 1940s, Bachelard made several attempts to understand the dynamics of imagination, along with the nature and formative forces of language, through an open-ended, inductive approach organized heuristically around a literary exploration of elemental images (fire, water, air, earth), rather than through a deductive approach led by a priori principles and concepts (as had been the case in traditional epistemologies and certain applications of psychoanalysis). At this time Bachelard's philosophy was being gradually nourished in the fertile soil of the phenomenological movement that had begun yielding fruit in France since the delivery of Edmund Husserl's celebrated lectures on phenomenology at the Sorbonne in 1929 and the subsequent publication of his *Cartesian Meditations* in French. Although Bachelard would not explicitly align his studies with this movement until several years later (and not without first qualifying its methods through his own findings),[5] his self-critical and practical philosophical style epitomized from the outset a fervent commitment to the phenomenological "attitude of crisis and wonder"[6] in the face of phenomena that present themselves to human experience in science or imagination. Bachelard's philosophical itinerary thus exemplified the agility of a mind forever open to questioning, revision, adventure, and discovery.

While Bachelard pursued questions of time, space, matter, and language in the late 1930s, testing a number of approaches (epistemological, psychological, poetic), Maurice Merleau-Ponty (1908–1961) was just starting to compose *The Phenomenology of Perception* (1945), where he would ultimately announce that phenomenological philosophy "is not the reflection of a pre-existing truth, but, like art, the act of bringing truth into being" (xx). Merleau-Ponty's avowal that phenomenology "is as painstaking as the works of Balzac, Proust, Valéry, or Cézanne by reason of the same kind of attentiveness and wonder, the same demand for awareness, the same will to seize the meaning of the world or of history *as that meaning comes into being*" (xxi, emphasis added) happened to capture the essence of Bachelard's practical explorations in the sciences and literature, which would lead in his later years to a mature articulation of his ontology.

The chapters collected here endeavor to highlight ways in which Bachelard was already beginning to carry the possibilities of the phenomenological movement in France to deeper and subtler levels, primarily by examining his distinctive mode of meditation in ushering the birth of knowledge from the recesses of world and being: a type of dream-thought (*pensée rêvée*) he would identify as "anagogic reverie" in *The Philosophy of No* in relation to scientific thought,[7] and "poetic reverie" in relation to adventures in literary imagination or art. The latter is most precisely defined in *The Poetics of Reverie* (5–6) yet is intimated as early as *Intuition of the Instant* (10, 56). Bachelard's characteristic mode of meditation is closely examined by a number of authors in this volume.

When engaging with established philosophical or scientific paradigms, however, Bachelard adopted a distinctive polemical style, a dialectic approach he had started developing since the early 1930s and laid out most succinctly in his *Philosophy of No* (1940). This approach could be qualified as a "critical hermeneutics" moved not by a wanton will to negate (as the book's title might suggest at first glance) but by a need to confront preconceptions—by reopening and subverting founding questions in order to rethink reified paradigms from novel perspectives, often illumined by recent scientific discoveries in physics, chemistry, or depth psychology. These discoveries would turn out to have profound ontological and hermeneutic repercussions, as attested in the works of scholars later influenced by Bachelard's oeuvre, such as Georges Canguilhem and James Hillman in the fields of health, medicine, and psychological insight, or Patrick A. Heelan and Don Ihde with regard to the physical sciences and technologies.[8]

Alongside such critical hermeneutics, Bachelard would adopt what poet Jean Lescure described as a "method of sympathy" in approaching literary or poetic discourse (II 64–71). This hermeneutic practice also took root early in Bachelard's career with his reading of Roupnel's *Siloë*, as laid out in his introduction to the *Intuition of the Instant* (1932). Bachelard in fact strove consistently to attune his hermeneutics to the specific nature of each text, phenomenon, or question at hand—hence the mutability of his methods and discursive styles, depending on the call of the case. In this volume the reader will be able to witness several hermeneutic attitudes at work within Bachelard's own texts, as well as in the variety of critical approaches to his oeuvre—some of which stand in sharp contrast, while others complement or reinforce one another in surprising ways.

Reception of Bachelard in Continental Philosophy

In a recent study, *Home: A Concrete Bachelardian Metaphysics* (Oxford: Peter Lang, 2011), Miles Kennedy offers a sustained and provocative discussion of Bachelard's ontology vis-à-vis Heidegger's renowned project of being-in-the-world, as well as the thought of Jean-Paul Sartre, Jacques Derrida, Simone de Beauvoir, Luce Irigaray, and other leading figures in twentieth-century existentialism and continental philosophy. In his opening chapter, Kennedy makes the unsettling claim that Bachelard's original insights were often "borrowed" by his French colleagues and employed at times reductively or without due acknowledgment (*Home*, 1–24). This rather cavalier attitude toward Bachelard's oeuvre among his contemporaries in continental philosophy might be explained in part by Bachelard's early allegiance to Brunschvicg's analytical rationalism (an approach which in those years had lost popularity among French continental philosophers despite its new critical-historical thrust)[9] and his appointment as chair of History and Philosophy of Science at the Sorbonne—not to mention his autodidactic and widely exploratory philosophical methods, too audacious for some when it came to his hermeneutic recovery of alchemical symbolism, for instance, after his own pungent criticism of its imagery and practices from the strict perspective of scientific epistemology.[10]

Surprisingly, however, Kennedy makes no allusion in this study to the work of Merleau-Ponty, who appears to have had contact with Bachelard during the late 1940s and 1950s when teaching concurrently at the Sorbonne and its neighboring Collège de France. This exception is perhaps due to Kennedy's focus in his book on the ontology of Bachelard's *The Poetics of Space* (with its mature notion of "dwelling" in the world), more than on his earlier work on the "elemental imagination," which had palpable influence on Merleau-Ponty's notions of the "imaginary" and the "flesh of the world" (VI 245, 267).[11] Yet Merleau-Ponty also appears to have critically predicated his "indirect ontology" in *The Visible and the Invisible* on the "direct ontology" proposed by Bachelard just a few years earlier in *The Poetics of Space*, a poetic ontology closely discussed by Glen Mazis in his piece for this volume (part 2, chapter 8).[12]

Later, in the introduction to *The Poetics of Reverie* (1960), Bachelard would highlight the subtle difference between the phenomenological approach he had been developing since the early 1940s and Merleau-Ponty's approach in *The Phenomenology of Perception* by emphasizing what he considered to be the "primacy of imagination" underlying perception (PR 1–15, especially 13–14). Bachelard had expressed interest in Merleau-Ponty's studies as early as *Earth and Reveries of Will*, teasing out examples of "intentionality" described in his colleague's magnum opus (ERW 39–41). During those years one finds only a few brief references to Bachelard in Merleau-Ponty's works: an allusion to the sacramental notion of Bachelard's "elements" of imagination in a 1948 radio lecture,[13] and another to the "superexistence" of a work of art in "Indirect Language and the Voices of Silence."[14] Yet judging by the working notes to *The Visible and the Invisible*, by the early 1960s Merleau-Ponty had come to a deeper appreciation of the ferment of Bachelard's thought within French phenomenology and in the development of his own ideas with regard to the roles of the "elemental imaginary" in perception, the "flesh of the world," "chiasmic intertwining," and even the "*Stiftung* of a point in time" (VI 245, 267). In fact, Merleau-Ponty's critique of Bergson's theory of time had long exhibited sparks of contact with Bachelard's arguments in *Intuition of the Instant (*1932), *The Dialectic of Duration* (1936), and "Poetic Instant and Metaphysical Instant" (1939)[15]—particularly with respect to the way Bergson's notion of continuous duration tends to dissolve past, present, and future into the amorphous tide of the élan vital, without giving enough weight to the pulsating role of the ethical subject at the very heart of this élan.[16]

Merleau-Ponty's new project—though cut short by his premature death in 1961—was fortunately carried forward by creative phenomenologists who would follow in his steps and beyond, prompted by his fertile proposals. Whereas his living legacy endured and flourished over the ensuing decades, Bachelard's critical relevance for Merleau-Ponty's project remained virtually unexplored in continental philosophy.[17]

From early on in his career, meanwhile, Michel Foucault had begun to detect the significance of Bachelard's thought within continental philosophy and culture[18]—drawing attention, in particular, to the subversive element in Bachelard's philosophical outlook and style, most vividly captured in the following excerpt from an interview recorded in 1972:

> What strikes me the most about Bachelard is that, in a way, he plays against his own culture with his own culture. In traditional education, as well as in the popular culture we inherit, there are always a certain number of established values: things one must read and others one need not read, works considered highly significant and others negligible; there are renowned people and less significant people. There is a hierarchy—you know, that whole celestial world with its thrones, dominations, angels, and archangels—all this is well hierarchized, and roles are very precisely defined. Bachelard knows how to disengage himself from this ensemble of values, and he knows how to disengage himself simply by reading everything, and by confronting everything with everything. He reminds me, if you will, of those skilled chess players who manage to capture the biggest pieces with pawns. Bachelard does not hesitate to oppose Descartes to a minor philosopher or an imperfect or eccentric eighteenth-century scholar. He doesn't hesitate to bring together in the same analysis the most important poets and a minor anti-poet he might have discovered by chance while browsing in a small bookshop. By doing that, he does not mean to reconstitute the "great global culture"—if you will, that of the West, Europe, or France. It's not about showing that it is always the same great mind [*Esprit*] that lives and swarms everywhere. My impression is, on the contrary, that he tries to seize his own culture through its interstices, its deviances, its minor phenomena, its dissonances.[19]

Bachelard Entering the Third Millennium

As Edward S. Casey and Kristupas Sabolius reveal in two of the opening pieces in this volume, "The Difference an Instant Makes: Bachelard's Brilliant Breakthrough" and "Rhythm and Reverie" (part 1), Bachelard was indeed a pioneer in discovering and illustrating how *reverie*—as a subversive mode of thought responsive to the sudden, though subtle, call of the instant—is the preeminent faculty capable of *breaking open* human intuition to inchoate energies that brew in the umbral dimensions of the pre-perceptible. With regard to anagogic reverie's role in the sciences, Anton Vydra's essay "Bachelard vis-à-vis Phenomenology" (part 2) then points to Bachelard's ventures into the noumenal realm of possibility, perhaps too readily dismissed by those among his phenomenological contemporaries who, without his intensive background in microphysics, had yet to come to a full appreciation of its ontological potentials. Mary McAllester also addresses this key mode of scientific thought in her essay "Adventures of Consciousness" (part 2) in terms of pure mathematical ideas that Bachelard intuits hovering around real phenomena (NSS 58)—possibilities that can break open astonishing paths to *realization* via the poetic exercise of mathematical reverie.

Alternatively, in the phenomenal realm of art, although we may subconsciously partake in such latent potentialities from the outset as living embodied creatures, Bachelard's waking-working reverie (*rêverie ouvrante-oeuvrante*) was intended to raise them to conscious awareness by teaching us to participate *attentively* in their invisible energies through the arts of contemplative listening and active expression (from lyrical poetry to metalwork). Such hermeneutic and ontological processes of disclosure, realization, and transformation—discussed respectively by Eileen Rizo-Patron and Glen A. Mazis (part 2)—would in turn make it possible for consciousness to harness and educate embryonic forces toward elected values or purposes: hence the ethical-political implications of Bachelard's philosophy.[20] The ethical implications of Bachelard's thought are addressed throughout this volume from a variety of critical perspectives—ranging from Richard Kearney's remarks on the categorical imperative of the "vertical instant" (part 1) to the essays by Madeleine Préclaire, Edward Kaplan, and Samuel Talcott on Bachelard's responses to the call and demands of "otherness" (part 4).

Although Bachelard opted not to adopt the existentialist ethos that predominated in continental discourse in the 1940s and 1950s (see Kennedy, 5–6, 142–44), nor to engage in heated debates on political philosophy that took ascendancy during and following World War II, he carried his critical activism into the hidden will and dynamics of the psyche—personal and collective—away from domains of consensual and partisan thinking. Having fought almost four years in World War I, more than a decade before being assigned as philosophy professor at the University of Dijon in the 1930s, Bachelard appears to have developed a mistrust of ideological discourse. No longer keen on rehearsing the inflexible gridlock it can lead to, instead he determined to find new paths toward opening the cultural psyche and helping to heal the spirit of his times. During the 1940s he was thus drawn toward a psychological depth-analysis of pervasive habits of feeling-thinking which he termed "culture complexes"[21]—attitudes and automatisms that could drive human behavior into obtrusive if not catastrophic impasses—through a painstaking study of language and imagery that tends to shape our very perception of the world.

Bachelard thus remained a philosophical trailblazer and resistance fighter within academia by opting to go "underground" via his decisive turn to the elemental imagination, wherefrom he struggled against a diseased environment and political establishment by first bracketing the din of ideological discourse in order to listen to the hidden pulses of the collective psyche, as expressed in dynamic imagery that arose in literature and the arts. Through this penetrating and solitary effort (even as he served as chair of the History and Philosophy of Science faculty at the Sorbonne), Bachelard was able to explore the hidden roots of the ills of his day and thereby to open up new ground. Pieces that especially highlight this cultural-political problem embedded in language and psyche, in our volume, are those by Eileen Rizo-Patron (part 2), Jason M. Wirth (part 3), and Samuel Talcott (part 4).

In the spirit of this intrepid thinker, several chapters gathered herein revisit areas of Bachelard's phenomenology that pertain to his ventures amid gaps or crossovers between the real and the imaginary, or between and among philosophical thinkers. For bold advances prompted by Bachelard's thought, see in particular Edward S. Casey's "Missing Land: Between Heidegger and Bachelard" (part 4), Jason M. Wirth's "The Heat of Language" (Part 3), and Samuel Talcott's "Environmental Politics" (part 4). Philosophical partners examined include ones from whom Bachelard drew inspiration or incitement (Novalis, F. W. J. Schelling, Henri Bergson, Edmund Husserl, Martin Heidegger, Jean-Paul Sartre, Henry Corbin, C. G. Jung, Martin Buber) and ones whose works were in turn spurred by Bachelard's unsettling proposals (Walter Benjamin, Michel Foucault, Henri Lefevre, Maurice Merleau-Ponty, and Jacques Derrida). Other prominent thinkers who may not have had contact with Bachelard yet whose works overlap with his in stimulating ways are also brought to the table (Hans-Georg Gadamer, Jean-Luc Nancy, and Gilles Deleuze). Salient among such dialogical analyses are Jean-François Perraudin's probe into Bachelard's polemic with Bergson (part 1), Anton Vydra's study of Bachelard vis-à-vis Husserl's phenomenology (part 2), Jason M. Wirth's symposium between Bachelard and other major philosophers on the tension between idea and image, Eileen Rizo-Patron's soundings of the Λόγος in Bachelard and Gadamer, Roch C. Smith's examination of Bachelard's "logosphere" versus Derrida's "logocentrism" (part 3), and two luminous accounts of Bachelard's spiritual encounters—the first with theologian and professor of Islamic studies Henry Corbin, by David L.

Miller (part 3), and the second with Jewish philosopher Martin Buber, by Edward K. Kaplan (part 4).

On the whole, Bachelard's work was aimed at responding to the call of the world's ever-nascent Λόγος—not to accomplished *givens* but to *gifts* that come as pleas, crises, or "coefficients of adversity" (to use Bachelard's phrase). This is a key aspect that Bachelard's phenomenological adventures shared, if tacitly, with those of his colleagues in continental philosophy, although Bachelard—especially during the 1940s—adopted more of a polemical intentionality vis-à-vis the perceived world than did his fellow phenomenologists, who focused on a vectorial intentionality less emphatic of the dynamic entanglements (*l'entrecroisement*) that Bachelard found persistently provoking/transforming subjects and objects, in unpredictable ways (WD 159–60; ERW 39–41; MR 182).[22]

Part 4 of our volume thus ends on an open note with a chapter from Madeleine Préclaire's *Une Poétique de l'homme*[23] on "Bachelard's Open Solitude," as well as two appendices: Bachelard's Preface to Buber (appendix A), featuring Bachelard's response to Buber's call in *I and Thou*, with its consequent summons to the "thou" of future readers, and Georges Gusdorf's personal testimony about his revered mentor (appendix B), which concludes with Bachelard posing a direct challenge to his reader and interlocutor.

Challenges of Translating Bachelard's Oeuvre

Although Bachelard scholarship continued virtually uninterrupted in the French academy after his passing in 1962,[24] one logistical factor that contributed to its relative eclipse in the English-speaking world toward the end of the twentieth century was the difficulty of gathering his prolific oeuvre into a cohesive array of publications in English translation.[25] The interdisciplinary nature of Bachelard's writings themselves—spanning scientific epistemology, psychoanalysis, depth psychology, philosophy of imagination, and phenomenology—is no doubt one of the reasons for its fragmented reception, along with the sporadic emergence of translations and critical analyses by scholars from diverse fields and schools of thought over the years. Yet the formidable task of translating his large body of work was valiantly undertaken, albeit in a scattershot approach, by different publishers and translators.

In the 1960s, Beacon Press published popular and influential translations of what were to become Bachelard's best-known works in North

America: *The Psychoanalysis of Fire* (1964, trans. Alan D. Ross), *The Poetics of Space* (1964, trans. Maria Jolas), and *The Poetics of Reverie* (1969, trans. Daniel Russell). These otherwise excellent editions did not include analytical indexes, which would have made them more accessible to scholarly study; moreover, the lexicon of key terms for Bachelard lacked both consistency and nuance, as different translators handled terms independently of each other, and certain problematic terms were introduced (such as "daydream" for the French *rêverie*, meant to connote a more lucid mode of attention than the aimless fantasies of a wandering mind). This sometimes made it difficult to correlate his philosophical ideas in more cohesive ways.

In the 1980s, the Dallas Institute of Humanities and Culture launched its Bachelard Translations Series under the direction of Joanne H. Stroud, who contracted with Éditions José Corti in Paris to publish all of Bachelard's works on the imagination in English: *Water and Dreams* (1983), *Lautréamont* (1986), *Air and Dreams* (1988), *The Flame of a Candle* (1988), *The Right to Dream*, a collection of essays and prefaces on art and literature (1988), *Earth and Reveries of Will* (2002), *Earth and Reveries of Repose* (2011), and his posthumous *Fragments of a Poetics of Fire* (1990). Each of these editions included helpful analytical indexes and illuminating editorial commentary.

Two anthologies of translated Bachelard selections in English were also published during those years, one with an extensive introduction by Colette Gaudin, *On Poetic Imagination and Reverie* (New York: Bobbs-Merrill, 1971; Dallas: Spring, 1987), and the second with selections from Bachelard's work in philosophy of science and poetics, including close textual analyses by Mary McAllester Jones, *Gaston Bachelard: Subversive Humanist* (Madison: University of Wisconsin, 1991). Several years earlier Roch C. Smith's comprehensive study *Gaston Bachelard* (Boston: Twayne, 1982) had appeared already tackling the cross-fertilization between his epistemology and his poetics despite their differences in philosophical approach and style.

Meanwhile, in the field of scientific epistemology, and on the question of temporality, Mary McAllester Jones was spearheading Bachelard studies in the United Kingdom, publishing translations of Bachelard's works with Clinamen Press in Manchester, UK—specifically, *The Dialectic of Duration* (2000) and *The Formation of the Scientific Mind* (2002). Also notable in the area of epistemology had been the earlier critical work of Mary Tiles, *Bachelard Science and Objectivity* (Cambridge: Cambridge University Press, 1984), and that of Patrick A. Heelan, author of the foreword to Bachelard's *The New Scientific Spirit* (1984, trans. Arthur A. Goldhammer). The only other book on Bachelard's philosophy of science published in English until then had been *The Philosophy of No* (1968, trans. G. C. Waterston). From Bachelard's collection of essays *Études* (1970), a single article entitled "Noumenon and Microphysics" has since been translated by Bernard Roy and published in *Philosophical Forum* (2006): 75–84. But all other works on scientific epistemology have yet to be translated into English. These include Bachelard's *Le Pluralisme Cohérent de la Chimie Modèrne* (1932), *Intuitions Atomistiques* (1933), *L'Expérience de l'espace dans la physique contemporaine* (1937), *Le Rationalisme appliqué* (1949), *Le Matérialisme rationnel* (1953).

In this volume, we are pleased to feature Edward K. Kaplan's newly revised English translation of Bachelard's 1938 "Preface to Buber's *I and Thou*." Also recently published is Eileen Rizo-Patron's translation of Bachelard's 1932 essay on the question of time, *Intuition of the Instant* (Northwestern University Press, 2013).

Alongside this ongoing translation venture, some illuminating analyses of Bachelard's contributions to continental philosophy have appeared in English during the last couple of decades, whether as book-length monographs, chapters in thematically-oriented volumes, or as articles in scholarly journals. Richard Kearney's *Poetics of Imagining* (New York: Fordham, 1998), for instance, sets Bachelard's philosophy of imagination beside that of Husserl, Heidegger, Sartre, Merleau-Ponty, and postmodern thinkers, dedicating a chapter to each, while Cristina Chimisso devotes her entire *Gaston Bachelard: Critic of Science and the Imagination* (New York: Routledge, 2001) to a study of the pedagogical orientation of Bachelard's oeuvre within its cultural and institutional context. Gary Gutting's *Continental Philosophy of Science* (Oxford: Blackwell, 2005) includes an excerpt from Bachelard's *Essai sur la connaissance approchée* (1928) in translation, with a critical commentary by Mary Tiles. During this time, individual essays on Bachelard's work were being periodically published in academic journals such as *Continental Philosophy Review*, *Religion and the Arts*, *Philosophy Today*, *International Studies in Philosophy*, and *Studies in History and Philosophy of Science*.

Most recently, new perspectives on specific issues of Bachelard's oeuvre have appeared in English as well—in particular, Miles Kennedy's *Home: A Concrete Bachelardian Metaphysics* (2011), a study of Bachelard's and Heidegger's differing notions of being and dwelling in the world, illustrated by a reading of Mark Z. Danielewski's novel *House of Leaves* (New York: Pantheon, 2000); and Zbigniew Kotowicz's *Gaston Bachelard: A Philosophy of the Surreal* (Edinburgh University Press, 2016), which highlights the "atomistic roots" of Bachelard's philosophy.

Finally, to help offset the thematic and disciplinary gaps in Bachelard scholarship among English speakers over the years, the State University of New York Press has just reissued, as part of its Contemporary French Thought Series, a revised and updated edition of Roch C. Smith's comprehensive introduction to Bachelard's philosophical oeuvre, with a fully annotated critical bibliography, under the new title of *Gaston Bachelard: Philosopher of Science and Imagination* (2016).

Notes

1. We use the phrase *phenomenological adventures* here not to refer exclusively to a school of thought but to suggest the dynamic processes of sedimentation-dissolution, activation-reduction, expansion-contraction by which our phenomenological world is constituted and critically recreated in Bachelard's accounts. The term *adventures* (related to both ventures and advents) is further meant to underline Bachelard's penchant for crossing the limits of the phenomenal, time and again, by reaching into the unknown to solicit the virtues of the noumenal.

2. See FSM 19. More detailed accounts on the intellectual context in which Bachelard's early thinking developed (including major influences on his thought) can be found in Roch C. Smith's *Gaston Bachelard: Philosopher of Science to Imagination* (Albany: State University of New York Press, 2016), 1–8; Mary McAllester Jones's *Gaston Bachelard: Subversive Humanist* (Madison: University of Wisconsin Press, 1991), 4–8; and Cristina Chimisso's *Gaston Bachelard* (London: Routledge, 2001), chaps. 2, 4, and 5.

3. Bachelard never abandoned the early epistemological interests awakened by the new scientific spirit, as attested by his books published between 1949 and 1953: *Le Rationalisme appliqué*, *L'Activité rationaliste de la physique contemporaine*, *Le Matérialisme rationnel.* Roch C. Smith, Mary McAllester Jones, and Cristina Chimisso present powerful arguments in the above-cited works (see n. 2) on the significance of Bachelard's epistemology of science for his developing theories of imagination.

4. See Bachelard's introduction (II 3–5), as well as the lyrical epigraphs heading each chapter, and those passages where Bachelard summons the reader "to return to the shores of Siloam where mind and heart become reconciled as they complement each other" (II 27). Most poetically revealing, in this regard, are the final pages of chapter 3 (II 52–54) and the conclusion (55–57).

5. Bachelard engaged in a practical and critical exploration of phenomenological methods after the mid-1930s, as Anton Vydra recounts in his essay "Bachelard vis-à-vis Phenomenology" (in part 2 of this volume). Although by the early 1950s phenomenology had attained thematic status in his critical philosophy (MR 1–36),

his commitment to its approach would be most eagerly articulated and demonstrated in *The Poetics of Space* (1957).

6. The attitude of "crisis and wonder"—which can be traced back to Husserl's "phenomenological reduction"—is clearly laid out in Bachelard's introduction to *The Poetics of Space* (xi–xxxi, esp. xi, xiv, xxviii–xxix), though one finds it already at work in his approach to the scientific challenges that called forth the revolutionary movements in twentieth-century science. Citing Eugen Fink, once Husserl's assistant, John Cogan here unpacks it in a lucid commentary that vividly reflects Bachelard's own practice: " '[I]t is in this wonder that the unsettling idea of a *genuine mode* of knowing the existent suddenly emerges from beneath the ordered, familiar world in which we are at home and about which we have fixed meanings concerning things, man and God, meanings which make certainty in life possible.' It is a 'genuine mode' precisely because it is not already decided what the nature of the existent and the nature of truth are. . . . The only 'knowing' that is original is the knowing that properly belongs to astonishment; because it is only in astonishment that man experiences the complete collapse of his traditional knowledge and pre-acquaintance with the world and with things; a collapse that is due entirely to a *new* confronting of the existent and a *new* projection of the senses of 'being' and 'truth.' . . . The way [Fink] uses [the term 'original'] in this passage heralds the sense of 'founding' invoked in the way phenomenology provides a ground for epistemology. Fink has told us that the astonishment in which philosophy begins is in no way 'merely a disposition, a feeling.' Rather, 'it is the fundamental disposition of pure thought; it is *original theory*.' . . . In astonishment a change and transformation of knowing occurs such that what we already know is reduced to mere opinion and even the very nature of knowing is altered. . . . Fink [thus] marks a distinction between the 'knowing' that stands in need of a foundation and the 'knowing' that does the founding. The knowing that does the founding is the original knowing of astonishment . . . and the door to sustained astonishment is opened by the rigorous performance of the phenomenological reduction" (John Cogan, "The Phenomenological Reduction," in *The Internet Encyclopedia of Philosophy* (ISSN 2161-0002, http://www.iep.utm.edu/phen-red/#H7, accessed June 30, 2015).

7. Bachelard wrote: "It is in [the] area of dialectical surrationalism that the scientific mind *dreams*. It is here and nowhere else that anagogic reverie [*rêverie anagogique*] comes into being, reverie which ventures into thought, reverie which thinks while it ventures, reverie which seeks an illumination of thought by thought, which finds a sudden intuition beyond the veils of informed thought" (PN 32/39, trans. modified).

8. Notable in this regard are Canguilhem's *Knowledge of Life*, where he examines the overcoming of "epistemological obstacles" in the advancement of biological cell theory (29), and Hillman's *The Force of Character: And the Lasting Life*, which shows how "reverie" can tap those deep intuitions whose moral force

can orient an entire life (183–84). While Patrick Heelan is a professed follower in the Heideggerian hermeneutic tradition, the seeds of Bachelardian inspiration can also be found in his work after he authored the foreword to the 1984 translation of Bachelard's *The New Scientific Spirit* (*Le Nouvel Esprit Scientifique*, 1934); see his essay "Why a Hermeneutics of the Natural Sciences?," *Man and World* 30 (1997): 271–98. Don Idhe's "material hermeneutics" was avowedly nourished by Bachelard's scientific epistemology, including (as in Heelan's case) his notion of "phenomeno-technology" (NSS x, xiii, 13). More recently, Bachelard's works are leaving their mark in the neurosciences, as noted by Michèle Pichon in her recent book *Gaston Bachelard: L'intuition de l'instant au risque des neurosciences* (Paris: L'Harmattan, 2012).

9. Alan D. Schrift, in *Twentieth-Century French Philosophy: Key Themes and Thinkers* (Oxford: Blackwell, 2009), 36–37, reports a divisive rivalry between two distinct modalities of philosophizing that had emerged from the introduction of Husserlian phenomenology in France in the late 1920s: "philosophies of rationality, knowledge, and the concept" (Cavaillès, Bachelard, Canguilhem) and "philosophies of experience, sense, and the subject" (Sartre, Merleau-Ponty). Although this blanket categorization tends to have been uncritically accepted, Georges Canguilhem claims in his book *Knowledge of Life* (New York: Fordham University Press, 155n5) that Bachelard's philosophy was far too subtle and complex to be categorized as "a philosophy of the concept." Jason M. Wirth's "The Heat of Language: Bachelard on Idea and Image" in this volume (part 3) will make this point patently clear.

10. On the seeming contradictions in Bachelard's early philosophical project, see his two 1938 publications, *Formation of the Scientific Mind: A Psychoanalysis of Objective Knowledge* and *The Psychoanalysis of Fire*. Bachelard, in fact, did not eschew contradictions but deliberately sought to explore their creative challenges and dynamics—not unlike some of his ancient pre-Socratic predecessors.

11. Bachelard's prolific work on the elemental imagination is briefly cited in Kennedy's *Home*, vis-à-vis Irigaray's metaphysics of Being-within or maternal space (107–8). Bachelard had long explored the imaginary of "flesh" (*la chair*)—starting implicitly with experiences of inner maternal warmth in *Psychoanalysis of Fire* (40–41), a poetics of living blood in *Water and Dreams* (59–60), and most ostensibly in *Earth and Reveries of Repose* (127–28, 130, 170–71, 181). In *Le Matérialisme rationnel* he would radically distinguish such "material reveries" from the "positive experiences at work in the world of tangible matters" (21), a line of epistemological research that has since paved the way for the recent surge in "materials science programs" in universities throughout the world.

12. In this 1957 text, which won the Grand-Prix National des Lettres in 1961, Bachelard proposed that the unfolding of being in the dynamism of a poetic image is "referable to a direct ontology" (PS xii), stressing that such a nascent ontology entails a break with previous knowledge at the moment when the new being of an image emerges in consciousness (PS xi, xiv, xix). Shortly thereafter Merleau-Ponty declared that "one cannot make a direct ontology. My 'indirect'

method (being in the beings) is alone conformed with being—'negative philosophy' like 'negative theology'" (VI 179). Possibly in response to Merleau-Ponty's objection, in *The Poetics of Reverie* Bachelard would further qualify his ontology by noting that "one can know states which are ontologically below being and above nothingness," where "the contradiction between being and non-being fades away" and a playful "sub-being (*moins-être*)" tries itself out as being without yet bearing being's full weight (PR 111).

13. Merleau-Ponty, *The World of Perception*, trans. Oliver Davis (New York: Routledge, 2004), 65.

14. Merleau-Ponty, *Signs*, trans. Richard C. McCleary (Evanston: Northwestern University Press, 1964), 57.

15. See Merleau-Ponty, *The Phenomenology of Perception*, trans. Colin Smith (London: Routledge, 1962), 276n1 and 415n1. See also Gary Gutting's comments in *French Philosophy in the Twentieth Century* (Cambridge, UK: Cambridge University Press), 116–17.

16. Given that their mutual friend and colleague Jean Wahl had asked Bachelard to direct the 1939 International Colloquium at Pontigny on the theme of "Destiny," it is unlikely that Merleau-Ponty and the young philosophers in France who were then turning to the concrete "moment" (Jean-Paul Sartre, Louis Althusser, Emmanuel Levinas, who became a naturalized French citizen in 1931, and Walter Benjamin who moved to Paris escaping the Nazis in 1933) were unaware of Bachelard's groundbreaking work on vertical time and the fertile instant. Although they did not cite him on this crucial topic, a stir was decidedly in the air—no small thanks to Bachelard. For a fascinating account of the history and legacy of the Pontigny encounters (to be resumed temporarily at Mount Holyoke College during World War II, and in the Norman village of Cerisy, after the old abbey at Pontigny was decimated by the Nazis), see Christopher Benfey's "A Violence from Within," in *Artists, Intellectuals, and World War II*, ed. C. Benfey and K. Remmler (Boston: University of Massachusetts Press, 2006, 1–13), and Jacques Derrida's chapter in the same book, "The Philosophical Model of a Counter-Institution" (46–55).

17. This long oversight is now being redressed by recent publications, such as *Imagination et Mouvement: Autour de Bachelard et Merleau-Ponty*, edited by Julien Lamy and Gilles Hieronimus (Lyon: Transversales Philosophiques, EME Éditions, 2015), Anton Vydra's comparative work on both phenomenologists (see Vydra's notes in chapter 6 below), and Glen Mazis's *Merleau-Ponty and the Face of the World: Silence, Ethics, Imagination and Poetic Ontology* (Albany: State University of New York Press, 2016), which addresses Bachelard's influence on Merleau-Ponty's development of his philosophy of flesh. At least since the mid-1940s, a tacit cross-fertilization had been underway between the works of these two philosophers, no doubt stimulated by the surge of artistic and poetic circles in France at the time.

18. See Foucault's 1954 essay "Dream, Imagination, and Existence," trans. William Forrest, published in Ludwig Binswanger's *Dream and Existence*, ed. Keith

Hoeller, as a special issue of *The Review of Existential Psychology and Psychiatry* 19, no. 1 (1984–85): 31–78.

19. Posted on YouTube on February 15, 2015: https://www.youtube.com/watch?v=am6TghIrYEc; English translation by E. Rizo-Patron.

20. These ethical-political implications were the critical focus of the recent 2012 colloquium at Cerisy (*Colloque à Cerisy-la-Salle*), celebrated on the occasion of the fiftieth anniversary of Bachelard's passing. The proceedings of this colloquium have been published in Jean-Jacques Wunenburger's edited volume *Gaston Bachelard: Science et Poétique—Une Nouvelle Éthique?* (Paris: Hermann, 2013).

21. Bachelard assigned the term *culture complexes* to collective tendencies grafted onto deeper personal complexes identified by Freudian psychoanalysis (WD 17; see also DD 153, PF 12, L 34). While Carl G. Jung had written about "feeling-toned *complexes*" decades earlier, in the mid-1930s Bachelard started developing the notion as a research tool along a parallel track, until he became familiar with Jung's work, which he strongly endorsed in his books after 1947 (ERW, ERR, PS, PR). In a 1957 interview with Alexander Aspel, Bachelard admitted that he had "received Jung too late" (cited in C. G. Christofides, "Bachelard's Aesthetics," *Journal of Aesthetics and Art Criticism* 20, no. 3 [1962]: 267–68).

22. Merleau-Ponty would later articulate such dynamics in *The Visible and the Invisible*, trans. Alphonso Lingis (Evanston: Northwestern University Press, 1968) under the rubrics of "reversibility" or "chiasm" (130–55), though he tended to describe it more as a structural condition or an act with two faces (263–65) than as a polemically productive force.

23. As stated in her preface, Madeleine Préclaire had considered entitling her book *Un chemin vers Siloë*, a phrase which—through its allusion to the healing fountain of Siloam (John 9:7)—suggests the forces of eternal renewal that inspired Bachelard's oeuvre until the end of his life. With this in view, the forthcoming English translation by E. Rizo-Patron is entitled *On the Way to Siloam*.

24. The impressive coterie of French continental philosophers whose thinking came under the impact of Bachelard's pioneering work during the twentieth century—despite its uneven reception—is remarkable. Besides Althusser (on the "epistemological break"), Sartre, Merleau-Ponty, Foucault, Derrida, and Irigaray, others deserving special mention here are Paul Ricoeur (on the development of his theories of language and poetic hermeneutics), and Canguilhem (in the fields of scientific epistemology and the health sciences).

25. Bachelard's advances in the field of the history and philosophy of science nonetheless appear to have had a lasting hold on American research, especially from the late 1940s onward—as attested, for instance, by the influence of his notion of "epistemological rupture" on Thomas S. Kuhn's "paradigm shift" theory in *The Structure of Scientific Revolutions* (Chicago: University of Chicago Press, 1962; 50th-anniversary edition, 2012).

Part 1

Adventures in Time

Chapter 1

The Difference an Instant Makes: Bachelard's Brilliant Breakthrough

Edward S. Casey

> Le temps ne coule plus. Il jaillit.
>
> —Bachelard, *L'Intuition de l'instant* (106)

One can read much, perhaps all, of the philosophy of the last two centuries—from Kant and Hegel to Bergson and James, from Husserl and Heidegger to Derrida and Deleuze—as a series of meditations on this one question: Is time continuous, or is it disruptive? Does it flow, or is it punctiform? The crux of the question, upon which any coherent answer depends, is often the status of the instant: Is it just a phase in time's ongoing movement? Or is it a decisive cut in time's streaming, something that brings time itself to a dead halt—at least momentarily?

This is not an arbitrary question, a mere artifact of doing philosophy in a certain way, much less a matter of staying within one's schooling in the field. It cuts to the heart of the matter: How do we experience time after all? Or (putting it less subjectively): What is time itself like? Does it occur in uninterrupted succession, one event after another with no breaks in between, or does it happen in punctuated units? These questions are asked equally of the creation of the world, of the way things are, and of how we take them to be. Here I shall focus on the experiential aspect of time-features that concerned a medley of thinkers in the last one hundred and twenty five years (dating from the publication of James's *Principles of Psychology* in 1890) and that qualifies all, or most, of them as "phenomenological" in some sufficiently generous sense. (Even Bachelard affiliated himself with this trend in his last works, most notably in *The Poetics of Space*).[1] It is from this largely phenomenological standpoint that my own brief contribution will be set forth.

A false start is often taken (I started taking it myself only a few minutes ago; I couldn't seem to help it): this is the antithesis between the continuity of duration as sheer becoming, a kind of gapless becoming on the one hand, and on the other, the discontinuity introduced by the instant conceived as a mere point, a cut, an interval, and so on. The contrast is that between time as a thickly flowing band that draws all differences into itself in what Bergson would designate as "heterogeneous multiplicity,"[2] and a punctiformity that disintegrates this same band into a powder of instants: in which the point (the "now-point" as Husserl called it) is at once indivisible and divisive. This is not just an antithesis, it is also an antinomy in which one can argue coherently for either model taken one at a time, yet one has to acknowledge that the two taken together are incompatible with one another.

It is into this very impasse that Bachelard boldly strode by reconceiving the instant not as a mere cut, nor a geometric point, nor simple location, but as a creative source of time itself. This is the thesis of Bachelard's remarkable book *Intuition of the Instant*, published in 1932 during the hegemony of Bergsonian thought in France. My aim is to explore different dimensions of this thesis than the ones that Bachelard, embroiled in a polemic with Bergson, emphasized in the space of such a short text. In what does the creativity of the instant consist? How may we understand this today?

A premise of his reconstrual of the instant is stated bluntly by Bachelard in *The Dialectic of Duration*, a sequel volume published four years later in 1936: "psychical continuity is not a given, but something constructed [*une oeuvre*]" (DD 19/viii, trans. modified). Constructed from what? From instants, concatenated rhythmic patterns that provide the sense or structure of continuity that we cannot afford to ascribe to the flow of duration itself. An entire "rhythmanalysis" ensues (DD 136–55), anticipating Henri Lefebvre's later employment of this notion in *The Production of Space,* a book that accomplishes for social space what Bachelard attempts to achieve in the instance of personal time.[3]

Apart from this special thesis, what is of most interest for us is the claim that the instant, far from being a desiccated or desiccating entity, is itself creative. Heidegger takes Aristotle to task for his analysis of time in terms of the punctiform now—the "now no longer" and the "now not yet"—leaving a void in the center of temporal experience which only the ecstasis of *Dasein*'s temporality in the form of its future-directedness can fill. Perhaps, however, we can reconstrue the now itself, the instant that occurs in (and as) the present, in a way that does not require such radical surgery and that restores to the present itself its own integrity and power. This is the direction suggested by Bachelard, who is not averse to ecstasy—he is perfectly capable of speaking of "the very ecstasy of the newness of the image" (PS xi)—but who proposes that there is something in the instant itself that is generative of the new that is the basis of temporal ecstasy. This is a unique flashing-forth from within the experience of time itself in the instant. Bachelard describes it as "the flare-up of being in the imagination [*la flambée de l'être dans l'imagination*]" (PS xiv/2). But it is not enough to replace one graphic metaphor with yet another more graphic one: flashing or flaring for ecstasy. Can we be more specific about what constitutes the inherent creativity of the instant? If so, then we might be able to support the radical view, first articulated by Bachelard, that the instant deconstructs the false antinomies of continuity versus discontinuity, duration versus the cut, becoming versus being, line versus point, and so on. We can do so by proposing not just a third term to set alongside two opposing terms, or some summation of all three, nor even a composite or assemblage in the manner of a Heideggerian *Versammlung*. The task for us, in the wake of Bachelard's breakthrough, is how to grasp this new sense of the instant taken as a source of the new itself, what Husserl cryptically called the "source-point [*Quellepunkt*]" that is at once "originary [*ursprünglich*]" and "creative [*schöpferisch*]."[4] But just how, where, and in what way is it creative? Bachelard himself tended to interpret it in terms of the "act/action," "decision," and especially "newness."[5] Here I would like to explore two additional parameters of the creativity of the instant: dimensions that are closely affiliated with newness and that are suggested, and sometimes explicitly mentioned, in Bachelard's analysis yet never fully pursued.

Human existence, doubtless all animal existence, is a jumpy affair, always on edge. Contrary to the assurance which we so often seek at personal and metaphysical levels alike—whether in settled dwelling or in the deliverances of a metaphysics of presence—the plain truth is that we experience our lives disjointedly, nomadically, in an ever-decentered and deferred way. Just as perception (the very paradigm of the epistemically stable source) takes place by way of quick glances, cast casually yet tellingly into every surrounding scene, so time (the putative paragon of continuous flowing) is lived in terms of disparate instants: now this event, now that one, then still another: not in a steady succession of discrete and datable occurrences but in upheavals of happenings and congeries of contingencies, whose corresponding emotional states are commensurately diverse. The live perceptual world is a glance-world—a world at a glance—where "time no longer flows, it leaps [*il jaillit*]" (II 60/106),[6] as Bachelard says so acutely. But in this *jaillissement,* this inconsistent gushing and unstable sprouting, we receive time's gift. And we do so in two guises: the *sudden* and the *surprising.*

The sudden is a subterranean but potent concept in Western thought. It first shows up officially in Plato's *Parmenides,* where as *to exaiphnes* it signifies what happens so quickly that it cannot be contained by the usual categories of thought—all of which valorize "determinate presence" in Heidegger's term for metaphysical notions that freeze Being rather than let it stand out into the open. The sudden cuts across such notions, just as it disturbs our ordinary expectations; it catches us conceptually defenseless as it were: a point not lost on Kierkegaard, who also recognized its importance in his *Philosophical Fragments.* Yet, for this very reason, it offers us insights not otherwise available—insights that can only occur all of a sudden, with a startle or a shock. These insights are in effect encounters with what comes upon us so rapidly that we have no chance to attend to it carefully, much less to cognize it in the usual patterns. We are in the domain of the *Aha Erlebnis,* but we are not limited to experience in any of its normalities and expectancies. We are "caught unawares," that is to say, unaware of what to say or do with what happens to us. Such suddennesses range from delicate but definitive moments of realizing that something is not working in a personal relationship to the experience of a poetic image—as in Bachelard's exemplary instance is a poetic image as "a sudden salience on the surface of the psyche" (PS xi)[7]—to events of epic proportions such as Kennedy's assassination or the 9/11 attacks. The fact that in the latter cases we almost always remember just where we were when we heard the catastrophic news is the placial equivalent of the temporal instant of reception.

Suddenness is a primary dimension of the instant: it qualifies the instant itself. Every instant occurs suddenly; there are no drawn out instants: what is drawn out in *distentio animi* (St. Augustine) is, rather, the moment, *der*

Augenblick, as well as what every instant proffers, its specific content: the very rapid arrival of what we had not exactly expected to be the case. (It follows that no expectation is ever fulfilled perfectly: gaps of excess or deficiency besiege even the surest best, disappointing or delighting us, either way.)

With the sudden we are already in the arms of the surprising. The two terms are coeval if not precisely coextensive. Only what happens suddenly can truly surprise me; and what surprises me arises suddenly. But the sudden is, strictly speaking, a predicate *of* time as instantaneous, while the surprising characterizes what arises *in* time: what "takes us over" (as "sur-prise" signifies in its original meaning), what supervenes in our lives, captivating us.

The surprising is a late modern, and by now a postmodern, avatar of wonder, that basic philosophical mood valorized from Aristotle to Descartes. If wonder is close to awe in its sweeping scope (ultimately, it is the world itself, or being-in-it, that is the proper subject of wonder, as both Fink and Heidegger suggest), surprise has a more restricted domain that is, however, no less significant. This is an arena of poignant intensity: of configurated events. Only something with shape can surprise; but the shape is not that of habitual perception or thought: it is a supervening shape that studs the field of the customary body. "I'm surprised to see you here," I say, though not amazed, not wonderstruck, not set back or overwhelmed. Instead, I find your recognizable presence something supererogatory, even gratuitous. I had just planned to give a talk at SPEP; I come into the prescribed room, and there you are: welcome or not, a distinct and distinctive entity in my purview, something to pin my glance on for an instant.

"For an instant": that is the point. The surprising, no less than the sudden, occurs in and as an instant, instantaneously. Even if it arises at the end of a long process of meditation or rumination, still it emerges in an instant. As I attend to something, turning it over carefully in my mind or perception, convinced that I have fathomed it fully, I remain subject to surprise at any moment.[8] Something like this happens in diverse domains: running steadily in training for my personal marathon, I feel bogged down within my ever increasing bodily limits until, one day, I am surprised—and certainly pleased—to discover that I can run one more lap of the quarter-mile track than ever before. Likewise in writing: Husserl wrote every day of his adult life, often repeating and restating ideas of the previous few days but then, in an instant, he was surprised to come upon a new spur of thought not hitherto accessible to him. It is as if Merleau-Ponty's distinction between the "habitual" and "momentary" body were suddenly to dissolve into one body of surprise. The very locution "surprised to [learn, hear, know] X" underlines the instantaneous character of surprise: the sharp prepositional "to" emphasizes the pointed discovery of what acts to surprise us.

Both the sudden and the surprising are creatures of the instant, together constituting its most closely fitting and effective armature. Linking them is a temporal structure I have not yet mentioned: the all at once, the *totum simul* that Aquinas attributed to God's perception of the created world. But I mean by it something much more modest, as invoked in the ordinary phrase "all of a sudden." All of a sudden we are surprised. In other words, the sudden and the surprising happen *tout d'un coup.* They co-occur, but in such a way that the occurring itself takes no time; or rather, it takes the stroke of an instant, which occurs by impaction as it were, all-at-once and here-and-now: "[W]hen it strikes, the instant imposes itself all in one blow (*tout d'un coup*), completely (*tout entier*)" (II 15/27). This is no ordinary but quite an extraordinary factor of time. For it does not happen in the ordinary taken-for-granted way—successively, in some linear or *nacheinander* fashion: an ineluctably horizontal model. Rather, it exhibits what Bachelard calls "verticality": "The aim [of a poetic instant] is *verticality* as depth or height—it is that stabilized instant wherein simultaneities prove, by ordering themselves, that the poetic instant has metaphysical scope" (II 58–59/104). But such an instant also has the phenomenological dimension on which I am insisting, in terms of which the sudden and the surprising happen together in an instant—not in the sense of the time they occupy or take up but as constituting the felt dimensions of the instant itself. And not just the poetic instant but any experienced instant: Bachelard's insight is widely generalizable. We experience every passing instant as refulgent with the surprising in its suddenness, and as sudden in its surprisingness: both together, the two-as-one in the temporal equivalent of Plato's indefinite dyad. But the members of this dyad are not the like and the unlike, the same and the different, the odd and the even; they are the deeply convergent, implosively so. So much so, that they arise both-at-once—altogether intertwined and temporally conterminous, even if not coincident in content.

What can we say about the relation of the sudden and the surprising to the novelty *(nouveauté)* that is Bachelard's own ultimate interest in his meditations on the poetic image? I shall conclude by ruminating on this last link.

The Bachelardian axiom goes like this: "Novelty is, in principle, always instantaneous" (II 21/37).[9] This is not just any "novelty"—but what Bachelard himself calls an "essential novelty"—namely, something essentially *new*. In what does such *newness* consist? In particular, three kinds of newness are here pertinent:

First, there is the new of the utterly unprecedented, the absolutely new—so new that it cannot even be designated "new" except in retrospect, when we realize just how new it was. So new, too, that we must devise a new kind or category for the new thing or landscape, feeling, or thought we have encountered: a kind irreducible to any previously known kind. Examples would be reading philosophy for the first time (it was Santayana for me), encountering a different civilization (say, Tibet), or seeing a new configuration of mountains (for example, the Crazy Mountains rising straight from the flat Montana plains).

Second, there are those things that are always essentially new, that cannot be what they are without being experienced as altogether new, yet somehow stay within the same kind or species: love for the nth time, reading a great book or seeing a great painting where the book or painting seems new each time (Proust's *Remembrance of Things Past*; El Greco's *View of Toledo*).

Third and finally, there are those things or experiences that are newly presented. In these, the new is winnowed from the old; it emerges from the familiar itself; such newness is not altogether new, but is new in relation to (and often despite) what has come before. Bachelard is especially struck by this form of newness, for example in the case of habit: "[H]abit is always an act restituted in its novelty" (II 37/64). As we can see in the case of attention, the very repetition of an act allows for the emergence of something new within it: as aspect of it never before noticed, an extension of it never before considered. In addition, habit brings with it another avatar not lost on Bachelard, who says strikingly that "habit is a routine assimilation of novelty" (II 37/64). Habitual practices, then, prepare us for the reception of the new—not the utterly new (nothing prepares us for that) nor even the new-each-time (which inheres in the complexity or density of an experience or a work)—but the new that just barely exceeds the routinely known: the new -just-now-arising as we may call it. If this last kind of newness is the most difficult to grasp (since routine itself may blind us to it), it is also the most frequently encountered.

What is most remarkable is that it is the instant alone that delivers each sort of newness to us. Or rather the instant as suddenly and surprisingly occurring: suddenly as clearing the ground, illuminating it like a stroke of lightning; surprisingly as thrusting forward something new on that same ground.[10] Nothing but an instant with this twofold power can open for us the prospect of the altogether new, often astonishing in its force or content (think of witnessing the sudden eruption of Krakatoa). What else but an instant can reveal to us the ever-new manifestations of the same depthless novel or the same person we love? And what but an instant can render us susceptible to the newly presented, to the unfamiliar that is drawn into the orbit of the habitual?

Bachelard is largely silent on the role of the instant in engendering the first two forms of newness. Yet everything he does say points to its indispensability in these contexts. When he speaks of "the vital force (*élan*) furnished by the radical novelty of *instants*" (II 37/65), we cannot help but hear in this deconstruction of Bergson the insistence that instants are the privileged, perhaps the exclusive, vehicles of the new in its sheer otherness as well as in its being the same as ever-different. Regarding its role in conveying this third sort of *newness*, Bachelard is explicit: "To seize habit in its essence, it is therefore necessary to seize it in its growth. Thus, by its incremental successes, habit becomes the synthesis of novelty and routine, and *that synthesis is crystallized through fertile instants*" (II 38/65, my italics). It is my contention that the same "synthesis"—a term Bachelard employs in a decidedly non-dialectical fashion—occurs in the first two forms of newness: a synthesis, however, that rightly retains its name only in contrast with the antithesis of point and line, cut and duration. Otherwise, it is a synthesis that continually undoes itself in time's "march of death" (in Husserl's stark phrase).

The undoing is the work of the instant in its dissolving, deconstructive potency. But the same instant is responsible for the doing, the creative work that is equally part of every instant and that is the focus of Bachelard's remarkable breakthrough. He saw, if not before than, better than anyone else, the creative potential of the instant. This is a potential glimpsed by Plato and Kierkegaard, Heidegger, and Benjamin (who relates it to "the sudden flash of recognition" in the *Arcades Project*), but not set forth as such until the publication of Bachelard's *Intuition of the Instant.* My aim, in this chapter, has been to extend Bachelard's basic insights into a still fuller acknowledgment of the unsuspected power of the instantaneous to deliver newness: newness of several sorts, all borne on the closely coordinated wings of the sudden and the surprising. The instant is creative and not merely divisive, efficacious and not just reflective, in its ability to bring what is truly new—new in ever new ways—into our grateful or startled ken.

A last remark is in order. By now we should be able to replace "instant"—a word still stubbornly suggesting a too determinate unit of time—with "instantaneously": the new comes to us less in an instant as a unit of time than *instantaneously*, where the adverb better conveys its surprising and sudden intervention. If we follow this path, we shall be less tempted to say that the instant brings the new (as I have just been tempted to say) than that, as the instantaneously occurring, the instant *is* the new: it is the new now, the now as news, the new itself insofar as we can know it, or at least as we can sense it: this, all of this, all at once in life as in poetry, in philosophy as in history, in word as in image.

Notes

1. See Bachelard's introduction to *The Poetics of Space*, where he spells out the principles of the phenomenological approach, which he proceeds to illustrate brilliantly in each of his subsequent chapters. See Anton Vydra's chapter 6 (below) on Bachelard's critical exploration of the phenomenological approach throughout his career leading up to his explicit endorsement of it in *The Poetics of Space.*

2. Henri Bergson, *Time and Free Will: An Essay of the Immediate Data of Consciousness,* trans. F. L. Pogson (New York: Dover, 2001), chap. 2.

3. See Henri Lefebvre's *The Production of Space*, trans. Donald N. Smith (Oxford: Blackwell Publishers, 2000), pp. 356, 405. More importantly, see his later *Rhythmanalysis: Space, Time, and Everyday Life, trans. Stuart Elden and Gerald Moore* (London: Continuum, 2004), as well as Elden's introduction to the book, which traces Bachelard's influence on Lefebvre's work (xiii, 9, 105n6).

4. On the now as "source-point" and its "originary" and "creative" character, see Edmund Husserl, *On the Phenomenology of the Consciousness of Internal Time*, trans. John Barnett Brough (Dordrecht / Boston: Kluwer Academic Publishers, 1991), 29f, 71, 74, 375.

5. Concerning action: "Real time exists only through the isolated instant, which is to be found wholly in the act, in what is actual, in the present" (II 30); also: "Because of its newness and its action, the poetic image has an entity and a dynamism of its own" (PS xii). Concerning decision: "Before the complicated process of the leap [into action] is actually set off, there has already been a simple, brutal instant of decision" (II 21). Concerning novelty or newness, among many passages, I again refer the reader to both *Intuition of the Instant* (II 15, 21, 32, 37–38, 46), and *The Poetics of Space,* where the "essential novelty of the poem" is seen as residing in an instantaneous image (PS xi).

6. *Il jaillit* could be variously translated as "it springs forth, it shoots up; it spouts or spurts; it jets or gushes; it bursts or explodes." Each of these English terms expresses an aspect of Bachelard's *jaillissement,* which is singularly suggestive.

7. Compare also PS xiv: "The poetic act itself, the sudden image, *the flare-up of being in the imagination,* are inaccessible to such investigations [i.e., as are found in certain psychoanalytical methods]" (my italics).

8. Pondering over attention itself, Bachelard concludes that "attention is . . . a series of beginnings; it is constituted by those mental rebirths that occur in consciousness when it heeds time's instants" (II 20/36).

9. This is spelled out as: "If novelty is essential to becoming, one has everything to gain by attributing such novelty to time itself: what is novel within uniform time is not being but rather the instant, which, in renewing itself, carries being back to its original freedom, to the initial accident or chance of becoming" (II 15/27).

10. I am not claiming that everything that is surprising is fully new: I can be surprised by the return of the familiar itself. In this case, I am engaged in the third form of newness, that is, in what is newly presented to me from within the customary context of the already known.

Chapter 2

Bachelard's "Non-Bergsonism"

Jean-François Perraudin

Translated by Eileen Rizo-Patron

Despite the distinctive polemical approach of Gaston Bachelard's "philosophy of no" vis-à-vis scientific and philosophical tradition, his accounts of time and imagination were significantly inspired by those of his renowned predecessor, Henri Bergson (1859–1941). My purpose in this chapter will be to show how Bachelard's critique of Bergson's theory of duration actually helps to advance a more prolific, therapeutic understanding of time and imagination than Bergson's account of the *élan vital* continuum had managed to reveal.

Gaston Bachelard first appeared on the French philosophical scene as an ardent polemical thinker. His philosophy of science was ostensibly developed against Meyerson's. But his liveliest, most persistent polemic was addressed to Bergsonism in particular. Not one of Bergson's key points escaped becoming the object of a dialectical reversal: his visualism, his pragmatism, his conceptions of *homo faber* and the imagination, his ontology, his vocabulary, his very images. From the *Essai sur la connaissance approchée* (1928) onward, a critique began to take shape against the Bergsonian thesis that the qualitative aspect of sensation eludes numerical and spatial determinations. Even on the literary end of Bachelard's work, in his posthumously published *Fragments of a Poetics of Fire* (1988), we read: "The poetic image is truly the work of a spoken instant, an instant one will fail to grasp in the attempt to plot it against the untorn and untearable continuity of Bergsonian consciousness" (FPF 7). If we transport this proposition onto the plane of creative imagination, it echoes the thesis of temporal discontinuity that Bachelard had developed explicitly against Bergson as early as *Intuition of the Instant* (1932) and *The Dialectic of Duration* (1936).

All commentators agree in recognizing in these texts a moment of essential divergence between Bachelard and the author of *Creative Evolution.* But numerous are those critics for whom Bachelard's philosophy of the imaginary reveals crypto-Bergsonian tendencies.[1] In *De l'Imagination poétique dans l'oeuvre de Gaston Bachelard*, for instance, François Pire writes: "After all is said and done, Bachelard is a Bergsonian when he proposes that the image provides access to a kind of knowledge that outmaneuvers the powers of intellect. The essential coincidence is between intuitionism and phenomenology."[2] Similarly, Pierre Quillet's splendid presentation of Gaston Bachelard in the series *Philosophes de Tous les Temps*, suggests that, among Bachelard's books on the imagination, only *Lautréamont* is in fact an "oneiric transcription" of his philosophy of time, while his books on the Elements and on Poetics somehow manage to reinstate Bergson's philosophy of duration: "Bachelardian imagination is Bergsonian intuition—yet somewhat freer, more penetrating, more transcendent, stripped of its empiricism and of late nineteenth-century evolutionism."[3] There is seductiveness in these remarks, especially the latter, which is nonetheless not entirely satisfying. We are struck, on the contrary, by the recurring critique of certain Bergsonian theses throughout Bachelard's works until the end of his career. I will here attempt to clarify this problem with the proviso that a more exhaustive body of research on Bachelard's critique of Bergson has yet to be carried out.

Bachelard's declaration that he accepted everything about Bergsonism except temporal continuity is well known. So let us begin by examining the import of Bergson's philosophy of time. This philosophy responded to two key concerns and to a third, less evident one, which nonetheless interested Bachelard the most. Bergson aimed, first of all, at assigning a limit to the positivistic imperialism that sought to reduce phenomena of consciousness to what is measurable and quantitative, by demonstrating that duration, which is assimilated to the very movement of mind, must translate into qualitative terms. By the same token, he aimed at defending the thesis of the freedom and spontaneity of mind by associating it with the creative duration of unexpected novelties. Finally—and this is where Bergson's philosophy fell short in Bachelard's estimation—it also found a need to outline some of the practical and therapeutic perspectives that would best assist us in using time, in better living time. This last point merits special emphasis, for Bachelard subscribed to the following proposal by Pierre Janet: "If we talk about knowledge of time, we have to arrive at ways in which we can protect ourselves against time and ways in which we can make use of it" (DD 50).[4] Does Bergson's philosophy of duration entail an equivalent project? If so, how does it address its challenges?

Bergson attempted to conjoin two aspects of lived temporality through consciousness. First of all, its flowing quality, its mobility, and its perpetually creative character—it is this aspect that is particularly developed in *Time and Free Will: An Essay on the Immediate Data of Consciousness*.[5] The images that best translate this intuition are most often aquatic: the very nature of duration, he later writes in *Creative Evolution*, is "a flux of fleeting shades merging into each other."[6] That which suggests duration is the image of a fresh watercolor, the mobile image of fluid nuances, the impressionism of blurred and interpenetrating boundaries (one might recall that Bergson was especially fond of Turner, while an uncompromising Bachelard preferred writing about Monet). Yet, as if to ward off a possible Heraclitean accusation, Bergson's term "duration" will come to suggest a certain permanence and organization underlying change. Images hence become more substantial. This is in fact the very pulp of *The Creative Mind*[7] and of that astonishing image of the snowball in *Creative Evolution*: "My mental state, as it advances on the road of time, is continually swelling from the duration which it accumulates: it goes on increasing—rolling upon itself, as a snowball on the snow" (CE 2)—an amazing and embarrassing image which, against its author's intent, seems to lead from temporality to space through the peculiar presence of the "road" of time. But this difficulty can be resolved if one understands that each consciousness receives its own impetus, its sloping curve, from the initial movement and continuum of the vital impetus (*élan vital*), a universal duration in which it partakes, and within which it is included.

That difficulty lifted, we might say that the snowball image condenses the essentials of Bergsonism as it will be critiqued by Bachelard. It in effect demonstrates that the past, folded over the present, tends to rejoin the future: here we have a compenetration of moments within the sensory-motor present expressed through the location of my body. This present is such that it allows me to use perceived images from my immediate past to orient myself towards the future possible action of my body in space. One could gather from this image that all past states are thus integrally preserved (it is the accumulated duration that continually causes our state of soul to expand) in such a way that it is the past itself that impels me towards the future. A perfect condensation of the entire substantialist and continuist concept of duration, much as that other statement from *The Creative Mind*: "It is not the 'states,' simple snapshots we have taken once again along the course of change, that are real; rather, it is flux, the continuity of transition, it is change itself that is real. This change is indivisible, it is even substantial" (CM 6).

Duration so described is fundamentally generative. It is that by which being is diversified into creatures and creations. In Bergson's words: "*Le temps est ce qui se fait, et meme ce qui fait que tout se fait*"—namely, "Time is what happens [generates itself]—and indeed what makes everything happen [be generated]."[8] This creation corresponds to a process of natural productive maturation—unpredictable, for sure, but capable of being relinked to the past through reflexive hindsight, in such a way that this philosophy of impersonal creation should never cease to affirm continuity. To create is never quite an inaugural act, for Bergson. On the contrary, the instant and discontinuity both belong to the order of illusion. This illusion is due to an imperfection in our faculty of attention, which does not grasp imperceptible, progressive modifications except when they suddenly become pregnant (CE 3). It has yet another origin: the very tendency of an intelligence associated with conceptual language to resort to space and always to address what stands out. Consequently, it is not surprising that the instant should have no privileged dimension in Bergson's philosophy. In *Creative Evolution* we read:

> A thousand incidents arise, which seem to be cut off from those that precede them, and to be disconnected from those that follow. Discontinuous though they appear . . . in point of fact they stand out against the continuity of a background on which they are designed, and to which indeed they owe the intervals that separate them; they are the beats of the drum that break forth here and there in the symphony. (CE 3)

Thus called upon by the melodic demands of the symphony-duration, the instant is not creative in and by itself, in Bergson's view. Rather, it is through the melody that duration brings change, much like sap brings fruit to ripeness. The task of intuition would then be to grasp the subtlest nuances in our mind, the will to work towards perfection and the plenitude of being. That which intelligence situates via isolated markers, here or there, as so many snapshots of a movement that is nonetheless indivisible, will appear to intuition rather as a movement "which corresponds to an inner work of *ripening* or creating" (CE 11, my emphasis).

Through this notion of intuition, one can discover within Bergson's philosophy what may be called a therapeutic perspective. Such a concern is evident, first of all, in chapter 4 of *Creative Evolution* where Bergson argues that the idea of nothingness is but a pseudo-idea that has given rise to the false problems of classical metaphysics: "The torturing problems, the questions that we cannot gaze at without feeling giddy and bewildered" (CE 275). This discussion is without doubt the essential source of Bergson's concept of duration, as Bachelard will show. Be that as it may, it does seem that for Bergson our consciousness of time is one that, while not necessarily afflicted with anguish, is still undeniably impaired—a consciousness which at bottom relishes its own impoverishment, namely, its impersonal character. Some might even say that the reduction of "conscious" life into discontinuous states—life thus refracted and fragmented by our demon of analysis—lends itself far better to practical life, to social existence, to the functions of language. Yet, against this, Bergsonian intuition is a movement of conversion by which we cease to act so as to allow our life to flow—a dreamlike movement by which we install ourselves in the womb of duration, granting the present its maximum extension, encompassing our entire past history as in the panoramic vision of a person facing imminent death. Duration has not only a theoretical intent (that of providing an answer to certain questions such as substance, or of putting an end to "false problems" such as the preservation of memories), but also the immediate practical value of yielding satisfactions analogous to those of art—namely, the impression of enhancement, enrichment, an opening of our being within time. Thus, in a philosophy understood as the *intuition of duration* (and Bergson always responds to this view), "reality no longer appears as a static state, that is, as being; rather it affirms itself dynamically within the continuity and variability of its vital impetus. Whatever there was of frozen immobility in our perception is now melted down and set into motion. A great vital impulse (*élan*) carries all beings and things. We feel lifted, carried away, led by its momentum. We live more fully" (CM 131–32).

A snowball with the flame of inextinguishable memories sizzling at its core; a fresh watercolor with merging colors; an invitation to dwell within the landscape of sounds and movements of symphonic duration—learn how to make use of these incantations, and you shall *own* time—Bergson would say.

Now let us picture a skeptical land-dweller, sufficiently in love with water to reach amorously towards it, but who unfailingly encounters "the shadows and reflections upon the river's moving mirror, never quite the limpid stream. Like substance, duration delivers nothing but phantoms" (II 19/33). This same river water will eventually yield other visions in the philosopher from Champagne, of course. But let us take matters one at a time.

How is it that Bachelard was led to subvert the theory of temporal continuity? If at the onset of his meditation on Roupnel's *Siloë* in *Intuition of the Instant*, Bachelard still admits his closeness to Bergson, his philosophy of science soon prompts his detachment from the master. The determining moments in the evolution of the sciences can indeed be found, he claims, in their sudden methodological ruptures. The history of scientific rationalism is defined by victories over the past. In this sense, the past is not the substance of the present except in a dialectical sense: the past is almost always a state to be reformed. Later on, he will denounce what J. L. Backès refers to as the "unfortunate continuities" of prescientific thinking in the arts of simple association.[9] Such false continuities readily turn into epistemological obstacles, contributing to a failure in understanding and defining novel phenomena. It is in this sense that the alchemist gives himself over to hasty analogies, those which unjustifiably link the mineral with the living world (FSM, chap. 8) and which somehow make "heart" rhyme with "sun" (PF, chap. 5). Thus, the primary intuition in Bachelard's philosophy is that of *initiation*—an intuition whereby the mind *frees* itself from cultural programming. The diurnal person is one who truly begins a new day, free from memories of the day before, knowing that rationality lies ahead. Hence Bachelard's appeal: "Give us not the empiricism of your evenings, but the vigorous rationalism of your mornings" (PN 11). Nascence here stands over against maturation.

It is not without some hesitation that Bachelard ventures to refute the theory of continuous time. He admits this himself in *Intuition of the Instant* (II 8, 14, 16, 18). But two reasons determine his decision to opt against Bergson, in favor of Roupnel. The first can be traced back to the theory of relativity, from which Bachelard thinks he can draw an argument against the absoluteness of Bergsonian duration. Yet this argument is not very convincing, besides the fact that Bergson responds to it—in advance, as it were—in a lengthy note to *The Creative Mind* (217n5). It seems to me that this factitious discussion plays on a subtle shift in the meaning of the word "duration." Where Bachelard speaks of duration in the sense of that objective, creative reality capable of ordering forms, such that it can appear in *Creative Evolution* under the name of the life-force (*élan vital*), Bergson would defend himself by setting out to show that relativity cannot undermine the intimate duration of consciousness. Indeed, the space-time postulated by relativity theory has no being—existence is conferred, in Bergson's view, only upon that which is perceived by consciousness.[10] But, as it turns out, Bachelard's second argument addresses precisely this type of lived duration. Here we find ourselves redirected back to the psychological terrain of *immediate givens*. Rather than an argument, we should perhaps call it a counterproof. Despite a concerted effort to reach duration in all its simplicity and substantiality, consciousness can only grasp fragments, isolated events. This is what translates the above-cited phrase from *Intuition of the Instant* (II 18–19/33), which amounts to saying that the intuition of pure duration is ultimately unattainable.

The sole temporal reality for Bachelard is, consequently, that of the instant. This option is in part dictated by a question Bachelard asks himself—a question that cannot be answered by the theory of continuity—namely, how do we account for *beginnings*? If the past flows over into the present, how can an act be an absolute origin, a source of decisive change? The thought of continuous time belongs, in his view, to the order of affect: it is emotion that dictates this thought, and its role "is perhaps only to blunt ever-hostile newness" (DD 60).

The instant will provide a better account of the absoluteness of creation, of novelty, if one understands it as the tightening of consciousness which, in a state of sudden tension, will generate an act. Here we retrieve the notion of rupture: the truly creative or *founding* act establishes itself above the nothingness of a discarded past. The instant is an instance of will and spirit/mind (*esprit*)—the term *instance* here understood in the sense of an urgent entreaty—while duration appears as a hardening of life: "Idleness alone lingers; the act is instantaneous. Could we not say then, conversely, that instantaneity is an act" (II 12/23)? That which we have just established sheds light, in my view, on the paradoxical invitation found at the onset of *The Dialectic of Duration*—namely, to live a life of repose (DD 17). It becomes even more polemical with regard to Bergsonism. In Bergson's final therapeutic proposals, as we saw above, he was inviting us to retrieve within ourselves the vast and sweeping movement of universal duration in order to feel ourselves carried, lifted, and led by it. We could no doubt detect a contradiction here: the *volte-face* movement of consciousness detaching itself from all practical interest in life, on the one hand, and its even deeper immersion within the current of life, on the other. But what is at stake here is the effort to recover our human destiny within ourselves—not elsewhere. If it is thus necessary to detach ourselves from life's driving impetus (*élan vital*), it is not because it is a powerful force (Bachelard is far from proposing that we adopt an attitude of immutable tranquility), but because letting ourselves be carried away by it would be but a matter of imitative idleness since it would "lead us away from individual goals." Only by the ability to detach ourselves could we avoid reducing our own time to the time of others, to the social frameworks of duration, to the time of things, and to the time of life (II 59–60). In order to return to ourselves, we must seize this tension that prepares for an increment of being at the edge of the instant. It is in this sense that "pure consciousness will be revealed as the capacity for waiting and for watchfulness, as the freedom and the will to do nothing" (DD 18).[11]

This option will lead Bachelard to inquire into the human mind's power of negation, in such a way that he is able to situate his discussion *vis à vis* the Bergsonian thesis on the idea of nothingness.

That which can be called into question is, indeed, the resistance and impermeability of the temporal tissue in Bergson's account. Because he totally eliminates negation and, more broadly, nothingness from his own philosophy, Bergson ends up attributing too much substance and integrity to duration, situating all creative effectiveness *behind* the present, while consequently granting too little creative power to the present moment itself. Let me offer a brief sketch, in this regard, of the content of chapter 4 in *Creative Evolution*. Here the idea of nothingness appears as a theoretical chimera—an illusion of emptiness, the product of a slippage, on the speculative plane, regarding what we experience in the act of making. For it seems to us that our productions actually fill in voids, or that we are adding something where nothing was before. Attentive only to a very circumscribed area of being, Bergson argues, we do not realize that plenitude, much like the life-force (*élan vital*), is given once and for all. In fact, "we are so deeply immersed within these regional realities, that we cannot extricate ourselves from them" (CE 273). In the same way, if we inquire into the effective content of the idea of nothingness, we see that it always entails repose: I cannot fictitiously eliminate being from myself without discovering plenitude in myself. I cannot represent my own annihilation other than by doubling myself, by resurrecting myself. Finally, from the psychological point of view, the idea of nothingness is but the feeling of disappointment when, as I wait to encounter one thing, I find myself facing another. Emptiness cannot be understood other than by reference to an intuition of plenitude.

This is no reason, however, not to think conversely—and since Bergson's argument is subtended by a logic of affirmation and negation, it could be countered by saying that every affirmation entails an antecedent negation

(DD 32–33). The history of sciences has taught us that nothing positive is given in advance. The positivity of first affirmations is precisely what fetters thought within a kind of dogmatism that must be refuted. It does seem, indeed, that every positive act starts with a negation. Whether it is in the sciences or even in the domains of ethical life and artistic creation, there is always much to undo or to repudiate, much to set to rest in oneself. It is always on the basis of this "will to negate" that one can come up with other possibilities. Gains can thus be made through a constant effort at self-transcendence, at transcending duration. Bachelard points this out and reproaches Bergson for not having given proper consideration to these modes of transcendence in his philosophy (DD 27): imprudence and risk, he claims, will provide the sudden relief from temporal platitude that Bergson's philosophy fails to provide. That relief is the instant.

From this viewpoint, duration is not given—rather, our temporality is something to be realized, to be created. After having refuted Bergson's idea of duration, it may be hard to believe that Bachelard will proceed to reintroduce it as an overlay upon his theory of temporal discontinuity. The question is: How to construct a well-woven duration, how to coordinate instants? The question is not to reestablish a continuity that never existed, but rather to know how instants might benefit from cohesion among themselves. To what kind of risk or imprudence should we deliver ourselves so that a productive resonance, consolidation, or coherence may be established among instants? In this regard we might well ask: Why did Bachelard not explicitly devote a reflective essay to the question of "moral time"? Indications of his thought on this issue, though brief, can nonetheless be found in *Intuition of the Instant* and in his essay "Poetic Instant and Metaphysical Instant." They foreground the values of love and generosity, along with rationality: "To strengthen the heart, it is necessary to reinforce passion with morality, to discover the general reasons for loving" (II 52/92–93). It will be necessary to look for temporal coordination in sympathy and in all that contributes to progress in us. Hence, "there is but one principle of continuity within the forces of the world—namely, the permanence of rational conditions, the conditions of moral and aesthetic success" (II 54/94–95). We might ask ourselves: To what type of imprudence must we deliver ourselves so that instants may develop solidarity along the lines of progress? This question could be accompanied by another: what are the models of such imprudence? Beyond these books about time, I would like to remind the reader that, for Bachelard, the history of human progress is animated by two heroic types which resemble the Bergsonian hero (however remotely, for they are not given to mysticism),[12] namely, the scientist who practices rational imprudence (the one who asks "why not?") and the poet who practices linguistic imprudence. These heroes benefit other individuals through their own dynamism.[13] So much for rational and aesthetic conditions. As for conditions for moral success, perhaps they should also be sought not within philosophy, which—like science—tends to distrust imagination, opposing image to concept, but within Bachelardian wisdom insofar as it endeavors "to make poetry and science complementary, to unite them as two well-defined opposites" (PF 2). And the purport of this wisdom is expressed in a comment recorded by his student Jean Lescure: "You are right in sensing that true humanity has all possibilities within its grasp, and that we must be persons of many means."

Given the restricted dimensions of this chapter, my goal here is not to offer an in-depth exploration as to how the imprudence of rupture and the conditions for the coherence of instants, if not of duration, are realized in different domains. Instead, I shall limit myself to offering some indications regarding Bachelard's philosophy of poetic imagination, insofar as it is in relation to this aspect of his work that the question of his "crypto-Bersgonism" (alluded to earlier) could have been posed. The thesis I wish to defend is clear. In his works on the imagination Bachelard does not abandon his conception of discontinuous temporality; he does not belatedly abandon himself to a sort of Bergsonism. It seems to me that one can reasonably defend the coherence of his thought.

To begin with, it is evident that Bachelard's notion of imagination—as it evolved after his critical texts, *The Formation of the Scientific Mind* and *The Psychoanalysis of Fire*—stands in stark contrast to Bergson's understanding of imagination. Here we find two concepts of human destiny that oppose each other. Against *homo faber*, Bachelard realizes early on that human beings have a poetic destiny (DD 22).[14] From *Water and Dreams* onwards, the distinction he draws between the formal versus material imagination provokes a polemic. Insofar as Bachelard privileges the latter over the former, he affirms the supremacy of an intimate knowledge of substances, through hand and body, over a Bergsonian knowledge of surfaces through vision. Thus, he writes: "Paste produces the *dynamic hand* which is almost the antithesis of the *geometric hand* of Bergson's *homo faber*. It is a medium of energy and no longer merely of form. The dynamic hand symbolizes the imagination of force" (WD 108). This contrast becomes even clearer if one places it alongside a statement from the introduction to *Air and Dreams*—a text crucial to understanding Bachelardian "imagination." In this work Bachelard shows that the classical notions of imagination suffer from a verbal obstacle found in the very word that designates this faculty. As a result, the imagination has been defined as the faculty of forming images. Under such conditions, the image is nothing but the unreal yet analogical form of another form (and it is in this sense that Sartre devises his own theory of the *analogon*). But to stop here amounts to ignoring the dynamic aspect of the imaginary. In his desire for imagination to recover its true prerogative—namely to liberate us from the thrall of reality—Bachelard will insist on its iconoclastic character by describing it as "the faculty that *deforms* images furnished by perception; it is above all the faculty that frees us from initial images and *changes* them" (AD 1/7, trans. modified). Bergson, by contrast, holds onto a classical conception of imagination. Take this example from the introduction to *Creative Evolution*: "A mind born to speculate or to dream, I admit, might remain outside reality, might deform or transform the real, perhaps even create it—as we create the figures of men and animals *that our imagination cuts out of the passing cloud*" (CE xi, my emphasis). Even here, the opposition between dreaming and acting is only apparent. Carving and cutting out (the Bergsonian individual succumbs to a "tailor complex") are so many acts common to perception, intelligence, and imagination, since the latter "parodies" the work of intellectual life (TFW 136–37). The origin of these three faculties is none other than the vital imperative that makes us artisans whose function it is to fabricate tools, to project structures upon the world—structures that support our altogether pragmatic understanding of things. Yet how poor this assimilation of imagination by perception seems to us—this momentary arrest of ordinary everyday figures (people or animals) within the passing clouds. It is true that this is an attractive and amusing game. But if imagination were nothing but that, it would not engage us intimately, as it sometimes does. We would not feel that movement which draws us to the sun as it sinks towards those beaches in the sky, that movement which links flying with swimming as it discovers an inner corporeal correspondence.

Imagination is not, for Bachelard, the representational imagination we find in Bergson. Yet it can appear as a rival to intuition. If indeed, for Bergson, intelligence and imagination cannot seize the diversity of elusive nuances within the flow, a conversion of consciousness can make it coincide, by contrast, with its own movement, with duration. In Bergson's words: "The intuition we refer to bears primarily upon internal duration. It grasps a succession that is not a juxtaposition—namely, a growth from within, the uninterrupted prolongation of the past into a present which is already blending into the future" (CM 20). In this case, Bachelard would reply: "Since the poet unveils a *fleeting* nuance, we learn to imagine all nuances as a matter of *change*. Only the imagination can register nuances, seizing them in *full flight* as they shift from one color to another." Thus, even while it detaches itself from reality, the imagination advances in steady fashion insofar as it is faithful to a substance, and may hence be grasped as continuity (WD 17, 18, 185; see also PR 19–20, 127–28). The valid continuity of reverie, those fortuitous moments of coherence that endow it with the value of monotony are indeed evident in certain rules and unifying principles of images. We have, for instance, the dream of swimming that can be pursued in midair, the tree that serves as a channel between earth and sky; or the house which similarly serves as a link between the memory of our lived childhood and the immemorial, that deep memory of childhood reverie that antecedes personal history (see PS 5–8).[15] In a certain sense, then, imagination realizes Bergsonian intuition, but it cannot be confused with it because it is not a faculty that can be explained merely in terms of psychic causality. Such a faculty does not take shape in one fell swoop, in Bachelard, but will give way—with increasing clarity—to the purely linguistic dynamic of reverie.[16] That which the philosopher calls the "verbal imagination" in fact appears in the preface to his two books on Earth reveries. Without completely renouncing the psychic or even unconscious causality of the image, he clearly demonstrates in these two works that language has a certain substance, that words have not only a surface but also a hidden core, their own magnetic power. Thus he writes: "In the ardor and brilliance of literary images, ramifications become multiplied; words are no longer mere signifying terms. They do not delimit thoughts; they harbor the future of the image" (ERW 5/7, trans. modified). This thesis of the creativity of language will be even more clearly stated from *The Poetics of Space* onward.

Such a philosophy of language is foreign to Bergson. In his view language, much like intelligence, applies to space. It is social and aims at an immediate communication accessible to all. In the end, it stabilizes and arrests that which it expresses. It is quite understandable, then, that any attempt to translate the unique experience of an elusive and always novel spiritual reality should fall short of its mark. Such a translation could only provide an imperfect and ultimately illusory equivalence. In this sense, for Bergson, the process of naming kills the spirit: "In short, the word with rigid contours, the brutal word, which stores up the stable, common, and consequently impersonal element in the impressions of humanity crushes, or at least conceals, the delicate and elusive impressions of our individual consciousness" (TFW 132, trans. modified).[17] But this critique does not hold up except to the degree that Bergson appears to misunderstand the specificity of poetic language altogether. Poetic language is a vitality of the word which creates, in its flight, a reality bursting with nuances that surpass the reality signified by natural language. The poetic image is always "a little above the language of signification," writes Bachelard (PS xxiii). And a few lines further down he adds that "poetry puts language in a state of emergence, in which life becomes manifest through its vivacity. These linguistic impulses, which stand out from the ordinary rank of pragmatic language, are miniatures of the vital impulse (*élan vital*). A micro-Bergsonism that abandoned the thesis of language-as-instrument in favor of the thesis of language-as-reality would find in poetry numerous documents on the intense life of language" (PS xxiii/10). It is admissible that such an instrumental conception of language should be the target of Bergson's critique of the concept; yet one may be surprised to find it still at work in his conception of art, and in what he calls its "images." For Bergson, language and imagination always appear as translations.

What is it then that constitutes the process of artistic creation in Bergson's view? The process, in his account, unfolds in two stages. First of all, it is a viewing of things from the level of disinterested intention. The artist attempts to become attuned with the flow of life. In this regard, there is no great difference between the Bergsonian philosopher and the artist, for at the core of their respective experiences one finds the intent to coincide with the essential thrust of creative duration. "The intention is just what the artist tries to regain in placing himself back within the object by a kind of sympathy, in breaking down, by an effort of intuition, the barrier that space puts between him and his world" (CE 177). Stopping here, an artist's intent would be purely contemplative. Bergsonian intuition is, in other words, roughly equivalent to art, minus the mediation of signs. Second, the task of the artist consists in finding mediating images (words, paintings, musical notes). If such images are mere metaphors, they will be more or less opaque, depending on the genius of the creator. If the poet's inspiration is such that his words virtually vanish before me, then I have some chance of participating in the creative event so long as I myself succeed in communing with the creative intention of their original insight. Such is the attitude of the Bergsonian reader or auditor of poems—and this qualification is already significant: the philosopher does not want to become enmeshed in the most patent materiality of words, in their graphic materiality: "When a poet reads me his verse," Bergson says, "I can interest myself enough in him to enter into his thought, put myself into his feelings, live over again the simple state he has managed to break up into phrases and words. . . . Now, I need only relax my attention and let go the tension that there is in me, for the sounds, hitherto swallowed up in the sense, to appear to me distinctly, one by one, in their materiality" (CE 209). For Bergson, then, the true listener of poetry is one who cuts through the materiality of language, rather than one who lingers in words. Good poetry, in his view, must aim towards the total transparency of signs. But isn't such transparency precisely what characterizes the effectiveness of instrumental, communicative language? Bergson is not describing poetry, here, but everyday prose (rather strange for a contemporary of Valéry!).

On the other hand, as already noted, Bachelard grants top priority in poetry to the creative aspect of language, to the flesh of words, and to their power of surprise. That is how he comes to demonstrate (in *The Poetics of Space* and *The Poetics of Reverie*) that the literary image has no past. Much as there are epistemological *ruptures* in scientific progress, might there not be a place for poetic ruptures as well? And why not posit a poetic equivalent to epistemological *obstacles*? The poet's art must indeed begin with repudiation—a repudiation of the individual and anecdotal past, and a rejection of the cultural past. In this sense it is worth noting that, from *Water and Dreams* onward, Bachelard denounces unfortunate continuities under the rubric of "culture complexes" (when the watery word stumbles as it utters the insincere dreamer's learned language of bookish mythologies).[18] The authentic poet, on the other hand, discovers in works of tradition not a series of word-recipes, but new possible futures for a rejuvenated imagination (PS xxviii–xxix). Similarly, he rejects the expression of habitual states of mind from his intimate past: the poetic image must suddenly place us beyond life, in a sphere where nothing but the felicity of poetic saying remains. This characteristic of the poetic image leads Bachelard to uphold the bold idea of pure sublimation—a vertical movement in which the verbal imagination liberates itself from libidinal affects. In this sense, there is no longer any tie between the novel present of the image and the past (see PS xi, xii, xxvff.). Better yet, the image is that which creates in us a new being which colors our affective self. It is through the image that our world expands: "[I]t expresses us by making us what it expresses; it is, in other words both a becoming of expression and a becoming of our being. Here expression creates being" (PS xix). At the same time, this outpouring of verbal energy (*élan vocal*) expresses a repudiation of horizontal time—that of our social memory and of the long-drawn-out duration of things. Delivered from psychoanalytical material, Bachelard seems to revive in these texts a mode of thinking that his books on the elements had partly toned down—namely, what had been represented in terms of vertical time in his essay "The Poetic Moment and the Metaphysical Moment," where he offered abundant advice on how to live a non-life that rises above horizontal time. Through the difficult refusal to refer himself to lived, psychological duration, the poet pledges his freedom: "Only then does a person reach the autosynchronous reference point at the center of himself, stripped of all peripheral life. Suddenly all commonplace horizontality disappears. Time no longer flows. It shoots up [*il jaillit*]" (II 60/106, trans. modified).[19]

I shall now return to the Bergsonian use of the image—this time a positive one—and to Bachelard's attendant critique. This critique does not exactly apply to what Bergson calls the "mediating image" between a philosophical intuition and its utterance in *The Creative Mind* (chapter 4), but to what Lydie Adolpe calls "the substitute image [*l'image pour autrui*]" in *La dialectique des images chez Bergson*. This book effectively formulates the back-and-forth movement that Bergson calls "to-and-froing [*va-et-vient*]." When the focus is on understanding an intuitive aim, a reader should mistrust and go beyond the banality and rigidity of language, in Bergson's view. Even as it becomes necessary for a writer to transmit the intuition, the words chosen still matter little to him—that is, the semantic region from which the philosopher will draw them seems arbitrary. Hence the choice of images so often borrowed from the social context.[20] Bachelard protests precisely against such choices, for in his view a genuine image cannot be social. In this industrialized era of prefabricated products, who can readily grasp the disdain Bergson injects into his expression "ready-made garment" (CE 48), for instance, to criticize the common use of ready-made concepts? Against the great bourgeois who liked having his own clothes personally tailored, an almost proletarian humor becomes patent in this Bachelardian exclamation: "For a ready-made garment is all that is needed, of course, to clothe a poor rationalist" (PS 75). Bachelard in fact proceeds to suggest that certain Bergsonian images, fabricated for an always identical application, are themselves too easily classifiable. The Bergsonian image of the "drawer," in particular, is never more than a metaphor: that is to say, the expression refers to a reality that remains removed from it, that precedes it, "at the most it is a fabricated image, without deep, true, genuine roots" (PS 74–75ff.).

Finally, Bachelardian imagination cannot be confused with intuition, and even the recourse to a "phenomenology" without great rapport with Husserl could not clarify matters. A claim to the contrary rests, in my view, on a rather imprecise understanding of the nature of "reverie." To the degree that Bergsonian intuition is primarily obscure, and that the recollection of past being is obtained through the relaxation of intellectual activity—while the detachment of interest, dreaming, and imagining are considered to be under the sign of a "lesser being [*moindre être*]"—one might be tempted to emphasize the diluting features of Bachelardian reverie and to identify it with intuition. So doing, however, one would fail to realize that reverie is always accompanied by effort, in Bachelard, for it is practiced as a rupture with habitual modes of thought. When one seeks to demonstrate the identity between intuition and reverie, the suggestion is that imagination is no more than a misty sympathy with things whereby consciousness finds itself slackened and half asleep, as if the movement toward reverie were always a descent! Thus, Pierre Quillet can say: "A scientist's insight is possible through a process of mental concentration, whereas reverie is a *dilution*, an expansion," even adding that "death and reverie entail a similar dilution" (Quillet, 148–49). Bergsonian intuition is on the side of the anteperceptive: it is pure aim and foresight (*visée et vision pure*); hence it is also antepredicative. This single trait allows us to distinguish it from the imagination as described in *The Poetics of Space* and *The Poetics of Reverie*—namely, at once a linguistic reality, a promotion of being through a rupture with the past, and the bearer of a verbal future, as expressed in this Bachelardian passage: "Phenomenology is set up to consider the poetic image in its own being, distinct and independent from any antecedent being, as a positive conquest of the word" (PR 3).

Phenomenology must allow us to grasp the image in its specificity, that is, not as a phenomenon of psychic pressure, but as a being irreducible to interpretation.[21] It must facilitate a productive reencounter with the image, through a telepoetry open to multiple readings (AD 124–25). It will require us, in other words, to experience the image in its creative flight. Phenomenology thus drives image consciousness in the direction of "an increment of consciousness," as Bachelard says, "in a moment of extreme tension" (PR 4, 5).

We believe it crucial, moreover, to highlight the fact that the cogito of the dreamer has nothing to do with the kind of somnolence often attributed to it and that Bachelard is not at all tempted to "return to, or become submerged within, the homogeneity of *prima materia*."[22] The introduction to *The Poetics of Reverie* is quite clear on this issue. In this text Bachelard establishes a distinction between two kinds of reverie. One is devoted to the elusive inconsistency of dreams, which rarely promote poetic being.

Bachelard describes it as follows: "It is common to inscribe reverie among the phenomena of mental relaxation. It is lived out within a distended time that lacks any binding force. Not guided by attention, it most often lacks memory. It is an escape from reality, without always finding a consistent unreal world. By following the 'slope of reverie'—an ever-downward slope—consciousness relaxes, becomes dispersed and, consequently, becomes obscure" (PR 5). This reverie that daydreams is not authentic reverie. The other one, which interests Bachelard, consists of an "I speak," which is the immediate given of its cogito. It is a working consciousness, a consciousness of working. The only way to distinguish it from the former is by placing the adjective "poetic" before it, restoring the etymological sense of the word "poetic" (Gk. ποίησις, creative production): "The reverie we wish to study is a *poetic* reverie, a reverie that poetry places on an upward slope—one which can follow a growing consciousness. This reverie is one that is written, or that at least promises to be written" (PR 6). Thus Bachelardian imagination is but the subject transported within language, this taut consciousness, open to the world in the imprudence of poetic discourse. Such imagination is the function of a verbal force (*élan vocal*) rather than of an unconscious life impulse (*élan vital*). Most definitely, then, the appearance of the phenomenological method in Bachelard cannot be interpreted as the sign of a resurgence of Bergsonian thought. It seems to me that the thesis of coherence prevails.

In *Air and Dreams,* Bachelard wrote: "I believe we could make Bergsonism more prolific (*multiplier le bergsonisme*) if we could root it more vitally in its own rich images by examining them in terms of their matter and dynamics" (AD 256/291, trans. modified). *Multiplier le bergsonisme* certainly does not mean overturning it in Deleuze's sense of "overturning Platonism." Rather, it suggests "setting it astir" by demanding more movement from it, showing the way towards heightened mobility and creative possibilities even within the microscopically diverse regions of images, intensifying the plurality of its temporal rhythms in order not only to *have* or *own* time, but to more fully *be* time.

This is why I have felt justified in speaking of Bachelard's non-Bergsonism, highlighting its main features in the sense that his "philosophy of no" does not gratuitously pursue a "will to negation [*volonté de négation*]" but rather a dialectical multiplication—that is, the spawning of possibilities which, while critically incorporating the object of their negation, also expand or better yet propagate it (PN 115–17/135–37). If the Prometheus complex is "the Oedipus complex of intellectual life" (representing that which impels us to know and to risk as much as, or even more than, our fathers), and if Bergson was for Bachelard something like a father or a master, then never will a master have been better served.

Notes

1. See Michel Mansuy, *Gaston Bachelard et les éléments* (Paris: José Corti, 1967), 257, 325.

2. See François Pire, *De l'Imagination poétique dans l'oeuvre de Gaston Bachelard* (Paris: José Corti, 1967), 190.

3. Pierre Quillet, *Bachelard* (Paris: Seghers, 1964), 118; hereafter cited as Quillet.

4. Cited by Bachelard from Pierre Janet, *L'Évolution de la mémoire et de la notion du temps* (Paris: Chahine, 1928), 19.

5. Henri Bergson, *Time and Free Will: An Essay on the Immediate Data of Consciousness*, trans. F. L. Pogson (1910; New York: Harper and Row, 1960). Originally published as *Essai sur les données immédiates de la conscience* (1889); hereafter cited as TFW.

6. Henri Bergson, *Creative Evolution*, trans. Arthur Mitchell (New York: Modern Library, 1944), 3. Originally published as *L'Evolution créatrice* (1907); hereafter cited as CE.

7. See Bergson's second lecture, "The Perception of Change," in *The Creative Mind: An Introduction to Metaphysics*, trans. Mabelle N. Andison (Mineola, NY: Dover, 2007), 121–27. Originally published as *La Pensée et le mouvant* (1934); hereaftercited as CM.

8. Translator's note: The bracketed translation of Bergson's line from the French *La Pensée et le mouvant* (3) is intended to highlight Perraudin's focus on the *generative* role of Bergsonian "duration." Mabelle Andison translates it as "Time is what *is happening*, and more than that, it is what causes everything to happen" (CM 2). A third option for *se fait* would be "time is what is made" (MM 150, see n. 10). Yet Perraudin reads Bergson's time (duration) not only as a *passive happening* but as a *reflexive generation*. The question of time's agency in such a "generative happening" remains open.

9. See Jean-Louis Backès, "Sur le mot 'continuité,'" *L'Arc* 42 (1970), 69.

10. Henri Bergson, *Matter and Memory*, trans. Nancy Margaret Paul and W. Scott Palmer (New York: Zone, 1988), 147. Originally published as *Matière et mémoire* (1896); hereafter abbreviated as MM.

11. Bachelard's therapeutic proposals in *The Dialectic of Duration* might be said to anticipate key principles in "Mindfulness Training" recently being promoted in the fields of education, cognitive therapy, meditation, and healing. Worth consulting on this topic are Mark Williams and Danny Penman, *Mindfulness* (London UK:

Little Brown, 2011); Donald McCowan, D. Reibel, and M. S. Micozzi, *Teaching Mindfulness* (New York: Springer, 2010); and Tim Ryan, *A Mindful Nation* (New York: Hay House, 2012), to mention a few.

12. See Bergson's account of exceptional human beings in *The Two Sources of Morality and Religion*, trans. R. Ashley Audra and Cloudesley Brereton (New York: Henry Hold, 1935), 25–26, and chapters 1–2. Originally published as *Les Deux sources de la morale et de la religion* (1932).

13. At an international conference in Geneva in 1953, Bachelard characterized the role of scientists and creators as one of "optimal paternity."

14. Translator's note: See Bachelard's distinction between *homo faber* (human beings as makers of objects, or reproducers of forms) and *homo aleator* (human beings as explorers of possibilities, capable of transforming themselves and their world) in Mary McAllester Jones, *Gaston Bachelard: Subversive Humanist* (Madison: University of Wisconsin Press, 1991), 10, 40, 60, 140. See also McAllester's introduction to *The Formation of the Scientific Mind* (FSM 9).

15. Here, again against Bergson, Bachelard entrusts to "space" the possibility of recovering our memories and, even more, the immemorial—a latent future that imagination could write, or at least intend to write.

16. On this subject see Michel Georges Bernard's essay "L'imagination parlée" in *L'Arc* 42 (1970): 82ff.

17. Translator's note: By rendering *le mot brutal* as "the rough and ready word," Pogson's translation in *Time and Free Will* does not convey the violence that Perraudin highlights in this Bergsonian passage. See the French edition, *Essais sur les données immédiates de la conscience*, 98; see also *Laughter: An Essay on the Meaning of the Comic*, trans. Cloudesley Brereton and Fred Rothwell (1911; London: Macmillan, 1913), 117, 130.

18. Translator's note: Bachelard had begun to illustrate the notion of "culture complexes" in *The Psychoanalysis of Fire* (e.g., the Prometheus complex, the Hoffman complex, etc.), but it was in *Water and Dreams* (17) that he first articulated a working definition for these prereflective attitudes and habits of the cultural psyche.

19. For other possible translations of the French *il jaillit*, see Edward S. Casey, "The Difference an Instant Makes: Bachelard's Brilliant Breakthrough," in this volume (note 6).

20. Lydie Adolphe, *La Dialectique des images chez Bergson* (Paris: Presses Universitaires de France, 1951), 15–160.

21. Translator's note: See Bachelard's critique of those types of "interpretation" that reduce poetic images to definite concepts or psychoanalytic contents (e.g., PS xx; FPF 25).

22. Georges Poulet, "Bachelard et la conscience du soi," in *Revue de Métaphysique et Moral* 1 (January–March 1965): 15.

Chapter 3

Vertical Time: Bachelard's Epiphanic Instant

RICHARD KEARNEY

In an essay entitled "Poetic Instant and Metaphysical Instant," Bachelard declares that "poetry is instant metaphysics" (II 58).[1] This concise and formative essay composed in 1939—just one year after he made his famous turn from science to poetics—sees Bachelard deliver one of his most succinct accounts of what he calls "vertical time." He defines the poetic moment as the "principle of an essential simultaneity in which the most scattered and disunited being achieves unity." We are concerned here with a "complex" instant that gathers and concentrates at once several simultaneities. So doing, it cuts across and shatters the continuity of sequential time (II 58). "Time no longer flows. It shoots up [*il jaillit*]" (II 60/106).

Bachelard is here throwing down the gauntlet to Bergson as he pursues an argument begun in his *Intuition of the Instant* (1932) and *The Dialectics of Duration* (1936), where he had boldly confessed his philosophy as "Bergsonism without continuity."[2] Some of the key insights proposed in his more sustained analyses of time are brought to a head from a poetic standpoint in this brief essay, yet all three texts equally challenge Bergson's philosophy of time as continuous duration, or what in his posthumous *Fragments of a Poetics of Fire* Bachelard will characterize as the "untorn and untearable continuity of Bergsonian consciousness" (FPF 7).

Bachelard claims that every "real" poem signals a stopping of ordinary clock time, introducing instead a dimension of "verticality," in depth and in height (II 58–60). Where prosaic time is horizontal and continuous (like Bergson's), poetic time is discontinuous and disruptive. Echoing Coleridge's definition of poetry as the "yoking together of opposite and discordant qualities," Bachelard maintains that the poetic instant is a "harmonic relationship between opposites" (II 59). Confronted by successive antitheses of ordinary time, the poet refuses to comply; s/he resists the tyranny of chronological sequencing by transmuting antithesis into "ambivalence." S/he substitutes simultaneity for succession. This is the moment which Bachelard calls "rapture" and "ecstasy" when the person—author or reader—is compelled to value or devalue (II 59), that is, to explode the continuum of world time, electing instead to move upwards or downwards in a rupturing moment of verticality—a sort of Jacob's ladder without explicit recourse to the divine (we shall return to this point below).

It is at this juncture in his analysis that Bachelard introduces his curious and central notion of androgyny: "More intuitively speaking," he writes, "a well-knit ambivalence is revealed through its temporal character: instead of masculine, vigorous time which thrusts forth and conquers, instead of gentle, submissive time which weeps and regrets, we have the androgynous instant. The mystery of poetry is androgynous" (II 59). This was a theme that Bachelard would return to time and time again in his various psychoanalyses of the elements—exercises in poetic depth psychology, belatedly influenced by Jung as well as by hermeneutic trends in phenomenology.

Bachelard goes on to enumerate a number of productive paradoxes surrounding the poetic instant: first, the holding of a plurality of contradictory events within a single moment (II 59); second, the "no" to the horizontal time of "other people, of life and of the world" which coincides with a "yes" to the emancipation of the deeper person "imprisoned in horizontal time" (II 60); third, the repetition or reliving of the past in terms of a certain "smiling regret," a singularly ambivalent emotion, for Bachelard, which transcends both melancholic nostalgia and naïve optimism (II 61). This most sensitive of ambivalences takes place, he says, in vertical time "for neither of its moments—smile or regret—precedes the other." Neither causes the other. "Here, feeling is reversible or, to put it better, being's reversibility is *imbued with feeling*: a smile regrets and a regret smiles, the regret consoles" (II 61).

This fascination with the poetic conjunction of opposites inclined Bachelard to seek for images not only in poetic literature itself but also in related notions of the *coincidentia oppositorum* in depth psychology and alchemy. But it is perhaps in the nautical notion of "*le point vélique*" that we find his favorite analogy, as several of his Sorbonne students attested. This describes a very specific convergence point of energies when the pressure of wind on sail is met with a countervailing resistance from the waves against the vessel itself. In this moment of opposing forces—sail versus sea—we witness a singular equipoise of intensities, a fertile commingling of immobility and movement, a still point that generates dynamic propulsion. And this double pressure on canvas sail and sea-born hull actually produces a humming sound. The boat literally *sings.*[3]

Bachelard also gives several examples of poets who epitomize these paradoxes. On the poetic effects of Mallarmé's "syntactical inversions" (of language and of time), he writes: "Reading Mallarmé, we are often struck by a sense of recurrent time capable of rescuing bygone instants. We can then experience, belatedly, those instants which should have been lived: a feeling all the more remarkable as it is stripped of regret, repentance, or nostalgia. It is simply fashioned from *wrought time*, which manages on occasion to insert the echo before the voice, denial within avowal" (II 60). This anticipates Bachelard's later development of his famous notion of "reverberation [*retentissement*]" in *The Poetics of Space* (1957) and *The Poetics of Reverie* (1960).

For Baudelaire—another minstrel of the "poetic instant" according to Bachelard—a poem does not unfold or evolve; it is "knit": and the resulting tissue of knots comprises a series of ambivalences—being and non-being, light and dark, the horror and ecstasy of life (II 60, 62). These clustered ambivalences include, crucially, a chiasmus of verticality and time which cuts across the normal linear flow of narrative drama. It prefers caesura to maturation, eruption to evolution. Hence the privileging of the genre of poetry over fiction in almost all of Bachelard's works. When Baudelaire speaks of "correspondences," for example, he is not simply speaking of a transpositional code of sensual analogies (as is so often thought). He is, rather, presenting "a summary of sentient being in a single instant (II 62)"—sensible simultaneities invoking deeper metaphysical correlations that cannot be experienced in chronological time (which for Bachelard also seems to include dramatic or narrative time).

In the aggressive intensity of the poetic instant, time plunges and rises vertically—and "for no good reason [*ohne warum*]." It is free, in other words, from causes, motivations, plots, and developments. One oscillates between rapture and collapse within a single present, as Prince Myshkin does, for example, in Dostoyevsky's *The Idiot,* in the epileptic moment preceding his famous "falling fits." In this epiphanic instant, Myshkin realizes that beauty is at once a horrifying power *and* the only thing that will save the world. He witnesses a liminal now-point when past and future crisscross and undergo a strange reversibility, a moment at once dark and illuminating, terrifying and jubilant. "It was from the fit that all the darkness came, from the fit that the 'idea' came too," Dostoyevsky tells us.[4] In such vertical epiphanies we hit upon that strange consolation without hope for something outside itself and without nostalgia for a past that is past. Here, as Bachelard boldly puts it, we discover "all that detaches us from cause or recompense, all that denies our private history, even desire itself—(for) all that devalues both past and future . . . is contained within the poetic instant" (II 61).

While Bachelard clearly privileges the genre of poetry over fiction or drama when it comes to the metaphysics of the instant, I think it can be countered that there are also striking examples of vertical temporality at work in certain modernist novels like Joyce's *Ulysses* or Proust's *Remembrance of Times Past.* As with Dostoyevsky's *The Idiot*, these novels are narratives constructed around certain vertical moments of "epiphany" which cut through the linear plot line and liberate the story into a series of circular reprises—for example, Marcel's involuntary memories as he enters the Guermantes' soirée in the final section of the novel or Molly's rupturing of the mock-heroic odyssey as she attests to the epiphany of the first kiss. In both cases, chronological time is upended and reversed, as past and future are reinscribed in a timeless moment: Marcel's reliving of his entrance to San Marco in Venice as he stumbles on the cobblestone in Paris; and Molly's reliving of the kisses of Gibraltar and of Howth Head in the here and now—"Yes I will Yes." It is perhaps unfortunate that in his analyses of the poetic moment Bachelard did not elaborate more frequently on how it might work in fictional and dramatic literature as it does in poetry per se.[5]

If poetry was Bachelard's favorite literary genre, phenomenology became his preferred philosophical one. This is especially obvious in later works like *The Poetics of Space*, but it is already implicit in earlier writings. The emancipatory power of the poetic instant might, for example, be said to recall Husserl's phenomenological *epoché* where our natural expectations and presuppositions are suspended in order to fully attend to "the things themselves." (Bachelard advocates a phenomenology of imagination in *The Poetics of Space*, and certainly read Husserl, Heidegger, Merleau-Ponty, and Sartre, though he disliked Sartre's residual Cartesian dualism.)[6] And while Bachelard does not often cite religious literature, one might recall, borrowing from a non-Western tradition, that special suspended moment of decision before battle, when Arjuna is instructed by Krishna in the *Bhagavad Gita* on the virtues of vertical time, namely, action without desire or reward: a notion retrieved and developed in the Buddhist idea of the empty moment as a free detachment from the horizontal cycles of *samsara*: as in the famous Heart Sutra—"form is emptiness, emptiness form." This, of course, is an emptiness that is not empty but fuller than the greatest fullness itself: another deep ambivalence conjured in the eternal instant. Indeed one might suspect an oblique rapport here between what Buddhism calls the empty form of time and Bachelard's claim that while "formal causality takes place within an instant, in vertical time . . . efficient causality develops horizontally, in life and in things" (II 61).

Bachelard does not limit his analysis of the instant to poetics—though he clearly privileges this idiom. He resists the temptation of literary solipsism or closure when he admits that the poetic instant also involves (1) a "*metaphysics* of the immediate," (2) a *psychology* of "fundamental ambivalence," and (3) a "*morality* of the instantaneous" (II 58, 61, 62–63). Though Bachelard would explore the first two areas in his later texts on depth psychology and ontology, from *The Psychoanalysis of Fire* (1938) to *The Poetics of Space* (1957), the claim for morality might come as something of a surprise to those wont to think of Bachelard as a neutral scientist turned literary aesthete. But Bachelard is no advocate of symbolist self-regard or "art for art's sake." He makes the bold claim in his 1939 essay on the poetic instant that imagination is the wellspring of ethical as well as poetic values. That the poetic instant is existential, as much as it is linguistic. This is boldly stated in the conclusion to his essay, where he demarcates his own position, once again, from the Bergsonian theory of *la durée*. I quote the passage at some length as it merits keen consideration:

> The categorical imperative of morality has nothing to do with time as duration. It does not retain any sensory cause; it anticipates no consequence. It steers a straight course, vertically, into the time of forms and persons. The poet here becomes a natural guide for the metaphysician who seeks to understand all the powers of instantaneous connections, the fervor of sacrifice, without succumbing to the divisions of a crude philosophical duality of subject and object, nor being detained by the dualism of egotism and duty. The poet brings a subtler dialectic to life. He reveals at the same time, in a single instant, the solidarity of form and person. He proves that form is person and person is form. Poetry thus becomes an instant of formal causality, an

> instant of personal power. It loses interest in what merely shatters or dissipates, in a temporal duration that disperses echoes. It seeks the instant. (II 62–63)

We shall return to the question of Bachelard's ethics in our concluding remarks.

It was actually in his book *Intuition of the Instant* (1932), published seven years before the pivotal *Messages* essay, that Bachelard had first developed his analysis of vertical time. Here he defined the instant as a sudden burst of consciousness calling for an acute act of *attention* (II 11–12). One experiences the instant, he claims, as an act of concentrated *will*, and will is to be understood as a radical moment of *decision* that is simultaneously a deep moment of attentive *listening* (II 20, 56). The act of will, as an act of auditory imagination, is a response to the incoming instant. "When it strikes," writes Bachelard, "the instant imposes itself all in one blow, completely; it is the agent of being's synthesis" (II 15). Such a burst of consciousness is experienced as an instant of "invention" (>Lat. *invenio-invenire*): a *discovery* and *creation* that is simultaneously active and passive, receptive and dynamic.

Bachelard returns to this paradox of vertical time in *The Formation of the Scientific Mind*, published just one year before "The Poetic Instant and the Metaphysical Instant." Here, speaking with his scientific hat on, he claims there are "critical moments" when one species changes from a previous species by "a decisive function" (FSM 26). This amounts, he says, to a form of radical mutation: an event of temporal rupture which is also a function of inventiveness. "Through the spiritual revolution required by scientific inventiveness, humankind becomes a *mutating* species, or a species that needs to mutate, that suffers if it doesn't change" (FSM 26). This is, of course, a million miles from the unbreachable continuity of Bergsonian consciousness. (And within yards of the philosophy of *coupure* that so influenced later structuralist thinkers like Althusser and Foucault. This structuralist aspect of Bachelard's philosophy is often neglected.)

The paradigm of mutation as metamorphosis is the same phenomenon captured in *The Psychoanalysis of Fire* (first published the same year as *Formation of the Scientific Mind*), where Bachelard speaks of the decisive act of imagination as a power to make a newborn babe out of a monster (PF 110). Or again in *Lautréamont* (1939) where he analyzes Ducasse's poem *Maldoror* as what he calls "instant language," namely the expression of a psychic force suddenly to become language without causal antecedence in previous thoughts (L 55). This instant of creative aggression and fracturing typifies, for Bachelard, the poetry of Lautréamont and the "good surrealists." It marks an inaugurating power, a gratuitous beginning where the sudden will to change is accompanied by a deep joy of decision (L 56). This instantaneous time is far removed from the clock time of everyday life. It is the moment of the transformation of forms, of awakening to a surreality beneath and beyond ordinary notions of the real. It is the magic of metamorphosis in the abrupt emergence of a poetic image (L 87). In this sense, poetics—no less than philosophy and morality—is an act of "willed origins" (RD 179). Or as Bachelard puts it in *Air and Dreams*, "valorization *decides* being: this is one of the great principles of the imaginary" (AD 74).

True to a central paradox of phenomenology, Bachelard holds that we disclose and create *at one and the same time*. This bilateral action is exemplified in his image of an artist-craftsman liberating the gem out of stone, the reverie of the crystalline substance representing at once an *instant* and an *eternity* (ERW 232/302). It is also invoked in Bachelard's 1938 preface to the French edition of Martin Buber's *I and Thou*, when he speaks about the genuine encounter between two persons as a special "synthesis of event and eternity" (P 271).[7] Such real encounters involve a curious crisscrossing of mutual questioning and surprise. Nothing is established in advance; both partners are exposed to radical novelty:

> Someone exists in the world, unknown to you, then, suddenly, in a single encounter, before knowing him, you recognize him. A dialogue begins in the night, a dialogue which, through a certain tone, completely involves the persons, "Michel, is that you?" And the voice answers, "Jeanne, is that you?" Neither one needs to answer, "Yes, it is I." For if the questioned person were to transcend the questioning, and forego the infinite grace of the encounter, he would then descend into monologue or confession . . . into the dull narrative of wishes and woes. He would say what he is, before saying what, through the encounter, he has become. The Instant of the human Person would be quite enfeebled, quite weakened, muffled, entirely deprived of the vector of futurity that sympathy just launched. (P 271)

This tone of mutual curiosity and astonishment, captured in the stammering of the I faced with the Thou, epitomizes what Bachelard refers to as an auditory imagination—a double tonality of aspiration and inspiration, of giving and receiving. "The ear then becomes *active*," as he puts it, "since lending an ear is wanting to respond" (P 000). And here we see how Bachelard's phenomenology of the instant involves a radical ethics of empathy, based on the Buberian insight that relations are not about poles, points, and centers but about *vectors*. The self for Bachelard, as for Buber, is less a substance or cogito than a dynamic relation to the endlessly surprising other.

Bachelard's philosophy of the instant takes the form of a phenomenology of relations understood as sympathy, reciprocity, and surprise. But Bachelard's phenomenology is unique in many respects. It reverses Gadamer's prioritizing of *Erfahrung* (continuous temporal experience) over *Erlebnis* (the discrete discontinuous moment). It challenges Sartre's priority of futural negations and intentions over the pure present, and it radically transforms Heidegger's reading of the *Augenblick*; for rather than seeing the authentic moment of decision, like Heidegger, as a recapitulation of past time and projection of our most proper possibilities in death, Bachelard sees it as an occasion of intense jubilation in the present as such. Less a question of being-towards-death than of being-towards-birth.[8]

In the poetic instant, in short, the temporalizing horizons of "before" and "after" dissolve to reveal a bare inaugural moment. This is the moment when a lightning bolt of cosmic time traverses personal time in a fire of intimate intensity (FPF 34–35). It is what Bachelard, in a favorite trope, calls a "phoenix poetic flash": an explosion where the death of linear time is reborn as vertical time, a natal event often caught in those special poems of an instant (T. S. Eliot's kingfisher, Matthew Arnold's Empedocles), great poems which combine "an instant in a man's life with an instant in the life of a world" (FPF 104). It is this break, insists Bachelard, this very interruption of the natural attitude of language, habit, and chronology that allows the "nascent Λόγος" of being to emerge as language. For here the advent of the poem signals an upsurge of new being—mortality giving way to natality, again and again. This Λόγος of the "phoenix flash" is best understood, suggests Bachelard, in the mode of reverie, that attitude of attention which combines will and decision with a deep receptivity towards an incoming gift. All of which occurs in a single instant of intensity. This is how Bachelard describes the crucial event: "When these flashes of fire, lightning or flight surprise us in our contemplation, they appear to our eyes as *heightened, universal moments*—not so much ours as given to us, moments which mark memory and return in dreams, retaining their imaginary dynamism. We might term them, in fact, phoenixes of reverie" (FPF 32)—that is, instants that give rise to reverie.[9] And, of course, the phoenix is, in myth and metaphor, a bird that rises up from ashes, resurrected from the caesura and cessation of mortality. For, as Bachelard reminds us in *Intuition of the Instant*, "although time will no doubt be reborn, it must first die" (II 6).

Such passages conjure up several associated images in the biblical tradition. But while Bachelard's notion of the instant seems extremely close, at times, to Christian (and more specifically Pauline) notions of the kairological or eschatological moment that cuts through time, his analogies are more commonly drawn from Greek and classical sources. Just as his psychoanalytic preferences are for Jung over Freud, his spiritual preferences seem to be for pagan and alchemical sources over biblical ones (though this is never stated in any dogmatic or polemical way). Rather than speaking of the eschaton coming like lightning crossing the sky (Matthew 24:23–27; Luke 17:22–24)—a key biblical passage for Kierkegaard's instant and Heidegger's *Augenblick*—Bachelard opts instead for poetic and classical allusions.[10] In short, he opts for a phoenix flash rather than the famous "flash of fire [*shalhevetjah*]" in the Song of Songs (8:6), the burning bush of Exodus 3:15, or the Pentecostal fire of the Acts of the Apostles. Bachelard is more wont to cite Empedocles than Jesus, Mallarmé than Maimonides, Baudelaire's *fleurs du mal* rather than the beatific *fleurs du lys*. And though he does, for example, devote an essay to Chagall's Bible in the posthumously published *Right to Dream* (1970), referring to prophets and their moral message, it is telling that even here the biblical reference is couched in an artistic allusion to a contemporary painter of folk dream and reverie. We should not forget the telling fact that while his seminal *Intution of the Instant* is actually a reflection upon Gaston Roupnel's *Siloë*, a retelling of the episode in John 9:7, where the blind man is cured by Jesus after bathing in the pool of Siloam, Bachelard does not once refer explicitly to its biblical origin.[11]

Why this discretion?—we may well ask. The option for poetic over confessional terminology is, I think, significant. But, careful, I am not suggesting for a moment that Bachelard is in any way antireligious or an advocate of militant atheism like Sartre or de Beauvoir. No, I suspect rather that Bachelard's attitude expresses his deeply humanist commitments as: (1) a scientist, (2) a phenomenologist, and (3) a citizen of the French République. Each of these three commitments requires a suspension of explicitly confessional and partisan religious language in favor of more secular idioms, which does not of course mean that sacred and spiritual experiences—clearly central to Bachelard's whole understanding of the poetic moment—cannot be probed and sounded. Indeed, terms like "grace," "spirit," and "resurrection" recur frequently throughout his writings. And in *Intuition of the Instant* he does not hesitate to speak of "the irruption of an absolute" (II 10) or of "the Creator's acts" (II 28). But when Bachelard does reference such notions, it is almost invariably in the idioms of poetry, philosophy, and myth. Here cosmic mystery traverses and truncates chronological time without explicitly announcing a coming kingdom or eschatological advent (although it does not, of course, exclude it either).[12]

Bachelard's poetics, in sum, bear witness to the pure moment which speaks from itself, which watches and listens to the "thing itself" as it springs forth into creative language. His poetics attest to vertical time as a landing site for the gift of the fabulous, the upsurge of the marvelous, without attributing this to any one religious tradition. When he does make religious allusions, these are invariably oblique, indirect, and pluralistic, as, for example, when he juxtaposes a reference to an Indian saint (Narayana) with one to a Greek seer or to an alchemical sage, without batting an eyelid. He never invokes the authority of any particular religious tradition over another, Western or Eastern, so we might reasonably conclude that Bachelard prefers a poetics of the instant that is preconfessional and thus open to all religious and non-religious experiences alike. And in this he may be described as a true phenomenologist of the spiritual imagination, a poetic pioneer, in his unique way, of interspiritual hospitality.

Let me conclude with a few brief words about Bachelard's ethics of the instant which, I believe, accompanies and supplements his poetics of the instant. This can be broadly classified under three rubrics: (1) an ethics of *empathy*; (2) an ethics of *attention*; and (3) an ethics of *emancipation*. As I have already mentioned the first, in Bachelard's close affinity with Buber's ethics of relation above, let me focus here on the last two. The ethical attitude of attention takes the form of a vigilance and receptivity towards the gift of the moment, a chance event that is at once fortuitous and gratuitous. This relates directly to Bachelard's notion of the "accident," as when he writes that there is only one general law within "a truly creative evolution," namely, "that an accident lies at the root of every evolutionary attempt" (II 13). This accident is literally *ac-cidens*, that which befalls us in a single blow, understood not as an abstract nothing (as in Bergson's evolution) but as the well-spring of reality itself in its beginning, its nascence, what he calls "the absolute of a birth" (II 13). An ethics of attention is thus one which discovers a true "occasion" of natality in a mere chance accident (*Zufall*), a moment of epiphany in rupture, of fertile *devenir* in the radical discontinuity of time. And so doing it transmutes mere contingency into a "destinal center." But whether this accident is an ex-nihilo advent of transcendence or an eruption from a forgotten dimension of immanent being is never resolved by Bachelard. What is clear is that a special attention to the accident as *arche* of new beginnings is at the heart of Bachelard's ethics. This attention is an act of both vigilance towards what comes and of audacity to listen and receive it. For as he writes in the opening chapter of *Intuition of the Instant*: "Intellectual courage consists in actively and vitally preserving this instant of nascent knowledge, of making it the unceasing fountain of our intuition, and of designing, with the subjective history of our errors and faults, the model of a better, more illumined life" (II 4).

This brings me finally to Bachelard's third ethical category—emancipation. The instant comes not as an imposition but as an event. It does not coerce but persuades. For in liberating us from the ineluctable flow of *durée*, we are released into the option of generosity. Bachelard speaks accordingly of being free to "receive the gift of a fertile instant . . . as an essential novelty" (II 32), that is, unconditionally, as if unbound by the ties of habit and routine. Here we experience chance as something which induces and solicits without condemning us to absolute necessity. The instant as lacuna, gap, aperture, caesura invites us to replace the *élan vital* with an *élan vocal*[13]—it replaces mute determinism with the liberty of poetic speech, the power to say "yes" or "no." Like the maiden in Denise Levertov's poem, *Annunciation*, the self for Bachelard is fundamentally free in its moment of decision.

> She was free
> to accept or to refuse, choice
> integral to humanness.[14]

It would be hard, I think, to find a better motto for Bachelard's ethics of the vertical instant.

Notes

1. This piece by Bachelard was first published as "Instant poétique et instant métaphysique" in the French review *Messages: Métaphysique et poésie* 2 (1939). References to this text correspond to the version published in *Intuition of the Instant*, translated by Eileen Rizo-Patron (Evanston: Northwestern University Press, 2013),

58–63. See also J. A. Underwood's translation in *The Right to Dream* (Dallas: Dallas Institute, 1988), abbreviated in this volume as RD, 173–78.

2. While, on its face, this might sound like professing "Christianity without Christ," Bachelard's relation to Bergson's philosophy was quite subtle and complex, as Jean-François Perraudin demonstrates in "Bachelard's Non-Bergsonism," in this volume.

3. Bachelard's image of *le point vélique*," recorded initially by Jean Lescure in *Paroles de Gaston Bachelard, Mercure de France* (May 1963), is cited by Pierre Quillet in *Bachelard* (Paris: Seghers, 1964), 9–10.

4. Fyodor Dostoyevsky, *The Idiot,* trans. Richard Pevear and Larissa Volokhonsky (New York: Vintage, 2003), 229.

5. Bachelard's tendency to bracket "narrative plot" in his literary analyses might best be described as a methodological *choice*, rather than as a blind spot, however. Two studies which focus on the role of poetic insight *in narrative* include Bachelard's essay "The Narrative of Arthur Gordon Pym" (1944), which analyzes Edgar Allan Poe's novel of maritime adventure, highlighting its twofold demand of vertical versus horizontal time, dream, and narrative (RD 101–11), and "Séraphîta" (1955) an essay that celebrates Balzac's mystical novel (on "the doctrine in action of the Christian Buddha," as Balzac described it), comparing its vertical movement to that of Dante's *Divine Comedy* (RD 93–99).

6. In his chapter on "the phenomenology of roundness" in *The Poetics of Space*, Bachelard reveals a close familiarity with the work of Karl Jaspers, as well. Citing from *Von der Wahrheit* (Munich: R. Piper, 1947), he proposes to trim down his "*Jedes Dasein scheint in sich rund*" (50) to "*das Dasein ist rund*" in order to make it "phenomenologically purer": "Because to add that *it seems round* is to keep a doublet of being and appearance, when we mean the entire being in its roundness. . . . It is not a question of observing, but of experiencing being in its immediacy" (PS 232, 234).

7. Edward K. Kaplan's translation of Bachelard's preface to Martin Buber's *I and Thou, International Studies in Philosophy* 35, no. 1 (2003), 89–94, is revised and reprinted in this volume as appendix A.

8. "Rather than the continuity of life," writes Bachelard, "it is the discontinuity of birth that ultimately needs to be explained. It is at the moment of birth that one can measure the true power of being. This power is, as we shall see, the return to the liberty of the possible, to those multiple resonances born from the solitude of being" (II 39).

9. Elaborating on the cosmic dimensions of T. S. Eliot's phoenix-kingfisher, Bachelard notes: "The poet experiences this instant of active light as a veritable emergence of time (*relief du temps*). Cosmic time seems here to heighten ordinary time" (FPF 34/68, trans. modified).

10. Bachelard also describes the phoenix as a "bird moving at lightning speed" (FPF 33). On this suggestive image, see Eileen Rizo-Patron's Bachelardian

study of "lightning" in Shelley's *Prometheus Unbound*, in "Bachelard's Subversive Hermeneutics," *Religion and the Arts* 10, no. 3 (2006): 355–73.

11. While Bachelard alludes to a "divine redeemer" in *Intuition of the Instant*, he abstains from identifying him by name. In his words: "The force of time is wholly condensed within that novel instant where sight awakens, near the fountain of Siloam, touched by a divine redeemer who in one gesture grants us joy and reason, and the way to eternal being through truth and goodness" (II 54).

12. Bachelard's poetic instant might be fruitfully compared to Benjamin's notion of the dialectical image "in which the Then *(das Gewesene)* and the Now (*das Jetzt*) come into a constellation like a flash of lightning" (Walter Benjamin, *Benjamin, Philosophy, History, Aesthetics*, ed. Gary Smith [Chicago: University of Chicago Press, 1989]). The Messianic instant, or *Jetztzeit,* is here described as "dialectics at a standstill," transcending all temporal chronology and sequence: "For while the relation of the present to the past is a purely temporal, continuous one, the relation of the Then to the Now is dialectical—not development but image, a leaping forth (*sprunghaft).* Only dialectical images are genuine (i.e., not archaic) images; and the place one happens upon them is language" (49). (I am grateful to Mary Anderson for bringing this reference to my attention.) A similar notion of the Messianic instant was developed by another Jewish philosopher, Emmanuel Levinas, in *Totality and Infinity* (Pittsburgh: Duquesne University Press, 1969). I have found no evidence to suggest that Bachelard was influenced by these "messianic" notions of the instant (disseminated after Bachelard had written the *Intuition of the Instant*), or that Benjamin or Levinas were influenced by Bachelard (who avoided religious or political allusions in his discourse, restricting his phenomenological studies instead to poetics).

13. It was Jean-François Perraudin who first remarked on Bachelard's *élan vocal* in contrast with Bergson's *élan vital.* See his piece "Bachelard's Non-Bergsonism" (see chapter 2).

14. Denise Levertov, *Selected Poems* (New York: New Directions, 2003), 162.

Chapter 4

Rhythm and Reverie: On the Temporality of Imagination in Bachelard

Kristupas Sabolius

In his early writings, Gaston Bachelard argues that the structure of our perception of temporality is given by the constructive activity of human consciousness, which by accumulating repetitions forms the impression of continuity. He claims that time can only be observed in instants—moments that neither intertwine nor innately interact with each other. Bachelard obviously opposes Bergson's position on the "indestructible unity" of duration (II 9), which would prevent the possibility of creative novelty. If one accepts the view of time as primordially continuous, the true originality of creation becomes senseless since, according to Bergson one must always deal with the phenomenon of evolution as a presence in constant movement, not only coming from the past to the future, but also interrelating with the past and being grounded in the past. Yet, according to Bachelard, duration can only be experienced through ruptures in time, that is, through a purposive linking of active instants that are inherently disparate or isolated from each other (DD 91–100).

It seems that Bachelard, on the one hand, offers an insight into the "systematic nature" of temporal organization and, on the other, takes on the very difficult challenge of reconciling the self-sustaining autonomy of the moment with its vital insertion in the sinuous stream of duration. That is why it is "rhythm," as a repeated event, that emerges as the key means of articulating the manner of our perceptions. The capacity of consciousness to focus, understand, and communicate is shaped by the dozens of patterns of recurrent activity, creating, at any one given moment, a person's internal state.

> In the orchestra of the world there are instruments that often fall silent, yet it is false to say that there is always some instrument playing. The world is *conducted* in keeping with a musical measure imposed by the cadence of instants. If we could hear all the instants of reality, we would understand that an eighth note is not made up from fragments of a half note but, rather, that a half note *repeats* the eighth note. It is from such repetition that the *impression* of continuity is born. (II 26–27/46, emphasis mine)

One could argue that the stability of any object is based on the consistency of the rhythm of its existence. This chair, this tree, this house maintain their being through consistent repetitions of themselves. The famous Heraclitean insight—all things are in flux, hence there can be no knowledge of them—here finds a new resolution. Rhythm is the Λόγος, the principle according to which all things undergo change in intelligible ways—that is, rhythm is what determines the nature of the vibratory flux that resides in all beings. If the world is an orchestra, it is only by the constitution of such rhythmic repetitions that the symphony of identity is performed. Bachelard has a clear and definite answer to the question, What comes first? The succession of repetitions always precedes the continuity of flow.[1]

The Structure of Time

It is obvious that reality cannot merely be described as the harmonic sound of the spheres. There are different types of concurrent rhythms that pursue each other, subordinating the human situation to myriad polyphonic experiences. But Bachelard clearly distinguishes several levels of duration in *The Dialectic of Duration* (*La dialectique de la durée*, 1936) and is thus able to generalize a "hierarchical layering" of durations in the human psyche by means of the concept of "temporal consolidation." Through this temporal consolidation, durations constructed within particular levels of human experience are organized in an open hierarchy (DD 94–95). Consequently, "this yields a model of how human experience as a whole is structured in time on two axes"—vertical and horizontal (DD 108–12).[2]

The chronological time of our daily routine evolves horizontally, through the series of repetitive events and practices that form the schematic patterns of our actions. The "naturalism" of this understanding stems from the combination of biological and sociocultural cycles ranging from seconds to years: respiration, daily feeding habits, the alternation of day and night, working and resting hours, seasonal variations, the celebration of national and personal holidays, and so on. The so-called irreversible one-way direction of progress is structured by similar modes of exercised activities and therefore turns easily into a constant flow of clichés as well as trivial formulas of behavior. However, as critic Noël Parker notes,

> [In Bachelard's account] the vertical axis . . . is one along which we can pass from one level of the hierarchy to another, higher one. And the lower levels are subordinate to the higher ones because the latter are higher in the sense that they may order the lower-level durations in a wider order. Moreover, ordering them in durations, the higher levels may also modify their inevitable one-way direction in time, and hence their causality. Moving up the hierarchy along the vertical axis thus brings a degree of freedom to manipulate and reorganize the durations/causalities lower down. Hence, Bachelard refers to this vertical axis as the "axis of liberation." (Parker 81–82; DD 111)

It is ultimately the imagination that provides us with this liberating power of verticality, fostering the temporal *décalage* (breakage, rupture), distorting the regularity of the perceived world and dissolving its recurring sequences. "Imagination allows us to leave the ordinary course of things" (AD 3). In the case of an up-surging image, the order of horizontal schematic reiterations is interrupted, and temporality is expanded into an instantaneous experience of altered rhythms. Dreaming uplifts the human psyche to inchoate primary experiences. This verticality in itself is anything but normal—rising and falling dislodges consciousness from any kind of ordinary, habitual routine. Due to the psychosomatic organization of human being, the movement upward and downward occurs by warping the standard directions of our mobility: jumping, climbing, squatting, crouching, diving, falling all implicitly change the amplitude of our orbital paths. But for Bachelard "man *qua* man cannot live horizontally" (AD 11): the capacity of imagination reveals a unique dimension of human interaction with the world.

> At the very heart of psychic phenomena there will be a real *verticality*. This verticality is no empty metaphor; it is a principle of order, a law governing filiation, a scale along which someone

> can experience the different degrees of a special sensibility. Finally, the life of the soul, all the delicate and discreet emotions, all the hopes and the fears, all the moral forces that are involved in one's future have a *vertical differential* in the full mathematical sense of the word. (AD 10)

Although standard cycles are transformed through verticality, this doesn't mean that their rhythms cease to exist: they turn into different kinds of repetitions. Poetic reverie possesses its own specific temporality that attunes us also to primordial experiences of time. In this context Bachelard speaks of "the hour of strawberries, the hour of peaches and grapes [*l'heure de la fraise, l'heure de la pêche et du raisin*]," which are occasions of psychic renewal in harmony with the change of seasons (DD 151/147). We have to reorganize our psychic activity according to vitalizing, though often hidden, constellations of rhythms. As a method, rhythmanalysis hence looks everywhere for the occasions of rhythms, trusting in their natural correspondences with one another (DD 151–52). In collaboration with poetry, it cultivates an intense sensitivity to the surroundings, while yielding an active and vibrant repose, or—to use the words of Pinheiro dos Santos, the Brazilian philosopher, whom Bachelard cites in the last part of the *The Dialectic of Duration*—"a lyric state of mind [*un état d'âme lyrique*]."

> Liberated in this way from habitual sequences of events, poetry becomes once again the model of rhythmic life and thought. It can thus offer us the best possible way of rhythmanalyzing our spiritual and mental life, in order that the spirit/mind (*l'esprit*) may regain its mastery of the dialectics of duration. (DD 154/150, trans. modified)[3]

It is as if the experience of a poetically stimulated imaginary process promotes reconciliation with our lost harmonious temporality: the return to the paradise of primordial fluxes that occur in our correspondence with the cosmological pulse. As Bachelard says, "The imagination given temporality by the word seems to me to be the humanizing faculty par excellence" (AD 12).

We have to add a short remark here—namely, that a skillful and innovative Bachelardian analysis contemporaneously yields some doubts or caveats about the need to *refute* the concept of duration as an essential quality of time. It seems that the idea of rhythm as reuniting the originality of nature and creation could be in accord with Bergson's understanding of continuous temporality, unless the notion of the "instant" is emphasized as a distinct and not interrelated point, granting it a spatial rather than a temporal existence. In fact, to avoid falling into a collision of mere theoretical schemata, Bachelard himself must develop a certain explanation of duration. This leads him to admit that instants are immersed in nothingness, and only the latter is continuous. In his words: "Time is . . . continuous as possibility, as nothingness. It is discontinuous as being" (DD 44).[4] Thus the introspection of a virtual duration behind our constructed experience of duration remains, though conceived in negative terms. Without further elaboration of this provocative perspective on Bachelard's "nihilism," we would add that "vertical time" could then be interpreted as a term suggesting a potential mode of temporal extension—perhaps similar to the one Bergson had in mind while describing his observation of melting sugar.[5] Bergson's "*Je dois attendre . . . que le sucre fonde*," one might claim, refers to a *rhythmical* dimension analogous to the experience of "*l'heure de la fraise, l'heure de la pêche et du raisin*."

This becomes even more obvious when one notices that, although Bachelard is inclined to deal with formulas traditionally attributed to the definition of substances, their linguistic character is poetic rather than scientific. And it seems that a geometrically or spatially rigid concept of the instant turns out to be rather an obstacle as it does not facilitate the possibility to grasp the properly dynamic, pulsating circulation of temporal meaning that Bachelard tries to suggest. In material imagination the concept of the interchange of the inner depths of subject and object gains a temporal exposition. The further step would include a chiasmic reversion of the double perspective of spatial characteristics.

> A salutary rhythm of introversion and extroversion comes to life in the worker's spirit. But if one truly invests an object with form, if one *imposes* a form on it in spite of its resistance, then introversion and extroversion become more than mere psychological orientations, or indexes of two opposing types of human psychology. They are types of energy, evolving as they interchange. (ERW 24–25)

Hence the equivocal statements that may lead to seemingly metaphysical or even mythological speculations should be considered in light of the intrinsic temporality of rhythms. The claim that "it is through the image that the one who imagines and the thing imagined are most closely united" (ERW 3/5) does not refer to a magical process of emanation or spatial fusion. Rather, this becomes possible only through the rejection or destruction of images as static structures—"in the dynamic critical activity of imagination which Bachelard calls *iconoclasm*. The iconoclastic function serves to demystify not only the immobilizing prestige of reality but also the 'fascinating' power of imagination itself."[6] The imaginative encounter with reality does not entail the immersion of one substance in the other. Even as the dreamer involves him/herself in reverie, the act of reunification is performed according to the rules of an *altered* vertical temporality. The rhythms of the imagining consciousness and the rhythms of matter reach the highest coincidence, amplifying the experience of the very given moment and creating a cosmological resonance that helps us to commune with the world. Meditating before a fire, for instance, we are led into a condition "beyond time, beyond space"—*hors du temps, hors de l'espace* (PR 193/166)—a liberating state of not being chained to a concrete place or to a horizontal repetition of patterns of behavior. This is how imagination concentrates "the cosmos-creating self"—*le je cosmisant* (PR 203/175).[7]

Resonance and Reverberation: The Logic of Imagination

Bachelard offers two concepts that bring about an altered temporality of material imagination: resonance and reverberation. *Resonance* is a dynamic condition through which the world discloses its imaginary opportunities: it oscillates with larger amplitude at some frequencies than at others. Under its sway, the rhythm of consciousness and the world-rhythm can come into accord. *Reverberation* technically means a further step, that is, the change of configuration of our rhythmical settings through the intrusion of an alien pulse. A single and immediate image can touch the whole world by its echoing repercussion. Describing its advent as the "opposite of causality," Bachelard found in reverberation the "real measure of the being of a poetic image" (PS xxi), for reverberation effectively enters subjectivity as a vibration that cuts through conventional borderlines, and dissipates the subject–object distinction. We are possessed by external rhythms; the so-called depth of our interiority is affected by this alien energy; we vibrate in tune with alien rhythms. In a way, this could be considered as a process of depersonalization that opens a possibility of transgression in our experience.

> This is where the phenomenological doublet of resonances and reverberation must be sensitized. Resonances are dispersed on the different planes of our life in the world, while reverberation invites us to give greater depth to our own existence. In resonance we hear the poem, in reverberation we speak it—it is our own. Reverberation brings about a change of being. It is as though the poet's being were our being. The multiplicity of resonances then issue from the reverberation's unity of being. (PS xviii/6; trans. modified)[8]

This transformation affects all parts of consciousness, penetrating both body and mind—the whole entity is literally permeated by a content which comes "from outside." Its sonority moreover extinguishes the surface/depth dualism. It is as if depth, for the dynamic imagination, is paradoxically more immediate than surface: it touches directly on the beyond, and it musically overwhelms the things it touches. "The exuberance and depth of a poem are always phenomena of the resonance-reverberation doublet. It is as though the poem, through its exuberance, awakened new depths in us" (PS xix),

Bachelard's insights in his understanding of rhythm anticipated Deleuze's subsequent analyses of Francis Bacon's paintings (1981) in intriguing ways,[9] although—as we shall see—they both adopted very different theoretical perspectives. *Mutatis mutandis*, Deleuze came to focus on the same aspect of "altered poetic temporality," yet as exposed in the perceptual intensity of a visual work of art: "paint the sensation, which is essentially rhythm" (Deleuze 60). Rejecting narrativity and representational interpretations, the text of *The Logic of Sensation* provides us with acoustic metaphors and helps to suggest the type of experience we encounter when faced with Bacon's paintings:

> In the simple sensation, rhythm is still dependent on the Figure, it appears as the *vibration* that flows through the body without organs, it is the vector of sensation, it is what makes the sensation pass from one level to another. In the coupling of sensation, rhythm is already liberated, because it confronts and unites the diverse levels of different sensations: it is now *resonance*, but it is still merged together with the melodic lines, the points and counterpoints, of a coupled Figure; it is the diagram of the coupled Figure. (Deleuze 60–61)

Deleuze not only identifies rhythmical structures in Bacon's art, but also registers the regime of their development. If every painting is fundamentally a movement, the vector of its evolution is marked by the level of engagement or—to speak in temporal terms—by increasing the rhythmical activity that occurs in and through sensation. Resonance is an amplification of this temporal experience that simultaneously decreases the determination of object-forms. Hence Bacon's paintings do not represent the correlation of forms and colors, but rather are the condition under which the liberation of forces turns out to be possible. Figures and colors are no longer the qualities of things, but start to function as overwhelming forces themselves. And, as it turns out, an analogical kind of temporal dynamism can also be found in Bachelard's writings.

Indeed, Bachelard's own literary and artistic interpretations had long endeavored to avoid the logic of signification, which presupposes the stratification of layers and the referential distinction between signifier and signified. Psychoanalysis, adopting this latter approach for instance, "looks for the reality beneath the image but fails to perform the inverse search: to look beneath the reality for the absolute image" (ERW 15). In other words, for Bachelard an image should not be treated as a sign. An image does not "mean," but rather *engages us* in the dynamic transformation of time. "We always think of the imagination as the faculty that *forms* images. On the contrary, it deforms what we perceive; it is, above all, the faculty that frees us from immediate images and *changes* them" (AD 1). So the experience of the *imaginaire* is the experience of a condensed process of modification. The psyche is always led by a *hunger for images*. "It craves images" (ERW 15). For this reason, perhaps, Bachelard constantly dissociated himself from the concept of formal imagination, which gains its articulation only by delimiting itself to the final stage of images conceived as visual products. "We could say that a stable and completely realized image *clips the wings* of the imagination. It causes us to fall from the state of dreaming imagination that is not confined to image, and that we may call *imageless imagination*, just as we speak of *imageless thought*" (AD 2).

Formal imagination is, therefore, reproductive imagination and, as such, is based on the perception considered as prior in time. It still refers to the distinction of object-forms and presupposes the judgment of the qualities of the things. Its function consists of recreating the "faint copy" of sensations; its creativity is reduced to a poor imitation of perception.

Bachelard, however, is keen on finding completely the opposite: "[A]n image may *precede* perception, initiating an adventure in perception" (ERW 3). Impoverished imagination, imagination ruled by clichés (that is, still horizontal), stems from cookie-cutter visual samples. This process has been well registered by thinkers and writers. The world is normally given in this state inundated with a noisy triviality that is difficult to escape. According to Deleuze, "there are psychic clichés just as there are physical clichés—ready made perceptions, memories, phantasms. There is a very important experience here for the painter: a whole category of things that could be termed clichés already fills the canvas, before beginning. It is dramatic" (Deleuze 71–72). Irvine Welsh also offers a stunning example of this particular interconnection between imagination and perception, constantly jeopardized with airtight shallowness that prevents us from seeing: an image may be the cause of blindness. In his short story "The Granton Star Cause," Boab, a twenty-three-year-old loser, meets God, who is a hobo-like bloke in a pub. Boab is given an explanation: if God looks familiar, "that's cause ye've nae imagination"; "Ye see ays n hear ays ye imagine ays."[10]

The challenge of material imagination sets a clear goal—to liberate one's capacity for reverie and to escape from the entrapment of surrounding ready-made patterns. This is far more difficult than it seems at first sight. Imagination should be exercised and developed as if it were a kind of physical training. Despite the fact that one frequently considers imaginative experiences to be either a form of the sporadic flow of mental trash or, on the contrary, a fulfillment of egoistic desires, neither of these trajectories really helps to enhance the capacity to operate the resources of the *imaginaire*. According to Bachelard, imagination, which is often treated as a vagabond activity, turns out to be most powerful when concentrated on a single image. One needs to improve the endurance, strength, and speed control of the psyche. This is how, by approaching the dialectic of imagination and will, the ground for a possible synthesis of the imagination of matter and the imagination of energy could be prepared. His first book on Earth, the most obdurate of elements, is hence devoted to countering the reigning doctrine of the primacy of the real: "The counsel to *see well*, at the base of the culture of realism, all too easily outweighs my own paradoxical advice to *dream well*, to remain faithful to the oneiric archetypes deeply rooted in the human unconscious" (ERW 2/3, trans. modified).

This by no means can be interpreted as a repudiation of formal imagination. Material imagination is not "better" than formal imagination. Rather, it seems that Bachelard is trying to focus on the level of engagement that occurs in material reveries. As Touponce puts it, "this experience of intimacy at the heart of matter was for Bachelard always linked to the body, our childhood bodies, where the image is an act of the hand, a magical gesture working with valorized substances."[11] Intimacy is a condition of concentrated experience, an experience that cannot be replicated without reducing its intimate character to triviality or formality. To a certain extent, it is an experience of altered temporality, the temporality of common time shared by those who are involved in a "secret event."

> A Copernican revolution of the imagination can therefore be formulated if we take care to restrict ourselves to the psychological problem of *imagined* qualities. Quality should not be sought in the object's *totality*, as the deep sign of substance; it should instead be sought in the *total adherence* of a subject who is deeply committed to what he or she is imagining. (ERR 59)

Rather than concentrate on *what* one imagines, on the formal creativity of imagination, always producing unseen forms and inventing new images, Bachelard invites his reader to learn *how* to imagine, to improve the procedures of the intentionality biased to the matter of things. One must carefully pursue the motion of reverie, to study its dynamics and to get integrated in its trajectories in order to be open to the true discoveries. As Bachelard had suggested years earlier, in his first book on temporality, fantasies tend to be egoistic, self-flattering, ephemeral (II 52)—an insight found also in Freud, and later in Lacan. It is indeed by renouncing oneself that the dreamer meets the cosmological challenge. One must stop speaking and start listening in order to follow the logic of imagination. Resonance and reverberation require not only attention and concentration, but also the capacity to obey a deeper will of imagination. A psyche longing for creative awakenings will *allow* the incursion of what may initially seem to be alien and dangerous.

> By experiencing the curious condensation of imagery and energy that characterizes work with matter, we experience for ourselves the synthesis of imagination and will. This synthesis, largely ignored by philosophers, is nonetheless the first synthesis to consider in a dynamology of the human psyche. One desires truly only that which one imagines richly. (ERW 18)

The Temporality of Material Imagination

But what does it mean—to "*dream well*" (ERW 2)? Although Bachelard does not constantly use temporal metaphors, his understanding of imagination should always be considered in light of the performativity of rhythms. Thus what is "penetration" in space is marked by resonance and reverberation in time. Henri Lefebvre, inspired by Bachelard and Pinheiro dos Santos in his book *Rhythmanalysis*, will later expand on Bachelard's account with insights on how rhythms function at the intersection of space and time.[12] "Rhythm is easily grasped," he writes, "whenever the body makes a sign; but it is conceived with difficulty. Why? It is neither a substance, nor a matter, nor a thing" (Lefebvre 64). According to Lefebvre, although rhythm has all these aspects, it cannot be reduced to them, as it implies something more. This "something more" is energy, which "unfolds in a time and a space (a space-time)" (Lefebvre 65). It is as if rhythm would mark the junction of time and space which occurs only through energetic flow and which consitutes the third unifying dimension of the world. Energy is what time and space have in common.

Bachelard's "*dreaming well*" might then be a way to master the expenditure of energy accomplished in accordance with a rhythm. To make our case, let us begin by reading the following passage, where Bachelard sums up his accounts of dynamic material imagination:

> I might mention here a few short works in which I have recently examined, under the name of *material imagination*, the astonishing need for "penetration." Going beyond the seductive imagination of forms, it thinks matter, dreams matter, lives in matter, or—what amounts to the same thing—it materializes the imaginary. I felt justified in speaking of a law of the four material imaginations, a law that *necessarily* attributes to the creative imagination one of the four elements: fire, earth, air, or water. Several elements, of course, can intervene to constitute a particular image. There are *composite* images, but the life of images has a more demanding purity of filiations. The moment that images form a series, they designate a primary matter, a basic element. Even more than its autonomy, the physiology of the imagination obeys the law of the four elements. (AD 7)

Bachelard's celebrated distinction between two forms of imagination—formal and material—seems to gain a whole new meaning here. "Formal imagination" is seduced by the objective qualities of images, operating by blocking the dynamism of consciousness and suspending its rhythms in the realm of vision; whereas "material imagination" is infected by four elements, since it not only performs the act of penetration but is also materialized by the world: imagining here turns into direct contact with one of four elements. Liberated from schematic formality, it discovers the true essence of matter: fire, earth, air, or water which is not a concrete object, but a *stoicheia* in the Greek sense of the word, the primordial force lying at the heart of all things. This mutual interchange is fulfilled as a resonating expansion of periodic amplitudes: thereby realizing intensification, which synchronizes the imagining consciousness with cosmological rhythms. "A psychology of imagination that is concerned only with the *structure of images* ignores an essential and obvious characteristic that everyone recognizes: *the mobility of images*" (AD 2). This is why material imagination is inseparable from and immediate to elemental matter—rather than being fixed in the physical substances of things, it dances a cosmological tango, following a series of movements that match the speed and rhythm of the music of the four elements.

The importance of the material imagination is witnessed by the polyvalent reveries that arise in the actual encounter with the four elements. It seems that Bachelard does not even try to reduce the ambiguity of the latter experience. The mobility of images, its fluid and undetermined character, should rather be intensified and amplified. The awaiting resonance thus ushers us into the dialectics of oxymoron.

> These reveries play upon the greatest of all contradictions: the contradictions of resistant matter. They awaken demiurgic impressions in the worker's soul. It seems that reality is conquered in the very heart of matter, and in the end, the greatness of the victory obscures the ease of its attainment, transporting the worker to the regions where the will is liberated from the phantasms of primal impulse. (ERW 35)

Bachelard often criticized the approach of psychoanalysis as fundamentally based on the premises of rationalization. For instance, Lacan's claim that the subconscious is structured as a language intrinsically pressuposes that its chaotic appearance can be clarified, that is, reduced to a rationally comprehensible system. For Bachelard, on the contrary, to comprehend an image means to be involved in the "flickering of ambivalence" which enables us to sense the whole dynamism of its relationship. When it comes to the sensory imagination, "one might posit the *indeterminacy principle* for affective response analogous to the *uncertainty principle* posited by microphysics, which restricts the simultaneous determination of static and dynamic descriptions" (ERW

58). According to him, the function of ambivalence in images is much more active than antithesis in the realm of ideas. The detailed examination of an image allows us to recognize its magnetically controversial character. It easily assumes moral, aesthetic, and even erotic qualities, at the same time constantly maintining the surplus of meaning which goes beyond any attributed determination. "Images carry out quite subtly the massive battle of wills which rages at the core of our being, using one essential ruse—the technique of revealing and concealing by turns" (ERW 26). We tend to categorize, group, and deliver judgments about images, but we never really master them. They always exceed their explanations, while containing and handling contradictory meanings as valid. This why the imagination should be considered as "the center from which the dual orientations of all ambivalence—extroversion and introversion—extend" (ERW 26).

Hence the material imagination is always at least twofold: it is accomplished as a collision of both our will and an alien will. And as an experience of being affected, it evolves through the process of alienation, offering to feel the voices of the Other which integrally belong to self-existence. It is as though the conscious self were guided by the released spontaneity of the subconscious. This process of dissociated psychism is an annihilation of the self-containment of "false subjectivity" by accumulating an amalgam of contradictions.

> Thus, for example, the freedom *from* the world affected by the dynamic function is converted into the material imagination's freedom *for* the world. And precisely because of this poetic interplay, the world for which we are now freed is always other than the world from which we are freed. In the discovery of this other world, the self discovers its "other" self. (Kearney 110)

One has to suspend the functions of "ego commands" to allow the impact of the "foreign power" in order to reach the paradox of comprehension—a paradox which is such because it legitimizes contradictions.

> The imagination has the power to multiply the inner qualities of things [*l'intimité des substances*]; it inspires the will to *be more*, not evasively but prodigally, not contradictorily but drunk with oppositional tendencies. The image is the individual differentiating itself to ensure its own evolution [*pour être sûr de devenir*]. (ERW 19/26)

It is not by chance that Bachelard uses the word "drunk" (*ivre*) here. Individuals affected by alcohol to the extent of losing control of their faculties or behavior could not in any way cultivate Descartes's *clara et distincta perceptio*. On the other hand, one might be led by obscure and captivating visions that expand comprehension by complicating determinations and integrating oppositions. This logic of impossibility works faster than the process of doubting and accessing rationality. If thinking means slowing down, imagination tends to intensify speed:

> In this realm . . . every image [is] an *acceleration*; in other words, the imagination is an "accelerator" of the psyche. Imagination goes *too* fast, systematically. This is a banal characteristic, so banal that one may easily forget to signal its importance. If we were to pay closer attention to the mobile fringe of images that rings reality, and correspondingly, to the transcendence of self inherent in the act of imagination, we would comprehend the human psyche for what it is—a driving force. (ERW 19)

Despite its energizing dynamics and exceeding speed, the material imagination sets its own conditions of time experience. Acceleration may not reach the resonating effect, unless cultivated patiently. Then, again, another paradox is constituted: the slow-fast motion. The rapid evolution of a driving imaginary force is harnessed by the slowness of concentration. It seems that Bachelard has a solution for how to master the protean character of fantasies. One can find passages where the necessity of the adjustment of different durations is emphasized:

> This *lithochronos*, or temporality based on a stone's hardness, can only be defined as the active time of work. A temporality whose dialectic is defined by the effort of the laborer and the resistance of the rock, it operates as a kind of natural and bracing rhythm. It is this rhythm that endows work with both its objective efficiency and its subjective tonicity, adding important new dimensions to the *temporality of opposition*. (ERW 16)

The activity of work is articulated according to the logic of colliding temporalities—and it is in this realm that one encounters the specific intensity of material imagination. We work insofar as we engage ourselves in reveries of confrontation with reality. Thus the resistance of matter stipulates the temporality of opposition. This is a temporality that requires our unconditional participation in the performed activity. In this way the protracted time of applied efforts meets the acceleration of imagination. Here a resonance occurs through the attention and concentration that are drawn forth.

> In our dreams of matter, we envision an entire future of work; we seek to conquer it through labor. We take pleasure in the projected efficacy of our will. It should not be surprising then that to dream material images—yes, simply to dream them—is to invigorate the will. It is impossible to remain distracted, indifferent, or detached while one dreams of resistant matter clearly imagined. (ERW 17)

No doubt one must be sensitive to these durations of matter in order to become attuned to them. Bachelard is very precise in disclosing the modalities of these rhythms, which might differ chronologically from our psychosomatic cycles, but could still remain analogous to them cosmologically.

> Decomposition and fermentation, two distinctly different *material temporalities*, work matter dialectically like systole and diastole work the heart. Here are sure signs of *dialectic duration*, a duration which finds impetus only in the successive pursuit of contradictory impulses—first a destructive maturation that seeks to reduce all to dust, and then a purified blending of ferments that works to achieve consistency. By this double movement it seems that *the molten matter kneads itself.* (ERW 67)

Here a particular example serves as a helpful rhythmical analogy. The dialectics of blood circulation corresponds to the chemistry of dough. Although they are not synchronized, a certain pertinence can be sensed: it is as though the capacity to feel one's heart beating evokes an understanding of concealed material temporality. This double movement is always ambivalent. In order to discover the frequencies of matter, one needs to become attuned to the modulation of one's own primordial pulse.

Analogically, for Deleuze, the dialectics of the heartbeat, the process of the heart muscle contracting and relaxing, pumping and filling with blood, seems to give a clue—if not to articulate—the laws of temporality of the experience at the level of sensations. By painting the sensation, Francis Bacon had offered us a condensate of motion which actively distorts the chronological perception of time, awakening the dimension of systole and diastole—the dimension that is already intrinsic in corporeal experience. This is why Deleuze chooses to focus on the most active and deforming type of rhythm—the fall.

> The fall is what is most alive in the sensation, that through which the sensation is experienced as living. An intensive fall can thus coincide with a spatial descent, but also with a rise. It can coincide with a diastole, a dilatation or dissipation, but equally with a contraction or systole. It can coincide with diminution, but equally with an augmentation. In short, everything that develops is a fall (there are developments by diminutions). The fall is precisely the active rhythm. (Deleuze 68)

It goes without saying that the function of Bachelard's material imagination is not equivalent to Deleuze's logic of sensation. But, in a way, a certain analogy could be drawn with an energetic character found in Bacon's paintings. It is by registering the modulation of intensified experience—that is, the accumulation of active reality that cannot be submitted to the subject-object distinction—that the reality of rhythmic flows is grasped, and one can claim that Deleuze's concept of sensation is "imaginational." The latter observation could be endorsed as well by the aspect of reality in which amalgams of concentrated forces are confronted. These forces are shaped by musical (ergo rhythmical) analogies: "Force is closely related to sensation: for a sensation to exist, a force must be exerted on a body, on a point of the wave. . . . It is in this way that music must render non-sonorous forces sonorous, and painting must render invisible forces visible" (Deleuze 48).

Conversely, material imagination could be marked as related to "sensations," since, avoiding the cultivation of merely subjective faculties, it also works "in connection with forces." Both Deleuze and Bachelard emphasize the energetic dimension which precedes any schematic shaping: "Through our material and dynamic imagination we experience the knot's external form awaken in us an internal *force* which longs to vanquish. This internal force, in privileging our muscular will, gives structure to our innermost being" (ERW 41). The materiality of imagination, for Bachelard, seems analogous to an awakening of sensation, for Deleuze. This is also the reason why Bachelard applies the method of phenomenology which "is essentially a dynamology and [why] a materialist analysis of work must be accompanied by an analysis of the energies involved" (ERW 33). His research avoids the exploration of mental patterns in our consciousness. On the contrary, if applied with mastery, it is the psychic drive of these forces that masters the kinetic character of fantasies by increasing it to the maximum and enabling us to experience the dynamic power of imagination. Being immersed in material imagination paradoxically entails becoming attuned to genuine temporality, awakening a latent rhythmical essence, undergoing the exertion of forces, stimulating the resonance of comprehension, and, therefore, possibly fulfilling the cosmological openness of the psyche to the world. In this kind of reverie it is ultimately the world itself that is reverberating its concealed truth through our intentional activity, the world that is being embodied and accomplished by us, and in us.

Our conventional understanding of imagination tends to be governed by the supremacy of the formal over the material. This supremacy conceals the fundamental role of reverie, which needs to be rediscovered and would redeem it from its systematic dependency on realism by exploding its object-like appearance. If the world is an orchestra, none of its instruments could be heard without the impact of a driving *imaginaire*. Bachelard contributes a lot to elucidating the paradox of this dynamic process, which accumulates contradictions and operates through the close proximity of imagination and will. Material reveries reach their resonating accomplishment through rhythmical motions, which, deeply rooted in primordial temporality, simultaneously awaken actual corporeal experience or, to put it in Deleuze's terms, the experience of living sensations.

Notes

1. As we intend to demonstrate further on, such "repetitions" cannot be reduced to automatic replicas of what came before. Each instant, in Bachelard's account, brings originality (variations) in its pulse, as it helps to transform, preserve, or dissolve an existing form, habit, or structure (II 44, 47, 49, 50).

2. Cited and discussed in Noël Parker, "Science and Poetry in the Ontology of Human Freedom," in *The Philosophy and Poetics of Gaston Bachelard*, ed. Mary McAllester (Washington, DC: Center for Advanced Research in Phenomenology, 1989), 81; hereafter cited as Parker.

3. My amended translation partly reflects that of Noël Parker, who translates *l'esprit* in this case as "spirit" (Parker 84), although it also means "mind" (as translated by Mary McAllester Jones in *The Dialectic of Duration*).

4. The full context of Bachelard's admission reads: "We believe [however] that we must give ourselves rather more than just temporal possibility characterized

as an a priori form. We need to give ourselves the *temporal alternative* that can be analyzed by these two observations: either in this instant nothing is happening, or else in this instant something is happening. *Time is thus continuous as possibility, as nothingness. It is discontinuous as being.* In other words, we start from *temporal duality*, not from unity. We base this duality on *function* rather than on *being*. When Bergson tells us that dialectic is but the relaxation of intuition, we reply that this relaxation [*détente*] is necessary to the renewal of intuition and that, from the standpoint of meditation, intuition and relaxation give us proof of the fundamental *temporal alternative*" (DD 44, emphasis added).

5. See Henri Bergson, *Creative Evolution*, trans. Arthur Mitchell (New York: Henry Holt, 1911), 9–10.

6. Richard Kearney, *Poetics of Imagining* (New York: Fordham University Press, 1998), 109; hereafter cited as Kearney.

7. See the example of Mélusine in Jacques Audiberti's *Carnage*, discussed by Bachelard in *The Poetics of Reverie*, 202–5.

8. English translator Maria Jolas here uses the terms *repercussions* or *reverberation* alternately for Bachelard's *retentissement* (see *Poétique de l'espace,* 6). My amended translation keeps the term *reverberation* to reflect Bachelard's consistency in his use of terms.

9. Gilles Deleuze, *Francis Bacon: Logique de la sensation* (Paris: Éditions de la différance, 1981), translated into English as *Francis Bacon: The Logic of Sensation* (London: Continuum, 2003); hereafter cited as Deleuze.

10. In Irvine Welsh, *The Acid House* (Scotland: Jonathan Cape, 1994), 130.

11. F. W. Touponce, *Ray Bradbury and the Poetics of Reverie: Gaston Bachelard, Wolfgang Iser, and the Reader's Response to Fantastic Literature* (San Bernardino, CA: Borgo, 1998), 32.

12. Henri Lefebvre, *Élements de rhythmanalyse* (Paris: Syllepse, 1992), translated into English as *Rhythmanalysis: Space, Time and Everyday Life,* trans. S. Elden and G. Moore (London: Continuum, 2004); hereafter cited as Lefebvre.

Part 2

Adventures in Methodology

Chapter 5

Adventures of Consciousness: Bachelard on the Scientific Imagination

MARY MCALLESTER JONES

"There are no big problems," Bachelard once said, adding by way of explanation that "big problems begin in a small way," for insights are gained by opening what he describes as "very small doors and very small windows."[1] This chapter seeks to open one of these "small doors," a way into an important aspect of Bachelard's work, namely, his conception of consciousness. Reference to the scientific imagination may seem paradoxical, and doubly so when linked to Bachelard's idea of the "adventures of consciousness." This phrase, "adventures of consciousness," is used movingly as he concludes the last book published during his lifetime, *The Flame of a Candle* (1961), for he is old and ill while writing this meditative reflection on his work on both poetry and science. He raises a series of questions about the possibility of such adventures, ending on a note of nostalgia for what he calls "strictly ordered thought" as the mind strains towards ever more rigorously developed works (FC 78). Bachelard seems indeed to aspire to existence as tension—pulled forward and forward again to something beyond, to something above, and to regard the "adventures of consciousness" (FC 77/111) as deriving from this tension. Tension is an idea that Bachelard chooses to emphasize here, clearly central to his conception of thought, existence, and consciousness. Moreover, Bachelard's readers can experience the demand of this tension, for not only does the book end with a question mark, but it also puzzles them with paradox when, for instance, he regards reverie as leading to a possible loss of being (we know that he conceives it otherwise) and presents an image of himself as sitting before a blank sheet of paper (we know that we have just read a book he has written). These, I would suggest, are fruitful paradoxes because they oblige us to think and consequently to embark on our own "adventures of consciousness."

Let us begin by pushing at the small door of the scientific imagination, to which Bachelard refers in a positive way—and quite briefly—in just four works, in 1934, 1940, and 1951. Given his extensive critique of the scientific imagination in *The Formation of the Scientific Mind*, published in 1938, these positive references seem contradictory, especially so in view of the evidence in the text that it had been underway well before 1936.[2] It would seem then that there are two different yet coexisting conceptions of the scientific imagination in Bachelard's thought. The scientific imagination he indicts is an obstacle to scientific thinking, which has to be "psychoanalyzed," as he puts it, that is to say cured of the mental inertia caused when images are espoused. What are these images? They are concrete images, rooted in everyday experience, in realism, sensualism, and direct intuition, their very evidence serving to block thought because, as Bachelard puts it, "you think as you see and you think what you see" (FSM 109). Unchecked, these images tend to accumulate unconscious values, stifling questions and mutilating thought: they are dangerous, he argues, because they are the opposite of abstract, discursive scientific thought, and they must therefore be combated. Given this thoroughgoing critique of the scientific imagination, how is a different view of it possible?

Towards the end of *The Formation of the Scientific Mind* (1938), Bachelard stresses the role of mathematics in modern scientific thought, twice using the French phrase *l'effort mathématisant*—the efforts of mathematics (FSM 246/249). This phrase is reminiscent of one used earlier, in *The New Scientific Spirit* (1934), where he had implicitly compared mathematics and poetry in writing about *l'effort poétique des mathématiciens*—the poetic strivings of mathematicians (NSS 32/35), which he describes as creative and realizing. Both phrases occur in discussions of mathematical "realization," in which Bachelard argues that mathematics creates a reality against that of "first objects" (FSM 238–39/234) and the "given world," so that "reality crystallizes along the axes provided by human thought, and new phenomena are produced" (FSM 246/249). The word "poetic" with its etymological sense of "making" serves to emphasize this creativity, jolting readers out of a positivistic, utilitarian view of science. It has another function too, for it leads us to connect mathematics and poetry and so to reflect differently on the scientific imagination. The connection between mathematics and poetry is firmly established when Bachelard goes on to declare in *The New Scientific Spirit:* "It is in the realm of aesthetics that we may find synthetic values comparable to the symbols of mathematics. When we think of the beautiful symbols of mathematics, wherein the possible and the real are conjoined, the images that come to mind are Mallarméan" (NSS 58/60). He then quotes from Mallarmé's *Divagations*: "One dreams of them as of something that might have been. With reason, because none of the possibilities that hover about a figure, as ideas, must be neglected. They belong to the original, even against probability" (ibid.). Bachelard reinforces the connection between mathematics and poetry when, commenting on this quotation, he adds that "in the same way, pure mathematical possibilities belong to the real phenomenon, however unlikely this may be, given the first lessons we learn from immediate experience." Mathematical symbols and poetic images are therefore both conceived as exploring and also sustaining possibility. Far from blocking thought, the scientific imagination extends it.

Referring to the scientific imagination may well seem paradoxical, for not only does Bachelard limit himself to mathematics here, but he also avoids the word "imagination." Indeed, it is not until 1951 that he will give it a positive sense in an epistemological work, when in *L'Activité rationaliste de la physique contemporaine* he writes about "the non-Cartesian imagination that must be placed at the beginning of modern scientific culture" (ARPC 66).[3] The idea of the "non-Cartesian imagination" is crucial, illuminating retrospectively his earlier adumbrations of the scientific imagination. Having compared mathematics and poetry in *The New Scientific Spirit*, Bachelard had also compared chemistry and poetry in a conference paper given in 1934, in which he presented a critique of the concept of "epistemological frontier."[4] Arguing that scientific thought transcends the frontiers of immediate observation, that it "supposes reality before knowing it and only knows it as a realization of its supposition" (É 80), Bachelard here stresses that there are more possibilities in reason than in nature—for instance, more chemical substances exist in the laboratory than they do in nature. He then reinforces his point by declaring that "some chemical bodies created by humankind are no more real than the *Aeneid* or the *Divine Comedy*. In some respects, it seems to us no more useful to talk of the frontiers of chemistry than of those of poetry" (É 83). Why make this comparison between chemistry and poetry? It does indeed seem paradoxical given that he himself had previously described chemistry as "that most experimental and positive of sciences" (PCCM 7). The comparison forces us to think differently, to understand that modern chemistry also explores possibility, that it creates its substances. Bachelard's third positive reference to poetry in an epistemological work is in *The Philosophy of No* (1940), where it is the turn of physics to be compared to poetry. Here he outlines what constitutes in his view the *ars poetica* of physics,[5] asking "What poet will sing this pan-pythagoreanism,[6] this synthetic arithmetic which begins by giving to every being its four quanta, its four-figure number, as if the simplest, poorest, and most abstract of electrons already had, of necessity, more than a thousand faces" (PN 32–33/39–40). Again, poetry is associated with possibility and with synthesis. And again, the word "imagination" is absent.

Initially, Bachelard associates imagination with perception: "it is with our retina that we imagine," he states in an article entitled "Le Monde comme caprice et miniature" published in 1933–34, adding: "We cannot transcend the retinal conditions of the imagination" (É 43).[7] A very similar statement is made in *The New Scientific Spirit* (1934): "It must not be forgotten that *we imagine with our retinas*" and consequently, he says, our imagination can take us only as far as our senses can (NSS 132/136). He warns against the use in science of images that are based on everyday knowledge—waves, particles, atoms, electron spin—because they hinder the non-realist, synthetic thought of modern science. Interestingly, as we have seen, Bachelard finds in poetry a model of this synthetic thought. Interestingly too, it is after writing his first series of books on poetic imagination that he formulates the idea of a "non-Cartesian imagination" in modern science, less wary perhaps of referring to the scientific imagination now that he has studied images that are manifestly non-retinal. Why does he refer to the scientific imagination as "non-Cartesian"? The context in which this phrase occurs is a discussion of the complex, dual image ray-wave, as opposed to the simple intuitions of ordinary knowledge. The term "non-Cartesian" underlines both this complexity, which is against Descartes's notion of "simple natures," and also the importance of synthetic thinking in modern science, which has broken with Cartesian analysis. Thus, the non-Cartesian imagination is, in Bachelard's view, a fundamental aspect of modern scientific thought—he places it, we must remember, "at the beginning of modern scientific culture"—which advances rather than obstructs the complex syntheses of modern science. This is clearly a very different idea of the scientific imagination from that put forward in *The Formation of the Scientific Mind.*

The non-Cartesian imagination makes us think back to the non-Cartesian epistemology Bachelard outlines in the last chapter of *The New Scientific Spirit,* and in particular to the conception he proposes there of the non-Cartesian cogito. Having argued that Cartesian methods and ideas are no longer tenable in modern physics with its complex synthesis of geometry, mechanics, and electricity (NSS 143/147), Bachelard compares Descartes's observation of a piece of wax with the way microphysics would deal with it (NSS 165–171/170–177), and in doing so he challenges Descartes's belief in the permanence of the I that thinks. Noting that Descartes did not see that "the mobile character of objective observation found its immediate reflection in the parallel mobility of subjective experience," Bachelard affirms, "If the wax is changing, then I am changing" (NSS 167/172). And as he concludes this discussion, he stresses the difference between what he calls "subjective meditation," which seeks clear, complete knowledge, and "the objective meditation that takes place in the laboratory," which is incomplete, progressive, and in need of "a complement whose existence it always supposes" (NSS 170–171/176–177). This distinction between subjective and objective meditations helps us understand the nostalgia Bachelard expresses at the end of *The Flame of a Candle* for "strictly ordered thought" (FC 78), for thought that is ordered by something beyond it, by the complement it supposes, and also his aspiration to existence as tension, "pulled forward and forward again to something beyond, to something above." In a similar way, his conception of the non-Cartesian cogito helps us understand his idea of the "adventures of consciousness."

What are the connotations of the word "adventure"? It suggests danger and risk, journeys and new experiences. While it may at first seem odd to associate such ideas with consciousness, Bachelard does in fact use this vocabulary—though not the word "adventure"—when developing his conception of the discursive, non-Cartesian cogito in his article "Idéalisme discursif" (1934–35).[8] Consciousness is not a given, he argues, for "I need to think something in order to think myself as someone"; if I doubt that something, then I lose both it and myself, and I have to reconquer slowly both objective truth and consciousness (É 87–88). The process of objectification involves consciousness of past errors, and Bachelard observes, "We have to go astray in order to get somewhere" (É 89). Rectification—the correction of past errors—means that we leave what he calls "the kingdom of appearances" and "empirical bondage" (É 94). Bachelard then develops this in a way that retrospectively helps us to understand his idea of the "adventures of consciousness." Not only does the mind discover and try out its independence from experience, he says, but my consciousness of objective error is also consciousness of "my freedom of orientation," and this "liberated, reflective orientation is in fact a potential journey out of my self, in search of a new intellectual destiny" (É 94). Thus, when I think against past objective errors, I think towards the future, I set out on a journey towards the objective unknown that is also an adventure of consciousness. For Bachelard, "consciousness of intellectual being is accompanied by consciousness of intellectual becoming. The mind is revealed as a being to be taught, that is to say, as a being to be created" (É 90). The adventures of consciousness are not optional in Bachelard's view, but essential to our becoming, to our human being.

The "small door" of Bachelard's idea of the scientific imagination has opened onto his conception of consciousness and of human beings. We have seen that for Bachelard, the scientific imagination is a fundamental aspect of modern scientific thought, with its syntheses, its exploration of possibility, and its creativity. The non-Cartesian imagination exemplifies the freedom of the scientific mind, its transcendence of reason and reality, and its endless reconstruction of thought and of consciousness, so illustrating what he means by the "adventures of consciousness." These adventures are by no means aimless wanderings; they are quests, if you like, quests whose every twist and turn is governed by what we strive to know. The idea of adventure had a very personal meaning for Bachelard, as we see from the last series of lectures he gave at the Sorbonne before he retired in 1954, at the age of seventy. In his account of these lectures, published in *Un Été avec Bachelard*,[9] Jean Lescure notes Bachelard's "will to make his philosophy an adventure, a creation" and records "an image, an idea of adventure" that Bachelard uses in attacking philosophers of Being[10]—namely, the nautical image of a "center of effort [*le point vélique*]," an image he turns into a dynamic image of human beings (192). Lescure explains how Bachelard modifies this "center of effort": while it is usually defined as the point on a sail at which the forces exerted by the winds come together, Bachelard "constructs it at the intersection of this resultant force and the resistance of the sea to the ship's progress." This is evidently a complex image of adventure—an image expressing great tensions—where progress is effort against forces opposing it. Bachelard then turns it into an image of human beings: he urges his students, Lescure says, to feel their own "center of effort," the point at which "adversity, the resistance of the immobile, that is to say the resistance of Being, is opposed by everything that humans have *to do* and *make*" (ibid.). Work, Bachelard argues, is a necessity; it is our history and our destiny. There is poignancy in these last lectures, for Bachelard's work as a teacher is coming to an end. There is poignancy too when, a few years later, he concludes *The Flame of a Candle*, for he senses that his work as a writer is now ending: "Is there still time for me," he asks, "to rediscover the worker I know so very well, and to bring him back into my engraving?" (FC 78/112, trans. modified). This word "engraving" is an interesting one, reminding us of Bachelard's very perceptive responses to the engravings of Albert Flocon,[11] in which he stresses the engraver's work, action, and "constructive will" (RD 55–57, 72–73, 81, 87–88/DR 71, 72, 76–78, 108, 117) so that for Bachelard an engraving signifies work. If he leaves us with an image of work, it is because in working—in the work of thinking and imagining, of writing and teaching—we experience "maximum existence, existence as tension," as he puts it, and indeed the "adventures of consciousness."

Notes

1. "De la Nature du rationalisme," in *L'Engagement rationaliste*, a collection of articles by Bachelard, preface by Georges Canguilhem (Paris: Presses Universitaires de France, 1972), 53. This essay was originally a conference paper given in 1950.

2. In *The Formation of the Scientific Mind*, Bachelard refers to *The Dialectic of Duration*, published in 1936, as a book he is planning to write.

3. Bachelard's ambivalence about this term nonetheless persisted. Even in his 1957 interview with Alexander Aspel he suggested that "if there is a mathematical imagination, it should be called something other than imagination" (cited in C. G. Christofides, "Bachelard's Aesthetics," *The Journal of Aesthetics and Art Criticism* 20, no. 3 [1962]: 268). In *The Philosophy of No*, he had alluded to its function under the rubric of *reverie anagogique* or "anagogic reverie"—translated by G. C. Waterston as "anagogical dreaming" (PN 32/39).

4. "Critique préliminaire du concept de frontière épistémologique," in *Études* (É), a collection of articles by Bachelard, ed. Georges Canguilhem (Paris: Vrin, 1970). This essay was originally a conference paper given in Prague in 1934.

5. Bachelard is referring implicitly here to Verlaine's poem "Art poétique" ("*Ars Poetica*," or "The Art of Poetry"), which begins: "Music before all else, / And for that prefer the Odd [as in "odd numbers"] ("*De la musique avant toute chose, / Et pour cela préfère l'Impair*"). Playing a variation of this theme, Bachelard writes: "Mathematics before all else . . . and for that prefer odd numbers . . . In short, the *ars poetica* of physics is written with numbers, with groups, with spins [*De la mathématique avant toute chose . . . et pour cela préfère l'impair. . . . Bref l'art poétique de la Physique se fait avec des nombres, avec des groupes, avec des spins*]" (PN 32/39).

6. Bachelard seems to be referring here to the Pythagorean doctrine that numbers are the first things in the whole of nature.

7. "Le Monde comme caprice et miniature" was originally published in the journal *Recherches philosophiques*, 1933–34, and later in *Études* (25–44).

8. "Idéalisme discursif," *Études* (87–97), was also originally published in *Recherches philosophiques*, 1934–35.

9. Jean Lescure, *Un Été avec Bachelard* (Paris: Luneau Ascot, 1983), 190–208. Twenty years before this, Lescure had published a shorter form of his notes: "Paroles de Gaston Bachelard: notes sur les derniers cours de Gaston Bachelard à la Sorbonne." *Mercure de France* 348 (1963).

10. Bachelard pointedly criticized those philosophers of Being who presumed to "overtake being in its totality" (PR 166). Bachelard himself would forge a new path to a "poetic ontology," unfolded in this volume by Glen Mazis in chapter 8.

11. See Bachelard's "Introduction to the Dynamics of Landscape" (55–70), "Albert Flocon's 'Engraver's Treatise'" (71–74), and "Castles in Spain" (75–90) in *The Right to Dream* (RD), trans. J. A. Underwood (Dallas: Dallas Institute, 1988).

Chapter 6

Bachelard *vis-à-vis* Phenomenology

Anton Vydra

As is well known, the French philosopher of science Gaston Bachelard allied at least the poetic aspect of his philosophy with the phenomenological movement that developed during the twentieth century. To define his philosophy of science, on the other hand, he found it necessary to rupture the boundaries of the phenomenological tradition by introducing, among other notions, the theory and practice of *phenomeno-technology* (NSS 13). Nonetheless, accepting Gaston Bachelard as a phenomenologist is still controversial in phenomenological circles. *Stricto sensu*, one might say, Bachelard does not belong to "the phenomenological canon." Let us, therefore, examine some of the possible justifications for this judgment.

I would like to present here several cases that illustrate why placing Bachelard among phenomenologists is so controversial. These cases will show that Bachelard used certain concepts in ways that at times differed from their customary use in Husserlian phenomenology. First of all, there is his particular use of the term "phenomenon," which in certain respects better resembles Kant's understanding of the term, but in other respects also the Husserlian "phenomenon." Second, in his book *Le Rationalisme appliqué* (*Applied Rationalism*, 1949), Bachelard addresses the question of "the given" (*le donné*) in a way that deserves special notice. Finally, the difference between his attitudes toward "thing [*la chose*]" and "matter [*la matière*]" in relation to the phenomenological notion of the "thing itself [*die Sache*]" is interesting. Some phenomenologists might maintain that his views show that he was not a phenomenologist. I will argue, however, that Bachelard can be considered a phenomenologist—indeed one who was seeking to develop a more open and pluralistic conception of phenomenology.

Many other influences certainly came into play, such as the historical context and the acceptance of Husserl within the French philosophical scene during Bachelard's lifetime. Husserlian phenomenology came to be increasingly well known in France during this period, while undergoing several subtle shifts away from Husserl's own project along the way. Phenomenology offered new impulses for various thinkers such as Koyré, Minkowski, Sartre, Merleau-Ponty, Wahl, Marcel, and of course Bachelard.

This chapter contains four sections. After contextualizing Bachelard's changing perspectives on the phenomenological method and its applications, the first section will tackle the key question of the concepts of *phenomenon* and *noumenon*—especially as Bachelard understood them during his early years—for he did not agree with one of phenomenology's chief precepts, namely, its stark conception of *phenomena* without reference to *noumena*. He criticized this philosophy, in other words, because it pushed this problem out of play. *Noumena* did not play a significant role in Husserlian phenomenology; yet, as we will see, for Bachelard a genuine phenomenology ought to include some notion of *noumenology*. The second section will discuss the viability of a "non-classical phenomenology" by which Bachelard opened up new areas for phenomenological inquiry (one might even call it a "non-phenomenology," in line with the critical dialectics outlined in his *Philosophy of No*). This idea may initially provoke some confusion but, if examined carefully, also much food for thought. The third section will show what it means for Bachelard to accept, refuse, or revise phenomenological attitudes. The fourth and concluding section will summarize these reflections, suggesting how and why Bachelard can be regarded as an authentic phenomenologist. Let me then open the discussion with the question of phenomenology itself.

Evolving Perspectives on Phenomenology

A retrospective glance at his work may show that Bachelard came to regard phenomenology as an approach best be applied to specific sorts of research, especially in areas for which there is no appropriate method derived from the natural sciences (for example, in the study of the oneiric functions of consciousness). However, we need to examine more carefully what Bachelard understood by "phenomenology."

The Poetics of Reverie (1960) begins with Jules Laforgue's words: "Method, Method, what do you want from me? You know that I have eaten of the fruit of the subconscious" (PR 1).[1] What "method" was Bachelard alluding to in this motto? Judging by its overall context, one straightforward reply would be: the *phenomenological* method. But such an answer calls for explanation. My aim in what follows is not to present a detailed comparative study of the relationship between Husserl's and Bachelard's phenomenologies (ultimately, such a study already exists),[2] but to highlight several features which are crucial for Bachelard's understanding of the concept of phenomenology within his methodological sphere of thinking.

First, it is important to note that while in his books about the philosophy of science Bachelard suggested setting "classical phenomenology" in abeyance (in order to revise it by incorporating working concepts such as *noumenology* and *phenomeno-technology*), in his books about the poetic imagination he would set out to explain why he made a methodological choice in favor of a phenomenology. In his later poetical works, he even situated phenomenology in polemical opposition to psychoanalysis (the latter having been his original method of research on the imagination)—considering phenomenology to be, in some cases, a more productive method than psychoanalysis. Nonetheless, he continued to regard both psychoanalysis and phenomenology as valuable methods for inquiry on verticality: the former descending to depths of human consciousness to face its tangled shadows; the second ascending to heights of human consciousness and sudden inspiration (FPF 23).[3]

Where do the inspirations for Bachelard's use of phenomenology come from? *Prima facie*, it seems that he is referring to Kant when he uses the terms *phénomène* and *noumène*, but also when he creates neologisms on their basis, such as *pyromène* (PF 58/103) or *bibliomène* (ARPC 6). Of course, Bachelard does not interpret the terms phenomenon and noumenon in a strictly Kantian way. For example, when discussing phenomena of modern physics and objects in motion inspired by Heisenberg's uncertainty principle in *The Philosophy of No* (1940), Bachelard writes: "*[T]he space of ordinary intuition in which objects find themselves is only a degeneration of the functional space in which phenomena are produced.* Contemporary science wants to know phenomena and not things. It [science] is not 'thing-oriented [*chosiste*].' A thing is merely an arrested phenomenon [*phénomène arrêté*]" (PN 94/109, trans. modified). Several pages earlier, however, he had written of a hypothetical chemical substance as a "genuine noumenon," which Kantianism would not accept, though "non-Kantianism" would (by which Bachelard means Kantianism rectified on the basis of modern scientific knowledge). This noumenon is a possible substance that we conceive (*raisonne*) when the structural formula exists for it (PN 51/60). In other words, if there is a structural formula that is theoretically affirmed and rational, then we can admit the real possibility of a substance that is expressed by it (even if no experience is yet available to demonstrate it). That is why such substance is "invisible," even if it is possible a priori. Of course, a noumenon is "the product of our *nous*, of our intellect," as Cristina Chimisso suggests. In her view: "By arguing this . . . Bachelard goes against the fundamental principles of Kant's conception of *noumenon*."[4]

Thus, according to *The Philosophy of No*, a phenomenon is not a static thing with a certain form, but a transforming object in a state of becoming. The term "arrested phenomenon" suggests that a static thing is an insufficient description of a phenomenon. Bachelard affirms this also in the area of modern (non-Aristotelian) logic, which can no longer be merely "thing-oriented [*chosiste*]" either. Logic must "re-incorporate things in the movement of the phenomenon," and it must study "new dynamized objects"—as do other modern sciences (PN 95/111). In this text, the term "noumenon" expresses the *possibility* of some chemical substance that exists with regard to an existing structural formula. If there is a theoretical possibility for the existence of something without a viable experiment, we can say it is a "noumenon";[5] whereas, if there is the theoretical possibility of existence coupled by an experimental validation of some sort (not by direct observation, as a thing of simple Euclidian localization, but through real effects as in the case of a photon), we can then say it is a "phenomenon."

Does the phenomenology of *The Philosophy of No* (1940), however, reflect Husserlian phenomenology or only Kantian phenomenology? We may indeed detect a Husserlian influence (even if Bachelard here does not directly cite Husserl) when we read: "Contemporary scientific thinking begins by an *epoché*, a placing of reality between parentheses [that is, a bracketing of reality]" (PN 28/34). But Husserlian phenomenology is not associated with the problem of noumena. We can find in *The New Scientific Spirit* (first published in 1934) the first mention of "phenomenology" in Bachelard's works. It was published at a time when Husserlian phenomenology was just becoming known in France. Husserl had delivered lectures at the Sorbonne in 1929, and these lectures became a basis for his later *Cartesian Meditations*. Simultaneously, the first monographs and translations of Husserl's works had begun to appear. Yet, should the phenomenology of *The New Scientific Spirit* also be understood as Husserlian? In this book, Bachelard's distinction between phenomena and noumena also occurs—a distinction which is far from being Husserl's. Could we argue that Bachelard's notion of "a primitive given [*une donnée primitive*]" refers to Husserl's *principle of all principles*? Rather, it seems here that he intended to allude to the positivistic concept of phenomenon as observable reality (NSS 11). In the following section, we must study Bachelard's divergent confrontations with phenomenology in other texts.

Phenomenology of Matter

In *Le Matérialisme rationnel* (*Rational Materialism*, 1953), Bachelard discusses "classical phenomenology," against which he posits his own revised version of phenomenology—here described as a *phenomenology dirigée* (a guided or reoriented phenomenology):

> Classical phenomenology complacently characterizes itself in terms of intentions (*visées*). Consciousness is thus associated with a purely directional intentionality. Hence, phenomenology attributes to [intentionality] an excessive centrality. [Intentionality] is a center from which lines of research emanate.[6] It is committed to all the immediate claims of idealism.
>
> Suddenly, *material* obstacles appear as contradictions so total, so irrational, that we would waste our time in trying to solve them. We then return to the center of intentions in order to begin to contemplate again. Signs, labels, or names of objects all respond to intentions. We organize all this in formal science, in the system of significations, in Λόγος. However, the contradictions posed by the material cannot be so easily ignored. Projections (*visées*) thus contradicted by the experience of matter provoke disharmonies in intentionality, discordances (*décoordinations*) within living being. The absurdity of the intended world echoes the baselessness (*la gratuité*) of our projected intentions. Thinking no longer works upon the encountered obstacle; it no longer persists within a determinate experience; it does not prolong its efforts beyond its initial failures. It is content simply to shift its intentional focus elsewhere. (MR 11)
>
> [. . .]
>
> We are [here] facing a cultural situation in which phenomenology cannot purely and simply return to "things themselves," because working consciousness (*la conscience au travail*) must rid

> itself of its original outlook and overhaul its research attempts. In a final analysis, scientific consciousness does not encounter the world based on a preliminary designation of [preconceived] matters. It aims (*vise*)—beyond things—toward matter. It begins by way of negation: it disclaims the object in order to discover matter. (MR 24)

Therefore, Bachelard makes a distinction between *classical phenomenology* (which he calls a *phenomenology of the object*) and this new phenomenology, which he calls "a *phenomenology of matter* [*matière*]" (MR 37).[7] Yet, why does Bachelard call the former phenomenology "classical"? He seems to understand that term as a development of the phenomenology of the directly intended object, which happens to be more typical of Sartre than of Husserl. He believes that phenomena should not be too closely identified with the obvious: the "visible." In addition, he questions the classical concept of matter (*matière*). Having been so influenced by Einstein, Bachelard himself now conceives matter as *energy*. He therefore views classical phenomenology as a reactivation of naïve realism, of substantialism, or even of thing-oriented (*chosiste*) epistemology (NSS 39, 64).

Bachelard's revised phenomenology, on the other hand, seems to anticipate the "phenomenology of flesh" later to be elaborated by Merleau-Ponty in *The Visible and the Invisible*,[8] where flesh (*la chair*) is described not as an object or thing in the external world, but in relation to the ancient notion of the "elements" (VI 139, 140). Although here Merleau-Ponty differentiates his concept of "flesh" from the traditional understanding of "matter," he admits the crucial influence of Bachelard's understanding of "elemental matter" in his definition (VI 267). For Bachelard the primary characteristic of such elemental matter, however, is *resistance* (MR 10).[9] Even in his early works on material imagination, he had described matter as a pervasive resistance that provokes effort (WD 159–60), at times persistent effort (ERW 146–47).[10]

Working consciousness, or obstinate consciousness (*la conscience opiniâtre*), is, in particular, confronted by matter's resistance which frustrates our efforts by provoking "disharmonies in intentionality, even discordances within living being," as we have seen in the above-quoted passages from *Le Matérialisme rationnel* (MR 11, 24). We are not faced here with static things, on which we have fixed our tranquil, passive gaze. Instead, we work with matter which is incessantly transformed, matter which cannot be conceived in its "arrested" form, but only amid its dynamic processes of permanent change. The often cited phenomenological example of a "cube" would thus need to be supplemented, as we can see, with examples of mass, paste or glue (ERW 87–93).

In these reflections Bachelard appears to be referring mainly to Jean-Paul Sartre's interpretation of phenomenology. Sartre had published *L'imaginaire* in 1940, where he had claimed that consciousness is made up of complex structures that intend (*intentionnent*) certain *objects*. To help explain imaginative consciousness, there he had used the example of the cube—an example later taken up by Merleau-Ponty (VI 140)—as well as that of a sheet of paper (Sartre 20, 23). In doing so, however, he did not consider the material milieu that surrounds and permeates an intending subject. We could further think about the difference between these two phenomenologies by comparing two attitudes toward the fine arts (the history and practical implications of which are addressed by Rizo-Patron in chapter 7). While the phenomenology of objects tends to see clearly drawn objects in a stable form, the phenomenology of matter is more impressionistic, as it envisions swarming brush strokes swirling around, even within the hardest appearances.

Accepted and Unaccepted Phenomenology

The following problem lies in the notion of "givenness [*le donné*]," because in *Le Rationalisme appliqué* Bachelard asserts that this notion tends to assume an exclusively passive ability to receive:

> According to Husserl . . . a subject presupposes as "existing" everything that is given (*donné*). In the mind, there is a correspondence between givenness and an ability *to receive*. Such dualism seems to us not holistically tight enough, not systematically reciprocal enough. By using an indispensable neologism, we would replace this mere receptivity (*recevoir*) by an ability to *accept delivery* (*réceptionner*) in the sense used in the contemporary technical world. The ability "to accept delivery" revises the supposition of existence about which Husserl speaks. It leads one to refusing badly defined, poorly coherent contents as "not-existing." (RA 43)

We have translated *réceptionner* as "to accept delivery" in the sense that one who accepts it can equally refuse it, especially if one knows nothing certain about it (as in the saying, "don't buy a pig in a poke"). In the same way, the scientist could respond to certain modes of givenness (without, at least, indirect proofs) by refusing or placing it in abeyance. The quotation expresses that we must not automatically accept everything that is given in primal (naïve) intuition, but we should rationally affirm such phenomena that have been prepared and produced by rational consciousness.

Let me reflect on one more note to the text of *Le Rationalisme appliqué*. It is true that in section 29 of the *Cartesian Meditations*, to which Bachelard refers above, Husserl writes about the "given [world]" as "always existing and . . . always presupposed [*immer vorausgesetzten*]."[11] Bachelard may have been familiar with the translation by Levinas[12] and Pfeiffer (*toujours présuposée existante*),[13] but Husserl does not mention here the ability to receive as a corresponding *activity* of a subject, spirit, or mind. What is more, presupposing the existence of a given objective world does not necessarily mean, in Husserl, presupposing the existence of every single thing that might initially *appear* to intuition. The term "existence" is nuanced in Husserl (for example, when he considers modes of reality in section 25), and the author of the *Cartesian Meditations* often speaks (especially in sections 23–26) of the affirmation or verification (*Bewährung*) of validity for everything that truly exists. This would agree with Bachelard's adaptation of it with the term *réceptionner*.

What can we say, then, about Bachelard's attitude toward Husserl, as it is revealed in this short paragraph from *Le Rationalisme appliqué*? For him, Husserl is a partner in a polemical discussion,[14] but not an unapproachable authority with unchallengeable views. That is why he examines and teases out such views, submitting them to the vocabulary of his own philosophy, and at times rejecting some of them. Bachelard wants to set in motion a philosophy that is in an ongoing process of correction or rectification. He does not outright reject other philosophical attitudes and methods but wants to help push them beyond their limits, to urge us to pay attention to unexplored areas. As Georges Canguilhem remarked, Bachelard's intent is not to overthrow (*torpiller*) other philosophers, but to look for new stimuli for their thinking.[15]

Of course, we can find places in his works where he rejects certain ideas as unacceptable. For example, in *The Flame of a Candle,* he scorns philosophical theories that define the being of familiar things in terms of their "instrumentality" (*ustensilité*) (FC 65/92, trans. modified). While Bachelard does not mention specific philosophers, in this case his allusion is evidently to Heidegger's notion of *Zeughaftigkeit*.[16] In support of this claim we would cite Jean Lescure's notes from one of Bachelard's last lectures at the Sorbonne, where he comments on Heidegger's analysis of Van Gogh's shoes as *Zeug* and *Schuhzeug*.[17] As we saw above, Bachelard finds a related problem in the case of Sartre: the direct intentionality toward the object.[18]

Beyond such negative criticism of some phenomenologists' statements, however, we can find a number of positive rectifications or developments of their thought in Bachelard's works. Consider, for instance, passages from three texts belonging to approximately the same period (1949–1953), in which the term "noumenon" is still used. The first passage below is drawn from *Earth and Reveries of Repose* (1948), the second from *Le Rationalisme appliqué* (1949), and the final one from *Matérialisme rationnel* (1953).

> Since the development of philosophical thinking has discredited the notion of the noumenon, philosophers now turn their sights away from [the] admirable constitution of noumenal chemistry, which represents the great systematics of material organization in the twentieth century.
>
> Contemporary philosophy's lack of interest in the sciences of matter is but another aspect of the negativism of this philosophical method. By adopting *one* method, philosophers reject others. By studying only one type of experience, philosophers close themselves off to other types of experiences. Thus, highly lucid minds will sometimes close themselves off in their lucidity, ignoring the multiple glimmers of enlightenment that emerge from the obscurer zones of psyche. (ERR 8/11, trans. modified)

Is it necessary to name the method here critiqued by Bachelard? The term "noumenal chemistry" used in this passage harks back to Bachelard's earlier essay, "Noumenon and Microphysics" (1931–32), where he had described the "noumenon of microphysics" as a complex structure—"neither a mere metaphysical posit nor a conventional rallying sign" (NM 80/É 18), but rather a dynamic "center where notions converge" (NM 83/É 23–24, trans. modified). In that earlier text he had set noumenology against "phenomenography" (NM 80/É 19). The latter, for him, only *describes* observed phenomena on the basis of common experience. The passage cited above from *Earth and Reveries of Repose* expresses Bachelard's nostalgic disenchantment regarding the development of philosophical thinking and, in particular, the direction of contemporary French philosophy which was then following a path quite different from the one he had suggested pursuing.

The second passage to quote, where Bachelard still uses the term "noumenon," is from *Le Rationalisme appliqué* (1949):

> One can describe an object in two ways: either as what we perceive, or as what we think. The object is here both a phenomenon and a noumenon. As noumenon, it is open to a future of perfecting not actually present in the object of common knowledge. A scientific noumenon is not a simple essence; it is an *evolution* of thought (*progrès de pensée*]. . . . To fully characterize [it], one would need to speak of a "nougonal noumenon"—of an essence of thought that engenders new thought. (RA 109–110)

By phenomenon, in this passage, Bachelard means *a perceived* object of common knowledge. A phenomenon is an object of perception; a noumenon is an object of thought or, more precisely, a vibrant focal point of unfolding *comprehension*. In his latest known essay on the philosophy of science, entitled "Le nouvel esprit scientifique et la creation des valeurs rationnelles" (1957), Bachelard will write that scientific experience does not concern the "immediate observation of phenomena"[19]—an assertion that echoes the distinction had made years earlier in *The New Scientific Spirit* between common observation and scientific observation (NSS 12). The "perceived" phenomenon of common intuition is, in his view, not an original phenomenon; it is a phenomenon of "phenomenography," and it is far from a scientific phenomenon in the genuine sense, as we saw above. Bachelard does not attack the observational method as such but stresses that modern scientific observation breaks through the veil of direct sensory experience.[20] Such external observation is for him a type of passive and rough empiricism, which poses an obstacle to the evolution of the modern scientific mind. "Thus, when we go from observation to system, we go from dazed eyes to closed eyes [*des yeux ébahis aux yeux fermés*]" (FSM 30/20, trans. modified). Through this terse and provocative phrase, Bachelard exposes an interesting feature of the phenomenology of closed eyes—a phenomenology that could otherwise be described in Pascalian language: Bachelard wants to help phenomenology become a rigorous scientific method that zeroes into hidden nuances and dynamic relations. In fact, *strenge Wissenschaft* is, within this context, a science of nuances.

The third and last text where Bachelard will explicitly use the term *noumenon* is *Le Matérialisme rationnel* (1953). There he ultimately makes the claim that the noumenon of a phenomenon of radiation is a kind of energy frequency (*enérgie fréquencielle*) without which we could not understand the concept of radiation. It is then possible, in his view, to describe the relation between the phenomenon and noumenon as the chiasmic doublet (*l'entrecroisement*) of *observation* and *comprehension* (MR 182). We can *observe* radiation if it appears to us, if it is a phenomenon; but we can *comprehend* it only through this idea of energy frequency.

Phenomenology and Poetics

Bachelard's latest works focus exclusively on exploring the nature of poetry and reverie. His sharpest shift in diction occurs in *The Poetics of Space* (1957), when he says in the introduction that he must forget everything in what he considers to be his arsenal or reservoir of knowledge up to that time (both his learning and his own habits of philosophical research). When he faces a novel poetic image, he considers all his preceding effort ineffectual (PS xi). Moreover, when he writes about "the cultural past" in that same passage, one must understand the French expression *culture* in the sense of "erudition," knowledge acquired through study and reading of scientific works. Describing Bachelard's work in this area, several authors even speak of Bachelard's "phenomenological turn."[21] Surely, in the introduction to his unfinished *Fragments of a Poetics of Fire*, we can see the outline of a somewhat changed (more nuanced) perspective:

> In order to teach the philosophy of science I was obliged to keep myself informed, taking my lessons from the members of the scientific community in which I found myself, all actively engaged in scientific research. But I had need of solitude as well, the solitude of reverie, of my own reveries. I hope to explain here how these reveries became working reveries in me, how reverie works one's inner being. (FPF 9)

The claim is quite different from the claim of *The Psychoanalysis of Fire* (1938) in which Bachelard was "demonstrating human errors" (PF 5). We are exploring a new area of phenomena. Prima facie, it seems—when one reads consulting his latest texts—that Bachelard has abandoned his rationalistic positions. But that is far from true. For him, rationalism constantly renews philosophy, and, more particularly, he points out that "to be a *rationalist* by oneself, in the margins of the scientific activity of one's day, is no longer possible. It is necessary that one educate oneself in rational company" (FPF 8). Of course, discursive rationalism demands the presence of a scientific community, polemical discussions, and productive contradictions. "But I had need of solitude as well," Bachelard adds. The principles of the phenomenological method used in his philosophy of sciences remain the same in his research on imagination and reverie. For example, in the modern sciences (such as chemistry or physics) immediate, naïve sensory experiences (sensory observations, sensory knowledge) are not essential for scientific work. Similarly, in the imagination, sensory perception is not necessary for the emergence of the phenomenon of a poetic image. Bachelard often emphasizes that imagination and reverie are not like perception (perhaps in disagreement with the phenomenology of Maurice Merleau-Ponty). "The eye which dreams does not see, or at least it sees with another vision. And this vision does not consist of 'leftovers.' Cosmic reverie makes us live in a state which must be designated as *ante-perceptive*," he writes in *The Poetics of Reverie* (PR 174). And when he writes about images of roundness in *The Poetics of Space*, he asserts that "the phenomenological problem [is] very clearly posed," because "[s]uch images cannot be justified by perception" (PS 232–33). And we can see this point being made in at least one more place in Bachelard's last lectures at the Sorbonne, when he spoke about Van Gogh's paintings of Arles, claiming that if we look at the painting "we do not perceive landscape, we imagine it" (cited in Lescure, 121).

Bachelard's research into "oneiric consciousness" might resemble Husserlian phenomenology yet more closely, even though poetic language and reveries are far removed from Husserl's concerns and from his style of phenomenological inquiry. Bachelard expanded the area of phenomenology in that he showed new possibilities for this research. How does oneiric consciousness behave? How does reverie operate? How should we describe the relation of imaginative consciousness to the phenomenon of the image? What is this limit-zone of consciousness where images emerge—the zone Bachelard called *limbo* (PR 109, PS 58)?

Of course, I do not want to assert that Bachelard identified with Husserlian phenomenology, because the distinctions between both phenomenologies persist. Norimichi Osakabe summed up one difference: Husserl, he suggests, tried "to describe and to analyze the structures of pure consciousness in relation to phenomena without projecting value judgments," whereas Bachelard's "philosophy leads ultimately to morality, because self-consciousness is formed in a Bachelardian world only by valorizing phenomena."[22]

This claim could return us to *The Philosophy of No* in which Bachelard coins the notion of the "epistemological profile" (PN 34–43). There he shows that an objective consciousness is formed by several philosophies, several doctrines, of which one may be broader, another more penetrating, but together forming the complex of our knowledge.[23] Similarly, we could say about Bachelard's "profiles of imagination" that they assist in determining characteristic features of individual consciousnesses through the *valorization* of phenomena—for example, by adhesion to one of the four elements. Maurice Merleau-Ponty offered an accurate explication of this in one of his radio lectures: "He [Bachelard] shows how each element is home to a certain kind of individual of a particular kind, how it constitutes the dominant theme in their dreams and forms the privileged medium of the imagination which lends direction to their life; he shows how it is the sacrament of nature which gives them strength and happiness."[24]

In his *Poetics*, following his books on the four elements, Bachelard develops a new type of phenomenology—a phenomenology of well-being, of consciousness at home. There are many different homes for different human beings, and phenomenology can inquire into the relations of consciousness to these various milieus of human beings and things. Here, I could also mention Miles Kennedy's analysis of Bachelard's concrete metaphysics and his rectification of Heidegger's notion of *Dasein*'s "fundamental mood" of being-in-the-world, which in Bachelard's contrasting view "carries human being's consciousness to that first home."[25] The term *home* refers not only to the home of the lonely individual; home is a place of warmth and conviviality with other people, beings or things. Home is an essentially intersubjective phenomenon. Reverie may stand in contrast to sociality, but it is not tantamount to "loneliness" or "isolation."

We can say that the familiar milieu of Bachelard's life was formed by the books of poets:

> We are in the presence truly of a *gift of the imagination*, offered simply in the simplest of intimacies . . . between a book and its reader. Literary imagination is an aesthetic object offered by a writer to a lover of books. The poetic image might be characterized then as a direct relationship between two souls, a contact between two human beings pleased at the chance . . . to speak and to listen, a renewal of language in the raising of a new voice. (FPF 10–11)

Conclusion

In this study, I have interpreted some crucial passages in Bachelard's writings in which he confronted the various phenomenologies of his contemporaries. Of course, in order to understand a philosopher, one must try to understand not only particular assertions, but also the whole context of his or her thinking. I have tried to do this in relation to Gaston Bachelard throughout this chapter. I have tried to show the meanings of some of his core notions (such as "phenomenon," "noumenon," "phenomenology") and *how* he changed his thinking about them.

First, I demonstrated what Bachelard's notion of phenomenon and of phenomenology was, and in what sense he suggested that we move beyond so-called "classical phenomenology." The neologisms that he coined (for example, phenomenography, noumenology, and the famous term of "phenomeno-technology") should be seen as part of his contribution to refining and advancing thought by proposing an ever self-renewing philosophical method. His arguments concerning phenomenology were addressed not only to Husserl, but more often to Sartre, Heidegger, Minkowski, or Merleau-Ponty (RD 82).[26] Bachelard believed that if phenomenology is to be a truly scientific project, as well as a vital method of inquiry in the humanities and the arts, it must be subjected, time and again, to dialectical discussion and argument among philosophers.

There is not just one—unique, closed, and untouchable—phenomenology. Bachelard has indeed provided many provocative points of discussion that can lead to a more open and vigorous phenomenology.

Notes

1. Bachelard's posthumously published *Fragment of a Poetics of Fire* starts, by contrast, with a motto from Rimbaud's poem *Morning of Drunkenness*: "We affirm you, method! We don't forget that yesterday you glorified each one of our ages" (FPF 27).

2. See Bernard Barsotti, *Bachelard: Critique de Husserl; Aux racines de la fracture Épistémologie/Phénoménologie* (Paris: Harmattan, 2002).

3. In the following chapter on "Bachelard's Hermeneutics," Eileen Rizo-Patron will explain Bachelard's *diméthode* (dual method) as a hermeneutic alternation between psychoanalysis and phenomenology.

4. Cristina Chimisso, "From Phenomenology to Phenomenotechnique: The Role of Early Twentieth-Century Physics in Gaston Bachelard's Philosophy," in *Studies in History and Philosophy of Science*, part A, 39 (2008), 387.

5. These attitudes of Bachelard toward noumenal reality seem to have had their origins in a Schopenhaurian reading of Kant. See especially Arthur Schopenhauer, *The World as Will and Representation*, vol. 1, trans. J. Norman, A. Welchman, and C. Janaway (Cambridge: Cambridge University Press, 2010), section 24, where Schopenhauer writes about *qualitas occulta*. A good example is his allusion to Euler's understanding of the essence of gravitation in terms of attraction, but "this fine mind saw a shimmering [*of this principle of attraction*] in the distance; he hurried to turn back in time, and in his anxiety, seeing all the contemporary fundamental views threatened, even sought refuge in old absurdities that had already been debunked" (Schopenhauer, 152). These words are reminiscent of Bachelard's polemics with the "convenientism [*commodisme*]" of Henri Poincaré (PN 120/141).

6. Bachelard here appears to be citing Sartre's *L'imaginaire: Psychologie phénoménologique de l'imagination* (Paris: Gallimard, 1940): "Intention lies at the center of consciousness: it intends (*vise*) its object, thus it [intention] constitutes it as it is" (27); hereafter cited as Sartre.

7. See also ERW 85–89.

8. Merleau-Ponty, *The Visible and the Invisible*, trans. Alphonso Lingis (Evanston, IL: Northwestern University Press, 1968); hereafter cited as VI.

9. Rizo-Patron's "Bachelard's Hermeneutics" (chapter 7) offers an illustrative analysis of matter's resistance, with its ethical and therapeutic implications in Bachelard's philosophy.

10. See Bachelard's confrontation with Merleau-Ponty, through his distinction between Merleau-Ponty's *phenomenologie du vers* (phenomenology toward), which governs "perception," and the *dynamology du contre* (dynamology against), which governs "action" within a resistant world, as described in *Earth and Reveries of Will* (ERW 41/55–56). See Merleau-Ponty, *Phenomenology of Perception*, trans. Colin Smith (London: Routledge, 1962), 101. Similar reflections can be found in the phenomenology of Michel Henry. See Jaroslava Vydrová, *Cesty fenomenológie. Fenomenologická metóda neskorého Husserla*. Pusté Úl'any: Schola Philosophica, 2010), particularly where he explores the possibilities of Henry's notion of "effort" and "resistance" for Husserlian phenomenology (137).

11. Edmund Husserl, *Cartesian Meditations: An Introduction to Phenomenology*, 7th ed., trans. Dorion Cairns (The Hague: Martinus Nijhoff, 1982), 63.

12. It is striking that Bachelard never mentioned Emmanuel Levinas in his works (and, conversely, Levinas never mentioned Bachelard) in spite of the fact that they agreed on similar points. Róbert Karul has recently shown an example of this similarity in his discussion of the terms *il y a* in Levinas and cogito[3] or vertical time in Bachelard's, *Dialectic of Duration*. See Róbert Karul, *O bytí bez subjektu. Sproblematizovanie Levinasovho čistého bytia* (Pusté Úľany: Schola Philosophica, 2012), 137–44.

13. Edmund Husserl, *Méditations cartésiennes: Introduction à la phénoménologie*, French trans. Emmanuel Levinas and Gabrielle Pfeiffer (Paris: A. Colins, 1931), 54, my emphasis.

14. In *The Philosophy of No*, Bachelard notes that two persons are truly able to hear one another only after they have contradicted one another—for, as he concludes: "Truth is the daughter of discussion, not of sympathy" (PN 114).

15. Georges Canguilhem, *Études d'histoire et de philosophie des sciences concernant les vivants et la vie* (Paris: Vrin, 2002), 195.

16. John Macquarrie and Edward Robinson translate this notion as "equipmentality" in Martin Heidegger, *Being and Time* (Malden: Blackwell, 2005), 97.

17. See Jean Lescure, *Un Été avec Bachelard* (Paris: Luneau-Ascot, 1983), 198–99, where he records Bachelard's allusion to Heidegger's analysis of Van Gogh's *Old Shoes* in "The Origin of the Work of Art" (*Poetry, Language, Thought*, trans. Albert Hofstadter [New York: Harper Colophon, 1975], 33–37). For another take on this issue, see Roch C. Smith's discussion of Heidegger's reading of truth in this painting through the lens of Derrida's critique, in "Bachelard's Logosphere and Derrida's Logocentrism: A Distinction with a *Différance*" (chapter 10 in this volume).

18. See Lescure, "Paroles de Gaston Bachelard: Notes sur les derniers cours de Bachelard à la Sorbonne," *Mercure de France* 358 (1963), 118–30, especially 121; hereafter cited as Lescure.

19. Bachelard, "Le nouvel esprit scientifique et la creation des valeurs rationnelles," published in *L'Engagement rationaliste*, ed. Georges Canguilhem (Paris: Presses Universitaires de France, 1972), 89–99, quote on 97.

20. In *Earth and Reveries of* Repose, he calls it "the veil of Maya, the veil of Isis" (ERR 7/10).

21. Christian Thiboutot, Annick Martinez, and David Jager, "Gaston Bachelard and Phenomenology: Outline of a Theory of Imagination," in *Journal of Phenomenological Psychology* 30 (1999): 1–17.

22. Norimichi Osakabe, "De la psychanalyse à la phénoménologie," *Études de langue et literature françaises* 38 (1981): 111–21, especially 118.

23. In Bachelard's words, "each philosophy gives only one band of the notional spectrum and it is necessary to group all the philosophies to obtain the complete notional spectrum of a particular piece of knowledge" (PN 42).

24. Maurice Merleau-Ponty, *The World of Perception*, trans. Oliver Davis (London: Routledge, 2004), 65.

25. Miles Kennedy, *Home: A Bachelardian Concrete Metaphysics* (Oxford: Peter Lang, 2011), 145.

26. We have reflected upon the theme of the relation between Bachelard and Merleau-Ponty in two recent articles. See Anton Vydra, "Pojem živelnosti u Merleau-Pontyho a Bachelarda" (The notion of spontaneity in Merleau-Ponty and Bachelard), in *Fenomenologie tělesnosti*, ed. Petr Urban (Prague: Filosofia, 2011), 143–55. Also, Anton Vydra, "L'image et l'affectivité: Le problème du sujet dans la notion bachelardienne d'imagination," *Archiwum historii filozofii i myśli społecznej* (Archive of the history of philosophy and social thought) 57 (2012), 179–94.

Chapter 7

Bachelard's Hermeneutics: Between Psychoanalysis and Phenomenology

Eileen Rizo-Patron

In the "Essentials of the Phenomenological Method" (1960) Herbert Spiegelberg cited Jean-Paul Sartre's work on the psychoanalysis of matter (*Being and Nothingness*, 1943) as one of the pioneering examples in hermeneutic phenomenology after Heidegger's analytics of *Dasein* and its fundamental moods (*Being and Time*, 1927). What made these projects "hermeneutic," in his view, is that they delved into deep structures of human experience in an attempt to understand meanings not immediately available to phenomenological description.[1] Yet what Spiegelberg's account failed to mention is that Sartre's psychoanalysis of matter had itself been prompted by Gaston Bachelard's earlier hermeneutics of matter in *The Psychoanalysis of Fire* (1938) and *Water and Dreams* (1942).[2] In these two works—followed by his series on the elemental imagination[3]—Bachelard gradually developed and fine-tuned a hermeneutic approach to phenomena that lie beyond the apparent reach of the senses, placing at our disposal a new phenomenological tool in the study of *imagination* and *matter*: a meditative mode of thinking he coined "poetic reverie"—a waking/working reverie (*rêverie ouvrante/oeuvrante*) which, unlike daydream, leads to increments of consciousness and a sharpening of insight through its focus on emerging variations in wonder-filled images capable of tempering the psyche and revealing unforeseen value (WD 113; AD 115–16; ERW 70; PR 5, 182). Bachelard never abandoned standards of phenomenological discipline in doing so, but instead carried them to levels of unprecedented subtlety.

This chapter will attempt to retrieve key features and working principles of Bachelard's hermeneutics of the elemental imagination—developed largely during the middle period of his career (1938–48)—with the purpose of casting light on its aesthetic, therapeutic, and ethical implications. In order to place Bachelard's understanding of the elemental imagination in perspective, however, let me first offer a synopsis of his multifaceted understanding of "matter"—from his early *Intuition of the Instant* (1932) to his posthumous *Fragments of a Poetics of Fire* (1988). In *Intuition of the Instant*—a study on the nature of "time" inspired by Gaston Roupnel's philosophical drama *Siloë* and by twentieth-century scientific discoveries and quantum physics (II 31)—Bachelard had proposed that "matter" is composed of the "rhythm-habits of being" (II 40–41). Endorsing Roupnel's thoughts on evolution and discontinuous progress, he proceeded to describe the formation of nerve and muscle fibers in animate beings, for instance, as "materialized habit[s], made up of well-chosen instants, strongly bonded together by a rhythm" (II 42). In an argument against Bergson's theory of temporal continuity as the uninterrupted flow of an élan vital, Bachelard furthered the claim that the woven fabric of our lived experience—our bodies, histories, perceived worlds—is recurrently ruptured and rewoven through such cadenced acts, or rhythm-habits, in response to the appeal of creative possibility granted us at the stroke of every instant, even if we often fail to heed its challenge for renewal due to unconscious or habitual attachment to a well-patterned past (II 43). Matter is thus described, in this early text, as the ever-emergent and decaying fabric of pulsating time, as the creative-destructive function of instants concretely "realized" along the intentional axis of our vital projects, desires, values—a phenomenon analogous to rhythmic crystallization processes in the inanimate world, yet one that remains open to transformation (via critical ruptures and reorientations) amid the malleable dance of animate and conscious being, as this dance rises and falls to the tune of our incarnate *responses* to the promise of possibility.[4]

In *The Dialectic of Duration* (1936), his second book on time, Bachelard would resume his argument with Bergson, yet focusing now on the periodical need to unravel matter, this tightly knit habit of time[5]—to dissolve the "ill-made durations" he discovers ensnaring human consciousness and desensitizing the psyche to the redemptive gift of a novel instant (DD 21, 136).[6] From this point on, questions of *liberation* and *healing* begin to emerge as guiding motifs or aims underlying Bachelard's philosophical quest—namely, how we might assist in unclogging and renewing the chiasmic dance between flesh and soul, matter and spirit. This passionate concern would soon become most patent in his works on the imagination of the elements, written during his "psychotherapeutic period" in the 1940s, to be resumed in his two final works: *The Flame of a Candle* (1961) and *Fragments of a Poetics of Fire* (1988).

While Bachelard's writings on scientific epistemology after *Intuition of the Instant* would continue into the 1950s under the Promethean sign of "progress,"[7] his elemental hermeneutics seemed to follow the opposite path of "regress"—what alchemists before him had symbolically termed a *regressus ad uterum*—namely, an effort to get back in touch with the force field or hidden matrix wherein our worlds are first conceived and given meaning. This "return to the mother" is not to be understood in terms of the Freudian Oedipus complex (as an attachment to the biological mother, or to our inherited past) but as a return to the subtle environment of our worlds in an effort to *transform the mother tongue*, understood as the congealed patterns of feeling and thought that tend to shape our worldview (PR 46). This critical move is illustrated, for instance, in the novels of Irish writer James Joyce (1992–41), as he sought to recreate himself and his world in the "silver womb of imagination,"[8] or in the work of Peruvian novelist José María Arguedas (1911–69), whose *Deep Rivers* features a plague-ridden Andean community striving to burst open what they called "the mother of the fever" (an atmosphere of ill habits and beliefs holding its people in thrall) through the *élan vocal* of improvisational song.[9]

Later in this chapter, I will address the question of how Bachelard tackles what he initially coined "ill-made durations" (DD 21) and later "culture complexes" (WD 17)—namely, those repetitive patterns that have powerful effects on the ways our worlds get constituted and organized at personal, collective, and material levels. But let us begin our examination of the distinctive features of Bachelard's elemental hermeneutics[10] by foregrounding the role of the "reader" in his philosophical discourse.

An Allegorical Figure?

Wedged within the rift between Bachelard's two bodies of work on the philosophy of science and poetry, one can detect the figure of an "alchemist" emerging rather early in his writings on scientific epistemology, and later again in relation to poetic psychology, creating provocative tensions and links between the two. While as a historian of science Bachelard had derided alchemical work for its imagistic projections, which act as epistemological obstacles to scientific progress (FSM 61, 194), in his writings on imagination, starting with *The Psychoanalysis of Fire*, his critical attitude suddenly shifted toward an exploratory sympathy vis-à-vis alchemical yearnings—a sympathy which would lead to his rereading alchemical treatises at a slower pace, under a different light, as he began to delve into the world's inner soul and to participate in its subtle transformations (PF 54). It is the intermittent reappearance of this equivocal figure throughout his works that leads me here to propose that the Bachelardian "alchemist" be read as an allegory of the "reader"[11]—provisionally, of course, since Bachelard never attempted to develop a systematic, hermetic hermeneutics.

For the purposes of this chapter, we will adopt a broad definition of "allegory" as "a form of art or discourse that sustains simultaneously *both* literal and abstract levels of meaning." Caution should nonetheless be exercised when summoning "allegory" to elaborate on Bachelard's hermeneutics: for one thing is to use the term to evoke some of the heuristic figures he deploys to help illustrate his interpretive theory (for example, *anima, animus, prima materia*, crucible, mortification, sublimation, magnetic stone, elixir, and so on), and quite another to characterize Bachelard's elemental hermeneutics as "allegorical" (a type of textual explication that seeks to decipher "a determinate message hidden beneath apparent meaning"), as Blanchot characterized the "hermeneutic conception of psychoanalysis" in his essay "Vast as the Night."[12]

Although later in *The Poetics of Space* (1957) Bachelard would himself describe his approach to literary texts as a "hermeneutics" and a "phenomenology of what is hidden" (PS xxxiii, 9), it is crucial to differentiate such a reading practice from the exegesis of ready-made strata of determinate meaning assumed to be deposited within certain literary images. For the virtue of Bachelard's elemental hermeneutics lies, rather, in its capacity to release the *emergent possibilities* of imaginary matter within poetic texts and artworks, much in the way Albert Flocon's engravings are capable of *exposing elemental forces* hidden in matter, as Bachelard points out in his essay "Introduction to the Dynamics of Landscape" (RD 55–56). One of my main objectives here is to begin to show how this may be so.

In *The Poetics of Space* Bachelard notes that what is essential in what he calls a "literature of depth" is that good poets will say only *just enough* to set a reader on the threshold of reverie. Such poets hope that their words, animated by deep personal experience, will carry a sonority capable of "reverberating" far beyond their formal figures, stirring a chord at the limits of transpersonal memory, perhaps beyond memory itself, in the field of the immemorial. For "all we communicate to others," Bachelard insists, "is an *orientation towards what is secret* without ever being able to tell the secret objectively. What is secret never has total objectivity" (PS 13). Already a decade earlier, in *Earth and Reveries of Will*, he had remarked on the stark distinction between *allegory*—understood as a figure "contrived after the fact" to represent a concept or hidden idea—and a *material image* rooted in oneiric energies that pulsate before their names are ever spoken and that can only be sounded out through reverie (ERW 304–5). Bachelard never ceased to stress the importance of this rich "indeterminacy" and open-ended life of poetic images—thus laying down one of the key principles of his elemental hermeneutics. Any strict matching of image and concept (as in the case of a bisemic allegory) would risk arresting creative reverie, which can alone expose the life of images.

A key difference between a "psychoanalytic hermeneutics" and Bachelard's "phenomenological hermeneutics" is, therefore, that Bachelard regards symbols as open-ended *invitations to dream,* whereby a reader is called to participate in the transformative pulse of literary images through what he called *mental homeopathy* (a sympathetic correspondence between an elemental image and a soul's subtle rhythms); whereas classical psychoanalysis tends to offer a system of *mental allopathy* where symbols are confronted with concepts indicating the social or external origins of mental trauma (ERW 303).

Formal versus Material Imagination

This notion of "mental homeopathy" in poetic understanding, which Bachelard would later translate in terms of "reverberation" (PS xiii, xviii, xxi), is rooted in the ancient Greek notion of μέθεξις (participation), a concept often backgrounded in Western aesthetics in favor of *mimetic* theories of art.[13] The increasing focus on this "participation principle" in Bachelard's works on imagination suggests that it lies at the crux of his elemental hermeneutics—a "hermeneutics of sympathy"[14] that deserves special attention in terms of its phenomenology and its implications for a philosophy of art.

In *Water and Dreams* Bachelard had first used the phrase "*substantial mimesis*" (WD 28), but by the time he wrote *Air and Dreams* he shifted to calling it "*substantial participation*" (AD 8). As he further employed this principle in his hermeneutics, he came to identify it explicitly with the essential participation (μέθεξις) discussed in Plato's *Phaedrus* (250d). Thus, alluding to Platonic μέθεξις in an intriguing passage I shall return to below, he wrote: "It appears that *participation in the idea of the beautiful* determines an orientation of images that in no way resembles the tentative orientation arrived at by the formation of concepts" (AD 65, emphasis added).

Initially, however, instead of thematizing the contrast in modern aesthetics between the principles of *mimetic representation* and *substantial participation*, Bachelard framed the distinction through a discussion of the eidetically oriented *formal imagination* versus the dynamically oriented *material imagination.* In *Water and Dreams* he critiqued modern literary education for having restricted itself to cultivating a clear, formal imagination. While dreams or reveries are most often studied only for the development of their forms, he lamented, we tend to forget that their life is rooted in the *pulse of matter*:

> With a succession of forms we do not have what we need for measuring the *dynamics* of transformation. The best that can be expected is a description of this transformation from the outside, like a pure kinetics. Such kinetics cannot appreciate forces, drives, and aspirations from within. The dynamics of dreams cannot be understood if we separate it from the dynamic quality of the material elements that dreams work over. We are looking at the mobility of the forms of dreams from the wrong perspective if we forget its internal dynamic quality. In the final analysis, forms shift because the unconscious becomes disinterested in them. What binds the unconscious, what imposes a dynamic law on it in the realm of images, is life in the depths of a material element. (WD 129–30)

Bachelard's focus here is on the reader's participation in the dynamic transformations that elemental reveries can evoke, rather than on capturing the visual forms they adopt along the way. For the material images that most attract us tend to correspond to those elements that vie for predominance in our psyches, often governing the passions and ideals of an entire life (WD 3–5). Hence the urgency to work through such images—*weighing* them in our hearts to resolve their ambivalences within ourselves—rather than simply describing their patterns from an aesthetic distance (WD 18).

This Bachelardian distinction between *formal* and *material* imaginations could also be retraced to the distinction between two types of ποίησις articulated in Plato's dialogues: the notion of ποίησις found in the *Republic* as the *imitation* of ideal essences (10:595a–602c), versus the type of ποίησις described in the *Symposium* (211e–212a) and *Ion* (534b) as an offspring of *participation* in the substance of inspiration or divine radiance that gives life to ideas and things.

Considering, however, that the ostensible framework of Bachelard's developing thought had been twentieth-century science—above all the "new scientific mind" from Einstein's special theory of relativity (1905) to later advances in quantum physics[15]—it is likely that Bachelard's hermeneutic shift from *representation* to *participation* was initially inspired by scientific discoveries in quantum physics, such as the Heisenberg "indeterminacy principle"—which proposes that an observed phenomenon is intimately affected by the very event and mode of observation (NSS 122)[16]—only subsequently to discover its corroboration in ancient Greek intuitions. Yet, given Bachelard's evident attraction to premodern philosophies and alchemical literature, one could argue that his elemental hermeneutics was actually sparked by the *galvanic encounter* between "quantum thinking" and "premodern reverie" in his philosophical meditations.

Bachelard kept insisting, in any event, on the difference between representational knowledge that purports to *reflect* reality through image-concepts, versus dynamically *partaking* in its nature by communion or "substantial participation."[17] While admitting that "a genuine communion is necessarily temporary," he described it as a knowing whereby one imbibes the essence of what is known—and is transformed by it (L 68–69). Most instructive, in this regard, is Plato's insight in the *Phaedrus* (250d, 7) that a "beautiful thing" is not merely a copy of the "idea of beauty" but that it actively partakes in beauty's essence by making it manifest. Such manifestation, according to Gadamer, defines beauty itself.[18] A person in the act of beholding "beauty" is seized and transfigured by its radiance—at times even becoming able to express it, as if a "community of essence" had been awakened by a force of *poetic induction*.[19] This may well be what Bachelard had been trying to suggest through his earlier-cited remark that the "idea of the beautiful" sets in motion an *orientation of images* more vibrant and alive than the discursive one arrived at by the formation of concepts (AD 65, 82).

Participation in such "substance of inspiration"(PR 7), however, always depends on the reader's willingness to submit to what Bachelard once called "the verbal *induction* of a poet's style" (RD 141), where he revealed his scientific background as he described the phenomenon in terms of "electromagnetic induction." This idea also recalls Plato's figurative description, in the *Ion*, of "magnetic forces" of inspiration that emerge from a divine power likened by Socrates to the "stone of Heraclea"—a stone that *animates and empowers* poets and performers who may then act as links in a chain of inspiration, finally to transmit its divine force to a captive audience (*Ion* 533d–e).

In light of this phenomenon of induction, one can infer—albeit allegorically—that Bachelard regards certain poetic texts as proverbial "philosopher's stones" capable of drawing out the latent energies in other "stones" (readers' souls) while assisting in their distillation and transmutation. There is no such thing as idle contemplation, Bachelard insists. We bring our destinies into play whenever we read poetic texts (L 59), and that is because such texts *question us*, drawing out the "dark elements" of our personal and collective imaginations into the light of awareness. The Bachelardian model of textual exegesis relies, however, on the reader's own *work* "pen-in-hand," as summoned by the lure of a text, rather than on the adoption of a passive stance indiscriminately subject to *daimonic* possession on the one hand (PR 4), or a purely removed critical attitude on the other. Therefore, while Bachelard's theory of "reading by poetic induction" may be analogous to Ion's account of the rhapsode's ecstatic performance of Homeric poems, it recontextualizes the hermeneutic event by inserting it into the realm of *writing* which introduces, by necessity, an element of will and skill (τέχνη) into the process of poetic induction so that it is no longer an issue of the reader's passive submission to the *daimonic* power of a poetic text. For Bachelard will insist that "in submitting passively to such wonder, one does not participate profoundly enough in the creating imagination" (PR 4). The Bachelardian reader must *work* at both unfolding the elemental forces of a text and transmuting one's self, by responding to its material images through lucid written reverie (*reverie oeuvrante*).

Matter as "Otherness"

As Paul Ricoeur often reminded us, a "hermeneutic imagination" is first and foremost an imagination that is "responsive to something other"—to living texts, to the suffering of others, to the world of action—rather than a purely "projective imagination" that proceeds according to a subjectivist aesthetics.[20] Even though Bachelard has at times been charged by critics for falling into the latter attitude,[21] I submit that Bachelard's imagination is fundamentally "hermeneutic" in its attentive responsiveness to the solicitations of matter understood as a mode of otherness—namely, as a vital dimension of the life-world with an apparent will of its own (ERW xv). For, as defined in his books on the four elements, Bachelardian "matter" alludes to a power both real and virtual—a force both oneiric and empirical that transcends the consciousness and control of the subject intending it.

Richard Kearney makes a good point when noting that for Bachelard (unlike Sartre) "matter does not signify an intractable and viscous resistance to freedom. It is rather a *call* to our freedom, the very paste of possibility from which we must wrest new forms" (PI 107). Nonetheless, Bachelard recognizes that such "paste of possibility" can incorporate a fair degree of resistance once it has settled in our collective psyches and worlds, generating what he terms a *coefficient of adversity* (WD 159). Such adversity is further explored in his Earth books, with their focus on compact materials that hardly lend themselves to oneiric play (ERW 39). In these cases, contemplated matter tends to assume an oppressive countenance—as in the blacksmith's trials in Lönnrot's *Kalevala* (ERW 114ff.), in Huysmans's petrifying reveries (ERW 159ff.), or in the imagery of Dante's devouring inferno (ERW 306–7)—all of which give voice to the perennial human struggle *against* catagenetic forces and substances: matter that blocks our way; matter that paralyzes us; contaminated matter; decaying matter; even radioactive matter.[22] Not every substance is as generously yielding to human reverie as is paste. Bachelard's "matter" is thus never passive: it is an elemental "force" of emergence and stability, resistance and destruction, germination or putrefaction, attraction or gravity[23]—a force that nourishes even while it challenges our freedom, provoking our *work* in response to otherness and awakening creative ingenuity, particularly in response to suffering.

But neither is matter's "otherness" totally alien: it is an otherness in which we are thoroughly enmeshed at the bodily level. It is easier to dissociate from the body when it doesn't respond to our will. But matter, for Bachelard, is also the deep trace of *habits* of the "world unconscious"[24]—the often-estranged product of our world's collective becoming: sediments embedded in our bodies and souls, manifested as the traits of the race. The contradiction between matter as "viscous resistance" versus matter as "paste of possibility" may thus be only apparent—*resistance* and *possibility* being but two faces of the same coin. Nonetheless, Bachelard sees them as opposite poles in a state of chiasmic tension that might turn explosive if we to allow our worlds and psyches to lapse into rigidity.

In his Earth books, Bachelard hence describes the "*dream* of substance" as unfolding against "*phenomena* of substance" (ERR 37). The resistance of a hardened world in fact prods us to dream and struggle *against it* rather than be subdued by its stubborn boundaries. Again, his favorite figure to illustrate this agonistic struggle is the alchemist tempering matter in his fiery crucible. For material imagination, Bachelard reminds us, "is essentially a matter to be transmuted" in the crucible of consciousness (AD 242). Years later, Bachelard will in fact revisit the patient and laborious processes of alchemy in a remarkable passage from *The Poetics of Reverie*, surprising his readers this time by portraying the alchemist as "an *educator of matter*" (PR 76). Unlike the chemist whose one-time intellectual exercise seeks the definitive formula for a pure compound, he writes,

> As soon as [the alchemist] has finished one distillation . . . immediately starts the distillation anew, again mixing dead matter with the elixir, the pure with the impure, so that the elixir *learns*, as it were, to liberate itself from its soil. . . . In alchemy we are not faced with intellectual patience, but we are within the very action of moral patience, which searches out the impurities of a consciousness. (PR 76)

This figure of the "alchemist as educator of matter" along with the figure of the "reader as alchemist," which traverses Bachelard's work, brings us to Bachelard's key notion of *reading as the education of "the imaginary mass that we are"* (AD 259–60)—a morally charged matter that is constantly becoming manifest through the images produced and reified by ourselves and our culture (whether it be in everyday speech, the arts, or mass media), as well as through our most intimate responses to others, to nature, or to poetic imagery in solitary reverie (AD 249, 259).

Such an educational process is not concerned with priming a student for success in the social world. Instead, for Bachelard, it takes on cosmic moral dimensions as it alludes to an elemental awakening of consciousness. Drawing on examples from seventeenth-century alchemical literature suffused with allegorical overtones, he notes that when alchemists, for instance, collected "the elixir of early morning dew" to mix in with the impure matter in their crucibles, they imagined themselves participating in the intimate becoming of the world (*anima mundi*), by dreaming of dew as a seed of daily renewal. Not only were alchemists always on the lookout for that pure dew which the universe rarely provides, but they worked at distilling and redistilling whatever they did find, in order to eliminate superfluities and produce a pure germ that might act as an absolving force (ERW 251–52). Shifting back and forth from "the alchemist" to the pronoun "one" (the reader) in his discourse,[25] Bachelard would here proceed to play a suggestive—if chimerical—variation on a well-known Heideggerian theme:[26]

> One is then certain to experience being-in-the-world (*l'être-dans-le-monde*) because one is a being-becoming-the-becoming-of-the-world (*l'être-devenant-le-devenir-du-monde*). Alchemists assist the world in its becoming by actually participating in its realization. They are *agents* of the world's becoming. (ERW 251)

For Bachelard this means that "humankind imagining" acts no less than as "the transcendent aspect of Spinoza's *natura naturans*" (WD 10), participating in nature's own creative agency. And this transcendent aspect of nature takes on concrete manifestation through what Bachelard (now through a variation on Spinoza) will term "literature *litteraturans*"—namely, literature as an *agency of creative evolution*, rather than simply as a created product (RD 140). Such living literature includes *the work of reading* as the hermeneutic unfolding of possibilities set in motion by poetic works which summon us endlessly to distill and redistill "the imaginary mass that we are" through poetic reverie.

Hermeneutics of Culture Complexes

In *The Formation of the Scientific Mind*, we recall, Bachelard had described humankind as "a species that needs to mutate, that suffers if it doesn't mutate" (FSM 26). Only a few years later in *Water and Dreams* he would add the surprising claim that "we suffer through dreams, and are cured by dreams" (WD 4). This provocative remark from his second book on the material elements condenses a controversial yet decisive claim that would mark Bachelard's work during this "psychotherapeutic stage" of his career. In *Earth and Reveries of Will*, citing the work of Robert Desoille[27] on the waking dream, Bachelard would note that patients who make an imaginary effort to descend into the inner world of matter by dreaming, for instance, of "entering into a rock" through some surface irregularity, may find themselves facing a sort of "inner cyst" or moral concretion they feel compelled to break up or dissolve (ERW 304). Such psychic concretions (or ill-made durations) appear to be akin to what Freudian psychoanalysts term "complexes" to designate affective knots that can potentially block a personality or thwart freedom of thought. In his books on the material imagination written during and after World War II, Bachelard proceeded to develop an exploratory body of work on what he would hence identify as "culture complexes," namely, *intersubjective mindsets* that appear grafted onto psychoanalytic complexes, continuing the transformation of psychic energy from primal to more elaborate cultural forms (WD 17–18). Such culture complexes, he discovered, typically manifest through affectively charged language in the liminal zone of material imagination, between consciousness and unconsciousness[28]—a zone that Bachelard also refers to as the "penumbral Heraclitean shadows" where reverie reigns (WD 6; PR 36). In *Water and Dreams,* he defines them as "prereflective attitudes" (WD 7)—that is, habits of feeling that tend to govern our thought processes, shaping our experiences and destinies so long as they remain unquestioned and unexamined (WD 17).

Bachelard warns us that, at times, even a culture's founding myths and loftiest ideals can devolve into dangerous *culture complexes.* A paradigmatic example is the Greek myth of Prometheus, one of the defining motifs of the Western psyche which fuels the modern belief in unlimited technological progress and the possibility of intellectual mastery or domination over nature and society. In *The Psychoanalysis of Fire,* Bachelard had recognized that when such myths become lodged in our psyches through uncritical transmission, they tend to sediment in the life of imagination as "affective complexes" analogous to the "epistemological obstacles" laid out in *The Formation of the Scientific Mind* (24 and passim). Yet such culture complexes are not necessarily negative, as appears to be the case with the Promethean complex that Bachelard also extols, despite its dangers. He in fact defines them as "hinges of ambivalence" which can potentially foster creativity as much as they might fester into raging neuroses (WD 167). They constitute the charged matter that nourishes our cultural styles—adding dynamism to our expressions and acts (PF 19; L xi). Nonetheless, if they turn into unquestioned automatisms or obsessions, they readily become obstacles to human evolution, resulting in destructive forms of psychosocial and degenerative ills.[29] It is here that hermeneutics and the arts come to play a *critical* therapeutic role in Bachelard, not only by raising such impulses of the individual and collective psyche to awareness through symbolic expression, but also by their ability "to transform oneiric energy into moral energy" (AD 112).

To illustrate this latter point, it would help to reflect on Bachelard's *Lautréamont* (1939), a striking case study of the implications of the "aggressive imagination" or hidden will then driving the Western soul, as expressed in the poetics of Isidore Ducasse's *Chants of Maldoror.* Having experienced the tragic futility of World War I, where he fought on the front trenches from 1914 through 1919, Bachelard now understood that the moral bane unleashed upon the world toward the end of the 1930s could be confronted only by following the path of "descent" into the troubled depths of the "cultural psyche," or the European *Weltanschauung* of his days, through a painstaking examination of the imagery seething at the roots of the collective unconscious (with its *ambivalent* potentials for both destruction and liberation)—an examination which continued in earnest right through the Nazi occupation of France in the early 1940s and beyond.

While fleeing Nazi persecution before his tragic death in 1940, Walter Benjamin happened upon Bachelard's then recently published study of Ducasse's poetics. In his final letter to the director of the Institute for Social Research in New York, Max Horkheimer, on what he described as the perilous state of French literature during that decade, Benjamin included a critical review of Bachelard's *Lautréamont* (1939). Yet, while decrying the "Hitlerite mentality" so blatantly manifest in much of the literature of his times, he appears to have interpreted his fellow philosopher's effort to expose the roots of human violence in *Lautréamont* as betraying—through what Benjamin regarded as Bachelard's celebration of "Platonic violence" (L 78/135)—an underlying sympathy towards the type of "idealism" that had helped spawn Hitlerism.[30]

If one rereads Bachelard's analysis of Ducasse's *Chants of Maldoror* carefully to the end, however, one may notice that the point of his book had been rather the contrary: that understanding the nature of *human* violence—as distinct from animal violence—requires the *recognition* of it as a *willed choice*. The "moral guarantee of idealism" (L 78/135) that Bachelard discovered in human violence does not mean that he consciously or unconsciously celebrated it (as Benjamin inferred in this letter to Horkheimer), but that he recognized it as an act that *has gone through the filter of human imagination, intellect, and will*. Unlike violence in animals (who, for all we know, lack this element of "ideality"), human violence is not simply a blind impulse (the inevitable result of efficient causality) but a decision in the sense that a human being, because of the latent presence of free will at any instant in time, *is potentially capable of interrupting that very impulse (élan)*. Human beings can choose otherwise, yet we often *allow* ourselves to be driven by fear, rage, or the instinct toward self-preservation (over and above self-sacrifice for a moral value that transcends our individual selves). Nonetheless, human beings are innately endowed with the ability to choose whether or not to give *consent* to a raw élan vital, however pressed by animal impulse or personal desire.

While it is true that Bachelard avidly explored the poetic "force" of Ducasse's *Chants de Maldoror* by "activating" its dynamic imagery, his study of *Lautréamont* was tempered by the need to *transmute its powerful élan* through the adoption of what Bachelard proposed as the conscious practice of "*non-Lautréamontism*"—the conversion of what he called the impulsive "Lautréamont complex" through phenomenological "reduction"—that is, by abstracting and suspending its "vital" impulses. In the conclusion he clearly summed up his thesis:

> I undertook this long meditation on the work of *Lautréamont* with the sole purpose of writing a Psychoanalysis of Life. In the end, to resist images of fire [as we did recently in *The Psychoanalysis of Fire*] and to resist images of life is the same thing. A doctrine that resists everyday images, those images already created, already formed, already taught, must also resist everyday metaphors. It must also choose: should one burn with fire, break with life, or continue with life? For me the choice has been made. The new poetry and ideas demand a breaking off and a conversion. . . . No value is specifically human if it is not the result of a renunciation and a conversion. A specifically human value is always a *converted* natural value. (L 90–91/155; trans. modified)[31]

This movement of discontinuity—this *moral interruption* of the aggressive life-impulse exposed through Bachelard's activation of the "Lautréamont complex" and its transmutation into the attitude of "non-Lautréamontism" proposed in his conclusion (too belatedly for readers unable to finish the book because of pressing circumstances or the revulsion elicited by Ducasse's imagery in *The Chants of Maldoror*)—parallels the dynamics of the "epistemological breaks" and the transmutation in human thought that Bachelard had advocated for progress in the sciences—a progress which, since his *Intuition of the Instant* (1932), had essentially included "moral progress" in the sense of the subject's need for attentive responsiveness to the *cry of otherness* (to what Bachelard would later call the world's *coefficient of adversity*—that is, the world's resistance against the excesses of human subjectivity). The type of "break" or "conversion of subjectivity" so urgently called for in Bachelard's *Lautréamont* can, in other words, be read as analogous to the "epistemological breaks" he proposed again in his next book, *The Philosophy of No* (1940), whose moral and pedagogical implications would continue to reverberate until the end of his career in 1962.

Conclusion

We have seen how Bachelard's elemental hermeneutics proceeded as a probing dialectic between psychoanalysis and phenomenology, with its dual method (*diméthode*) of uncovering and transforming the reading psyche through a rhythmic process of phenomenological "activation" and "reduction" (L 69), analysis and synthesis. Bachelard would sum it up in his posthumous *Fragments of a Poetics of Fire*:

> In dreaming their way through the tangle of poetic imagery, phenomenologists are able to pick up where psychoanalysts have left off . . . These two approaches in combination, with their two opposing methods—one looking backward, and the other forward to a language shamelessly unsupervised; one focused on the depths, the other on the heights—might in their give and take, help pinpoint the articulation between impulse and inspiration . . . One must always maintain one's connection to the past, and yet ceaselessly pull away from it. A whole philosophy of language, then, must combine the teachings of psychoanalysis with those of phenomenology. (FPF 23–24/53–54)

Although in the last books published during his lifetime—*The Poetics of Space*, *The Poetics of Reverie*, and *The Flame of a Candle*—Bachelard opted to veer away from "sites of ill-being" as the focus of his poetic meditations to gravitate more and more towards "sites of well-being," cosmic reverie, and repose, his hermeneutics of the elemental imagination most often took its *points of departure* from disturbing images of matter in failed and marginal works (including alchemical treatises), or from cultural fragments or waste products that reveal unrecognized culture complexes.[32] Yet Bachelard's interest in retrieving this often overlooked matter—so resistant to elaboration—not only would associate his hermeneutics with psychoanalysis; it also anticipated those trends of deconstruction that look to marginal figures or to the suppressed writings and sayings that tradition tends to exclude.[33] Ironically, it is *Western tradition* that delivered the key metaphor in this case. For it was the "rejected stone" (Psalms 118:22)—what we most tend to spurn in ourselves and our worlds—that became the cornerstone of Bachelard's hermeneutic explorations during that fraught period in the 1940s.

As Pierre Quillet later noted in his book on Bachelard, "alchemy is the divinization of matter, much as Manichaeism is its abomination" (28). Especially in *Earth and Reveries of Will*, Bachelard stressed the need to accept the world's darkest, most resistant matter in our struggles toward sublimation and moral redemption. For beautiful matter, he realized, is matter that has gone through the crucible of evil and is born out of abjection. Here, inspired by Paul Claudel, he would write aphoristically in his native French: "*La belle matière co-naître de la matière abjecte*"—"beautiful matter is born from/with abject matter" (ERW 192/250, trans. modified).[34] Until the end, Bachelard indeed persisted in finding promise in fallen matter (however petrified or putrefied) as it emerged in his phenomenological explorations of the soul's intercourse with the world. And so we rediscover him today—at this, our own crucible in history—as we gather every elemental image that seizes us, in a patient effort to purify and temper it, until it sings.

Notes

1. Herbert Spiegelberg, "The Essentials of the Phenomenological Method," in *The Phenomenological Movement* (The Hague: Nijhoff, 1965), 694–701.

2. Sartre's critique of Bachelard's approach to matter and the material imagination appears in *Being and Nothingness* (trans. Hazel E. Barnes [New York: Washington Square Press, 1984], 765–84).

3. Bachelard's series on the elemental imagination was followed by *Air and Dreams* (1943), *Earth and Reveries of Will* (1947), and *Earth and Reveries of Repose* (1948). A decade later, he resumed these studies in *The Poetics of Space* (1957), *The Poetics of Reverie* (1959), *The Flame of a Candle* (1961) and his posthumous *Fragments of a Poetics of Fire* (1988).

4. Robert Inchausti strikes a chord with Bachelard's notion of the "instant" when he comments on the eschatological dimension of the moment in *Ignorant Perfection of Ordinary People* (Albany: State University of New York Press, 1991): "When seen from the perspective of an eschatological present . . . time is material for self-creation, not a limitation" (133). From this perspective—which echoes Bachelard's thesis in *Intuition of the Instant*—time appears as the"paste of possibility" to set an incarnational ethics into motion.

5. The term "habit," besides referring to an often-repeated action, evokes the image of the woven "cloak" of the perceptual world, a fabric ever open to weaving and unweaving.

6. Such "ill-made durations" will later be examined in Bachelard's works on the elemental imagination under the rubrics of "culture complexes" (WD 17) or "anthropocosmic complexes" (PR 123).

7. Bachelard's later works on scientific epistemology include *Les Intuitions atomistiques* (1933), *Le Nouvel esprit scientifique* (1934), *La Formation de l'esprit scientifique* (1938), *La Philosophie du non* (1940), *L'Activité rationaliste de la physique contemporaine* (1951), and *Le Matérialisme rationnel* (1953).

8. See Richard Kearney's reflections on Joyce's narrative art in *On Stories* (London: Routledge, 2002), 17ff.

9. José María Arguedas, *Deep Rivers*, trans. Frances Barraclough (Austin: University of Texas Press, 1978), 232.

10. These principles are not "axiomatic." They serve, rather, as heuristic attitudes that distinguish Bachelard's phenomenological approach to imagery from any objectivistic, empirical study.

11. Once Bachelard becomes acquainted with C. G. Jung's works, he will avail himself of certain Jungian distinctions to identify the ambivalences of critical reading "*in animus*" as compared with sympathetic reading "*in anima*" (PR 65).

12. Maurice Blanchot, "Vast as the Night," *The Infinite Conversation*, trans. Susan Hanson (Minneapolis: University of Minnesota Press, 1993), 318–25, 458n1.

13. One notable exception to this trend in modern aesthetics is the work of Owen Barfield, founding member of the Oxford "Inklings," an informal literary group comprised of such creative writers as J. R. R. Tolkein and C. S. Lewis. See Owen Barfield's *Poetic Diction* (New York: McGraw Hill, 1964).

14. Jean Lescure's characterization of Bachelard's approach to Roupnel's *Siloë* as a "method of sympathy" in *Intuition of the Instant* (II 64/138) invites us to characterize Bachelard's intimate reading of literary texts as a *hermeneutics of sympathy* that contrasts with the *hermeneutics of suspicion* adopted by authors such as Marx, Nietzsche, and Freud—not to mention with Bachelard's own critical hermeneutics of science (with its "epistemological breaks"), as succinctly summarized in *The Philosophy of No* (1940).

15. Mary McAllester Jones, *Gaston Bachelard: Subversive Humanist* (Madison: University of Wisconsin Press, 1991), 4ff; hereafter cited as SH.

16. Heisenberg's *indeterminacy principle* in microphysics had a profound impact not only on Bachelard's scientific epistemology but also on his poetics. He even came to characterize the minute dynamism of elemental images in terms of the "*Heisenberg principle for oneiric life*" (ERR 13), and the ambivalence of such images in poetic experience as the "*indeterminacy principle for affective response*" (ERW 58–59).

17. In *Air and Dreams* Bachelard cites a passage from Plato's *Phaedrus* on the soaring function of wings to illustrate this intimate communion (μέθεξις) with divine lightness and dynamism: "With its *aerial materialism* this participation gives a concrete meaning to the abstract doctrine of Platonic *participation*" (AD 68). For him, such soaring can best be evoked through pure poetry, as in the case of Shelley's "Skylark" more than through visual "representations" where the formal imagination predominates (AD 26, 56, 82).

18. Hans-Georg Gadamer, *Truth and Method*, ed. Garrett Barden and John Cumming (New York: Crossroad, 1985), 438.

19. See also Carl Gustav Jung's *participation mystique* in *Essays on a Science of Mythology* (Princeton: Princeton University Press, 1973). Although Jung describes it as an individual's participation in the *collective psyche*, rather than as elemental

communion, his *collective psyche* is itself rooted in the *material imagination* of the world unconscious: "The deeper layers of the psyche lose their individual uniqueness as they retreat farther and farther into darkness. Lower down . . . as they approach the autonomous functional systems, they become increasingly collective until they are universalized and extinguished in the body's materiality. . . . The body's carbon is simply carbon. Hence at bottom the psyche is simply world. . . . In the symbol, the *world itself* is speaking. The more archaic and deeper, the more *physiological* the symbol, the more collective and universal, the more material it is" (92). Bachelard picks up on this elemental participation of *self* and *world* again in *The Poetics of Reverie*: "When a dreamer speaks, who is speaking, he or the world" (PR 187–88)? But Bachelard conceives of such participation in terms of *mutually responsive* and *fertile interlacings* where, as Kearney notes, "the imagination finds itself in a world of which it is both the creature and the creator" (*Poetics of Imagining* [New York: Fordham, 1998], 110–11; henceforth cited as PI).

20. See Kearney's account of Ricoeur's "hermeneutic imagination" in *Poetics of Modernity* (New York: Humanity Books, 1999), xvi and chapter 7.

21. Insofar as Bachelardian imagination tends toward cosmic solitude, away from sociopolitical spheres, it has at times been criticized as non-hermeneutic, even solipsistic. Several chapters in part 4 of this volume, however, make the case for the ethical, intersubjective, and transsubjective thrust of Bachelard's philosophy. One of my aims here is to assist in shedding light on the ethical underpinnings of Bachelard's elemental hermeneutics. For him, "the moral life is a cosmic life: the world in its entirety seeks to be renovated" (WD 148; see also PI 7).

22. See *Earth and Reveries of Repose* (49–50/66) for Bachelard's example of contaminated air—contagious miasmas that mutate into swarms of locusts—cited from Friedrich Schlegel's *La Philosophie de la vie*, trans. M. l'abbé Guénot, 2 vols. (Paris: Prent-Desbarres, 1838), 1:296.

23. The point of Bachelard's *Earth and Reveries of Will* had been to study the earth element as an "activist force," hence its original French subtitle "*Essai sur l'imagination des forces* [*An Essay on the Imagination of Forces*]" and not—as it appears in its English translation—*An Essay on the Imagination of Matter*, the actual subtitle of Bachelard's *Water and Dreams*. Matter is typically "at war" with itself, as Bachelard would stress again in *Earth and Reveries of Repose* (44–57/58–78).

24. Compare Jung, *Essays on a Science of Mythology*. Bachelard did not view such unconscious matter as "impervious to sublimation," however. This is where his reading sharply differed from that of certain psychoanalytic trends. The resistance of unconscious matter—typically experienced as somatic suffering—provokes our conscious efforts at understanding. And such matter, in his view, is amenable to transmutation through the autonomous *absolving power of poetic language* (FPF 21–23; PS xxv–xxviii), even if at times it seems to withhold its grace—until the heart, perhaps, is ready to listen.

25. Also telling is Bachelard's use of the *present tense* here—a detail that helps induce a kind of experiential identification with alchemical work, often regarded as too remote for modern readers.

26. See Martin Heidegger, *Being and Time* (*Sein und Zeit,* 1927), trans. John Macquarrie and Edward Robinson (San Francisco: Harper and Row, 1962), part 1, sec. 2, 78–86.

27. Robert Desoille developed a psychology of the "waking dream" which focuses on the future of images rather than their past—a medical-psychiatric technique Bachelard called *psychosynthesis*, rather than *psychoanalysis*. Bachelard discusses Desoille's work at length in *Air and Dreams* (111–25), and *Earth and Reveries of Will* (302–9).

28. Pierre Quillet, *Bachelard* (Paris: Seghers, 1964), 85.

29. For an example of the struggle to overcome culture complexes, see my reading of Shelley's *Prometheus Unbound* in "Bachelard's Subversive Hermeneutics," *Religion and the Arts* 10, no. 3 (2006), 355–73.

30. See Walter Benjamin, *1940 Survey of French Literature* (written March 23, 1940, trans. David Fernbach), *New Left Review* 51 (May–June 2008), also available online, May 19, 2012: http://www.newleftreview.org/II/51/walter-benjamin-survey-of-french-literature (4–6).

31. In the first sentence of this passage from *Lautréamont*, the English translation makes a serious error by rendering in the *affirmative* what had been intended in a *negative* sense. The French edition reads: "La longue meditation de l' œuvre de *Lautréamont* n'a été enterprise par nous qu'en vue d'une Psychanalyse de la Vie" (155). Hence my correction of that line, as well as other minor amendments in the passage.

32. The violent images in *Lautréamont*—much as the images of suicide or slow death in *Water and Dreams*, and the devouring or decaying images in Bachelard's Earth books—reveal Bachelard's focus, during this "psychotherapeutic period" of his career, on the destructive dynamics of complexes. Although such "images of crisis and struggle" may not have attained the level of poetic freedom "above the language of signification" later to become the focus of his *The Poetics of Space* (xxiii), they already harbored the seeds of that possibility—as he suggested in *Lautréamont* and again in *Earth and Reveries of Repose* when he described the realm of poetic expression as an "autonomous universe" that offers itself—albeit without guarantee—"as a means of liberation from the three worlds envisaged by Binswanger's *Dasein* analysis, the *Umwelt* (surrounding world), the *Mitwelt* [interhuman world], and *Eigenwelt* [personal world]" (ERR 57/77).

33. Cf. John D. Caputo, *Radical Hermeneutics* (Bloomington: Indiana University Press, 1987), 264.

34. See Paul Claudel, "Traité de la co-naissance du monde et de soi-même," in *Art poétique* (Paris: Mercure de France, 1913), 59. The wordplay between *co-naître*

and *connaître* recalls the Husserlian precept that a subject in the act of knowing does not merely project its intentional aim onto an object, but "co-constitutes meaning." Also see Jean Grondin, *Sources of Hermeneutics* (Albany: State University of New York Press, 1995), 43, which traces the allusion to the etymology of *con-naître* as "to be born with" to Charles Péguy.

Chapter 8

Bachelard's Poetic Ontology

Glen A. Mazis

> For one who truly lives out the evolutions of material imagination, there is no figurative meaning: all figurative meanings retain a certain sensual value [*poids de sensibilité*]. Everything depends on determining the nature of this persistent, perceptible matter [*matière sensible*].
>
> —Bachelard, *Water and Dreams*[1]

Material Imagination as a Path to Ontology

Forging a new path for ontology is the notable achievement we owe to Gaston Bachelard. His writings articulate an ontology accessed through an imaginative development and explored through poetic reverie of what is *latent* in our perception of the world. His expression of nuance is as painstaking as an artist in detailing myriad concrete aspects of being within the varied elemental qualities of the world: air, earth, fire, and water. These descriptions offer his readers a galaxy of subtle ways in which the world *becomes*, disputing the insistence of the ontological tradition that being is accessed exclusively through reason and must be expressed in clear and distinct categorical discourse in order to uncover its universal and permanent aspects. Bachelard counters this tradition by revealing the power of a kind of imagination that develops the sensual presentation of the world to bring forth its deeper sense in poetic reverie, in which the vital meaning of the fleeting, the fragile, and the obscure is fathomed and added to our understanding of being. His own creativity is continually at play in locating the nuanced qualities of things in the world through a poetic language that brings forth the discoveries of reverie. Bachelard's writing uses metaphor and image as deftly as the poetic writings he explores. The literary writings are extended and deepened through an "ontological amplification," as he called it (PR 167). The importance of Bachelard's work, which I will attempt to present in this chapter, is that it arrives at a non-foundational ontology in which person and world are interwoven in the sensual manifestations of an ongoing becoming through an imaginative expression in poetic language that transforms the culturally dominant ontological understanding, as well as that of the mainstream of preceding European philosophy, in providing a transformative possibility for those who engage in its project.

Bachelard's access to another sort of ontology than the traditional one is possible, however, only by recognizing a mode of imagination other than the familiar "formal imagination," which arises only *after* perception by recombining sense contents into new forms. Such imagination, the focus of Western philosophical and cultural tradition for centuries, contrasts with what Bachelard introduced as the "material imagination" which affords access to our primal contact with the world. At the outset of *Water and Dreams*, Bachelard declares, "The imagining powers of our mind develop around two very different axes"—one that gives impetus to the formal cause, and another that plumbs the material cause—namely, "a *formal imagination* and a *material imagination*" (WD 1). Our primal sense of contact with the world, for Bachelard, is one that has imaginative dimensions within what is sensed: "Before becoming a conscious sight, every landscape is an oneiric experience" (WD 4). These levels of significance can become manifest through the workings of a material imagination that unfolds "images of matter, *direct* images of *matter*. Vision names them, but the hand knows them. . . . They have a weight, they constitute a heart" (WD 1). Already within our embodied insertion in the world, there is a felt affective relationship to things and situations around us that awaits further expression.

The affectivity entered through material imagination then arises through a *further* opening of this primal encounter with the world's materiality. In the beginning of *Earth and Reveries of Repose*, Bachelard writes: "[A]ll matter we imagine, all matter on which we meditate, is at once the image of interiority . . . these material images transcend sensations . . . material images engage us in a deeper affectivity" (ERR 3). This underlying affectivity is discovered through an intense hearkening to the sensual world. For, as Bachelard puts it, "[a]n emotional imagination lies behind a formal imagination. When symbolism draws from the heart itself, how much greater the visions become! The visions then seem to think" (WD 42). Layers of the world's sense can emerge from this felt understanding, but they call for the *work* of the material imagination to become manifest. Bachelard thus turns his readers towards discovering this "full sensual universe latent *within* imagined matter" (ERR 3/4, trans. modified). This prereflective dimension of the world, made manifest through the material imagination, will hence draw us beneath surface being and into the depths of becoming.[2]

Material imagination is "the primary imagination" which brings *forth* "those certainties borne by an immediate sensation" (WD 122). But the way the world appears to our senses emerges and undergoes mutations as the material imagination plunges into the *life of matter* (WD 129), tapping into the innumerable nuances silently spoken to us by things—what Bachelard calls their "murmurs" (WD 195). Thus, beyond the formal image which merely recombines previous categories, "a material image dynamically experienced, passionately adopted, patiently explored, is an *opening* in every sense of the word, in its real sense and its figurative sense" (ERW 24). In entering into the sensual encounter with the world, material imagination opens up its latent level of significance and becoming, especially if undertaken with the fervent engagement of an artist beyond the cold detachment that philosophy often borrows from traditional scientific methods. Although Bachelard seemed to reject such passionate engagement when he began psychoanalyzing the material imagination in *The Psychoanalysis of Fire* (PF 1–6), as this book progressed he realized that the very drive to "objectivity"—to purge science from any emotional coloring—was itself fueled by a passionate *will to intellectuality* (Prometheus complex) which, if unrecognized and untamed, could paradoxically block our very capacity to enter into deeper levels of existence. He later came to the realization that "material images"—when focused with *vigilant* fervor—can actually deepen our sense of existence: "This deepening reveals a double perspective: opening into the interior of the active subject and into the inner substance of the inert object encountered in perception" (ERW 24). Thus, in every engaging encounter with the substance of things in the world, we gain a deeper understanding of who we are, even as we deepen our sense of those things which have now entered our being.

This work of the material imagination is more than an enlargement of understanding, however. It is a transformation of being, indicated when Bachelard adds that "in working with this matter, this double perspective is reversed. The inner depths of subject and object interchange: a salutary rhythm of introversion and extroversion comes to life" (ERW 24). Unlike the well-known path of imagination as shallow fancy or fantasizing, here the imaginer *becomes* through a back-and-forth exchange with these depths of imagining—a motion which actually releases one *into* the world. As Bachelard says, "the imagination is nothing other than the subject transported into things" (ERR 2). This being transported into things is the vitality inherent in material imagination as contrasted with formal imagination: "Though forms and concepts harden rapidly, material imagination remains an active power. It alone can revitalize traditional images endlessly . . . It gives life back to forms by transforming them, for a form cannot transform itself" (WD 134).[3] Bachelard thus recognizes that what had been considered unintelligible in the philosophical tradition—the material, considered mute and senseless unless shaped by form—acts as an interlocutor that communicates a deeper sense, if hearkened to. The forms by which matter has been named can themselves be burst open and transformed. But, as he will insist, a kinetic description of external forms cannot truly grasp the forces, drives, or aspirations that prompt such transformations (WD 130). Only an imagination that *grows from within* the material elements that our dreams absorb and exude, inhale and exhale, can actually express the *dynamics* of transformation and the *becoming* of things.

This dynamism uncovered through material imagination thus calls for dissolving the distance of the objective stance, such that the imaginer's "*cogito* is [no longer] divided into the dialectic of subject and object" (PR 158). The vitality of this deeper sense of the world can only be stirred by the attuned attitude of the material imaginer, for "the energy and life of the image does not come from objects . . . The imagination is first and foremost the *tonalized subject*" (ERR 63). When the imaginer is attuned to the rhythms and nuances of things around her or him, then another sense of "quality" emerges: "And so, when the imagination has set us in the most attentive kind of sensitivity, we realize that qualities are not so much states for us, but processes of development, of becoming. Qualifying adjectives that are lived by the imagination [. . .] are closer to *verbs* than to *nouns*" (ERR 65).[4] What tradition tends to see as the objective qualities of things are actually dynamic manifestations of becoming. Bachelard writes, for instance, "Red is closer to redden than to redness. When imagined, red darkens or pales according to the oneiric weight of imaginary impressions. Every imagined color becomes a fragile, fleeting, ungraspable nuance. It tantalizes dreamers who wish to fix it" (ERR 65). Red as entered into through material imagination has waves and levels of sense into which the imaginer is enfolded as a becoming that deepens and interweaves with other beings.[5] This sense awaits material imagination's revival because it unfolds only as entered into as a process of participatory unfolding between person and world. Rather than a categorized quality, this *encounter* is a discerning sensitivity that enters the dynamism of qualities as distinguished by their nuances: "the world of reverie begins with the nuance" (PR 153). To trace out the process of this becoming, it is necessary to turn to Bachelard's method of poetic reverie.

Poetic Reverie and Writing

Bachelard's ontology acknowledges that access to *what is* begins with a sensual encounter with the world. Yet the traditional separation of the real and the imaginary is necessarily overcome as the material imagination draws out what is latently present in the sensual. In fact, our *perceptual sense* is itself dependent upon this imaginative drawing forth: "If imagination's function of openness is insufficient, then perception itself is blunted. We must find, then, a regular filiation between the real and the imaginary" (AD 7). The perceptual is in need of a *way* for material imagination to augment its dynamism and depth through further activity, and this activity is for Bachelard poetic reverie. Unlike the loss of consciousness so common to dream, such reverie bears the mark of a "manifest psychic activity" (PR 167). And since "imaginary life—*true* life—is animated by a pure literary image" (AD 253), this leads him to conclude that the manifestation of the depth of *what is* requires this distinctive sort of reverie which poetry sets on the track of "an expanding consciousness" (PR 6). Thus vitalizing, broadening, and deepening the sensual contact with the world, poetic reverie is not simply the opposite of nocturnal dream: poetic reverie is indeed crucial to another sort of ontology that ushers forth the deeper levels of world perception.

This means that a new *relationship* to the sensed world emerges in poetic reverie: "All the senses awaken and fall into harmony in poetic reverie. Poetic reverie listens to this polyphony of the senses" (PR 6). Here, the overlapping of the senses and the way they move into each other (such that sounds, for instance, have color as part of their deeper sense) comes to the fore. However, the polyphony latent in this sensual encounter still needs to be *expressed* to become manifest and explored. Poetic reverie is a reverie that comes about in moments of *composing* and then *reading* poetic language, or as Bachelard continues this statement: "[T]his reverie is written or promises to be written" (PR 6). The materially imaginative flow of language within poetry, its use of metaphor and rhythm, is the sort of writing that is able to communicate reverie's sense: "[I]t must be written, written with emotion and taste, being relived because it is written down" (PR 7).[6] Such written poetry is itself a process, another way to be in relation to the world and to language. Language already harbors references to other expressions of varied kinds that bring forward the past—subtle references carried by rhythm and sound as they are taken up poetically and written with renewed emotional attunement. Then the felt, the imagined, the sensed—including the echoes of other understandings of the world—all come together to permeate its expression: "The written word has an enormous advantage over a spoken one, because it can call forth abstract echoes in which thoughts and dreams reverberate" (AD 250).

Playing off these other registers contained in language, poetic writing now *intensifies* the writer's relationship to the moment of encounter with the world, making this writing a "polylogism"—a writing of many levels, unlike spoken language: "But it is especially its counterpoint that makes *written* poetry surpass any diction. . . . True poetry has several registers. . . . At least three levels are discernible in this multipronged polylogism, and they must find the place where words, symbols, and thoughts are in accord" (AD 248). The depth of interplay within poetic language opens language to the hidden latencies within sensual presentation. Poetic writing propels language into these depths that otherwise would be inaccessible. And, as it injects dynamism into language by quickening the material imagination (AD 250), literary language also provides the poetic force which transforms sensual acuity: "[T]his poetic force animates all the senses; reverie becomes polysensorial. From the poetic passage, we receive a renewal of the joy of perceiving, a subtlety of all the senses" (PR 162).

Poetic reverie will even lead Bachelard to call poets "born phenomenologists" who, by hearkening to the way "things speak to us," are able to achieve a more intense "contact with things" through their language (PS xxiv). Still more to our point, however, is what Bachelard highlights as "ontological significance" of poetic writing: "Because of its novelty and its action, the poetic image has an entity and dynamism of its own; it is referable to a direct *ontology.* This ontology," he affirms, "is what I plan to study" (PS xii). The novelty to which Bachelard points here is the way that poetic language breaks with the use of standard language that relies on static concepts or *definitive* intuitions about the world (PS 214–5). In other words, the instituted language of culture and metaphysics is a dualistic language that tends to reduce phenomena to strictly distinct and circumscribed meanings that convey a surface grasp of the world and a distanced, manipulative relationship to it. Poetic language will instead accent the usually taken-for-granted relations of sense, syntax, and semantics, setting them into motion even while retaining their surfaces. Hence, "by means of poetic language, waves of newness [begin to] flow over the surface of being" (PS 222). Paul Ricoeur similarly explains the power of metaphor as a "predicative assimilation" capable of breaking up conventional language use and opening new meaning by bringing together two aspects of things from differing regions of being, though without entirely doing away with the distance between them which may act as a productive *tension* between incongruence and congruence, remoteness and proximity.[7]

In Bachelard's view there must be this breaking open of standard language use for language to be poetic: "To deserve the title *literary image*, [a sign] must have the virtue of originality. A literary image is a nascent meaning. From it, the word—the old word—gets new meaning. But that is still not enough: the *literary image* must be enriched with a new *oneirism*. Such is the dual function of the literary image: to mean something different, and to make readers dream in another way" (AD 249). By forging unprecedented connections in poetic language, new senses emerge from the interplay as well as meanings that had been latent and now appear after having gained through the combination of what Bachelard calls the "reality" and "unreality" functions—the former from ordinary language use, the latter from material imagination (AD 7, PR 13). We know we need to cope with reality, but it is equally true that we need the function of the unreal to give fullness of meaning (AD 7). Examples abound in Bachelard's writing, but let us take one line he cites from a short poem by Jean Tardieu, "I walk the treadmill of myself." Such treadmill is unreal, of course, since none of us has an actual treadmill as part of our physiological make-up, but everyone can agree how this illuminates the reality of an aspect of our being that we experience daily as we trudge in circles within obsessive thoughts, worries, feelings, and ideas. In the same passage, Bachelard recognizes how poetic reverie gives "the I a non-I which belongs to the I" (PR 13). Not circumscribed by the strict boundary of ego-identity in poetic reverie, we find ourselves *in* all sorts of beings and objects which are not our ostensible selves, living in dimensions of our beings that *are* birds, stones, flowers, or doors—vital dimensions without which our being would be impoverished.

Poetic reverie thus transports us beyond ourselves into things, freeing us to experience an essential dimension of our being in the world—for we are *eccentric* beings, despite the concerted cultural and philosophical efforts to reduce us to *egocentric*, substantial individuals. Bachelard exclaims, "But what a spiral man's being represents! And what a number of invertible dynamisms there are in this spiral" (PS 214).[8] Taken up into this reciprocal becoming with the depths of the world just entered, human being moves past itself, then back into itself, always surprisingly transformed in the interim—not circling back, but always spiraling in becoming. This is the poetic response Bachelard regards as countering the dangers of self-enclosure, of trying to be the source of oneself, of one's own vitality and meaning—a self-mirroring which would make us static: "Poets lead us into cosmoses which are being endlessly renewed" (PS 23). Such eccentricity is a *differential* movement that reveals our being and the being of those things with which we are related and entwined: "Reverie is a manifest psychic activity [that] contributes documentation on differences in the *tonality of the being*" (PR 167). Yet, unlike a thinker's cogito, the dreamer's cogito is both a "diffuse being" and "the being of a diffusion. It escapes the punctualization of the *hic* and of the *nunc*. The dreamer's being invades what it touches, diffuses into the world. Thanks to shadows, the intermediary region which separates man from the world is a full region, of a light density fullness" (PR 167).

Taken into our being in poetic reverie are all those relationships that emerge through metaphor, rhythm, and the motion of meaning that crosses definite boundaries. There are myriad aspects of ourselves murmured to us by those beings that surround us elementally—whether in their fluid malleability, in the earthy resistance of clay and rock (ERW 8), or in the radiant calm of the blue sky overhead (AD 163). Such nuances are often not presented as discrete characteristics but as an encompassing atmosphere, as in the rounded landscape that awakens a serenity in Rilke that suffuses world and soul. The poetic does not yield an ontology of separate things in hard-edged juxtaposition of measurable quantities, but a diffuse, interrelated becoming most aptly described in Bachelard's phrase "light density fullness" (PR 167).

Still, the power of poetic reverie is greater than this diffusion, for its dynamism *bonds* the person with the sensed and imagined world. The depth of the "poetic force" described by Bachelard also entails a *hearkening to things* such that their felt qualities can captivate the soul through the experience of "reverberation [*retentissement*]." Such reverberations not only transport us into greater depths of the sensed world; they provoke an intimacy *beyond* the associative resonances evoked by their image-concepts, which are still ego-enclosed and hence distant (PS xviii). In the reverberations of poetic reverie, Bachelard writes, "a flower, a fruit, or a simple familiar object suddenly comes to solicit us to think of it, to dream near it, to help it raise itself to *the rank of companion*" (PR 154, emphasis added).

The underlying dualism of the European cultural-philosophical heritage, including the postmodern ethos, thus dissolves in poetic reverie. Bachelard here describes the mutuality of person and world as actually "touching and interpenetrating," for in poetic reverie "they are on the same plane of being" (PR 158). Moreover, a writer who is open to "the antecedence of being" (PR 111)—or what is present prior to recognition—feels carried along in poetic reverie by the motive force of language itself, as if the poem were *emanating* from the world and writing itself: "When a poet dreams . . . it seems as though contemplated nature helps in the contemplation, as though it contains within itself the means for contemplating" (WD 27–28). The sense of what *is* hence comes to us from the world as much as we move to grasp it—leading to a growing awareness of person and world as they exist *through each other*. Poetic reverie therefore displaces the self—not only from a substantial centered self to a diffused self within an interplay with the world, but also from the human claim to possess self-generating faculties to the recognition of a *shared process* with the beings it now relates with poetically.[9] With this in mind, it might be better to refrain from claiming that *we see the world*, and admit instead that *we see with the world*.[10] Poetry, the writing that embraces material imagination, expresses this enlacing with the world: "This pancalistic union of the visible and vision has been felt by innumerable poets; they have lived it without defining it. It is an elementary law of the imagination" (WD 28). If one imaginatively enters the depths of what is latent in one's first encounter with the world, the sense of this pancalistic relationship is so heightened that the poet-reader now feels even the words *on the page* are actually being murmured to him by the world.[11]

It is for this reason that Bachelard claims that *written* words have a voice, a virtual sound (not a literal one) to which one can hearken: "The literary image emits sounds that must be called . . . *written sounds*" (AD 249). In the literal silence of the written poetic text, there is a sounding of the world, a dialogue that comes before the spoken word.[12] Poetic reverie and writing thus led Bachelard not only to a non-foundational ontology of becoming, of pancalistic reversal between human being and world, but to articulate our modern need to enter a silent, fragile, and obscurely mysterious sense of being.[13]

Poetic Ontology: Its Role in the Augmentation of Being

In the modern world of ever-increasing haste and manipulation of other beings for utilitarian purposes, Bachelard recognized the power of the slower rhythm and pace of poetry, which allows another sort of dwelling in the presence of beings. In the section on "The Literary Image" that concludes *Air and Dreams*, he states: "By virtue of written poetry's slow pace, verbs rediscover the fine points of their original movement. Each verb is accorded, not the time of its expression, but the true time of its action" (AD 248). In the slowness of poetry's time, the reader enters into the presence of a verb as a becoming, a process of manifestation and unfolding meaning. Such poetic writing differs from one that would deploy verbs as external "thrusters" to expedite and execute matters. But this important difference applies not only in the case of poetic verbs, for "when an adjective makes its object blossom, written poetry, the literary image, allows us to live slowly the time of its blooming" (AD 248).

Here Bachelard also brings to our attention that poetry is truly "the first manifestation of silence." Moreover, it "leaves attentive silence alive beneath its images. It constructs a poem based on silent time, on a time which is not labored, rushed, or controlled by anything, on a time that is open to everything spiritual, on the time of our freedom" (AD 248). The manifestation of silence is indeed inseparable from this slower time that marks the poetic use of language. As Bachelard exclaims, "Poem: a beautiful temporal thing that creates its own tempo" (AD 248). Our capacity to enter into this slower pace is an expression of our freedom—*freedom from* frenetic activity and its obsessive drive to control the world; and *freedom to* cultivate the creative sensitivity that will allow the world and ourselves to become more fully manifest.

Even when recited, the words of poetic language convey at their heart *a silence*. But Bachelard insists that this silence cannot be understood as the literal absence of sound. Rather, poetic silence is a quality that stems from a kind of wonder and attention to the myriad details of beings present in a *hushed still openness*: "If we want to study this integration of silence into a poem, we must not reduce it to [a] linear dialectic of pauses and sudden starts through a recitation of the poem. We must understand that the element of silence in poetry is a hidden, secret thought" (AD 251). The silence of poetic language is about the depths of the hidden, the latent in what we sense, which can only become manifest by making language itself a kind of hearkening suspension. These moments of poetic reverie belong to a different sort of time:[14] "They are included in a different duration from experienced duration, in that non-duration which provides the great reposes experienced in an existentialism of the poetic" (PR 120). Rather than a time filled with "happenings," this is a time in which the existence of beings, as well as ourselves, comes more fully into register in its varied contingencies and nuances. Within this time, as we have seen, we have already moved beyond the dichotomies of presence/absence, being/non-being, real/non-real: "Thus . . . we can know states which are ontologically below being and above nothingness. In these states the contradiction between being and non-being fades away. A lesser-being [*moins-être*] is trying itself out as being" (PR 111). Within the still inchoate becoming of person and world that emerges at such moments of poetic contact "[t]his antecedence of being does not yet have the responsibility of being. Neither does it have the solidity of the constituted being which believes itself capable of confronting a non-being. In such a state of mind, one feels clearly that logical opposition, with its too bright light, erases all possibility of penumbral ontology" (PR 111). Although what becomes manifest in the poetic is not the clear and the distinct, its slightest shadings can nonetheless open up expansive realms of sense not glimpsed before, such that "sometimes one literary image is enough to transport us from one world to another" (AD 250). The worlds opened up through poetic language are manifested in "softened keys," through "a dialectic of light and shadow" (PR 111), in a way that is essentially at odds with our increasingly oppositional world of manipulation from a distance.

The philosophical tradition that preceded Bachelard's work was one which had little patience indeed with these phantom senses and fleeting phenomena, and could easily discount his path of ontology: "Philosophers of the strong ontology (*l'ontologie forte*) who overtake being in its totality and keep it integrally even in describing the most fleeting modes will quickly denounce this dispersed ontology which attaches itself to details, perhaps to accidents, and which believes it is multiplying its proofs by multiplying its points of view" (PR 166/144). The claim that only what is clear and distinct, unchanging and substantial is alone what counts as "being" loses access to the subtle variations of meaning and becoming that are often, if paradoxically, the locus of vitality and depth in human existence. Paying close attention to those first possibilities of primal contact in our sensual encounter with the world, and allowing material imagination to intuit its latencies, helps bring out those "differences in the tonality of the being" we mentioned earlier (PR 167). Nonetheless, the *differential ontology* Bachelard discovers emerging at this level of being's tonality is both penumbral and fragile. It is penumbral as it allows the obscure depths of what is encountered to be manifest only through images that are nuanced, mysterious, and open to unending exploration, for "no one ever finishes dreaming or thinking about a poem" (AD 252). It is fragile as it often trails shimmering beings that are elusive in appearance. This kind of ontology, as we saw above, requires a "subtlety of seeing" open to the pancalistic experience that "everything I look at looks at me" (PR 185, WD 27–28)—an experience that deepens our *bonds* with the world (PR 185).[15]

As we have suggested throughout this chapter, the modern insistence on the exclusive validity of a hard ontology versus Bachelard's poetic ontology has taken a heavy toll on our culture and philosophical tradition. Hence the urgency, on Bachelard's part, to contrast a dwelling with things in their imaginal depth with the manipulation of a so-called "objective" world that is actually under the sway of a metaphysics which thinks via static and geometric concepts "cast in the mold of linguistic fossils" (PS 214). To further draw out this threat (and expose its human repercussions), he turns to a poem by Henri Michaux entitled "L'Espace aux Ombres [Shade-Haunted Space]." Here Bachelard warns that, in a world governed by geometrized relations, human being is exiled from its living haunt (*the being of its shade*) as it falls into a dislocated existence amid a cacophonous bustle of activity. Those who live this way tend to erect a defensive borderline between inside and outside which they use to fortify a sense of reality and identity that ultimately causes them pain and drains the world of the possibility of being explored in its imaginal depths (PS 216–17). Refusing to enter the deeper becoming offered by material imagination and poetic reverie thus means, for Bachelard, losing part of our own being: "Literary images, when correctly dynamized, also dynamize the reader" (WD 185). It is only in this way that human beings and the world can enter a full relationship that manifests depths we would otherwise pass by. Hence, for Bachelard, "Literature is not merely a substitute for some other activity. It brings human desire to fruition. It represents an *emergence* of the imagination" (AD 249).

Paradoxically, without a poetic ontology, the *reality* of both humans and the world becomes empty. Without the imaginal, reality is barren—even hostile (ERR 2)—offering no hospitable place to be or to dwell in the world. We need poetic wonder to open up a materially imagined path and a home in the midst of other beings, in such a way that we can offer one another our deeper being.[16]

Notes

1. Translation amended (WD 145/198). In this chapter the term used for the presentation of beings by the senses will be "sensual" (rather than the oft-used

term "sensory"). It is meant to suggest a felt encounter with the world—before reflection and categorization—rich with affective, perceptual, imaginative, and intuitive levels of sense that can be further developed from their latency in the primal contact with the world. Bachelard himself remarks on this greater density of content in the *sensual*: "This density, which distinguished the superficial from the profound in poetry, is felt in the transition from *sensory values* to *sensual values*. I believe that the doctrine of imagination will be clarified only by a proper classification of sensual values in relation to sensory ones. Only sensual values offer 'direct communication.' Sensory values give only translations. Confusing the 'sensory' and the 'sensual,' writers have claimed a correspondence among *sensations* (highly mental data) and have therefore failed to undertake any study that considers poetic emotion and its dynamics" (WD 20).

2. Spurred by an image from Poe's "Descent into the Maelström," Bachelard declares, "This is a specific instance of that law I wish to repeat on every possible occasion: imagination is a becoming" (WD 103).

3. As Bachelard puts it: for "an imagination that develops in depth [. . .] everything is lost in the realm of the formal image, but nothing is lost in the realm of the material image" (WD 127).

4. David L. Miller's chapter in this book, "Gaston Bachelard and Henry Corbin: On Adjectival Consciousness" (chapter 9), offers an in-depth meditation on this issue.

5. As Bachelard states, "metaphors summon one another and are more coordinated than sensations, so much so that a poetic mind is purely and simply a syntax of metaphors" (PF 109).

6. The ontological implications of "written reverie"—including poetic translation—are examined further in part 3 of this volume ("Adventures in Language").

7. Paul Ricoeur, "The Metaphorical Process as Cognition, Imagination and Feeling," *Critical Inquiry* 5, no. 1 (1978): 143–59

8. In a footnote at the bottom of this page (PS 214n1), Bachelard laughs at himself for using an image that is "geometric" after having criticized the "geometricism" of modern language use and common sense. However, his poetic use of this image differs by its inclusion of details of dispersal, diffusion, and open-endedness—a dynamism which is quite at odds with the geometric reduction of beings to clearly defined, static boundaries of being and meaning.

9. Bachelard calls this shared process "the ambivalence which plays upon the two participles *seen* and *seeing*" (WD 28/42, trans. modified).

10. Bachelard, in *Water and Dreams*, cites numerous examples from Paul Claudel's works on the reciprocal relationship between knower and known based on his explorations of the idea of "co-naissance" (a "co-knowing" that also is a "co-birthing," a sense suggested by the double meaning in French between the hyphenated and typical usage of the word) in *Poetic Art*. See Paul Claudel, *Poetic Art*

(New York: Philosophical Library, 1948), especially 61–65. Bachelard foregrounds this key notion in *Earth and Reveries of Will*, as cited at the conclusion of Eileen Rizo-Patron's piece on "Bachelard's Hermeneutics" (chapter 7, n34).

11. In footnote 23 of *Air and Dreams*, Bachelard explains that he has borrowed the term "pancalism" from the American psychologist James Mark Baldwin, who uses it as part of his aesthetic theory. It was originally a medieval aesthetic term that implied not only beauty but also an interconnectedness of spirit and matter. Bachelard was also aware of these sources, and in *The Poetics of Reverie* he cites Novalis using the term in the same way that implies the painter's object becoming active in the painter's expression. Bachelard refers readers to James Mark Baldwin, "Pancalism: A Theory of Reality," in *Genetic Theory of Reality* (New York and London, 1905), chapter 15, 275ff (AD 49).

12. In *Poetics of Imagining* (New York: Fordham University Press, 1998), Richard Kearney has a deft way of expressing Bachelard's notion of the imaginal as an "audition": "Bachelard conceives of the imagination not as privation but as audition—an acoustics of the *other* than self" (103). See "Sounding the Living Logos: Bachelard and Gadamer" (chapter 12 in this book) for E. Rizo-Patron's development of this key hermeneutic question.

13. These descriptions may well be applied to Merleau-Ponty's ideas of "reversibility" and the "flesh of the world," also considered capable of being expressed only through poetic language and a poetic ontology, such as the one Merleau-Ponty gradually developed during his career and matured most fully in his latest works. The series of parallels with Bachelard's work are striking, indeed. Emmanuel de Saint Aubert's examination of Merleau-Ponty's unpublished notes and manuscripts informs us that Merleau-Ponty's interest in Bachelard's work was first aroused by Bachelard's 1942 publication of *Water and Dreams* (Emmanuel de Saint Aubert, *Du lien des êtres aux elements de l'être: Merleau-Ponty au tournant des années 1945–1951* [Paris; Vrin, 2006], 255) and continued at different periods of his unpublished notes and throughout his writing. The details of this influence and the overlap of Bachelard's and Merleau-Ponty's poetic ontologies are explored in part 3 of my book, *Merleau-Ponty and the Face of the World: Silence, Ethics, Imagination and Poetic Ontology* (Albany: State University of New York Press, 2016).

14. Kristupas Sabolius elaborates extensively on this theme in "Rhythm and Reverie: On the Temporality of Imagination in Bachelard" in the fourth chapter of this book.

15. The bonds between seer and seen "are active in both directions" (PR 185).

16. The important question of "hospitality" in Bachelard's ontology is specifically explored in Préclaire's and Kaplan's chapters in part 4 of this volume.

Part 3

Adventures in Language

Chapter 9

Gaston Bachelard and Henry Corbin: On Adjectival Consciousness

David L. Miller

In a 1986 lecture in Jerusalem, Jacques Derrida addressed the problem of how one can speak philosophically about matters whose nature is not that of a some-*thing*—for example love, meaning, being, spirit, soul, God—without objectivizing them. Derrida was continuing the Heideggerian query concerning whether a non-objectivizing thinking and speaking are possible.[1] The title of Derrida's essay was "Comment ne pas parler [How not to Speak],"[2] and during the course of his argument Derrida petitioned a perspective from Meister Eckhart. The latter, in his twenty-sixth sermon, *Quasi stella matutina*, argued that "soul" is a *bîwort*, a "by"-word, which in Latin would be *adverbum*, an "adverb,"[3] that is, a word placed "by" another word to qualify it.

"By"-Words

On this perspective, and contrary to conventional understanding, the word "soul" is not a noun because it does not name some-*thing*. Rather, it qualifies, modifies, gives quality and value to every-*thing*, as does an adjective or adverb. So, on this view it would be appropriate to say "soul-music" or "soul-food," but inappropriate to say "the care of the soul," as if there were a some-*thing* to take care of. Further, the soulful quality of music or food in, say, New Orleans, is sensed only by and through the body. Used properly as *bîworts*—according to Eckhart—there is no body/soul opposition. It is not that metaphysical discourse *should* be adjectival; it is that it *is* always and already, and only, adjectival—even if it employs nouns. These nouns do not name static physical things, even when they seem to. Rather, they refer to qualities and values. It is not entirely unimaginable that Derrida had in mind, wittingly or unwittingly, Gaston Bachelard, who had indeed argued that the soul of a discourse is embedded in a "by"-word. Bachelard's "by"-word was "adjective," a word that is placed *by* a noun to give it quality, just as an adverb is placed *by* a verb in order to qualify its action.

For example, Gaston Bachelard wrote the following in *The Poetics of Space*: "A gloomy life, or a gloomy person, marks an entire universe with more than just a pervading coloration. Even things become crystallizations of sadness, regret, or nostalgia. And when a philosopher looks to poets . . . for lessons in how to individualize the world, that person soon becomes convinced that the world is not so much a noun as an adjective. If we were to give the imagination its due in the philosophical systems of the universe, we should find, at their very source, an adjective. Indeed, to those who want to find the essence of a world philosophy, one could give the following advice—look for its adjective" (PS 143–44).

Beginning with the publication of *The Psychoanalysis of Fire* in 1938, Bachelard focused on the imagination of matter, the material imagination, especially its fundamental mythic and poetic tropes: earth, air, fire, and water. His perspective was that these words do not name some-thing(s), but that they—if I may put it this way—"ad-ject." They speak of qualities: earthiness, airiness, fieriness, and fluidity. A person does not look at some*thing* when contemplating material imagery; rather, one looks through the image at any- and every-thing, which is thereby given quality and value. Bachelard's observations concerning this are consistent, and they stretch from 1940 to 1960, that is, from his book *The Philosophy of No* through works on each of the mythic and poetic elements, to his late writings on light, fire, and candles. Typical of Bachelard's observations are the following: "Mass [in the physics of post-quantum mechanics] is an adjective" (PN 73). "The qualities of light and air [in Goya's paintings] are *adjectives*, which can help us to know the true *substance* of the countryside" (WD 26). "Each adjective has its privileged noun which material imagination quickly retains. *Coolness* [*fraîcheur*], accordingly, is an attribute of water. Water is, in a sense, embodied coolness. . . . When the substantial root of a poetic quality has been discovered, when the *matter* of the adjective on which material imagination works has really been found, all the well-rooted metaphors develop by themselves" (WD 32). "One fine adjective, clear, well-placed assonant, and voila! substance" (ERW 72).

Thus realizing that in conventional literary theorizing adjectives tend to be "absorbed into nouns," whereupon qualities become objectivized and what is substantive is regarded as concrete substance (ERR 60/83), Bachelard then developed a reverse hermeneutic strategy: namely, to reabsorb nouns into adjectives—often by entertaining clashing qualities[4]—hence reabsorbing nominalism into dynamic imagination. "Once imagination has set into motion an attentive sensibility in us" he writes, "we realize that qualities are not so much states . . . as they are processes of becoming" (ERR 65/89, trans. modified). This implies that adjectives have more a verbal than a nominal force. As Bachelard writes: "*Red* [*rouge*] is closer to *redden* [*rougir*, 'to blush'] than to *redness* [*rougeur*, 'a blush']" (ERR 65/89). So, "true fire is not fire itself. [True fire] is none other than flaming fire, burning fire, fuming fire, ashening fire" (ERR 37/50, trans. modified).

There is an additional issue that Bachelard attributed to an adjectival function: namely, verticality. "Adjectives . . . that convey the power of the imaginary," he wrote in *Air and Dreams*, "live vertically" (AD 104). But it is in his chapter "The Imaginary Fall" that he would learn—from Novalis among other poets—that such verticality initially acquires upward dynamism vis-à-vis a power that weighs down on all things (AD 104–9). A few years later, in *Earth and the Reveries of Will*, he again wrote: "Verticality is so impressionable a human dimension that it . . . permits an image to be elongated, stretching it in two directions at once, both upwards [*vers le haut*] and downwards [*vers le base*]" (ERW 263). Citing Schelling he would add: "Only the vertical axis has an *active* spiritual significance; width [*largeur*] is purely *passive* and material. The meaning of the human body resides more in its height [*hauteur*] than in its breadth [*largeur*]" (ERW 280, emphasis added). Such active dynamism will achieve its most intense focus in *The Flame of a Candle* (a year before his death twenty years later), where Bachelard writes: "An upright form soars up and carries us along in its verticality. . . . To communicate with the verticality of an upright object through imagination is to . . . participate in the hidden fire that dwells in beautiful forms" (FC 39).

Here, in the section on "the verticality of flames," Bachelard again writes in relation to the poetry of Novalis: "The most diverse beings are made substantive by [the verticality of] the flame. Only an adjective is necessary to make them more specific. A cursory reader will perhaps see no more here than stylistic play. But if he participates in the inflammatory intuition of a poetic philosopher, he will understand that the flame is the source for a living creature. Life is a fire. To know its essence one must burn in communion with the poet." It is at this juncture that Bachelard cites Henry Corbin, the historian of religion: "To use an expression of Henry Corbin, we could say that Novalis' formulas . . . raise meditation to incandescence" (FC 45/65).[5] Corbin, for his part, had written earlier that "ideas have a substantial, transcendental, angelic existence, and the relation of terrestrial persons with ideas is ordained according to the height of their world, not according to its breadth."[6] So what is the point about verticality? And what is the connection to Henry Corbin? I will return to the matter of verticality and incandescence in the concluding section of this chapter, but first I want to demonstrate the extent and significance of the connection between Bachelard and Corbin.

Gaston Bachelard and Henry Corbin

The relation between the thought of the poetic philosopher and the historian of religions is revealed in a correspondence between the two men, or at least from a series of letters from the former to the latter.[7] On December 31, 1955, Bachelard addressed the director of the collection *Bibliothèque Iranienne* in writing, not knowing at the time that this "director" was Henry Corbin himself—a lapse that turned out to be a bit awkward, since in the letter Bachelard spoke in glowing terms about Corbin's book *Avicenne et le récit visionnaire* and its author. Bachelard's words were as follows: "Henry Corbin, whose articles at the Eranos conferences I have read with attention, gives to me in this book a proof of a beautiful depth of meditation. . . . I do not wish to put down *Avicenna* . . . [A]ll of its pages captivate me. They make me think and dream."

In August of the same year, four months earlier at the Eranos Conference in Ascona, Switzerland, Corbin had written:

> Just as in the Dialectic of Love, one takes one's departure from sensible beauty in order to be elevated even to a meeting with the unique principle of all beauty and all ideas, so the adepts of hieratic science take for the point of departure precisely these apparent things, and the sympathies as have manifested between them and the invisible powers. Observing that all is in all, they have situated the foundations of the hieratic, being astonished to see and admire in initial realities the ultimate venues of being and in such ultimates also the proximate realities; in the

> sky there exist terrestrial things according to a fortuitous and celestial mode, and on the earth there exist heavenly things in a terrestrial condition. What other reason could one give for the fact of a heliotrope following by its movement the movement of the sun, and the selenotrope the movement of the moon, making a procession in the measure of their ability, with the cosmic flames?[8]

This is striking, because the line about the heliotrope was the very same sentence that Bachelard would cite in *The Flame of a Candle* to be published six years later (FC 60).

The connection between the thought of the two men was confirmed by Stella Corbin in a personal letter to me of October 10, 1983: "When Bachelard wrote *The Flame of a Candle* he had tried to see Henry in order to inquire about Persian poetry, but in those years Henry sought few contacts. So it was I who had taken *Terre céleste* to Bachelard. On that evening he showed me with emotion his copy of *Avicenne et le récit visionnaire*, a copy well used, pages scribbled with notes, phrases underlined."[9] Two letters from Bachelard to Corbin demonstrate the fidelity of the emotion and the connection. On May 13, 1956, he wrote: "Your Avicenna never leaves my table. But with each re-reading, I see in it more complexity. If you have the occasion of passing Place Maubert, knock at my door."[10] And on May 17, five years later, Bachelard wrote to Corbin:

> Dear Monsieur. For a long time I have been wanting to write to you. . . . Your book has such an importance that I would like to study it without ceasing in order to be able to speak to you about it in an appropriate manner. When I spoke to your belle-soeur [sic] of the usefulness that it would have for me to see the Iranian religion of fire, I believed that then I was touching the poetry of fire. . . . But where are the poems of the Persian poets? . . . In this deficit of little works, how important for me was the discovery of your book! It is the *élan* of verticality that I received from each page of *Terre céleste*. If I had known your work twenty years ago, what a stronger tone I would have given to my book *Water and Dreams*? Reading you, I imagine that I yet could have the power to speak of the dynamicity of human verticality.[11]

So it would seem, then, that it is no incidental matter when Bachelard says: "To utilize a formula of Henry Corbin, we could say that Novalis' text tends to carry meditation to incandescence," that is, to carry reflection to shimmering consciousness, radiation, resonance, iridescence (FC 45). Indeed, it was in that very book—the one that never left Bachelard's table and in which he had scribbled—that Corbin had written: "What is certain is that, in Avicennan terms, the contemplative intellect, Absâl, is ordained to the illumination that it receives from the Angel, but this illumination, the irradiation of Forms that it received, is also the very same light of which it is itself made. . . . Thus it is its own light that grows more intense, its own being that is progressively brought to incandescence."[12] And, for Bachelard, this incandescence is a quality of poetic imagery and imagination.

Poetry and Incandescence

Poetry—like adjectives—carries meditation and thought to incandescence. Coincidentally (or perhaps not so coincidentally), the American poet Wallace Stevens also mentions "adjective" in "The Man with the Blue Guitar," a poem that has to do with the verticality of fire, clearly implying an incandescence. Stevens writes as follows:

> The pale intrusions into blue
> Are corrupting pallors . . . ay di mi,
>
> Blue buds or pitchy blooms. Be content—
> Expansion, diffusions—content to be
>
> The unspotted imbecile reverie,
> The heraldic center of the world
>
> Of blue, blue sleek with a hundred chins
> The amorist Adjective aflame.[13]

On June 25, 1953, Stevens wrote to Renato Poggioli, his Italian translator, responding to a question the latter had posed about these lines. Stevens explained: "In this poem the amorist Adjective means blue (the amorist Adjective) as a word metamorphosed into blue as a reality."[14] But four days later, apparently Stevens had a second thought, so he wrote another letter, saying: "The other day I commented on 'amorist Adjective aflame.' Perhaps my explanation was a bit too expansive. The poem in which this appears is a poem that deals with the intensity of the imagination unmodified by contacts with reality, if such a thing is possible." And then comes the surprising sentence: "Intensity becomes something incandescent." Stevens goes on: "I took a look at this poem after I had written to you and thought that the metamorphosis into reality, while a good enough illustration, was misleading. The poem has to do with pure imagination."[15] Here Stevens uses the very same words that Bachelard fastens upon in Corbin, and apparently without knowledge of the work of either, at least as far as I have been able to determine.

Eight years after Stevens' letter, Bachelard would write: "The flame is an inhabited verticality" (FC 40). "Everything vertical in the cosmos is a flame" (FC 43). "The fire flowers [*feu fleurit*] and the flower lights up [*fleur s'illumine*]. These two corollaries could be developed endlessly: color is an epiphany of fire; and the flower is an ontophany of light" (FC 59/85). And, concerning precisely what this color is, Bachelard had concurred in advance with Stevens. The following had been published in 1938, fifteen years before the American poet's letter to his translator: "You may object that Novalis is the poet of 'the little blue flower,' the poet of the forget-me-not tossed as a pledge of imperishable memory over the edge of the precipice in the very shadow of death! But go down into the depths of the unconscious, find there with the poet the primitive dream, and you will clearly see the truth: the little blue flower is red!" (PF 41),[16] that is, the amorist adjective aflame.

Adjectival Consciousness

Adjectives modify, qualify, as in the poetic line: "the red wheelbarrow."[17] Adjectives give quality. They make matter *matter*. One might say that adjectives are not a part of speech, not a special kind of language, but that every language is a special form of adjective. It is a matter of seeing nouns and verbs, things and actions, being and doing, intelligible and sensible, as if valorized or, in the terminology of Bachelard and Corbin, verticalized.

The adjectival strategy is not to attempt to give life substance by imagining it nominally or nominalistically, thereby thinking that one had named some*thing*. Nor is it attempting to give substance life by verbing it, that is, turning it to program, recipe, behavior, activity, and thereby feeling that one is now doing *some*thing. Rather, it is an unveiling of a quality in any noun and in every verb, so that any noun and verb can be an adjective, can ad-ject, by being *carried to incandescence*. The world is an adjective, said Bachelard (PS 143–44).

To be sure, I am not speaking about adjectives. A problem with the talk concerning adjectives is that the word "adjective" is not an adjective . . . unless, of course, it is aflame. Adjectival consciousness supposes that sub-jects and ob-jects are ad-jects when the tra-ject-ory of their "throwing in and under [sub-ject]" and their "throwing out and away [ob-ject]" is qualified and is experienced as a "throwing toward [ad-ject]."

For example, in an image from a dream, the teacher (subject) with a raincoat (object) meditated to incandescence may become "the rain-coated-teacher" or the "teaching-rain-which coats," or "the moistening-of-teachings'-coating," and so on.[18]

Ad-jecting subjects and objects does not happen by an objective "throwing out" of intelligible ideas, nor by a subjective "being thrown down-and-under" by sensible experiences. Rather, it happens by allowing the reverie of what matters to be "thrown towards" *a possibility of deeper signification*—as in Stevens's "unspotted imbecile reverie," the "man with a blue guitar" in the poetry cited above. In Bachelard's words: "poetry is always a vocative [*la poésie est toujours un vocatif*]" (WD 121/164). It is always coming at you: ad-jecting.

In adjectival consciousness grammar is generative, utterance is performative, language is vocative, and speech is (in Heidegger's terms) e-ventful: "speech speaks," not egos.[19] For Bachelard it is an issue of "vocal imagination [*l'imagination parlante*]" (WD 189/253) and "vocal images [*les images parlées*]" (FC 4/5, trans. modified).

The vocative is a fundamental voice that addresses us directly. "Hey you!" Something is linguistically thrown in our direction, and, like an adjective, it may qualify, give quality to, a life. Something of the sort is thrown at the reader by this late poetic fragment by Rainer Maria Rilke:

> As long as you catch what you yourself threw into the air,
> all is mere skill and petty gain;
> only when you unexpectedly become the catcher of the ball
> that the Goddess, your eternal playmate,
> threw toward you, toward the center of your being
> in a precisely calculated curve, in one of those arcs
> reminiscent of God building bridges:
> only then is being able to catch the ball an ability to be
> cherished—

not yours, but a world's. And if you
were to have the strength and courage to return the throw,
nay, even more miraculous, if you had forgotten about
   strength and courage
and had already thrown . . . as the year
throws birds, the migrating flock
that an older warmth flings
across seas to a younger—only
through your daring is your play genuine.
You neither make throwing easier nor harder
for yourself. From your hands issues
the meteor and races towards its place in the heavens.[20]

It is in this meteoric manner that adjectival consciousness functions to carry material imagination to incandescence.

Notes

1. See Stanley R. Hopper, "Introduction," *Interpretation: The Poetry of Meaning,* ed. Stanley R. Hopper and David L. Miller (New York: Harcourt, Brace and World, 1967), ix–xxii.

2. Jacques Derrida, "Comment ne pas parler: Dénégations," *Psyché: Inventions de l'autre* (Paris: Galilée, 1987), 577–78.

3. *Meister Eckhart: A Modern Translation,* trans. Raymond B. Blakney (New York: Harper and Row, 1941), 222–23.

4. Bachelard elaborates further on this point: "In the realm of imagination, there is no value unless there is polyvalence. The ideal image must beguile us through all our senses and must call us into a world *beyond* the sense that is most obviously involved" (ERR 60/82, emphasis added).

5. The word "incandescence" is the same in French as it is in English. This sentence in the original French reads: "Pour employer une formule d'Henry Corbin, nous dirions que les formulas novalisiennes tendent à porter à l'incandescence la meditation."

6. Henry Corbin, "Pour l'anthropologie philosophique: Un traité persan inédit de Suhrawardî d'Alep," *Récherches philosophiques* 2 (1932–33): 393; my translation.

7. This correspondence was kindly made available to me before her death by Stella Corbin, wife of the late Henry Corbin; it is here published in my own translation with the permission of Mme. Corbin, to whom I am most grateful.

8. Henry Corbin, "Sympathie et théopathie chez les 'Fidèles d'Amour' en Islam," *Eranos Jahrbuch* 24 (1955), 199f. Here Corbin is citing Proclus.

9. Stella Corbin, personal letter to the author, October 10, 1983, quoted with her kind permission; my translation.

10. Bachelard, personal letter to Henry Corbin, May 13, 1956, quoted with the permission of Stella Corbin; my translation.

11. This letter from Bachelard to Corbin is published in Christian Jambet, ed., *Henry Corbin* (Paris: Éditions de L'Herne, 1981), 311–12; my translation.

12. Henry Corbin, *Avicenna and the Visionary Recital*, trans. Willard R. Trask (Dallas: Spring Publications, 1980), 238. Compare Henry Corbin, *Alone with the Alone: Creative Imagination the Sūfism of Ibn 'Arabī* (Princeton: Princeton University Press, 1997): "The idea of 'genesis' [in the doctrine of imagination] . . . has nothing to do with a *creation ex nihilo* and is equally far removed from the Neoplatonic idea of emanation; we must think rather of a process of increasing illumination, gradually raising the possibilities eternally latent in the original Divine Being to a state of luminescence" (126).

13. Wallace Stevens, "The Man with the Blue Guitar," *The Collected Poems of Wallace Stevens* (New York: Vintage, 1990), 172. The lines concerning the vertical flame are: "A candle is enough to light the world. / It makes it clear. Even at noon / It glistens in the essential dark. / At night, it lights the fruit and wine, / The book and bread, things as they are, / In a chiaroscuro where / One sits and plays the blue guitar."

14. Wallace Stevens, *Letters of Wallace Stevens*, ed. H. Stevens (New York: Knopf, 1977), 783.

15. Ibid., 785. Stevens is by no means the only poet to utilize the word "incandescence" as a description of poetic utterance. For example, in an essay on history and politics, Paul Valéry described "incandescence" as what Edward S. Casey has since called the "world at a glance" (Casey, *The World at a Glance* [Bloomington: Indiana University Press, 2007]). Valéry's description is as follows: "Physicists tell us that if the eye could survive in an oven fired to the point of incandescence, it would see . . . nothing. Nothing . . . and yet an infinitely potential nothing" (Paul Valéry, *An Anthology* [Princeton: Princeton University Press, 1977], 98). Octavio Paz has also invoked "incandescence" to describe the poetry of such a view—calling to mind Bachelard's notion of "l'intuition de l'instant" in his 1932 book by that title: "Poetry does not give us eternal life, but it causes us to glimpse that which Nietzsche called 'the incomparable vivacity of life.' The poetic experience is an opening up of the wellsprings of being. An instant and never. An instant and forever. . . . Poetry opens up to us the possibility of being . . . in a single instant of incandescence" (Octavio Paz, *The Bow and the Lyre*, trans. Ruth L. C. Simms [Austin: University of Texas Press, 1973], 139). In another work, Paz refers to the poetic "mirror reflections focused in another luminous body" as "not the eternity of religions, but the incandescence of the instant" (Octavio Paz, *Conjunctions and Disjunctions*, trans. Helen R. Lane [New York: Seaver, 1982], 135). Nor is poetry the only art to utilize such description. The painting of Stephen Hannock (b. 1951)

is referred to as "luminism." Hannock has said about his work that it is "about what the paint can do to create the illusion of luminosity," but he might as well have said "incandescence," as anyone knows who has seen his work. See Stephen Hannock, *Luminosity: The Paintings of Stephen Hannock* (San Francisco: Chronicle, 2000), 15; Jason Rosenfeld, Martha Hoppin, and Garrett White, *Stephen Hannock,* foreword by Mark C. Taylor (Blue Ridge Summit: Hudson Hills Press, 2009). The photographic technique of Mike Disfarmer (1884–1959) has been similarly described as "waiting for the moment of clarity, that instant when everyday flesh caught fire, when he could see the weight of blood and bones the spirit carried, and how beautifully, if wearily, they were carried after all" (quoted from Verlyn Klinkenborg's book review, "Far North," of Julia Scully's *Outside Passage: A Memoir of an Alaskan Childhood* [New York: Random House, 1998] in *The New York Times Book Review,* May 10, 1998: 7).

16. Concerning *The Psychoanalysis of Fire,* Bachelard had said to Jean Lacroix: "Tenez, Lacroix, j'ai fait ce qu'on ne devrait jamais faire, un livre autour d'une phrase qui chantait dans ma tête: elle est rouge la petite fleur bleue!" Cited in Gilbert Lascault, "Elle est rouge, la petite fleur bleue," *L'Arc* 42: 32; see also Vincent Therrien, *La révolution de G. Bachelard en critique littéraire* (Paris: Klincksieck, 1970).

17. William Carlos Williams, *Selected Poems* (New York: New Directions, 1969), 30.

18. An adjectival mode of meditative thinking has been adopted psychologically in work with dreams by James Hillman. See James Hillman, "Further Notes on Images," *Spring* (1978): 163–65, 172, and *Dream and the Underworld* (New York: Harper and Row, 1979), 62–63.

19. Martin Heidegger, *Unterwegs zur Sprache* (Pfullingen: Neske, 1975), 12: "Wie west die Sprache als Sprache? Wir antworten: Die Sprache spricht."

20. Quoted in Eugen Fink, "The Oasis of Happiness: Toward an Ontology of Play," trans. Ute Saine and Thomas Saine, *Yale French Studies* 41 (1968): 19–30, quote on 30.

Chapter 10

Bachelard's Logosphere and Derrida's Logocentrism: A Distinction with a *Différance*

Roch C. Smith

For Gaston Bachelard, author of some twelve books on the philosophy of science and another eleven volumes on the imagination, words hold a very special place. But their privileged position rests less on Bachelard's prolific verbal production than on his philosophical outlook. In his books on science, as one might expect, words, with their baggage of imprecision, are suspect, whereas this very ambiguity is seen as a source of their power in his works on the imagination. Yet, the point for Bachelard is not so much that the imagination accords special status to words over quantitative measurement, but rather that words themselves are the primary, often the singular means of imagining. Imagination for Bachelard is nothing if not verbal.

This notion is particularly prevalent in *Water and Dreams*, the first of his books on the four elements to be devoted exclusively to the imagination. After differentiating between the rather static, picturesque, and superficial *formal* imagination and the more dynamic, substantial, and internal *material* imagination in which, as he puts it, "*matter is the unconscious of form*" (WD 50), Bachelard, borrowing and adapting freely from depth psychology, determines that the most profound wellsprings of the imagination are verbal. If, in the realm of the imagination, matter is the unconscious of form, the most direct expression of the material imagination cannot be found in those imaginary works that depend on formal, visual qualities, such as painting. For Bachelard, the material imagination is most accessible through words, particularly through words that are intended to be read imaginatively. Not surprisingly, literature, and especially poetry, is the privileged medium of the material imagination: "In the final analysis the true domain for studying the imagination is not painting; it is literature, the word, the sentence" (WD 188). Initially, at least, Bachelard views literature as a means to the study of the imagination rather than as the object to be studied.

Six years later, in *Earth and Reveries of Will*, his emphasis has shifted slightly. Literature is still spoken of as a means, but this time the end is not only imagination generally, but specific art forms. Bachelard now sees the literary imagination as the key to all art, including, particularly, the plastic arts: "One has only to *write* one's painting, *write* one's sculpture. . . . Through *literary imagination* all the arts are ours" (ERW 72). Such a view may seem extreme, if not totally subversive, to a painter or sculptor, yet one finds the engraver Albert Flocon, in an exchange during the 1970 Cerisy colloquium on Bachelard, coming very close to agreeing: "Today's painters are quite convinced that what they do goes beyond words. For my part, after a relatively long experience that went from the abstract to the concrete, I think that, in a way, discourse can quite readily account for the image, although never fully so."[1]

Words, especially the words of imaginative literature, occupy a special place in the imagination because they are found at the imagination's source, in reverie. That is why Bachelard finds it possible, indeed necessary, to write *The Poetics of Reverie*. As he explains, "This reverie is written, or, at least, promises to be written" (PR 6). For Bachelard, there simply cannot be a reverie without words. Borrowing a phrase from the poet Henri Bosco, Bachelard explains what he calls "one of the axioms of the Poetics of reverie . . . 'All the being of the world, if it dreams, dreams that it is speaking' " (PR 187). Reverie precedes culturally acquired knowledge. Unfettered by rational constraints, reverie is the primitive subjective state in which words link the dreamer and the world. For Bachelard, all imaginative art stems from this verbal origin, and all art is therefore approachable through words.

Perhaps the most striking example of Bachelard's verbal primacy can be found in his 1960 essay on Chagall's Bible. For, nowhere else in his work do we encounter a more sustained demonstration of his view that visual arts must be verbalized. Chagall has transformed the written text of the Bible into a picture book, but Bachelard insists that the power of these paintings derives from their ability to become words. Bachelard delights in Chagall's work precisely because the cycle is complete: words become paintings that again are transformed into words. The role of Chagall's painting, in Bachelard's view, is to give the fullest quotient of reverie to words. Thus, it is not just that "Chagall reads the Bible, and . . . beneath his brush, beneath his pencil, the Bible becomes . . . a picture book, a book of portraits" (RD 7). For, Chagall's paintings also speak: "The colors become words. Anyone who loves painting knows full well that painting is a source of words, a fount of poems" (RD 8).

As an example, Bachelard points to Chagall's depiction of Adam and Eve and wonders whether the painter may "with his gaze stroke the lovely fruits of this earth without detaching them from the tree" (RD 9). From Bachelard's point of view this painting suggests a delegated temptation. Inspired by the painting, one can, if we are to believe Bachelard, hear Adam's words: "What is Adam saying to Chagall's Eve but: 'Come, my lovely one, know temptation, but only temptation. Stroke, but do not pluck,' or again, even more subtly: 'Do not pluck, but stroke' " (RD 9).

Yet it is not a question of Bachelard's particular verbal reverie being the only appropriate one, but of the inevitability of verbal reverie itself: "Anyone who dreams before this picture will find the words come to his lips. We can *see* the temptation, so we voice it, each in our own way" (RD 9/17, trans. modified). Chagall's paintings evoke reverie, and, as always, reverie for Bachelard is inescapably verbal: "It is for us, the dreamers, to *make these pictures 'speak'* " (RD 12, emphasis added). It can hardly be otherwise for a philosopher who regularly associates the visual with the inauthentic, superficial, formal imagination and who finds substance and authenticity only in the material imagination.

A decade before his introduction to Chagall's Bible, Bachelard had perceived in the global communication of radio certain implications for the imagination. His essay "Reverie and Radio" can serve as a paradigm of verbal primacy in Bachelard, for here the word truly has acquired cosmic proportions. Faced with the realization that, thanks to radio, "the whole planet is talking" (RD 167/216, trans. modified), Bachelard offers the notion of a sphere of words, akin to the biosphere, which he labels the "logosphere."[2] Radio goes beyond mere communication to fulfill on a daily, global scale the verbal reverie that, in Bachelard's view, is peculiarly human. Unlike the biosphere which encompasses all living things, the logosphere is strictly limited to the human species and, more particularly, to the expression of the human psyche: "We all of us speak in the logosphere. We are citizens of the logosphere" (RD 167). According to Bachelard, radio creates a logosphere that reinvents humankind as the voice of the world by expressing unconscious reverie: "It is through the unconscious, then, that this solidarity among the citizens of the logosphere . . . can find its realization" (RD 168). The logosphere is the result of a technical extension of the poet's voice which, as Bachelard suggests in *The Poetics of Reverie*, is particularly attuned to universal human reverie: "The voice of the poet is a voice of the world" (PR 188). Radio brings into reality the voice of the world; it makes universal the verbal reverie in which we all live. It is this materialization that Bachelard calls the logosphere.

Some sixteen years after Bachelard's essay, Jacques Derrida, in *Of Grammatology*, introduces the strikingly similar expression of "logocentrism." Like the term "logosphere," logocentrism refers to the universal privilege accorded to the spoken word in the contemporary world. Derrida defines it as "the metaphysics of *phonetic* writing . . . which was fundamentally . . . nothing but the most original and powerful ethnocentrism, in the process of imposing itself upon the world."[3] Both Bachelard's and Derrida's concepts point to what might be called the matrix of words within which modern humans live, but a crucial difference is that Bachelard's term is related to reverie, while Derrida is speaking of the universality of traditional Western philosophical discourse. Bachelard's term gives a *psychological* interpretation to a phenomenon of technology. Derrida seeks to expose the logocentric *structure* of philosophy. Yet, in this sense, both logosphere and logocentrism refer to hidden realities.

But whereas Bachelard sees the logosphere as a positive manifestation of humankind's universal verbal reverie through early twentieth-century technology, Derrida sees in logocentrism a contemporary philosophical impasse that demands escape from what might be called the established "word order." Bachelard celebrates the logosphere as a realization of his own intuitions; Derrida seeks to disclose that the end of the long logocentric tradition is in view. In fact, in a most fundamental way, Derrida's entire work centers on the revelation of logocentrism and the means of transcending it.

Derrida sees the first signs of a break when the written word frees itself from the logocentric tradition, when "the science of writing—*grammatology*—shows signs of liberation all over the world" (G 4). Grammatology is, in fact, an attack on the very heart of logocentrism, although by no means the only one. In *Margins of Philosophy*, for example, Derrida continues to probe for an exterior vantage point that will permit him to examine philosophy without being caught in the logocentric web when he asks: "Can one, strictly speaking, determine a non-philosophical place, a place of exteriority or alterity from which one might still treat *of philosophy*?"[4] And in a well-known essay, first published in 1968 and reproduced in 1972 as the first chapter of *Margins*, Derrida offers further examples of what it means to escape from logocentrism by returning to the notion of *différance,* which he had introduced in *Of Grammatology.* Continuing to insist on the centrality of *writing* in language, he calls attention to the "neographism" (M 3) of this French expression (no doubt Derrida, unlike Bachelard, would not be caught trafficking in neo*logisms*) in which the penultimate vowel *e* of *différence* has been replaced by the *a* in *différance.*

Essentially, the term brings together the notion of time and space, the idea of temporizing or deferring and separating or differing: "*Différance* as temporization, *différance* as spacing" (M 9). The notion allows Derrida to take his cue, albeit critically, from Saussurian semiology in order to attack the philosophical assumptions of logocentrism: "Whence . . . the transformation of general semiology into grammatology, this latter executing a critical labor on everything within semiology, including the central concept of the sign, that maintained metaphysical presuppositions incompatible with the motif of *différance*" (M 15). *Différance* may thus be thought of as a cultural motif that summarizes the waning of logocentric limits. In this respect it is the positive side of the logocentric coin. It leads to a deconstruction of logocentric assumptions.

Such a deconstruction is precisely the object of Derrida's 1978 book, *The Truth in Painting.* As with Bachelard, the visual arts acquire significance through a transformation into the realm of the verbal, although with Derrida the semiotic analysis of the painting's code as well as of commentary on the painting is infinitely more idiosyncratic than Bachelard's verbal reverie.

Derrida's point of departure, in fact, is not a painting but the following statement by Cézanne, in a letter to Émile Bernard: " 'I owe you the truth in painting and I will tell it to you.' "[5] In his introductory analysis Derrida reveals the ambiguity of this statement whose meaning may range from the direct *presentation* of truth in painting, the faithful *representation* of truth in painting, truth in *painting* as opposed to some other medium, and truth *about* painting. Cézanne's key statement opens the way for Derrida's four-stage examination of painting in which the common denominator is the line and the inevitable limit or margin that it suggests: "The common feature [*trait*] of these four times is perhaps the trait. . . . Discourses on painting are perhaps destined to reproduce the limit which constitutes them, whatever they do and whatever they say: there is for them an inside and an outside of the work as soon as there is work" (TP 11). We may recognize here the limits of logocentrism and, as usual, Derrida's purpose is to explore such limits in order to probe for a breach: "One space remains to be broached in order to give place to the truth in painting. Neither inside nor outside, it spaces itself without letting itself be framed but it does not stand outside the frame" (TP 11–12). As an example of this kind of *différance* in painting, I should like to look at Derrida's last chapter, entitled "Restitutions of the truth in pointing [*pointure*]," wherein the three earlier directions of the book come together and in which he concentrates on a particular painting by Van Gogh entitled *Old Shoes*.

The interesting point for Derrida is that this painting was the object of an analysis by Heidegger, with which the historian Meyer Schapiro took issue.[6] Heidegger, Derrida recalls, had sought to identify the shoes as those of a peasant man or woman. But according to Schapiro, Heidegger errs in attributing the shoes to peasantry: "Heidegger gets both the painting and the shoes wrong. By attributing them to some peasant man or woman, he remains in error . . . in imaginary projection, the very thing against which he claimed to put us on our guard" (TP 275). As presented by Derrida, Schapiro thus stands for the idea that truth in painting should be representational. In its rejection of imaginative projection, this position is exactly the opposite of that of Bachelard's verbal reverie. As Derrida himself makes clear, "Schapiro's attribution remains in the aesthetics of representation, and even of the most empiricist kind" (TP 318).

Heidegger's position, on the other hand, turns out to be much closer to Bachelard's. For Heidegger, as Derrida explains, the painting becomes words; it speaks: "It all looks, in the end, as though Heidegger had indeed not spoken of the picture. But far from evading it, he would, in this hypothesis, not have spoken *of* it in order to let *it* speak *itself*. Not made to speak but allowed speak. (Once they are painted,) these shoes talk, this thing produced by and detached from its subject begins to talk (about it), that's what Heidegger says a little later" (TP 323).

Yet Derrida is no less critical of Heidegger's search for revealed truth in Van Gogh's painting: "But in his case, by saying '*Bauernschuhe*' without asking himself any questions about this, Heidegger falls short of his discourse on the truth in painting, and is even more naïve than Schapiro. . . . The fact is that stepping backwards from a truth of adequation toward a truth of unveiling, whatever its necessity and its 'critical' force, can just as easily leave one practically disarmed when faced with the ingenuous, the precritical, and the dogmatic" (TP 318/363, trans. modified). Derrida rejects the notion that truth in painting can be reduced, either through representation (Schapiro) or revelation (Heidegger) to the signifier of a preexisting signified, as the logocentric tradition would demand.

As far as Derrida is concerned, Schapiro's attempt to rectify Heidegger's thought and Heidegger's particular interpretation of Van Gogh's painting *impose* an ideological order, an "ideological arraignment" (TP 325) of the kind he had denounced a decade earlier when writing of logocentrism. Schapiro's essay is viewed as an attempt to police Heidegger's critical discourse, which, in turn, attempts to police art itself: "Everything comes down to one of those reading exercises with a magnifying glass which calmly claim to lay down the law, in police fashion indeed" (TP 326).

Derrida seeks to escape from this logocentric order by searching for truth in the area that encompasses both the work and its margin, which, in the case of painting, Derrida identifies as the "*parergon*," and which he associates with Van Gogh's shoelace: "All the more so in that the *parergon* has here perhaps the form of this lace that attaches the inside to the outside, so that the lace (inside-outside), half undone *in* the picture, also figures the relationship of the picture with its outside" (TP 331). Just as the reality of global radio had served as a paradigm of Bachelard's verbal reverie, Van Gogh's painting, with its shoelaces weaving in and out, serves as a paradigm of Derrida's search for "truth in painting" and, in this chapter, "in pointing." In the spirit of *différance* Derrida defers a logocentric rush to understanding by playing on the similarities and differences between the French words *peinture* (painting) and *pointure* (stitching; shoe size). The *parergon*, embodied here by Van Gogh's painting, is Derrida's tentative response to the logocentric imposition of order. Because it transcends limits without cutting itself off from the work, because it avoids seeing difference as opposition, it is a form of *différance*:

> And then these laces, precisely, these loosened bonds do not seem to me to participate in a logic of the cut, but rather in the logic of stricture, in the interlacing of *difference* of (or as) stricture. . . . The logic of detachment as cut leads to opposition, it is a logic or even a dialectic of opposition. I have shown elsewhere that its effect is to sublate difference. Hence to suture. The logic of detachment as stricture is *entirely other*. Deferring: it never sutures. Here it allows us to take account of this fact: that these shoes are neither tied nor untied, neither filled nor empty. (TP 340/388–89, trans. modified)

In semiotic terms the truth in painting is at once in the signifier and the signified. On a more concrete level it may be sought partly within the frame or partly without, but it is never to be found exclusively in one domain or the other: "What pertinence is then left to the classical questions of identification, description, and attribution? What sense is there in knowing just whom or just what we are speaking of as we adjust? And especially in knowing if it happens inside the painting or outside the frame? It is naïve to ignore the appropriateness of these questions. It is no less so to confine oneself to them" (TP 344/393, trans. modified). Derrida demonstrates that Schapiro's and Heidegger's essays on Van Gogh's painting are dogmatic. This is because, despite different approaches, each seeks a form of referential truth in painting, a *literal* truth that can be *fixed* in words. In Derrida's estimation such a discourse is inadequate as an approach to truth in painting because of its presumptive certitude.

At this point Derrida may seem about as far from Bachelard as can be imagined. Bachelard revels in words; Derrida rejects logocentrism. Bachelard emphasizes verbal reverie; Derrida condemns naïve approaches to art. Yet, despite these apparent differences, they share the goal of avoiding dogmatism, of going beyond assumed limits, of expanding possibilities. This is essentially the meaning of *différance* for Derrida: "*Différance* is not only irreducible to any ontological or theological—ontotheological—reappropriation, but as the very opening of the space in which ontotheology—philosophy—produces its system and its history, it includes ontotheology, inscribing it and exceeding it without return" (M 6). For Derrida, the margin of any work is, in fact, not a limit but a potential extension of the work: "the margin is no longer a secondary virginity but an inexhaustible reserve, the stereographic activity of an entirely other ear" (M xxiii). By listening with this "other ear" when he examines the question of truth in painting, Derrida sees Van Gogh's work both as a particular painting—the *Old Shoes*—and as a statement about art that goes beyond the actuality of the work.

Throughout much of his work on science Bachelard repeatedly affirms the importance of transcending conventionally framed "immediate reality" in contemporary physics and chemistry. For example, as he reminds us in *The New Scientific Spirit* (1934), "Every new truth comes into being in spite of the evidence; every new experience is acquired in spite of immediate experience" (NSS 7). A few years later, in *Formation of the Scientific Mind* (1938), the appeal of what is immediately available will be labeled an "epistemological obstacle" (FSM 24–32), a notion that, like Derrida's logocentrism, summarizes the essential error to be avoided when searching for truth. Such an obstacle may take many forms, according to Bachelard, but in all cases it prevents the renewal of knowledge by insisting on facile continuity and unity. In Bachelard's view, science works by going beyond the margins of such assumed unity, much in the way Derrida will later describe *différance*. As Bachelard affirms: "Contrary to this however, scientific progress is at its clearest when it gives up philosophical factors of easy unification such as the creator's unity of action, nature's unity of plan, or logical unity" (FSM 26). How akin to Bachelard is the question Derrida poses in his introduction to *Margins of Philosophy* where he asks: "Can one treat of philosophy itself . . . without already allowing the ungraspable and imperial totality of an order to be imposed through this attempt at unity and uniqueness? If there are *margins,* is there still *one* philosophy, *the* philosophy?" (M xvi, trans. modified).

Since Bachelard, in the early stages of his work on the imagination, insists that "the axes of poetry and of science are inversely related to one another at the outset" (PF 2/10, trans. modified), his notion of a universal verbal reverie culminating in a logosphere may at first be seen as an egregious example of the logocentrism condemned by Derrida. Yet, the epistemology of science informs Bachelard's examination of the imagination in very subtle ways. In his books on the elemental imagination Bachelard applies a fundamental lesson learned from contemporary science when he insists on the imagination's power to create an existence that transcends initial or conventional impressions of reality. In *Earth and Reveries of Will,* for example he speaks of this power as a "sur-existentialism [that] . . . positions being in its reaction against such conventional givens (*le donné*), both external and internal" (ERW 92–93/121–22, trans. modified). Such a "being" would appear to have more to do with Derrida's notion of *différance* than with logocentric limits. In fact, some twenty years before Derrida's commentary on truth in painting, Bachelard himself sees in Van Gogh a particular example of the imagination's power to transcend margins when house and nest seem to be associated in the painter's reverie: "For the simplest image is doubled; it is itself and something else than itself. Van Gogh's thatched cottages are overladen with thatch. Thick, coarsely plaited straw emphasizes the will to provide shelter by extending well beyond the walls" (PS 98). As will be the case with Derrida, Bachelard sees a double register in Van Gogh's apparently simple painting: "For a painter, it is probably *twice* as interesting if, while painting a nest, he dreams of a cottage and, while painting a cottage, he dreams of a nest. It is as though one dreamed twice, in two registers, when one dreams of an image cluster such as this" (PS 98).

If we return to Bachelard's statement on the axes of poetry and science, we note that he said they were *initially* contrary to one another (*d'abord inverses*). What is to be avoided—and here I think Derrida and Bachelard converge—is the naïve application of rational approaches to art. Thoroughly familiar with contemporary scientific revolutions, Bachelard knows very well that science itself has discarded unified linear thinking in its own practice, as the subject of its inquiry has become increasingly ephemeral and indeterminable. The epistemological challenge in attempting to understand any form of art, to verbalize the work, as Bachelard would have us do, is to make sure one's approach does not destroy the work by insisting on a conceptual, linear, criticism: "In this domain, everything takes place simply and delicately. The soul is so sensitive to these simple images that it hears all the resonances in a harmonic reading. Reading on the conceptual level, on the other hand, would be insipid and cold; it would be purely linear" (PS 99).[7]

While his style and the sources of his thought are vastly different, Derrida draws the same fundamental conclusion when he seeks to explode the constraints of traditional modes of thought and expression. The explosion remains verbal; one does not escape from the logosphere any more than from the biosphere without encountering the void. But within the verbal milieu in which our minds operate, the work of both authors suggests that we must not be bound by the centripetal forces of traditionally rationalistic methodologies and established realities. Imagination, even in its most verbal form, demands escape from logocentrism. On this *différance* Bachelard and Derrida are both in agreement despite their differences.

Notes

1. Maurice de Gandillac, Henri Gouhier, and René Poirier, eds., *Bachelard: Colloque de Cerisy* (Paris: Union Générale d'Éditions, 1974), 284; my translation: "Les peintres d'aujourd'hui sont très convaincus que ce qu'ils font échappe aux mots. Personnellement, après une experience relativement longue, qui est allée de l'abstrait au concret, je crois que le discours, d'une certaine manière, peut très bien render compte aussi de l'image, encore qu'elle ne soit jamais épuisée par lui."

2. Writing in 1951, Bachelard could not have foreseen the ubiquity of planetary "speech" made possible by the internet. But such phenomena as the World Wide Web simply enrich his original observation that we now all live in a logosphere.

3. Jacques Derrida, *Of Grammatology*, trans. Gayatri Chakravorty Spivak (1967; Baltimore: Johns Hopkins University Press, 1974), 3 (emphasis added); hereafter cited as G.

4. Jacques Derrida, *Margins of Philosophy*, trans. Alan Bass (1972; Chicago: University of Chicago Press, 1982), xii; hereafter cited as M.

5. Jacques Derrida, *The Truth in Painting*, trans. Geoff Bennington and Ian McLeod (1978; Chicago: University of Chicago Press, 1987), 2, 255; hereafter cited as TP.

6. See Martin Heidegger, "The Origin of the Work of Art," in *Basic Writings*, ed. David Farrell Krell (New York: Harper & Row, 1977), 143–87. See also Meyer Schapiro, "The Still Life as a Personal Object: A Note on Heidegger and Van Gogh," in *The Reach of Mind: Essays in Memory of Kurt Goldstein*, ed. Marianne L. Simmel (New York: Springer, 1968), 203–9.

7. Louis Marin has attempted to establish parallels between verbal and iconic techniques of communication. See his "Toward a Theory of Reading in the Visual Arts: Poussin's *The Arcadian Shepherds,*" in *The Reader in the Text: Essays on Audience and Interpretation*, ed. Susan R. Suleiman and Inge Grossman (Princeton: Princeton University Press, 1980), 293–324, and his "On Reading Pictures: Poussin's Letter on *Manna,*" *Comparative Criticism* 4 (1982): 3–18. Such "readings" of visual art rely on the identification of structures drawn from language but common to each medium. Bachelard, on the other hand, clearly gives a privileged status to words themselves, that is, to semantic rather than semiotic elements, as the necessary means of imagining. As I have argued elsewhere, however, Bachelard's determination to avoid technical, "linear" readings does not preclude or invalidate more conceptual methods, provided these are attempted separately and are not the initial means of approaching the work. See my essay "Gaston Bachelard and Critical Discourse: The Philosopher of Science as Reader," *Stanford French Review* 5 (1981): 217–28, and my revised and updated *Gaston Bachelard, Philosopher of Science and Imagination* (Albany: SUNY Press, 2016), 134–36.

Chapter 11

The Heat of Language: Bachelard on Idea and Image

Jason M. Wirth

> Image—not allegory, not symbol of something other than itself: symbol of itself.
>
> —Novalis[1]

In the "Transcendental Analytic" of his imposing First Critique (1781), Kant denigrates examples as the "*Gängelwagen* of judgment" (A134/B173–74), the infantile go-kart of thinking that clings to images because it does not possess the wherewithal to proceed correctly on its own. Not only do examples usually fail to meet all of the conditions of the rule by which we would understand something; reliance upon examples also threatens to become an end in itself, "weakening" the intellect as it retains the examples while failing to learn the general principles. Images of a principle, therefore, are only for those who "lack judgment," which, Kant informs us in a footnote, is a symptom of stupidity or thick-headedness (*Dummheit*), an "irremediable defect." Indeed, one might say, not only is the image of a principle not the rule that defines the principle, but even more straightforwardly, *images are not ideas*, even when they are used to illustrate or exemplify ideas. Images have their own life within their own domain.

Kant, of course, was not the first or last to struggle with the chasm between image and idea.[2] Gaston Bachelard, too little read in recent years, made a profound contribution to the problem of thinking in and between this chasm. While it is obvious, for example, that Bachelard, beginning with his 1938 work *The Psychoanalysis of Fire*, radically shifted his attention from an occupation with natural science to a multipronged study of the poetic imagination, *the manner of this transition* between the two is less obvious. Bachelard's philosophy of science, furthermore, was no naïve encomium to representational thinking, and it insisted on the critical importance of the *rupture épistémologique*. Nonetheless, its domain was that of the *intellect or mind* and its conceptual arsenal. The poetic imagination, on the other hand, was in some very real sense the *miracle of images within the domain of the soul*. What a staggering thought, especially from a thinker who never abandoned his Promethean quest for scientific progress! How could a scientist ever speak of the soul, and even if he or she could, what could it possibly mean that the soul, already an enigmatic word, marks the prodigious miracle of the imagination's production of images? Is this not the domain of ideas on holiday and as such a renunciation of science's hard-won victory over fanaticism, superstition, and what both Kant and the post-Kantians derided as *Schwärmerei*?

The nub of such fears, in Bachelard's view, stems from an inadequate understanding of the discordant complexity of the ψυχή. The contemporary manner of speaking of the "psyche," especially in its scientific sense (psychology, psychoanalysis), conflates its antithetical dimensions, reducing ψυχή to the cerebrations of something like Aristotle's νοῦς, with some added complexes tossed in for good measure. In Bachelard's own repurposing of Carl Jung's adaptation of an ancient Latin distinction, the *anima* (the soul, the life principle, the "feminine") has been subjugated by the *animus* (the mind, the "masculine"). In retrieving the *anima*, Bachelard did not reverse the lopsided tendency of contemporary thinking with an equally lopsided position. In attempting to think the *anima*, it cannot be altogether isolated from the *animus* (despite the fact that it is its polar opposite) and vice versa. "The mystery of poetry is androgynous" (RD 174).[3] At stake are the distinctive trajectories within thinking, the *anima* and the *animus*, imagination and conceptualization, as well as the fullness of a thinking that holds together within itself these conflicting operations. Although they are irreconcilable, *anima* and *animus* name two aspects of a unitary process.

How then do idea and image, science and poetic imagination, even Nature and Art, belong together, despite their obvious and insuperable opposition? This is the question that guides the following four meditations on Bachelard and the problem of the imagination. In light of this question, I will bring Bachelard into dialogue with F. W. J. Schelling, Milan Kundera, and Jean-Luc Nancy.

Ideas and Image

In the beautiful introductory essay that frames his final and unfinished work on the poetic imagination, *Fragments of a Poetics of Fire*, Bachelard offers a formulation of the rift between idea and image in general as well as in the development of his own thinking:

> The invention of an idea and the imagination of an image are very different psychological exploits. Ideas are invented only as correctives to the past. Through repeated rectifications of this kind one may hope to disengage an idea that is valid. There is no original truth, only original error. Scientific ideas have a long history of error. The poetic imagination for its part has no history at all. It admits of no past preparation. The poetic image is truly the work of a spoken instant. (FPF 7)

Ideas subject themselves, via experimentation and reflection, to continuous refinement and in so doing develop a history, albeit a history characterized by disconfirmation and error. Concepts demand memory as well as the capacity to reconfigure, in light of error, what we remember. Error "by its very nature cannot be eliminated."[4] One might say that the life of a good idea is, echoing the late Nietzsche, always the ongoing history of an error. But these labors in which thinking continuously sobers itself and refines its arsenal move in the opposite direction of the profligate imagination. "An *idea*, in short, cannot be *imagined*. In fact, those who labor in the field of ideas are obliged to hunt images down" (FPF 7). In Kantian thick-headedness (or in flights of Kantian genius) we may try to imagine what we are incapable of understanding, but confusing the fruits of the imagination with the formal elements of thinking at best confuses the imagination with inventiveness and other kinds of creativity that more properly belong to the realm of ideas.[5]

When Bachelard, a teacher and researcher specializing in the philosophy of science, sought to explain the poetic image, however, something very curious happened. In attempting to explain the image that is "the product of a spoken instant" (FPF 7) through an idea, that is, in attempting to discern, even as the history of an error, the principle of the image, this particular *explanans* found itself fiercely contested by its *explanandum*. "I thought I might study images as I was accustomed to studying scientific ideas, as objectively as possible. I did not sense the paradox in studying the imagination 'objectively' though it was capable of bearing the unexpected even into language. I believed that through the sheer accumulation of examples I should come to discover rules" (FPF 3).

Instead of the rules that govern the consistent deployment of a hypothetical idea, he discovered *l'âme*, the soul, and this new surprise—one might even say, a surprising kind of surprise (he had not expected the unexpected to be unexpected in this way)—bifurcated Bachelard's thinking, prompting him to "lead two lives" (FPF 9). Is there a method for the imagination? The assumptions implicit in this question confuse the imagination with a scientific phenomenon and conflate the *anima* with the *animus*. The encounter with the poetic image demands not that one philosophize, at least in the sense of relying on universalizable abstractions, but that one "dephilosophize" oneself (PS 236/211). "Concepts and images develop on two divergent planes of the spiritual life" and the attempt to make them "cooperate" will produce "nothing but disappointments" (PR 52). Indeed, "images and concepts take form at those two opposite poles of psychic activity which are imagination and reason. Between them there is a polarity of exclusion at work. They have nothing in common with the poles of magnetism. Here, the opposite poles do not attract; they repel" (PR 53). However, it is important also to see that, although image and idea oppose each other, Bachelard always speaks of a unitary ψυχή and "spiritual life," however at odds with itself that it may be.[6] This is, so to speak, the unity (or non-duality) of an opposition.

One might say that something like surprise (*étonnement*), the sudden or instantaneous emergence of the unexpected, the unforeseeable, or, to use Schelling's precious term, the unprethinkable (*das Unvordenkliche*), paradoxically demonstrates the connection between science and poetry in their opposition. In the history of an error that marks the progress of a good idea, surprise is occasioned by the sudden appearance of the new, which produces an epistemological rupture. As Mary McAllester Jones articulates it: "If we are surprised, then we were in error. Moreover, surprise is an indicator of newness, of the progress of scientific knowledge" (Redemptive Instant, 125). Science is a discontinuous progression through disconfirmation (the surprise discovery, the unanticipated experimental result, the unexpectedly successful new hypothesis, and so on), but its success also has to do with the selectivity of the idea, that is, the idea's capacity not to speak to everything, but to isolate some aspect of the whole. In a sense, one might say that the idea is a diminution, the reduction of the whole to particular aspects. Focus winnows the large into the matter at hand. Samuel Taylor

Coleridge, himself both a master of the image and the concept (and deeply sympathetic to both Kant's and Schelling's respective experiments in thinking in this regard), made this point precisely in his unfinished work, *Logic*. The concept is not originary but depends on the double movement of focus:

> There are few who cannot recollect or place themselves in that state of mind in which their eye has rested either on a cloudless sky or the general aspect of the starry heavens or on a wide common bounded only by the horizon without consciously attending to any particular object or portion of the scene. There will be many too, I doubt not, [not] unwilling to confess that they have been sometimes in that state of mind which they could perhaps describe by no other term than that of thinking, and yet if questioned of what they were thinking about must answer nothing.[7]

In what action does the unthinkably large give rise to a thought? Coleridge continues: "We cannot distinguish or set apart one thing from another of the same kind without some degree of conscious attention to that from which we separate as well as to the thing so separated." Coleridge named the former "clusion" (that from which a distinction is made) and the latter "seclusion" (LO 54). The discursive idea sequesters and secludes.

For Bachelard, the progress of such seclusions is an unfinishable task—surprise by its very nature is the impossibility of achieving closure with any of our ideas for there is no particular time in which we can expect the unexpected to show itself. But there is a price for the history of an idea, for the wake of its progress by disconfirmation: the idea requires seclusion and concentration at the heart of the possibility of analysis. In a sense, one might say that in order to get more (to progress scientifically, to have a productive history of an error), one must settle for less (the idea's concentration of Nature into analyzable aspects of Nature). Scientific theories, when successful, are exclusionary, eliminating contesting accounts.

In the other part of his two lives, Bachelard discovered that the imagination moves in the opposite direction. As Eileen Rizo-Patron eloquently phrases it, "While Bachelard's writings on scientific epistemology . . . would continue into the 1950s under the Promethean sign of 'progress,' his elemental hermeneutics seemed to follow the opposite path of 'regress'—what alchemists before him had symbolically termed a *regressus ad uterum*."[8] It is critical to point out immediately that the *regressus ad uterum* has nothing to do with the psychoanalyst's verdict that our images are a sign of a regressive urge to return to our mothers. "How can such distant impulsions coming from an attachment to the mother be so constructive in the poetic language?" (PR 46). One might even say: what alchemists had *imagined* as a *return to the womb* is nothing less than to attempt *to imagine the imagination as such*. Since I do not want to jump the gun, I will hold this key thesis in reserve, and return to it explicitly later in the essay. For now, we can see that the imagination, the instantaneous appearance of the image, reverses the direction of the discursive idea (it abandons the shifting focus that makes possible the history entailed in progress). It does so by contesting the idea: the discursive idea is the ongoing attempt to determine something in particular, while the image breaks with the history of meaning. "Poetry opens up the meanings of words, suffusing them in an atmosphere of imagery" (ERW 5). Or in *The Poetics of Space*: "Language bears in itself the dialectic of open and closed. By meaning it closes, by poetic expression it opens up" (PS 222). The idea secludes, while the image expands. "The image cannot provide matter for a concept. By giving stability to the image, the concept would stifle its life" (PR 52). One might say that with the imagination, if we settle for less (abandon the idea), we get more (an expansion of our being). When we stop going forward and in turn go backward, we know less, but we can welcome more. Images "must be received in a sort of transcendental acceptance of gifts" (PR 65). We return to the source in the immense productivity of its surprises.

What is this return to the womb? How is it not only the discordant partner of the idea, but also an *image of the image* as such? How does one think the play between "broad daylight" and the "nocturnal side of the soul" (PR 53)? In the remaining sections, I will concentrate chiefly on the two late masterpieces *The Poetics of Space* and *The Poetics of Reverie*, although I will make brief use of some of Bachelard's other works on the poetic imagination (1938–1961).

As we return to *l'âme*, which is clearly not a scientific idea nor is it, strictly speaking, an image (for what image is here imagined?), we should clear the table. The womb, the source, the dark night of the soul—these might be images of the soul, but the soul itself is not its images. Bachelard is not speaking about a thing that can be conceptually analyzed, nor is the soul the mere fruit of a reverie. How to think the *anima*? Despite Bachelard's sympathy for Jung, it is not an archetype, at least in the sense that the soul does not really explain anything. If it is archetypal, then we must say that archetypes are not the unconscious rules that govern consciousness (as if they were a psychoanalytic variation of the Kantian schematism). The soul is archetypal only in the sense that it is elemental. Its traces—images—are themselves inexplicable. I also think that it is not wise to follow James S. Hans when he uses Derrida to accuse Bachelard of trucking in a metaphysics of presence. "Bachelard is really only chasing the endless series of traces in the linguistic system, traces not at all based on presence or immediacy but on absence and perpetual deferral. For Derrida, then, Bachelard's work is but one more metaphysical mystification of presence in a long series of mystifications dating back to Plato."[9] The soul's images are not only unexpected (radically futural in their disruption of the present), but, as we shall see, the soul is not the transcendent subject of images. *There really is no such thing as the soul.* It does not present itself to be properly conceived. Not only does it not present itself, but it also undermines the project of representation as such. Perhaps one could say that the term "soul" nominally names (thinks without identifying) the enigmatic temporality of the imagination. It names something like the ultimate clusion from which the imagination draws ever anew.

Eisemplasy

Bachelard approvingly quotes Pierre-Jean Jouve's claim that "[p]oetry is a soul inaugurating a form" (PS xviii) and refers significantly in his works to *l'imagination productrice.* In *The Poetics of Reverie,* he claims, presumably distancing himself from the early Merleau-Ponty, that even a phenomenology of perception must yield to a phenomenology of the productive imagination" (PR 14). The latter is a clear allusion to Kant's vexing struggles with *die produktive* or *erzeugende Einbildungskraft* in the First Critique (B152). The latter was the faculty of synthesizing the manifold into form (A120),[10] that is, into a comprehensible, rule-governed intuition of the sensible. Kant also called this "spontaneity" and the faculty of the a priori determination of the sensible. Things become even more volatile in the Third Critique, where we find it even more subtly pursued as the "*free lawfulness* of the imagination [*die freie Gesetzmäßigkeit der Einbildungskraft*]" (section 22). Furthermore, in the First Critique, Kant carefully distinguished it from the reproductive imagination (*reproductive Einbildungskraft*) (A100–102), which was *wiederzeugende* (producing again what has already been produced) and *nachbildende* or imitative. This last term should give us pause. The productive imagination produces the image (*Bild*), while the reproductive imagination replicates or copies the image—it literally comes "after" (*nach*) the image.

This distinction was already clearly in play in Bachelard's middle period when he distinguishes the "creative imagination" from the "reproductive imagination." The latter must be "ascribed to perception and memory" and as such is rooted in the so-called *reality function* (ERW 2/3, trans. modified). We reiterate what we remember having seen; that is, we imitate or replicate an image (*nachbilden*). The "creative imagination," on the other hand, produces the "*imagined* image": "Creative imagination functions very differently than imagination which relies on the reproduction of past perceptions, because it is governed by an *unreality function* every bit as powerful as the *reality function*" (ERW 2/3). The imagined image "may *precede* perception, initiating an adventure in perception" (ERW 3). In contrast, the force of the reproductive imagination, at least from the perspective of the soul, slows what it should quicken and kills what it should animate. The mere replication of even the most striking image quickly enters the turgid and stiff domain of the cliché. "An imitative image has no spark. Literature ought to surprise" (ERW 4).

Despite the famous consternation and perplexity in Kant's thinking regarding this explosive discovery,[11] *die produktive Einbildungskraft* was indispensable to post-Kantians like Schelling, Fichte, and Novalis, and it is clear that such figures inspired Bachelard.[12] Of the thinkers who took this provocation up in the wake of Kant, it was perhaps Schelling who thought it through most radically. For Schelling, *Einbildung* is the introduction (*ein*) of image (*Bild*) into that which is at first without image.[13] Presentation (*Darstellung*) itself is the *Einbildung* of Nature, Nature as a verb in its modes of giving birth to itself (*natura naturans*).[14] Schelling at times referred to this "expulsive [*ausstoßende*]" movement as the *In-Eins-Bildung*, that is, the conjunction of freedom and necessity (difference and identity) in a shared one. The many become one (*eins*) by virtue of coming into (*in*) image (*Bild*). Coleridge, for his part, attempted to render Schelling's term through his remarkable neologism *esemplastic*, derived from the Greek εις εν πλάττειν, to shape into one.[15] The shaping is "plastic" (from πλάττειν), indicating the productive movement from the formless to the formed. Coleridge also dubbed this "to coadunate," to make one with.[16]

In Schelling's important 1807 Munich address, *Über das Verhältnis der bildenden Künste zu der Natur*,[17] he speaks of the relationship of the plastic arts (literally, the arts dedicated to the emergence of image) to the question of Nature. If one can understand art, then one gains an insight into Nature and vice versa. In both Nature and art one "initially" discovers "the greatest severity [*Strenge*] of form"—"for without limits [*Begrenzungen*] the unlimited [*das Grenzlose*] could not appear" (UV 35). This is the first "appearance" of what Schelling, in a manner resonant of some of Bachelard's later formulations, calls *der schaffende Geist*, the productive spirit: it is "entirely lost in form" (UV 36). But over time, *die kommende Seele*, the coming soul, the advent of the soul, so to speak, "announces itself." Although pressed into form, it offers an initial hint that while form may have been the first word, it is not the last word. (As Bachelard made this point: "Dreams continue their growth despite the poems that express them" [WD 18].) This announced "lovely *Wesen*,"[18] some manner of being, is "neither sensible nor spiritual"—it belongs neither to the physical world of the concrete nor to the realm of ideas (UV 36). It is, rather, *unfaßlich*, ungraspable and incomprehensible. It is nonetheless available to every sensibility (*allen empfindbare*), and Schelling gives this *Wesen* its original Greek name: χάρις, which he translates as *die Anmut*, grace, favor, charm, and comeliness (UV 36–37).

One might say that a work becomes charming and graceful when body and soul are in harmony—"the body is form and grace is the soul, albeit not the soul as such, but rather the soul of form or the nature-soul [*Naturseele*]" (UV 37). A long-held Christian tradition claims that the soul is precisely what marks humans as unique. Each person is most fully her singular soul, an eternal soul (a singular essence) that stands before God. Schelling reverses this: "The soul in humans is therefore not the principle of individuality, but rather that through which one is elevated above all selfhood" (UV 38). To conceive of the soul as something, even something singular, is to think it, in Heidegger's sense, as something ontic. The soul, intimated in all form, has no form of its own. One might say, as we shall develop later in relationship to Bachelard, that it is a mistake to say that if it is not something, if it is not given in ontic orders, then it is nothing, the mere absence of presence. The soul is elemental and in this respect like water, which has no form of its own, but which can take the form of anything. Elemental water suggests something like Plato's χώρα, that which is formed, but which has no form of its own and which cannot as such be adequately conceived, but which can only be thought, amid the activity of its mythopoiesis, through a kind of bastard reckoning (*Timaeus* 52b2–3).

As form softens into an intimation of the watery element of its source, we can more deeply appreciate the allure of art and, in so doing, appreciate art as the trace of the soul of Nature herself. In fact, Schelling's *Naturphilosophie* is a radical experiment in thinking the *anima mundi* or *Weltseele* anew[19] with the help of science and philosophy. Bachelard for his part did not shy from the relationship of reverie and the cosmos: "The poet listens and repeats. The voice of the poet is a voice of the world" (PR 188). In art, Nature reimagines herself, finds another outlet for her productivity, in the poetic word, the word that in its own right is *natura naturans*. Poets "speak of the world in the language of the world" (PR 188), cosmic words which "weave bonds between man and the world" as the two "tonalities reinforce each other" (PR 189).[20] In the living *anima mundi*, one could speak with Bachelard of the "living being of the image" (PS 218).

In the third draft of *Die Weltalter* (1815), we find the following, quite striking, evocation of the soul:

> And awoken out of inactivity, the soul does not hate the contracting force but rather loves this confinement as the only way that it can come to feel itself and as that which hands over the material and the, so to speak, means, which are the only way that the soul can come out. Hence the soul does not want somehow to sublimate the negating force, neither in general nor as what precedes it. To the contrary, the soul demands and confirms the negating force and explicitly only wants to come out and be visible in it so that consequently the soul, unfolding from the highest, is always enveloped and retained by the negating force as if by a receptacle. (I/8, 278)

All of Nature expresses the soul of Nature, the instantaneity of what Schelling called an *ewiger Anfang*, an eternal natality that never comes to presence, but gives itself ever anew. Images are the ever-surprising adverbs of the soul. As Eileen Rizo-Patron expresses it: "Bachelard's imagination is fundamentally 'hermeneutic' in its attentive responsiveness to the solicitations of matter understood as a mode of otherness—namely, as a vital dimension of the life-world with an apparent will of its own. For, as defined in his books on the four elements, Bachelardian 'matter' alludes to a power both real and virtual—a force both oneiric and empirical that transcends the consciousness and control of the subject intending it."[21] One might call this elemental otherness, following Bachelard's own use of alchemical images, the dark matter of the imagination, or perhaps its χώρα. As Pierre Quillet said of Bachelard: "Alchemy is the divinization of matter, much as Manichaeism is its abomination."[22] Such Manichaeism, I would add, would denigrate Bachelard's "two lives" into the mere division of science and poetry, idea and image. The alchemy of thinking holds together both idea and image, despite their insuperable opposition.[23]

We may, as Bachelard happily contended, live in an age of image, but should we be so quick in our rush to embrace images? Is not this age also the rise, even the triumph, of flashy images that deceive and distract the intellect? American television news—that monstrosity of infotainment—seems to specialize in seducing the intellect with vague associations and flashy images, as if it were scarcely different than the orgy of advertisements that punctuate these supposedly balanced reports of important events and issues. The ascendancy of Donald Trump is a monstrous case in point. I think that this concern, one of the great anguishes of contemporary globalized human life, is important in itself, but it has little to do with what Bachelard is elucidating. I might say, in a peremptory fashion, that the cult of images is a new version of an old problem: the sophistry in which one deceptively presents images as if they were ideas. It is the problem of doing willful violence with images.[24] But this is a complex issue, and in order to appreciate the power of Bachelard's insight, we need to distinguish the dark matter of the soul's reveries from the violence of what I will here call, following Milan Kundera, "imagology."

Imagology as the Violence of the Image

The violent nightmare of Trump "politics" in the United States offers a new round in a lamentable history of something like the sophistry of the image. It is not enough to say that such projects present a worrisome, even odious, ideology. In Milan Kundera's novel *Immortality*, the narrator argues that "imagology has gained a historic victory over ideology."[25] After the profound and influential analyses of Hannah Arendt and the Frankfurt School, it seemed that nothing, least of all the truth, could escape the seeming omnipresence of ideology. But the narrator insists:

> All ideologies have been defeated: in the end their dogmas were unmasked as illusions and people stopped taking them seriously. For example, communists used to believe that in the course of capitalist development the proletariat would gradually grow poorer and poorer, but when it finally became clear that all over Europe workers were driving to work in their own cars, they felt like shouting that reality was deceiving them. Reality was

> stronger than ideology. And it is in this sense that imagology surpassed it: imagology is stranger than reality, which has anyway long ceased to be what it was for my grandmother, who lived in a Moravian village and still knew everything through her own experience: how bread is baked, how a house is built, how a pig is slaughtered and the meat smoked, what quilts are made of, what the priest and the schoolteacher think about the world; she met the whole village every day and knew how many murders were committed in the country over the last ten years; she had, so to speak, personal control over reality, and nobody could fool her by maintaining that Moravian agriculture was thriving when people at home had nothing to eat. My Paris neighbor spends his time in an office, where he sits for eight hours facing an office colleague, then he sits in his car and drives home, turns on the TV, and when the announcer informs him that in the latest public opinion poll the majority of Frenchmen voted their country the safest in Europe (I recently read such a report), he is overjoyed and opens a bottle of champagne without ever learning that three thefts and two murders were committed on his street that very day.
>
> Public opinion polls are the critical instrument of imagology's power, because they enable imagology to live in absolute harmony with the people. The imagologue bombards people with questions: how is the French economy prospering? is there racism in France? is racism good or bad? who is the greatest writer of all time? is Hungary in Europe or in Polynesia? which world politician is the sexiest? And since for contemporary man reality is a continent visited less and less often and besides, justifiably disliked, the findings of polls have become a kind of higher reality, or to put it differently: they have become the truth. Public opinion polls are a parliament in permanent session, whose function it is to create truth, the most democratic truth that has ever existed. Because it will never be at variance with the parliament of truth, the power of imagologues will always live in truth, and although I know that everything human is mortal, I cannot imagine anything that would break this power. (I 118–19)

At the time Kundera was composing—one might even say, imagining—*Immortality*, the Heidegger affair was ascendant, and the great philosopher was quickly falling from his pedestal. This is not to say that the question of Heidegger's politics, naïve and self-absorbed as it may have been, does not deserve philosophical scrutiny. While there were suddenly many books, essays, and conference panels devoted to this question, something decidedly unphilosophical was also beginning to take shape: a change in Heidegger's *imago*. No longer was Heidegger the daring thinker who ventured the ontological difference. He suddenly reappeared as a Nazi bastard. In fact, most people, if they have heard of Heidegger at all, probably only recall that he had some kind of relationship to the Nazi party. Heidegger? Oh, wasn't he that Nazi? Others took this fissure in his imagological status as an opportunity to dismiss or even excoriate him, all the time concentrating not on his thinking and writing, but on the scandal itself. Kundera: "If at the time I was writing these pages everyone decided that Martin Heidegger was to be considered a bungler and a bastard, it was not because his thought had been surpassed by other philosophers, but because on the roulette wheel of imagology, this time he landed on an unlucky number, an anti-ideal" (I 120).

Chris Hedges, in his recent and quite striking work, *Death of the Liberal Class*, argues that although the extinction of a significant leftist political voice in the United States was chiefly a matter of the Left betraying its own values, this abdication was abetted "by a shift from a print-based culture to an image-based culture."[26] The former ideally demanded care, fact-checking, and serious editorial vigilance. The ascent of the image (the increasing power of cable infotainment, endless political blogs, the ubiquity of the sound byte, the catastrophic shrinking of our attention spans, the chaos of the internet and social media, the erasure of the distinction between political opinion and political reporting, etc.) renders unrecognizable and undecidable the distinction between the "spinning of the real" and "the real itself." "Facts, opinions, lies, and fantasy" have all become "interchangeable" (DLC 207). This problem may be much older than the rise of the internet and television—its permutations are ancient—but it has in recent years taken on a new fury. "A populace entranced by these fragments, images, and spectacles, a populace that can no longer find the words to articulate what is happening to it, is cut off from rational discourse. It expresses reality through the use of selected and isolated facts, half-truths or lies that do not make sense. Illusion becomes true" (DLC 207).

Jean-Luc Nancy, in his beautifully nuanced collection of essays, *The Ground of the Image*, attempts to discern the difference, despite their ambiguous relationship, between violence and the image.[27] In thinking violence, Nancy begins with a simple and "anodyne" image: when confronted with a screw that stubbornly resists being extracted, one impatiently grabs a pair of pliers and yanks it out, ignoring both the "logic of the screw's threads" and the wood within which it is embedded (GI 16). "Violence does not participate in any order of reasons," and "it denatures, wrecks, and massacres that which it assaults" (GI 16). In this sense, Nancy speaks of the immense stupidity of violence, not in the sense in which Kant spoke of *Dummheit* (the inability to grasp principles as one finds oneself awash in the images that serve as examples), but in the sense of the vulgarity of *le con*. "It is not the stupidity that comes from a lack of intelligence, but much worse: it is the stupidity of *le con*. It is the calculated absence of thought willed by a rigid intelligence" (GI 16–17). *Le con*, the flathead, the stupid twat, thick as a brick and having shit for brains, is for Nancy violent in two ways, both as "slang" and as an "obscene and invasive image" (GI 17). The impatient recklessness of *le con* does not participate in the play of forces, but rather responds to them with a "sort of pure, dense, stupid, impenetrable intensity" (GI 17). Donald Trump, *le con par excellence*, who became president of the United States on a toxic stew of images and vague and often violent phrases and sentence fragments, demonstrates the incredible power of imagology.

This brings us to an ambiguity. One could say that in a certain way all images have an element of violence. *La veritable vérité*, truth that really is true rather than one of the many confidence games of sophistry, "cannot irrupt without tearing apart an established order. Truth ruins method despite all the latter's efforts" (GI 17–18). In addition to well-known ideas like Benjamin's "divine violence" or Heidegger's violence of truth setting itself into a work, we can say that Bachelard's thinking also has this element of violence. Not only does the epistemological rupture reduce our standing assumptions to the status of error, but reverie is also quite violent in the sense that the soul takes back the words that we have carefully calcified into our ideas. The relaxation and repose of the imagination should not be confused with the idyll in which the *anima* goes to sleep while the body remains awake. Nocturnal dreams are not the model for daytime reveries. The joy that is the repose of reverie is not only the violent loosening of received meanings (a violence against memory itself), but it is also the violence of the unexpected, the shock of the new.

This "terrible ambiguity" between the imagination of the true and the assault of the true is far from the last word.[28] Violence, at least in our allegedly postmodern age, feeds on the shadowy domain of this ambiguity. Violence attacks the true, replacing it with the pseudo-truth that is nothing short of the capacity of violence to force or impose itself on others, to insist on itself as if it were truth. Violence is the intensity of images and ideas insisting on themselves *ad baculum*. "The difference is that the true truth is violent because it is true, whereas the other type, its thick double, is 'true' only insofar as it is violent" (GI 18).

Imagology, one might say, begins with the fact that "violence always makes an image of itself" (GI 20), but this image is violence's attack on the real. All kitsch, for example, is the violence in which art is deprived of its power to reimagine and reexplore the real. Violence is about violence, while art, contrary to the false denigration of poetic imagination to careless and ineffectual fantasy, "touches the real—which is groundless and bottomless" (GI 25). Art is a kind of *violence without violence* because its force comes from being, to use Nancy's signature term, in "touch" with the real, which is not to say that art either represents or otherwise reveals the real. Bachelard also never assigns to the image the power of representation. Bachelard rather wrote of the "poetisphere" (PR 25), which demonstrates that a good, poetic book is "at once a reality of the virtual and a virtuality of the real" (PR 24). There is nothing to reveal, no reality to capture in a representation, not even the soul itself. There is no soul in a realm ontologically distinct from its images. Hence we could say with Nancy:

> Violence without violence consists in the revelation's not taking place, its remaining imminent. Or rather it is the revelation of this: that there is nothing to reveal. By contrast, violent and violating violence reveals and believes that it reveals absolutely. . . . It is the exact knowledge of this: that there is nothing to reveal, not even an abyss, and that the groundless is not the chasm of a conflagration, but imminence infinitely suspended over itself. (GI 26)

In direct contrast, Kundera's imagologue is a person of conviction and principle: he "demands of the journalist that his newspaper (or TV channel, radio station) reflect the imagological system of a given moment" (I 120). Imagology is the flathead's enraged, furious, malignant dogmatism, and it is a violence against the imagination's alliance with the event of truth. For Bachelard, even psychoanalysis, with which he had some limited sympathy (for example, its capacity to ameliorate traumatic events in the past), flirts with imagology. "Psychoanalysis looks for the reality beneath the image but fails to perform the inverse search: to look beneath the reality for the absolute image" (ERW 15).[29] For psychology and psychoanalysis to realign themselves with the ψυχή, however, they must first relax the hold of the concept of mind—to de-oedipalize and de-territorialize themselves in the sense made famous by Gilles Deleuze and Felix Guattari in *Anti-Oedipus*. This is nothing short of the imagination imagining itself. Concepts may describe the imagination, but they cannot explain it (poetry demonstrates that psychology and psychoanalysis, even philosophy, cannot give a proper account of the ψυχή). Discursive concepts can nonetheless still reverberate with the imagination imagining itself. It is to this issue that I now turn in my final meditation.

A Phenomenology of the Soul

Jean-Luc Nancy provocatively claims that the "image is always sacred," not in the sense that it is religious, which etymologically connotes a binding together (*religare*) of what is otherwise separate (mortals and God or the gods, immanence and transcendence). It has rather the opposite sense: The sacred "signifies the separate, what is set aside, removed, cut off." The image is sacred in the sense that it is *distinct* (GI 1), not yoked to something else beyond itself. The image does not bind itself together with its ground, as if the image revealed something beyond itself. The image is not a "translation of a state of the soul: it is the soul itself that presses and pushes on the image; or rather the image is this pressure" (GI 6–7). It would be a mistake to say that the soul is the ground of the image if by that one means that the image makes manifest its origins in a being called the soul.[30] There is no soul outside the immense proliferation of her surprises. "One can thus say that it appears as what it is by disappearing. Disappearing as ground, it passes entirely into the image. But it does not appear for all that, and the image is not its manifestation, nor its phenomenon. It is the force of the image, its sky and its shadow" (GI 7). The truth of the image has, as we have seen throughout this chapter, nothing to do with its capacity to represent something outside of itself, yet it allies itself with the non-violent violence of the event of truth. "Art marks the distinctive traits of the absenting of truth, by which it is the truth absolutely" (GI 13). Art is simultaneously the presenting and absenting of truth.

I think that Nancy's insightful description is itself something like what Bachelard dubbed a "phenomenology of the soul." The strangeness of this philosophical assignment should not be lost on us. In taking up the issue of the "poetic imagination" one must "forget his learning and break with all his habits of philosophical research" and "be receptive to the image at the moment it appears . . . in the very ecstasy of the newness of the image" (PS xi). Bachelard repeatedly emphasizes the novelty of the image: "[T]he poetic act has no past" (PS xi); "it is not an echo of the past" (PS xii). It appears instantly, and hence we see "the wholly unexpected nature of the new image" (PS xiii) and "the sudden image, the flare-up of being in the imagination" (PS xiv). The emergence of the poetic image from nowhere into imagined space marks the non-chronological "verticality" of the instant (RD 173).[31] Poetry, the fruit of the Λόγος, "puts language in a state of emergence" and therefore also "confirms the unforeseeable nature of speech" (PS xxiii). Indeed, it is a "*transformation of one's being through Language*" (FPF 12). It is "surprising," and its "images are therefore unpredictable" (PS xxvii). If psychoanalysis attempts to explain the origins of the poetic image in our earlier psychodynamic development, it finds itself powerless to account for the miracle of the image, its capacity to emerge as a *non sequitur* from our biographies (repressed or otherwise). Traditional psychology cannot address how a person becomes a poet not *because* of one's life, but rather *in spite* of it (PR 10).

Hence, Bachelard's own analysis "liquidates the past and confronts what is new" (PS xxviii). Or as Edward Casey clarifies, it is not so much that the new comes *in an instant*, but rather that it happens *instantaneously*, "where the adverb better conveys its surprising and sudden intervention." Hence it is not that the "the instant brings the new" but that "as the instantaneously occurring, the instant *is* the new: it is the new now, the now as news, the new itself insofar as we can know it."[32] Even in Bachelard's celebrated *topophilia*, the images of space are themselves subject to the temporality of their natality. In the myriad images that characterize the manners in which we come to be at home within the depths of the earth, the inexplicable emergence of the images within which we dwell indicate what he had already famously announced in 1932, six years before his explicit turn to the image: "*Le temps ne coule pas. Il jaillit.* Time no longer flows. It spouts" (II 60/106). Time does not flow or slip by. Like water, it suddenly gushes forth or spurts out, or like a flame, it suddenly flashes, lights up, shoots up, or like an idea, it suddenly alights, strikes, bursts forth. *Jaillir* is a strange verb, for its operation is shrouded in a wake of images. How does one speak to such time, which, as Nancy observed, "is both the blind spot and the obscure vanishing point" (GI 23)? Thinking ahead to the more than two decades of careful study of the image that comprised Bachelard's other life, one might say that *jaillir* names an instantaneity that could be understood as a verb whose subject is both enigmatic and absent *in* and *as* each of its presentations. It is a verb with no real subject, neither acting nor being acted upon, but presenting itself from itself, as if it were the productivity of the middle voice.[33]

Bachelard eventually called his study of the imagination "a phenomenology of the soul," documenting the "dreaming consciousness" (PS xvi). The soul? Few words flirt as readily with kitsch as the word "soul," but Bachelard recalls the distinction in German philosophy between *der Geist*, the mind, and *die Seele*, what is otherwise than the mind even as it is given with the mind, just as the *anima* reciprocally interpenetrates yet opposes the *animus*. The image is a "flicker of the soul" (PS xviii). In a sense, I think that one could say that under the rubric of a "phenomenology of the soul," Bachelard is proposing a *radicalization of psychology* or what he at the end of his life called a "psychologically active poetics" (FPF 10). "I shall never be anything but a psychologist of books" (PR 93). By *radical* I mean a psychology that attends to its origins in both the ψυχή and the Λόγος. Insofar as contemporary psychology has evolved into the study of the mind (*Geist, animus*), it attempts to give at least a quasi-scientific account—itself a diminution of the rich range of the Λόγος—of the image by locating its origins in things like past events, or mental structures, or cognitive aberrations. "The psychoanalyst . . . inevitably intellectualizes the image" (PS xx).[34] The ψυχή is not the mind (*animus*) per se, and the Λόγος is not an explanation. The ψυχή also names the *anima*, *die Seele*, the soul, and a phenomenology of the ψυχή attempts not to explain it, but somehow to describe it, to articulate it with language, "to consider the poetic image in its own being" (PR 3). In this way, Bachelard links the Λόγος specifically with phenomenology as it attends to—reverberates (*retentir*)—the movement of the ψυχή in language.[35] It charts and bears witness with language to the white heat or dark matter erupting within language. To the extent that one can speak of psychology, one could say that this is "the psychology of wonder from the phenomenological point of view" (PR 3).

Perhaps one could say—imaginatively—that the Λόγος witnesses the mythic element of the soul and is therefore a kind of *lucid dreaming*. The latter term, coined by the great Dutch writer and psychiatrist Frederik van Eeden (1860–1932), names the kind of dream within which dreamers become aware that they are dreaming. This awareness, simultaneously of the dream, yet at enough distance from the dream that it can name the dream as a dream, marks the tension in which the ψυχή and the Λόγος gain the requisite distance for the latter to become aware of the former. Of course, as the dream becomes lucid, it is breaking away from its nocturnal element and emerging toward reverie, where one might say that the Λόγος bears witness to the emerging image-inducing force of μῦθος. In fact, Bachelard quotes the "great" philosopher Schelling on this point: "One is almost tempted to say that language itself is a mythology deprived of its vitality, a bloodless mythology so to speak, which has only preserved in formal and abstract form what mythology contains in living and concrete form" (PR 37/32–33, trans. modified). On the one hand, one cannot have a purely mythological thought any more so than one can have any other kind of purely imagistic thought, for mythology is not a mythic image and the word "image" is not an actual image, but an abstraction, the image as conceived. This, of course, immediately draws our attention to the paradoxical relationship of image and idea within the discord of thinking itself.

At the same time, Schelling's own sense of mythology touches upon its refusal of all allegorical and metaphorical content. A myth does not mean something beyond itself: "Everything in it is thus to be understood as mythology expresses it, not as if something else were thought, something else said. Mythology is not *allegorical*; it is *tautegorical.* To mythology the gods are actually existing essences, gods that are not something *else*, do not *mean* something else, but rather *mean* only what they are."[36] The coming of images is mythic in the sense that images are tautegorical; that is, they come as themselves, not as bearers of a hidden meaning. Images are anti-oedipal: there is no complex, no tacitly operating subject, at the heart of their production.[37] As such, the mythic quality of the soul—indeed, the *soul as the myth of the myth*—links it to the Λόγος while simultaneously delimiting its range. As Markus Gabriel puts it in his recent study of this issue: "Schelling's concern is to safeguard the sense of mythology against Λόγος' project of absolutizing itself in the form of reflection. *Reflection is limited precisely because it is engendered by mythology and not the other way around.*"[38] The poetic imagination is tautegorical—the images come as themselves—and even the Λόγος, which in the rigors of reflection gains distance on the imagination, cannot in so doing extricate itself from it. In a sense, one could say, albeit quite imaginatively, that in the combined movement of μῦθος and Λόγος, the reflective capacity of the latter, its capacity to step back, allows it to dream lucidly, to think the thought that it is dreaming while it is dreaming. It can think the thought of the genesis of images while nonetheless in the thrall of that which it also holds at a conceptual distance. This is the ongoing balancing act between the violence of the imagination and the rigors of critical thinking.[39]

Of course, Bachelard's own term for this was not lucid dreaming, and it certainly was not the dream (*le rêve*), but rather *la rêverie*—"the free expansion of all *anima*. . . . It is doubtless with the reveries of his *anima* that the poet manages to give his *animus* ideas the structures of a song, the force of a song" (PR 67). This is not the mere fact of a consciousness as it daydreams (*rêvasse*), but the detailed making present of the Λόγος as it renews itself in a specifically *poetic* reverie (PR 6). One could say that *la rêvasserie* is the soul in its mere wandering, while *la rêverie* is the soul as it wonders, or, in its etymological sense, as it revels and raves, as it dreams in language wildly and "shamelessly unsupervised" (FPF 24), flaring up in inspired words. "Yes, words really do dream" (PR 18). Of course, these words are themselves caught up with images, and the soul does not reveal itself in the image of a Muse—this is the ruse in which we imagine that there "is a transcendent subject for the verb *inspire*" (PR 7).[40] If one is not careful, the Muse becomes the mark of the imagological: a transcendent subject *revealed* at the heart of the imagination. Nonetheless, while *le rêve*, nocturnal wandering, is the experience of a "delegated wandering" (PR 11)—dreams happen to us—*la rêverie* is not its diurnal analogue (daydreaming), nor is it mere idle musing. It is the unexpected advent of a new world, and, as such, it "gives us the world of worlds" (PR 13) and "puts us in the state of a soul being born" (PR 15). *Les rêves* issue from *Geist* or *animus*, while *la rêverie* expresses the natality of the *anima* (PR 19) in and as the images within which we dwell.[41]

This radical psychology is radical, therefore, in a second, more fundamental, sense. Not only does it attend to an originary sense of both ψυχή and Λόγος, but it marks these words as themselves addressing origination as such—"grasping the very essence" of the poetic image's "originality" (PR 3). The poetic image does not follow from the stockpile of received concepts, metaphors, even images, but marks the discontinuity of a new beginning, the fertility of the imagination's natality, coupling wonder with the joy of speech (PR 3). "The newborn poetic image—a simple image!—thus becomes quite simply an absolute origin, an origin of consciousness. In times of great discoveries, a poetic image can be the seed of a world, the seed of a universe imagined out of a poet's reverie" (PR 1). The imagination of the poetic image, that is to say, the image in its radical genesis, occurs, however, within language itself, upsetting its prevailing consensus of ideas and images. "As a general thesis I believe that everything specifically human in man is Λόγος. One would not be able to meditate in a zone that preceded language" (PS xix). Such a radical Λόγος of the ψυχή attends, one might say, to the ψυχή dreaming in the Λόγος. Language itself is filled with the relics of the tautegorical vitality of long forgotten reveries. The Λόγος in the reverie is not consciously rendering an account of anything, for the ψυχή dreams in images, not in concepts. "An *idea*, in short, cannot be *imagined*" (FPF 7). The poetic word is the Λόγος speaking in images and, as such, saying what has not yet been said and what could not have been anticipated in discursive language and as such "confirms the unforeseeable nature of speech" (PS xxiii) and "in its newness opens a future to language" (PR 3), a future beyond the contractions and seclusions of our ideas.

Not only is the image not an idea, it is also not a metaphor, at least insofar as the latter is understood as making sense of the image through something besides itself. "A metaphor gives concrete substance to an impression that is difficult to express. Metaphor is related to a psychic being from which it differs. An image, on the contrary, product of absolute imagination, owes its entire being to the imagination" (PS 74). Metaphors render something intelligible by locating an illuminating resemblance in something beside the image itself. Of course, metaphors are indispensible to language, and we struggle in vain to imagine a poetics free from the use of metaphor. The poetic image, in distinction from other elements of a formal poem, however, is true without fundamentally revealing anything. As Paul Celan remarks in his famous 1960 address "*Der Meridian*," poetry speaks to the "majesty of the absurd which bespeaks the presence of human beings"; there is no metaphor for this utopia, "hence the poem is the place where all tropes and metaphors want to be led *ad absurdum*."[42]

Poetic works, and the life of the imagination more generally, cannot wholly emancipate themselves from metaphors and ideas. In a sense Bachelard's phenomenology of the soul both *imaginatively conceives* (articulates an understanding of imagination even as its operation contests the assumptions of comprehension) and *conceptually imagines* (deploys ideas unmoored from their received understandings). Such a phenomenology, a kind of bastard phenomenology, brings philosophy to its edge, to the point where it confronts its nonphilosophical ground, its shadow, much in the way that Merleau-Ponty claimed, "What resists phenomenology within us—natural being, the 'barbarian' source Schelling spoke of—cannot remain outside phenomenology and should have its place within it. The philosopher must bear his shadow, which is not simply the factual absence of future light."[43] This question of philosophy's relationship to nonphilosophy demands, in turn, that one philosophize, impossible a task as it may finally be, about the activity of philosophy itself. In order to philosophize, Bachelard both conceives (a beneficiary of the history of philosophy) and dephilosophizes, that is, opens himself to the opposed pole, to the elementally nonphilosophical soul at the heart of the productive imagination. In their remarkable work, *What Is Philosophy?*, Deleuze and Guattari argue,

> The plane of philosophy is prephilosophical insofar as we consider it in itself independently of the concepts that come to occupy it, but nonphilosophy is found where the plane confronts chaos. *Philosophy needs a nonphilosophy that comprehends it; it needs a nonphilosopical comprehension just as art needs nonart and science needs nonscience.* They do not need the No as beginning, or as the end in which they would be called upon to disappear by being realized, but at every moment of their becoming or their development.[44]

A plane of immanence is the possibility of moving from the nonphilosophical to the prephilosophical. The latter "does not mean something preexistent but rather something *that does not exist outside of philosophy*, although philosophy presupposes it. These are its "internal conditions" and as such it "constitutes the absolute ground of philosophy, its earth" (WP 41). The plane of immanence is "like a section of chaos," a prephilosophical slice of the utterly nonphilosophical, and, as such, much like the winnowing of the Platonic χώρα, it "acts like a sieve" (WP 42). It is like a "desert that concepts populate without dividing up" (WP 36). Working in tandem, concepts allow the prephilosophical ground of philosophy to appear in thinking. The prephilosophical plane of philosophical concept creation is not itself a phenomenon, but a *planomenon* (WP 35), the manifesting of a plane of immanence, "the horizon of events, the reservoir or reserve of purely conceptual events" (WP 36).

Bachelard in his two lives presents his own, quite remarkable *image of thought*, discerning what by right belongs to the full complexity of the ψυχή (the contraction and expansion, the breathing—to borrow Schelling's image—of *animus* and *anima*). What is a reverie on reverie if not the imagination imagining itself? The *anima* restricts or condenses both when the *animus* conceives it (the *idea* of the soul can never be the *ideatum* of the soul) and when the *anima* imagines itself (the image as such is its own compression). The *animus* concentrates, contracts, focuses, and hence Bachelard speaks of the *animus* as that which "projects and worries" (PR 64), while reverie is the "free expansion of all *anima*" (PR 67). Expansion and contraction split and divide thinking—Bachelard led "two lives"—but for all that, one cannot speak of this schizoid condition as a duality. As Bachelard had already contended in 1938:

> The axes of poetry and of science are opposed to one another from the outset. All that philosophy can hope to accomplish is to make poetry and science complementary, to unite them as two well-defined opposites. We must oppose, then, to the enthusiastic, poetic mind the taciturn scientific mind, and for the scientific mind an attitude of preliminary antipathy is a healthy precaution. (PF 2)

The image of the schizoid ψυχή speaks to its full complexity, to its "syntheses" (PR 61): it is always becoming its own inner oppositions anew. Self-determination gives rise to reimagination and reimagination settles on its images, including the images that we attempt to conceive. "We are the unity of image and memory" (PS 16)—the retentive force of our cultivated and carefully retained ideas and the surging forth of our images. This "androgyny" (PR 84), or, one might say, following Nietzsche, this Dionysian-Apollonian tension of the whole, is the becoming of thinking: "The human being taken in his profound reality as well as in his great tension of becoming is a divided being, a being which divides again, having permitted himself the illusion of unity for barely an instant. He divides then reunites" (PR 90).

Who writes a book? Who reads a book? Is it the *anima* or the *animus*? This is irresolvable: "[I]mmediately the literary work, the literary creation would enter into the worst ambiguities" (PR 93). Perhaps the best that we can say is that the human "is a half-open being" (PS 222). The image, born of the unexpected, announces the futurity of the soul and hence the diversity of its beginnings. In this sense, as we have seen, we can imagine the soul as *ein ewiger Anfang*, "opening all the prisons of the being so that the human possesses all becomings" (PR 158)—what else is the *moi-rêveur* (PR 166/143) other than the waters of the productive imagination? Is there some master I that unites all of the imagined selves, some transcendental ego, some grammatical I that accompanies the unity of apperception? "Reveries, mad reveries lead life" (PR 170). It is always a mistake in the end to speak of *the* soul. "Poetry is never as unified as when it diversifies" (PR 25). Perhaps we could think of it in the way that the early Julia Kristeva adapted the Platonic χώρα to "denote an essentially mobile and extremely provisional articulation constituted by movements and their ephemeral stases."[45] It does not *represent* anything and has no axiomatic form, but "precedes evidence, verisimilitude, spatiality, and temporality. . . . It can never be definitely posited" (RPL 26).

Although it eludes representation and, indeed, further undermines the project of representation as such (ideas are the history of an error and images do not promote the aspirations of our ideas), the soul nonetheless speaks to an emancipatory, even "revolutionary," element of thinking: the capacity of the *anima* to dissolve what Bachelard called "unfortunate concretions" (PR 128). When W. E. B. Du Bois speaks of the souls of black folk, one can hear the pain of the concretion of life on the other side of the color line as well as the soul's simultaneous refusal of these forms. In the final chapter of the *Souls of Black Folk*, Du Bois, who was the first African American to do graduate work in Germany and who knew and esteemed the German philosophical figures upon which Bachelard draws, spoke of a "soul hunger" that is audible in black churches as the congregation performs the Sorrow Songs and gropes "toward some unseen power."[46] These Songs, reimagined—one might say, reanimated—from lifeless Anglican hymns, expressed the prayer that "sometime, somewhere, men will judge men by their souls and not by their skins" (214). Or one need only think of Aimé Césaire's poetry, which, under the moniker of negritude, unleashed the emancipatory reserve of an African unconscious. Even if such a strategy is in the end only provisional, Césaire's poetry opened up a whole new world in which the people of Martinique and beyond could dwell. "Softening" and "erasing the traumatic character of certain childhood memories" may be for Bachelard the "salutary task of psychoanalysis," but as it is softened, it does not disappear or "dissolve in nothingness. In order to dissolve the unfortunate concretions, reverie offers us its calm waters, the obscure waters which sleep at the bottom of every life" (PR 128).[47] In reverie, the abyss revealed to us in our nocturnal dreams is shown to be the superabundance of water, the eternal beginning, the inexhaustible fountain of images. "Dreams without a history, dreams which could light up only in a perspective of annihilation are in the Nothing or in the Water" (PR 147). Of course, we think water not only as an element, but as elemental, a way of thinking the elemental imagination as such.[48] In the ongoing revolution of poetic language, we see that because "in poetic imagery there burns an excess of life, an excess of language, I will be able to discover point by point the sense there is in speaking of *the heat of language*" (PF 13–14).

Notes

1. Novalis, *Philosophical Writings*, ed. and trans. Margaret Mahony Stoljar (Albany: State University of New York Press, 1997), 66.

2. In the Third Critique, Kant distinguishes between concept (*Begriff*) and idea (*Idee*). The latter can be aesthetic (an intuition of the imagination) or purely rational and, as such, transcend any cognizable object (e.g., the idea of freedom). Concepts, on the other hand, are employed to cognize actual objects (see §57, comment 1). In the present chapter, I contrast the realm of both ideas and concepts with the realm of images, and hence by *idea* I aim to include in the Kantian sense *both ideas and concepts* and to mark most broadly the *discursive* in all of its complexity.

3. Both Carl Gustav Jung's and Bachelard's deployment of the masculine and feminine elements of the *animus* and *anima* nowadays sound quaint at best and risk being offensive. It is beyond the scope of the present chapter to explore this complicated issue, but in passing I note that Bachelard is not speaking of the tendencies of women versus men and vice versa. His deployment of these principles ultimately undermines the possibility of self-representation, indeed of representation as such.

4. Mary McAllester Jones, *Gaston Bachelard, Subversive Humanist: Texts and Readings* (Madison: University of Wisconsin Press, 1991), 13. See also her important essay, "The Redemptive Instant: Bachelard on the Epistemological and Existential Value of Surprise," *Philosophy Today* 47 (SPEP Supplement 2003): 124–31; henceforth cited as Redemptive Instant.

5. "When psychologists speak of the 'imagination' of a mathematician, for example, this is as much as to admit the lack of a vocabulary adequate to describing the inventive and associative capacities of rational thought" (FPF 7). This being said, Bachelard held that chemists and mathematicians also think poetically. See Mary McAllester Jones's essay "Adventures of Consciousness: Bachelard on Scientific Imagination," in this volume.

6. On the dual function of language and the image-thought dialectic, see *Air and Dreams*.

7. Samuel Taylor Coleridge, *Logic*, ed. J. R. de J. Jackson (Princeton: Princeton University Press, 1981), 53; henceforth cited as LO.

8. Eileen Rizo-Patron, "Bachelard's Hermeneutics," 107–26 in this volume.

9. James S. Hans, "Gaston Bachelard and the Phenomenology of Reading Consciousness," *The Journal of Aesthetics and Art Criticism* 35, no. 3 (Spring 1977): 323.

10. In the first edition or "A" version of the Transcendental Deduction, we find the claim: "The transcendental unity of apperception thus relates to the pure synthesis of imagination, as an *a priori* condition of the possibility of all combination of the manifold in one knowledge" (A 118).

11. See Martin Heidegger, *Kant und das Problem der Metaphysik* (Frankfurt am Main: Klostermann, 1991); *Kant and the Problem of Metaphysics*, 4th ed., trans. Richard Taft (Bloomington: Indiana University Press, 1990); henceforth cited as KP with the page number of the Taft translation followed by the *Gesamtausgabe* edition. Heidegger suggests: "The original, essential constitution of humankind, 'rooted' in the transcendental power of the imagination, is the 'unknown' into which Kant must have looked if he spoke of the 'root unknown to us' for the unknown is not that of which we simply know nothing. Rather, it is what pushes against something unsettling [*das Beunruhigende*] in what is known" (KP 110/160). John Sallis observes: "The tension is obtrusive: On the one hand, imagination is that by which subjectivity is first constituted as such; on the other hand, imagination continues to be reduced to a mere power possessed by the subject. Imagination is freed with one hand, only to be suppressed, bound with the other" (John Sallis, *The Gathering of Reason* [Athens: Ohio University Press, 1980], 175). Kant downplayed the preeminence of the productive imagination in the "B" Deduction in favor of reason. As Heidegger argued: "In the radicalism of his questions, Kant brought the 'possibility' of metaphysics before this abyss. He saw the unknown. He had to shrink back" (KP 115/168). Reason's abyss—itself, following the spirit of Bachelard—an image and not an idea—would deny Kant the universality in which "to wander critically through the region of Moral Philosophy and to repair the indeterminate, empirical universality of popular philosophical doctrines concerning morals" (KP 115/168).

12. Margaret R. Higonnet makes a strong case for the unifying centrality of the productive imagination throughout Bachelard's works on the poetic imagination, especially through the influence of Novalis. "Beneath Bachelard's wide-ranging, apparently eclectic sampling of European and American literature lies a consistently Romantic poetic for which Novalis provides the main model" (37); "Bachelard and the Romantic Imagination," *Comparative Literature* 33 (Winter 1981): 18–37. The importance of Novalis is already evident in ERW during Bachelard's defense of the "magical idealism" of the creative imagination in Novalis: "To the productive powers of imagination must be credited every human faculty, whether pertaining to the world within or the world outside the mind" (ERW 3).

13. For more on the problem of the imagination in Schelling, see my *Schelling's Practice of the Wild* (Albany: State University of New York Press, 2015), chap. 6; for more on eisemplasy, see chap. 5.

14. *Natura*, after all, does not signify the set of all things but rather their "birth" (from *natus* "born," past participle of *nasci,* "to be born"). Using a distinction in Spinoza that Schelling held dear even as he critically transformed it, one could say that modern science studied *natura naturata*, already born Nature, but had lost the wisdom to think *natura naturans*, the progressive natality of Nature. For more on Schelling's critical relationship to Spinoza, see chaps. 2 and 3 of my *The Conspiracy of Life: Meditations on Schelling and His Time* (Albany: State University of New York Press, 2003).

15. Samuel Taylor Coleridge, *Biographia Literaria* (1817), ed. James Engell and W. Jackson Bate (Princeton: Princeton University Press, 1984), 168; henceforth cited as BL.

16. BL 168, editor's footnote.

17. F. W. J. Schelling, *Über das Verhältnis der bildenden Künste zu der Natur* (Munich: Felix Krüll, 1807); henceforth cited as UV. All Schelling translations are my own unless otherwise noted.

18. *Das Wesen* is traditionally translated as essence, although Schelling's use of this term is far from its use in the history of Platonism.

19. For more on the *anima mundi*, see *The Barbarian Principle: Merleau-Ponty, Schelling, and the Question of Nature*, ed. Jason M. Wirth with Patrick Burke (Albany: State University of New York Press, 2013), chap. 1.

20. "All important words, all the words marked for grandeur by a poet, are keys to the universe, to the dual universe of the Cosmos and the depths of the human spirit" (PS 198).

21. Eileen Rizo-Patron, "Bachelard's Hermeneutics," 107–26 in this volume. See also her insightful essay "Sites of Reverie: The Divinatory Hermeneutics of Gaston Bachelard," *Religion and the Arts* 8, no. 2 (2004): 200–22. In the third draft of Schelling's *Die Weltalter* we find the following claim: "Whoever has to some extent exercised their eye for the spiritual contemplation of natural things knows that a spiritual image, whose mere vessel (medium of appearance) is the coarse and ponderable, is actually what is living within the coarse and the ponderable. The purer that this image is, the healthier the whole is. This incomprehensible but not imperceptible being, always ready to overflow and yet always held again, and which alone grants to all things the full charm, gleam, and glint of life, is that which is at the same time most manifest and most concealed. Because it only shows itself amidst a constant mutability, it draws all the more as the glimpse of the actual being that lies concealed within all things of this world and which simply awaits its liberation. Among the most corporeal things, metals, whose characteristic gleam has always enchanted people, were *par excellence* considered as the particular points of light through which this being glimmered among dark matter. A universal instinct had an inkling of its proximity in gold which, because of its more passive qualities—its almost infinite malleability and its softness and flesh-like tenderness, all of which combine with the greatest indestructibility—, seemed most akin to that spiritual corporeal being. Even in one of those seemingly accidental plays of which we so often have the opportunity to notice, gold was used to designate the earliest age of the world in which the glory of nature still prevails" (*The Ages of the World*, trans. Jason M. Wirth [Albany: State University of New York Press, 2000], I/8, 283 [division/volume, page number]; standard pagination based on the edition established by Schelling's son is inserted in the body of the translation).

22. Quoted in Rizo-Patron, "Bachelard's Hermeneutics," 107–26 in this volume.

23. See the 1815 draft of *Die Weltalter*: "The belief in the general capacity of matter again to be elevated into spiritual qualities has been retained through every age with a constancy which alone would already allow us to infer its deep ground and which so coheres with the dearest and ultimate hopes of humans that it could probably never be eradicated. One must let the rabble have the conventional concept of alchemy. But what happens with the digestion and appropriation of food, when from out of the most diverse substances the same thing is always caused in the whole and when each part always draws precisely what is suitable to it? What happens with the initial formation of the fetus? Everything that occurs around us is, if you will, a constant alchemy. It is every inner process, when beauty, truth, or the good are liberated from the attached darkness or impurity and appear in their purity. (Though the alchemist begins again *from below—a prima materia* that they would like to carry *ad ultimam*). Those who understood that for which they sought, sought not for gold, but rather, so to speak, for the gold of gold, for what makes gold into gold, that is, for something far more general. Perhaps if there is an external effect by which matter was brought to coagulation like milk was brought to curdle by rennin, then there must also be an opposed potency by which, if it were in human hands, the effect of that coagulating force could either be sublimated or, to a certain degree, overcome. If all matter, in accord with its inner essence, is now exclusively singular and if the difference between corporeal things of the same echelon is perhaps more or less based on the concealment of that original being, then it would surely be possible, through a gradual overcoming of the obscuring potency, to transform the less precious into the more precious" (Schelling, *The Ages of the World,* I/8, 284–85).

24. See the discussion of the gratuitous violent imagery that Bachelard discovers in the Lautréamont complex (L 80–81/139), where he recognizes both its *dynamizing* and *dehumanizing* potentials (L 86, 90–91/148, 156). The distinction drawn in Bachelard is mostly between the "devouring" versus "poetizing" uses of imagination.

25. Milan Kundera, *Immortality*, trans. Peter Kussi (New York: Harper, 1992), 118; henceforth cited as I.

26. Chris Hedges, *Death of the Liberal Class* (New York: Nation Books, 2010), 207; henceforth cited as DLC.

27. Jean-Luc Nancy, *The Ground of the Image*, trans. Jeff Fort (New York: Fordham University Press, 2005); henceforth cited as GI.

28. One does not have to hold that one can ever get to the truth or that there are unassailably true positions in order to appreciate the distinction that I am trying to draw here.

29. It would be difficult to level these charges against a subtler model of psychoanalysis like that of Jacques Lacan. Nonetheless, the power of a book like *Anti-Oedipus* by Gilles Deleuze and Felix Guattari is that it offers independent arguments for the depth of the problem that Bachelard is here addressing; Gilles Deleuze and Felix Guattari, *Anti-Oedipus: Capitalism and Schizophrenia,* trans. Robert Hurley (1972; New York: Penguin, 1977).

30. One could take Nancy to be implicitly criticizing Bachelard at this point. After all, we find in Bachelard many formulations like: "All great, simple images reveal a psychic state" (PS 72) and cosmic reveries are a "state of the soul" (PR 16). This seems to contradict Nancy's insistence that the image is not a "translation of a state of the soul." I would not be sympathetic to this reading of Bachelard. As we have seen, a phenomenology of the soul is not a psychology or a psychoanalysis. The soul imagines images but is itself unimaginable. As we have seen, the soul is not a transcendent subject, and it does not speak to anything that is mathematically one. As we shall see, images are tautegorical, not signs of the soul.

31. For an insightful discussion on this point see "Vertical Time: Bachelard's Epiphanic Instant," 49–61 in this volume.

32. Edward S. Casey, "The Difference an Instant Makes: Bachelard's Brilliant Breakthrough," 19–28 in this volume.

33. For an excellent study of the problem of the middle voice in both Continental philosophy and especially the Kyoto School, see Rolf Elberfeld, "The Middle Voice of Emptiness: Nishida and Nishitani," trans. Jason M. Wirth, *Japanese and Continental Philosophy: Conversations with the Kyoto School*, ed. Bret Davis, Brian Schroeder, and Jason M. Wirth (Bloomington: Indiana University Press, 2011), 269–85. To be sure, as Bachelard also argues in *Intuition of the Instant*, this event requires human (poetic) presence: "The poet brings a subtler dialectic to life. He reveals at the same time, in a single instant, the solidarity of form and person. He proves that form is a person, and that a person is form. Poetry thus becomes an instant of formal causality, an instant of personal power" (II 63).

34. "The image was present, present in us and separated from all that past which might have prepared it in the soul of the poet" (PR 4). At this stage, Bachelard seeks to study the natality of the imagination, not the poet and her personal or cultural "complexes." As suggested in Rizo-Patron's piece on "Bachelard's Hermeneutics" (part 2), Bachelard studied "complexes"—unlike some psychoanalysts—as sites of a soul in combat or tension and therefore as ambivalent sites of potential creativity versus paralysis. This comprised the ethical charge of poetic complexes in his earlier studies.

35. "The goal of all phenomenology is to situate awareness in the present" (PR 4).

36. F. W. J. Schelling, *Historical-Critical Introduction to the Philosophy of Mythology* (1842), trans. Mason Richey and Markus Zisselsberger (Albany: State University of New York Press, 2007), 136.

37. Although Bachelard at one time used the imagery of the Oedipal in an original way, I am here alluding to its discussion in Deleuze and Guattari's *Anti-Oedipus*. There is no master structure of the subject operating mechanically at the heart of the psyche.

38. Markus Gabriel, "The Mythological Being of Reflection: An Essay on Hegel, Schelling, and the Contingency of Necessity," in Markus Gabriel and Slavoj Žižek, *Mythology, Madness and Laughter: Subjectivity in German Idealism* (London: Continuum, 2009), 62.

39. For a profound study of the complex relationship between μῦθος and Λόγος, see Marcia Sá Cavalcante Schuback's essay, "Ulysses at the Mast," in *The Gift of Logos: Essays in Continental Philosophy*, ed. David Jones, Jason M. Wirth, and Michael Schwartz (Newcastle upon Tyne: Cambridge Scholars, 2010), 11–26.

40. Bachelard: "Reality is a power of dreams, and dream is a reality" [*La réalité est une puissance de rêves, et le rêve est une réalité*]" (AD 13/21, trans. modified).

41. In his late work, *The Flame of a Candle*, Bachelard reiterates this point: "It is by way of the *animus* that the psychoanalyst studies dream images. For him the image is double, always signifying something other than itself. This is a caricature of the psyche. One racks the brain, to think, always to think. To enjoy images, to love them for themselves, would demand that the psychoanalyst accept a poetic education on the fringes of all such erudition. Hence fewer dreams by way of the *animus* and more by way of the *anima*" (FC 7).

42. Paul Celan, "The Meridian," *Collected Prose*, trans. Rosmarie Waldrop (Riverdale-on-Hudson: Sheep Meadow, 1986), 40, 51.

43. Maurice Merleau-Ponty, *Signs* (1960), trans. Richard C. McCleary (Evanston: Northwestern University Press, 1964), 178. See Bachelard: "Since life throbs most strongly in self-expression, where then is true life, excessive life, to be located? In what poem, what image? Human beings are never fixed in space or time as others think, and are not to be found even where they themselves tell others to inquire" (FPF 19).

44. Gilles Deleuze and Félix Guattari, *What Is Philosophy?*, trans. Hugh Tomlinson and Graham Burchell (New York: Columbia University Press, 1994), 218; henceforth cited as WP.

45. Julia Kristeva, *Revolution in Poetic Language*, trans. Leon S. Roudiez (New York: Columbia University Press, 1984), 25; henceforth cited as RPF.

46. W. E. B. Du Bois, *The Souls of Black Folk* (1903; New York: Penguin, 1989), 210–11.

47. "All the obliterations of the night converge toward this nothingness of our being. At the limit, absolute dreams plunge us into the universe of the Nothing. When this Nothing fills up with Water, we are already coming back to life" (PR 146). And speaking of water, who can forget Maya Deren's brilliant short evocation of the power of water, *At Land* (1944)?

48. On this issue one should see not only the middle works of Bachelard, but also John Sallis, *Force of Imagination: The Sense of the Elemental* (Bloomington: Indiana University Press, 2000). See also *On the True Sense of Art: A Critical Companion to the* Transfigurements *of John Sallis*, ed. Jason M. Wirth, Michael Schwartz, and David Jones (Evanston: Northwestern University Press, 2016). For one of the greatest experiments in the elemental imagination in recent years, I would recommend filmmaker Terrence Malick's masterpiece, *The Tree of Life* (2011), in which the elemental imagery of life defends itself against Job's charge that death and suffering are signs of the fundamental injustice of being. Malick cinematically imagines the imagination while simultaneously presenting it as the justice of becoming.

Chapter 12

Sounding the Living Logos: Bachelard and Gadamer

Eileen Rizo-Patron

> You built a temple deep inside their hearing.
>
> —Rainer Maria Rilke, *Sonnets to Orpheus* (1:1)

> But do we know how to welcome into our mother tongue the distant echoes that reverberate at the hollow center of words?
>
> —Bachelard, *The Flame of a Candle* (28)

Can the art and discipline of translation play a critical role in promoting a mode of thinking devoted to the poetic-philosophical task of ushering a living Λόγος into being? This chapter will explore this question by first revisiting Gadamer's hermeneutic reflections in a brief supplement to his *Truth and Method*, ultimately to focus on a remarkable insight on the essence of language that grows out of that meditation—an insight that will invite us, in turn, to delve into Bachelard's soundings of the Λόγος in his works on imagination. It is such a retrospective reading of Bachelard's work from the vantage point of Gadamer's hermeneutics that motivates the principal aim of this piece—namely, to show *how* Bachelard's practice of waking reverie in response to evocative language (found in literary, philosophical, or even scientific texts) presents itself not only as a viable way of probing the rich possibilities of the hermeneutic arts, but as a promising complement to Gadamer's philosophical hermeneutics. One of the critical questions that will need to be examined, however, is whether the practice of reverie in

Bachelard's poetic hermeneutics—ready as it is "to hearken to the demons of the inkwell" (FC 15)—is actually unconcerned with discovering the *truth* in a text, as some commentators allege, or whether it contributes valuable ways of awakening the inner ear and cultivating a mode of listening that is attuned to becoming—hence in effect fostering the birth of truth.

Gadamer's Hermeneutic Breakthrough

In a brief essay entitled "To What Extent Does Language Preform Thought?,"[1] Hans-Georg Gadamer (1900–2002) once reminded readers that language learning necessarily entails developing culture-specific ways of thinking and feeling, of forming opinions, arguments, and convictions according to a set of preformed articulations of meaning, and not merely acquiring words, idioms, or peculiar modes of expression. As Martin Heidegger revealed in his *Introduction to Metaphysics*, Western languages historically framed themselves in accordance with the "Λόγος of ratio" elucidated by Plato and Aristotle, which became gradually detached from the pre-Socratic notion of φύσις in Greek metaphysics.[2] It is this version of Western metaphysics that in time gave rise to our technological civilization with its Promethean ideals of mastering nature and society. The problem of linguistic relativity later foregrounded by linguists such as Wilhelm von Humboldt had already been announced, Gadamer recalls, in Nietzsche's proclamation that "God's most creative act was to create grammar," implying that human beings are first initiated into these schemas of perception and world mastery in such a way that we can never get behind the legacy of grammar (TM 493–94). Such linguistic heritage, Gadamer realizes, becomes a cultural heritage of forms and techniques of working, ideals of liberty and order—in short, a way of life.

Faced with the weighty evidence of twentieth-century European history, however, Gadamer was compelled to ask: To what degree has the patterning of Western thought actually *determined* our lives? Does it irrevocably limit our capacity to tune into latent energies or tacit realities that might *not* correspond to our concepts, fabrications, opinions, expectations? And what is the fate of *truth* in all of this? How much does language shape even our earliest experiences of the world? Might such programming not create prejudices or necessities that would force us to run down a path to the technological destruction of our own civilization and, even worse, the self-destruction of humanity (TM 494)?

These questions became all the more poignant as Gadamer reflected on the hermeneutics proposed in the first version of *Truth and Method*—a hermeneutics that emphasized the fundamental role of *language* in human experience as it involves us from the start in "hermeneutic circles" of understanding in our exchanges with the world and others. After his debates with Jürgen Habermas, however, Gadamer readily admitted that the linguistic patterning that shapes our minds and worlds is not necessarily a prison house (TM 495). He agreed with Habermas's observation that we do have some kind of prelinguistic experience of the world—for we respond naturally to gestures and are capable of intuitively understanding people's tones, facial expressions, laughter, including subterfuge, before conceptualizing them. Even more, he agreed that the very possibility of adopting a *critical stance* with regard to our own preconceptions and linguistic conventions already reveals that our human capacities exceed any fixed form of "instituted language," though perhaps not what he would term "the linguistic *virtuality* of reason" (TM 496).

By the time he wrote this supplement, Gadamer's most urgent question had thus become: How might we "succeed in turning the *pre-formed conceptual matter that we inherit* into *living fluid speech*"? (TM 493, my emphasis). This challenge turns even more critical when it comes to understanding *written* language, which tends to take the form of reified things and relations in our culture. Our entire world, Gadamer noted, is largely a "literary" one, administered by writing and transcription. Hence everything in writing calls for a "heightening of the inner ear" to be understood through layers of skillfully crafted, or thickly crusted, meaning. This is important not only in poetry but also in philosophy as in all genuine dialogue and translation. At this point, Gadamer called upon his students to hone their listening:

> You must sharpen your ear. You must realize that when you take a word in your mouth, you have not taken up some *arbitrary tool* which can be thrown in a corner if it doesn't do the job, but you are committed to a line of thought that comes from afar and stretches beyond you. What we do is always a kind of changing back that I want to call *translation* in a broad sense. To understand and read is already to translate, and to translate is to translate again. (TM 496–97, my emphasis)

Yet translation is typically enacted, in our daily transactions, as an unreflective process. Gadamer in fact defines such translation as "an *indivisible unity* of implicit anticipation, of presumption of meaning in general, and of the explicit determination *of what one presumed.* All discourse," he adds, "includes something of this anticipation and determination" (TM 497, my emphasis). Gadamer's definition, one might argue, applies particularly to our ordinary reactions to one another in daily life, to our prereflective interpretations of others so commonly manifest in interpersonal conflicts, mass media sound-bytes, or run-of-the-mill political debates. But such translation often entails the projection of our own a priori categories upon others,[3] revealing more about ourselves and our own thought patterns than it does about others and what they are trying to say to us. Gadamer describes such a form of thinking and speaking as a manner of habitual recitation, to be contrasted to that other mode of speech we might engage in at special moments of crisis or grace, when we are truly brought to listen and think on our feet, and from the heart.

It is at this point that Gadamer is struck by the insight that brings this brief meditation on language to a sudden end:

> The basic misunderstanding concerning the linguistic character of our understanding is one of language, as if language were an existing whole composed of words and phrases, concepts, points of view and opinions. In reality, language is the single word whose virtuality opens up the infinity of discourse, of discourse with others, and of the freedom of speaking oneself and of allowing oneself to be spoken. Language is not its elaborate conventionalism, nor the burden of pre-schematization with which it loads us, but the generative and creative power unceasingly to make this whole fluid. (TM 497–98)[4]

Bachelard's Soundings of a Poetic Λόγος

We now turn to Gaston Bachelard (1884–1962), whose philosophy, at first blush, might be described as coming from a hermeneutic pole opposite to Gadamer's. This epistemologist and philosopher of science in fact surprised the French academic world in the late 1930s with an unexpected change in focus toward an intensive study of imagination and poetic language. My aim in what follows is to show that even while Bachelard exhibited a style of thought unlike Gadamer's, following a primarily inductive mode of philosophical inquiry, his findings anticipated and in certain ways went beyond some of Gadamer's hermeneutic insights by illustrating *how* it is that readers most readily come in touch with language's *generative force*.

Bachelard arrived at some of his most fruitful discoveries through an exploratory reading of poets and philosophers in his works on the elemental imagination (1938–1948).[5] Towards the end of his career, he would have a chance to marshal and fine-tune his key hermeneutic discoveries in the introduction to *The Poetics of Space* (1957), where he proposed the cultivation of a mode of reading and listening that attunes itself to the pulse of a text by first adopting a vigilant *attitude of crisis* with respect to our preconceptions, and bracketing our initial reactions to words. To tap into the vibrant life of a literary image or phrase, Bachelard would then invite us to experience its reverberations (*retentissement*) in the manner of Minkowski's phenomenology. "In reverberation," he wrote, "a poetic image has sonority of being"—sonority not merely in the acoustic sense, but insofar as it can alter the entire tenor of life (PS xii–xiii). Here Bachelard was careful to distinguish between what he called the *reverberations* vs. *resonances* of an image, and to underline their complementarity:[6] while resonances are dispersed along the associational planes of our life-world, reverberations stir our being to the core; while resonances invite us to react to a poem, its reverberations seize us. The reverberations of a *single* poetic word can thus precipitate a decisive shift in our being (*virement d'être*). The tiniest *variation* of one image is hence capable of setting our *entire* linguistic mechanism into motion (PS xviii–xix/6–7).

The images Bachelard gathered over the years into his crucible of meditation had the virtue of placing us at the very "origin of the speaking being" to which Gadamer would later allude so conclusively in his supplement to his magnum opus. Learning to experience the reverberations of a new image by reading in what Bachelard termed waking reverie, we indeed "begin to feel a poetic power rising naïvely within us" (PS xix). Though we may then experience resonances and reminders of our past, by the time the striking image stirs the surface it has already taken root in our souls (PS xix). Given to us by another, we nonetheless feel we have created it: "It becomes a new being in our language, expressing us by making us what it expresses. In other words, the image is at once a becoming of expression, and a becoming of our being. Here expression creates being" (PS xix).

In one of his earlier books, *Air and Dreams* (1943), Bachelard had gone as far as to propose that the Word—the sacred poetic Λόγος that praises, prays, and sings—acts as "a prelude to *natura naturans*, which in turn produces the *natura naturata* that can be heard in the sounds and forms of created nature" (AD 98–99). But already in *Water and Dreams* (1942) he had been interpreting these notions creatively—inspired by Spinoza—when he proposed that "mankind imagining is the transcendent aspect of *natura naturans*" (WD 10).[7] His claim was that nature's transcendent aspect takes on concrete manifestation through literature when undertaken as an agency of creative evolution (literature *litteraturans*), rather than when understood simply as a created product (RD 140).

Bachelard's distinctive hermeneutics of poets, philosophers, and physicists—from Plato to Paz, from Heraclitus to Heisenberg[8]—could in fact be cited as a vivid example of such literature *litteraturans*. His already-cited variation of Heidegger's renowned theme of "being-in-the-world"[9] itself illustrates how readers are invited to imagine themselves as "being-becoming-the-becoming-of-the-world," not unlike those alchemists who regarded their task as assisting in the world's evolution by gathering its generative images, distilling them, and developing their possibilities through meditative reverie (ERW 251). Later, in *The Poetics of Space*, Bachelard would reiterate that "a poetic image which stems from the Λόγος is personally innovating" (PS xix–xx) and that approaching such an image with an objective attitude would risk stifling its reverberation by rejecting on principle the *transsubjective* depth at which the original poetic phenomenon begins.[10] Psychoanalysts, in his view, tend to intellectualize images by translating them too readily into reductive concepts that neither *sing* nor *dream*. The label "*traduttore, traditore*" would apply to interpreters in such cases (PS xx). Only a reading enlivened by intimate participation (PS xxxv, 162) could remain faithful to the living Λόγος of a text.

Toward the end of his life, in *The Flame of a Candle* (1961), Bachelard would provocatively compare such a hermeneutics that attunes itself to the reverberations of an image with the contemplation of a flickering flame at the edge of the seen and the unseen. As the intensity of a writer's imagery draws the reader in, like a flame (FC 1–2), one may begin to experience the tacit agony of a nascent Λόγος:

> A dreamer who has read the works of Franz von Baader finds muffled, miniature bursts of lightning in the cries of his candle. He hears the noise of a being that is burning, that *Schrack* that Eugene Susini tells us is untranslatable from German into French. Strange to say, the phenomena of sound and sonority are the least translatable elements from one language to another. The acoustic space of a language has its own reverberations. (FC 28–29)

One could always observe von Baader's "burning candle" from a safe aesthetic distance, of course, and reflect it on the surface of the mind (or the target language) as in a mirror. But when a writer's word strains toward a new meaning that trembles beyond its formal boundaries, moving beyond established thought, the only way for a reader-translator to do it justice is to plunge into the fluctuating field of its super-flame and let its intensity awaken something unforeseen. In such cases what is needed, in Bachelard's view, is "to explore with the ear those cavities in syllables that constitute the sonic core of a word, its inner matrix. . . . When the flame quivers, the eye moves and the lid trembles. But an ear entirely given over to an awareness of its own hearing has already heard the uneasiness of the light" (FC 28–29, trans. modified).[11] It is the latent energy of a demanding poetic image that dreams actively in us, moving us to cry, sing, pray, or color it anew. In this regard, Bachelard tenders a line that risks upsetting certain taboos about the inviolability of poetic *form*: "Dreams continue their growth," he claims surprisingly, "*despite the poems* that express them" (WD 18). Over and above the conventional features of literary language, Bachelard clearly grants precedence to the *oneiric energy* that gives rise to words in poems or reduces them to silence, at the stroke of an instant.

The translation of a text via "Bachelardian reverie" thus offers itself as an occasion for the reader's creative participation in what Dylan Thomas once sang as "the force that through the green fuse drives the flower"[12]—another way of thinking about the energy that both nourishes and consumes the flower of *language* as it does the flower of nature, or the flame of a candle.

Bachelard as "Dissident" Reader

It is paradoxical, nonetheless, that the scientific training that had fostered Bachelard's devotion to detail would itself lead him at times—when moved by the power of an image—into an apparent disregard of an author's specific words as "arbitrary tools" (incidentally setting off Gadamer's hermeneutic alarm). Let us then consider some of the dangers of "reading reverie" for the translator by examining Bachelard's reading of Henry David Thoreau's "Walking" (1863).[13] Bachelard sums up its theme in *Earth and Reveries of Will* by quoting what he detects as Thoreau's key motif: "I enter a swamp as a sacred place—a *sanctum sanctorum*. There is the strength, the marrow of Nature." At this point, Bachelard adds, "[Thoreau] goes on to declare his veneration for mud 'rusted with the blood of many a meadow' " (ERW 100).

In a critical essay on the role of reading and translation in Bachelard,[14] Kenneth Haltman points out that in the flurry of discussing the substance of Thoreau's essay, Bachelard managed to distort a line from its French translation, claiming that he only did so *to suit his own argument* about the fertile powers of maternal earth (RT 67–75). While Bachelard extolled Thoreau's veneration of "mud [*la boue*]" in his rendering of the line "*la boue, rouillée du sang de maints marais* [mud rusted by the blood of many a meadow]," the subject of Thoreau's sentence had actually been a set of agricultural tools (*le faucillon, l'écoubre, la bêche*) the last of which happened to be *la houe* (the "bog-hoe"). Bachelard could have misread *la houe* as *la boue* in the haste of transcription—perhaps driven by poetic zeal compounded by poor eyesight. But Haltman suspects, more seriously, that Bachelard took the French *la houe* as an "expendable tool," deliberately substituting the plural *rouillés* (rusty) with the feminine *rouillée* to make its reddish hue qualify the bloodied "mud" rather than the "agricultural tools" by which Americans have earned victories far more important than those gained by blood-stained weapons (RT 69).[15]

Haltman then concludes that Bachelard's reading offers but "revealing illustrations of his own ideas constituted *a priori* . . . in a manner less disciplined than Bachelard would have us believe" (RT 73). While technically justified, such a conclusion misses a key point. Just before the phrase that Bachelard transformed in French, Thoreau himself had elaborated on the image of fertility that had induced his French reader to see "living mud" beyond the "stained tools." When surveying a swampy property one day, Thoreau's narrator had found his employer up to his neck in the mud, swimming for his life. Nonetheless, he added, the fellow "would not part with it for any consideration, on account of the mud it contained," for it is said to be the task of the American to work the virgin soil, and he was intent on putting "a girdling ditch round the swampy ground and redeem it by the magic of his spade" ("Walking," par. 48).

Bachelard's link between "the *blood* of many a meadow" and the "sacredness of mud" was, therefore, no arbitrary projection. Thoreau had been exalting that very lifeblood when he wrote: "I enter a swamp as . . . a *sanctum sanctorum*. There is . . . the marrow of Nature" (RT100). One might even argue that Bachelard's transcription and comment of Thoreau's text followed the magnetic lure of its imagery,[16] despite its technical transgression. For poetic texts such as Thoreau's "Walking" call for a hermeneutics that grants at least equal sway—if not primacy—to an imagination attuned to the Λόγος of φύσις that underlies—both nourishing and corroding[17]—

the more technically formalized Λόγος *as ratio* that prevailed in modern thought. In such cases, our French phenomenologist would even challenge his students with this proposal:

> Since the poet dares to write an extreme reverie, the reader must dare to read it to the point of a kind of beyond of reader's reveries—without reticence, without reduction, without worry about objectivity—even adding, if it is possible, his own fantasy to the fantasy of the writer. Reading always at the summit of images, stretched toward the desire to surpass the summits, will give the reader well-defined exercises in phenomenology. (PR 204)

The question is how beneficial such *exercises* can be for students of philosophical hermeneutics, particularly those engaged in the translation of philosopher-poets, despite the occasional transgressions and obvious pitfalls—or perhaps even *thanks* to them.

Challenges of Translating Bachelard

In order to address that lingering question, let me conclude this reflection by closely examining a passage from *Intuition of the Instant* which illustrates Bachelard's attitude and emerging view of translation,[18] while simultaneously offering a sketch of his philosophical approach to Gaston Roupnel's *Siloë*. Aside from the general hermeneutic interest of the passage, its specific interest lies in that it draws on a provocative line on the nature of "truth" from Samuel Butler's *Life and Habit* (1910), which Bachelard cites from Valéry Larbaud's French translation:

> Alors que les romans de M. Roupnel sont animés d'une véritable joie du verbe, d'une vie nombreuse des mots et des rythmes, il est frappant que M. Roupnel ait trouvé dans sa *Siloë* la phrase condensée, tout entière ramassée au foyer de l'intuition. . . . Nous avons donc repris les intuitions de *Siloë* aussi près que possible de leur source et nous nous sommes efforcé de suivre sur nous-même l'animation que ces intuitions pouvaient donner à la méditation philosophique. . . . [U]ne intuition ne se prouve pas . . . elle s'expériment en multipliant ou même modifiant les conditions de son usage. Samuel Butler dit justement: "*Si une vérité n'est pas*

> *assez solide pour supporter qu'on la dénature et qu'on la malmène, elle n'est pas d'une espèce bien robuste*."[19] (*L'Intuition de l'instant* 7–8, emphasis added)

My recent translation of Bachelard's book into English (Northwestern University Press, 2013) included the following retranslation of Butler's line from Larbaud's French rendering: "*If a truth is not sturdy enough to endure distortion and rough handling, it does not belong to a very robust species*" (II 4, emphasis added)—its aim being to salvage the powerful metaphor of "truth as a living species" which had ostensibly triggered Bachelard's reading. As it turns out, this metaphor had only been latent in Butler's original English version, which actually read: "Unless a matter be true enough to stand a good deal of misrepresentation, its truth is not of a very robust order, and the blame will rather lie with its own delicacy if it be crushed, than with the carelessness of the crusher."[20] The mutations undergone by the text's translation into French and then back into English soon became apparent, prompting the critical question whether or not such retranslations—if truthful or legitimate—can be fruitful and, if so, what they might teach us about the import of such exercises on attuning the inner ear through translation practice.

At this very point in his text, Bachelard proceeds to argue that it is through the very *deformations* to which he has subjected Roupnel's theses in *Siloë* that readers will be able to weigh their *true force*. Nonetheless, he adds this caveat:

> If the integrity of Roupnel's text is much too deformed by our arabesques, readers may always restore its unity by returning to the mysterious source of the work. . . . [For] the same key intuition keeps reemerging in this book. Roupnel tells us, moreover, that its strange title is truly intelligible only to himself (*Siloë* 8). Is this not a way of inviting his readers to bring their own Siloam, the mysterious refuge of their personality, to the threshold of their reading? (II 5/8)

The implication in Bachelard's allusion to the "mysterious source of the work" to which readers are always invited to return is that every living text is animated and steered by the force of a hidden element that acts as an underlying spring capable of giving rise to a plume of poetic and semantic possibility. Although throughout his works Bachelard alludes to such a source through a variety of metaphors—a "secret hearth [*foyer secret*]" (II

3/8), a "destinal center" (PS 9), an oracular site that urges a text into the "fluid substance of its future" (RD 48–49, 141)—it remains nonetheless an elusive force that cannot be objectively determined, but only divined by awakening the inner ear to its latent call, to its unique reverberation, so that the subject may intimately participate in its vital Λόγος—stirred anew each time, as if for the first time.

In view of the various examples cited in this study, my concluding wager would thus be that readers—in their education through the practice of Bachelardian reverie in a hermeneutics of poetic and philosophical works—might grow increasingly attuned to, and adept at, experiencing (1) the timely birth of *philosophical truths* of a personal, sociopolitical, ecological, scientific, or spiritual nature; (2) the *flowering of language* itself, through its evolving sonority and emerging variations over time; (3) the becoming *of their own being*, through creative mutations in thinking and feeling habits which include somatic patterns and processes. For, as Bachelard was to discover, every live phrase vibrates bearing a subtle tune or *line of force* (L 83), a virtual *nerve fiber* that acts as a neurotransmitter between soul and body (PS xxiv, 220). Hence the ontological and evolutionary potentials of poetic language that Bachelard kept announcing since his earliest writings, and with increasing conviction in his later works.[21]

After rereading Bachelard's seminal *Intuition of the Instant* we may be left wondering whether the springs of *Siloë* evoked in Roupnel's philosophical drama—and ostensibly inspired by the pool of Siloam where a blind man gained his sight in the Gospel according to John (9:7)—might not have alluded, after all, to that vibrant poetic element that Gadamer had been divining and reaching for in his supplement to *Truth and Method*, when he described language as that "single word whose virtuality opens up an infinity of discourse"—as "the generative and creative power unceasingly to make this whole fluid" (TM 498).

Notes

1. This piece, first published in 1970 in Gadamer's *Gesammelte Werke*, vol. 2 (199–206), was later included as a supplement to *Truth and Method*, trans. Sheed and Ward, ed. Garrett Barden and John Cunning (New York: Seabury, 1975), 491–98. Henceforth *Truth and Method* is cited as TM.

2. See Heidegger's study of the historical consequences of this abstraction of the rational Λόγος from nature's living φύσις in *Introduction to Metaphysics*, trans. Ralph Manheim (New Haven: Yale University Press, 1959), 178–94.

3. In the practice of written translation, early drafts typically betray the expectations we project upon an author's words, in our attempt to make sense of them as we initially incorporate them into our own idiom or the target language. Subsequent revisions may reveal, however, that the source text implied different meanings or harbored fertile ambivalences worth bringing to the fore, as I hope to illustrate in this study.

4. The German *zu verflüssigen*, translated here as "to make fluid" (literally "to become liquid") is translated by Weinsheimer and Marshall as "fluent." It could also be rendered as "to be set into motion."

5. See my chapter "Bachelard's Hermeneutics" (chapter 7) in this volume.

6. See also Kristupas Sabolius's detailed analysis of Bachelard's "reverberation-resonance doublet," in "Rhythm and Reverie," chapter 4 of this volume.

7. This Bachelardian remark resonates with an insight inspired by Kant's *Critique of Judgment* (highlighted for me by Dennis J. Schmidt during a graduate seminar at Binghamton University) that "*Art is the self-production of Nature at the site of its final purpose.*" This would imply that Art is *natura naturans* at the site where Nature finally attains consciousness, awakening to its own creative power and transcendent implications.

8. Most thought-provoking are Bachelard's own "translations" of Heisenberg's *indeterminacy principle*—from the realm of microphysics to micropsychology—in *Earth and Reveries of Will* (58) as well as *Earth of Reveries of Repose* (13).

9. Bachelard's deft variation on Heidegger's famous theme has already been cited and discussed in chapter 7.

10. This passage is mistranslated in Maria Jolas's version of *The Poetics of Space*, which states that the "transsubjectivity of the image could not be understood in its essence through the habits of *subjective* reference alone" (PS xv). Bachelard's French text states exactly the reverse: "cette transsubjectivité de l'image ne pouvait pas être comprise, en son essence, par les seules habitudes des références *objectives*" (*Poétique de l'espace*, 3, emphasis added).

11. Conscientious translators are familiar with those moments when—because of a troubling ambiguity or an idiomatic mismatch between source and target languages—the text to be translated requires them to take a *poetic leap*. In such cases, the reader is compelled to engage in a creative act by moving beyond familiar thoughts into an agonic zone where thought must be generated anew.

12. See Dylan Thomas, *The Poems of Dylan Thomas* (New York: New Directions, 1952), 90.

13. In *La Terre et les reveries de la volonté* (131–32; cf. ERW 100) Bachelard based his reading of Thoreau's text on Léon Bazalgette's French translation, "Marcher" (*Désobéir* [Paris: Rieder, 1921], 222, 224). On this point, see Kenneth Haltman's endnotes to his translation of *Earth and Reveries of Will* (ERW 325).

14. Kenneth Haltman, "Relire et traduire: La Découverte du sens cache dans le texte Bachelardien," in *Bachelard dans le monde*, ed. Jean Gayon and Jean-Jacques Wunenburger (Paris: Presses Universitaires de France, 2000); henceforth cited as RT.

15. Thoreau, "Walking," in *Walden and Other Writings* (New York: Modern Library, 1981); here I cite this essay by paragraph numbers as available online, http://www.bartleby.com/28/15.htmlne. Thoreau's line reads: "The weapons with which we have gained our most important victories, which should be handed down as heirlooms from father to son, are not the sword and the lance, but *the bush-whack, the turf-cutter, the spade, and the bog-hoe, rusted with the blood of many a meadow*, and begrimed with the dust of many a hard-fought field" ("Walking," par. 49; my emphasis).

16. An earlier passage from Thoreau's "Walking" offers yet another guide for interpretation: "What is it that makes it so hard sometimes to determine whither we will walk? I believe that there is *a subtle magnetism in Nature*, which, if we unconsciously yield to it, *will direct us aright*" (par. 21, my emphasis).

17. Bachelard devoted part of chapter 2 in *Earth and Reveries of Repose* (1948) to Nature's corrosive powers—the virtues of decay and death—not only to its nourishing powers (ERR 46–55/62–75). As poignantly stated in the opening lines of Dylan Thomas's poem, "The force that through the green fuse drives the flower / Drives my green age; that blasts the roots of trees / Is my destroyer" (*The Poems of Dylan Thomas,* 90, lines 1–3).

18. Although Bachelard is mostly concerned with the explication or unfolding of texts, the art of translation offers a fertile context to try out what he liked to call "our temptation to be a poet"—a temptation he endorses (FC 15) and celebrates (RD 141, PS xxii). Poetic translation is indeed a field where Bachelard's hermeneutics can be critically tried and tested, since it demands acute attention and sensitivity to a text's hidden resonances and reverberations, while requiring readers to push beyond its limits, so that form can be transmuted into energy and converted back into form. Such a task demands a translator's total engagement—aesthetic, cognitive, and ethical—since the new life and direction we choose to impart to a text by our *will to logos* is inevitably a matter of responsibility, not just for our sake but for those who will follow.

19. Bachelard's note cites Samuel Butler, *La Vie et l'habitude*, trans. Valéry Larbaud (Paris: La Nouvelle Revue, 1922), 17.

20. Samuel Butler, *Life and Habit* (London: Fifield, 1910), 1.

21. The question initially raised by Bachelard in *The Dialectic of Duration* (1936) about the possibility of creative evolution via poetic language (DD 22) would find an emphatic response in *Air and Dreams* (1943): "As soon as we put language in its proper place, at the height of human evolution, it is revealed in its double effectiveness: it bestows on us the virtues of clarity and the powers of dream . . . A philosophy concerned with human destiny must . . . be an openly living language. It must study the *literary being* candidly, because [he or she] is the culmination of thought and dream" (AD 266/302; trans. modified). See also PS 222.

Part 4

Adventures in Alterity

Chapter 13

Reverie and Reverence: Bachelard's Encounter with Buber

Edward K. Kaplan

> Perhaps, you will ask, "Are you sure that legend is the true one?" Does it matter what the reality located outside of me might be, if it has helped me to live, to feel that I am and *what* I am?
>
> —Charles Baudelaire, "Windows"[1]

Gaston Bachelard both dramatizes and elucidates how poetic imagination can sensitize us to the world and to other people. And yet his works on creative reverie convey an overall impression of reading and fantasy as insulated from the cares of daily life. A closer look, however, reveals that Bachelard's analysis of dreaming consciousness strives to nurture a deeper affiliation with the other, akin to what Martin Buber calls "dialogue." Bachelard's sympathetic preface to the 1938 French translation of Buber's *I and Thou* authorizes us to seek correlations between these two modes of being in the world, solitary and communal.

Bachelard and Buber

Ethical consequences were always of concern in Bachelard's thinking. In 1938, the year he published *The Psychoanalysis of Fire*, he contributed a substantial preface to the French translation of Buber's *I and Thou* (German original, 1923).[2] Buber's theory of dialogue assumes the autonomy of two individuals who then become partners in communication. The gulf between them may be overcome through a process Buber calls "encounter," leading to mutual "recognition," reciprocal communication, and "inclusion." As Bachelard summarizes: "The encounter creates us: we were nothing—or nothing but things—before being united" (P 272/8–9).

The human individual is ontologically complete only in relationship. Bachelard describes the "two inseparable magnetic poles" of I and thou as energy producing: "I am a person if I am linked to a person. Detaching myself from my brother, I destroy myself. Losing concern for my brother, I abandon God" (P 272/10). Such is the ethical plenitude of being human, in Bachelard's response to Martin Buber, pointing to its religious foundation.

Bachelard's foundation, however, remains verbal, poetic, as he coordinates the ontology of "persons" and "things." The world first takes on personal meaning through projected desire: "A *participation* of the person endows things with such obvious poetic values that the whole language is magnified by it" (P 273/11–12). Bachelard then lyrically asserts his own poetic faith:

> What do flowers and trees matter to me, and fire and stones, if I am without love and without a home! We must be two—or at least, alas! we must have been two—in order to comprehend a blue sky, to name a sunrise! Infinite things such as sky, forest, and light find their names only in a loving heart. And the breeze of plains, its gentleness and its palpitation, is first of all the echo of a tender sigh. Thus the human soul, enriched with a chosen love, vivifies great things before little ones. The soul says *thou* to the universe right after it feels the human exaltation of the *thou*. (P 273/11)

The pathos of Bachelard's "alas!"—alluding to the loss of his wife early in their marriage—helps explain his later insistence on the pleasures of solitude made possible by abundant reading and systematic reverie. For him, such aesthetic projection which "vivifies great things before little ones" becomes the royal path of reconciliation with the world. As he puts it in *The Psychoanalysis of Fire*, "far from being a *description* of the objective phenomena, it "inscribe[s] human love at the heart of things" (PF 51/93).

Moreover, Bachelard's notion of "valorization"—attributing an affective value (usually positive) to images or substances within reverie or aesthetic contemplation—prepares a transition from imagination to ethics: "It is not knowledge of reality that makes us love reality passionately. It is *feeling*, the first and fundamental value. As for nature, we begin by loving it without knowing it, without really seeing it, by actualizing in things a love that has its basis elsewhere. Then we search for its details because we love it as a whole, without knowing why" (WD 115/155). By stepping out of the self, reverie can lead to reverence for the world and for others.

Aesthetics flows into shared life as the imagining individual seeks to establish a responsible connection with the world. The decisive mark of the ethical is "reciprocity," which Bachelard calls "the most precious Buberian category" (P 274/13). Bachelard clearly distinguishes contemplation of nature or of objects from reciprocal communication between persons: "The *noumenon*, which gets lost in the vagueness of an open-ended meditation with regard to things, is suddenly enriched as it is grasped and understood by another mind. The clearest *noumenon* is thus the meditation of one mind by another mind, and so the two souls, in a common glance, are closer, more convergent than the pupils of their eyes" (P 274/13–14)!

From Autonomy to Mediation

Writing on Martin Buber, Bachelard rejects the lone individual as the model of full human being. It is true, however, that Bachelard's phenomenology contributes to a metaphysics of autonomous imagination by emphasizing its freedom from external constraints: "Humankind is a creation of desire, not a creation of need," he asserts as early as *The Psychoanalysis of Fire* (PF 000).[3] What Bachelard calls "the function of the unreal" is a universal human force of transcendence which is at least as necessary to mental health as the "reality function." His ethical ambition in that respect was to reestablish imagination in its living role as guide for human life (AD 181/209).

Bachelard repeatedly explains how poetic reverie conveys happiness, as the solitary dreamer transcends the tensions between his desires and the oftentimes hostile objectivity of the world (PR 157–58/135–36). Freedom of will is the touchstone. He devotes an entire chapter of *The Poetics of Reverie* (1960) to the phenomenological structure of daydreaming in order to explain how the dreamer feels released from any responsibility. Reverie remains absolutely free, or at least *it feels absolute*, for the fantasizing self creates a veritable cosmos of which he or she is the center. The inner world of daydream encounters no intrusion of perceptual reality:

> [The person of reverie] lives by his reverie in a world homogeneous with his being, with his demi-being. [He] is always in

> space which has volume. Truly inhabiting the whole volume of his space, the man of reverie is from anywhere *in* his world, in an *inside* which has no *outside*. It is not without reason that people commonly say that the dreamer is *plunged* in his reverie. The world no longer poses any opposition to him. The I no longer opposes itself to the world. In reverie there is no more non-I. In reverie, the *non* no longer functions: everything is welcome. (PR 167/144, trans. modified)

Subject is no longer opposed to object, images no longer opposed to presence. "The dreamer's being invades what it touches" (PR 167). Or so it feels.

Solipsism is a commonly used term in philosophy for this experience of encompassing fullness. Here the subject is, ontologically speaking, consubstantial with the dream ("a world homogeneous with his being"). The relationship of consciousness to its content is here radically in favor of the self: "the man of reverie and the world of his reverie are as close as possible—they touch each other; they interpenetrate.They are on the same plane of being; if the being of man must be linked to the being of the world, the *cogito* of reverie would be stated thus: I dream the world, therefore, the world exists as I dream it" (PR 158/136).

How, then, do we enter the domain of ethical responsibility, if the "outside" world is not ostensibly present to the "*cogito* of the dreamer" (or lucid dreamer)? Here I underscore what I call the question of reality, which Baudelaire poses rhetorically at the end of his prose poem, "Windows," the epigraph of this chapter: "Does it matter what the reality located outside of me might be, if it has helped me to live, to feel that I am and *what* I am?"[4] With Socratic irony Baudelaire provocatively implies that, as a poet, as a writer, reality does *not* matter. My own assumption, however, is that "yes, reality *does* matter." Gaston Bachelard himself suggests this tension, and posits this premise, in the various dialectics of real versus unreal explored in his works on science and poetics.[5]

Bachelard's phenomenology of reverie indeed both anatomizes and transcends solipsism. He takes a crucial step into the world as he locates heterogeneous elements within the seemingly homogeneous unity of dreaming self and content of consciousness. For even though "the function of the unreal" seems to triumph, in practice it has not entirely displaced (or replaced) the reality function: "Thanks to shadows, the intermediary region which separates man from the world is a full region, of a light density fullness. The intermediary region softens the dialectic of being and non-being.

Imagination does not know non-being" (PR 167/144, trans. modified). If there is no nothingness within reverie, what of the "intermediary region" that separates but also links the dreaming person to the outside? Its "light density" implies that there is permeability to the world.

Human beings are composite creatures, and the dialectic of imagination versus reality is only one aspect of our multiplicity. We are constituted by much more than the radical phenomenological moment, and people function on several planes of consciousness. We are at one and the same time thinker, dreamer, and realist. The utopias of imagination do not, in practice, preclude an ethical challenge.

Mixing the Real and the Ideal

An *amalgam* of perception, memory, and imagination softens the dialectic of "reflexive" solipsism versus "transitive" ethics (Kaplan 5–6, 21–23). Reverie can perform a synthesis, in addition to liberating us through autonomous creativity. In fact imagination can draw upon concrete perceptions and memories that it enriches with values: "True images are *engravings*. Imagination engraves them in our memory. They deepen lived memories, displacing them to become memories of imagination" (PS 31–32/46, trans. modified). These memories can become revivified and infused with fresh affectivity through actual contact with the world, as well as through reading and dreaming: "For we have in our memories micro-films that can only be read if they are illumined by the living light of the imagination" (PS 175/161, trans. modified).

The imagination highlights certain memories by restoring the idealized aspects of our early impressions. Powerful dormant reveries are reawakened for their value component as remembered experience: "The remembered past is not simply a past of perception. Since one is remembering, the past is already being designated in a reverie as an image value. From the very beginning, the imagination colors the paintings it will want to see again. In order to delve into the archives of memory, one must recover values beyond the facts. . . . In our reveries, we make impressionist paintings of our past" (PR 105/89–90, trans. modified). Reverie is a technique for reliving our past in such a way that we may more freely reconcile ourselves with reality, past and present, orchestrating facts and desires.

Self-integration is achieved through such links between inner and external experience. Bachelard's methodological preface to *The Poetics of*

Space (1957) revises the psychological orientation of his books on the four elements; he applies the phenomenology of Eugene Minkowski to examine how the poetic image can echo on the affective level as well as reverberate deep into the dreaming-reader's distant past (PS xii–xiii/12).[6]

> The resonances [outer echoes] are dispersed on the different planes of our life in the world, while the reverberations invite us to give greater depth to our own existence. In the resonance we hear the poem, in the reverberations we speak it—it is our own. The reverberations bring about a change of being. It is as though the poet's being were our being. The multiplicity of resonances then issues from the reverberation's unity of being . . . the poem possesses us entirely. This grip that poetry acquires on our very being bears a phenomenological mark that is unmistakable. The exuberance and depth of a poem are always phenomena of the resonance-reverberation doublet. (PS xviii–xix/6–8; trans. modified)

Bachelard explains how a sort of transsubjectivity transpires. The assumed contact with another person (the poet) is produced, in large part, by both echoes and reverberations within the reader.

Bachelard's key notion of "phenomenological doublet" of ideal and real is the foundation of his ethics. His prime example is childhood, the original season and locus of such syntheses. He devoted a full chapter of *The Poetics of Reverie* to childhood reveries, exploring how the surface echoes and inner reverberations of poetic reading can be integrated so as to enhance our relation to the world as it truly exists:

> In our opinion, it is in the memories of this cosmic solitude that we ought to find the nucleus of childhood which remains at the center of the human psyche. It is there that imagination and memory are most closely bound together. It is there that the being of childhood binds the real with the imaginary, that it lives the images of reality in total imagination. And all these images of cosmic solitude react in depth in the child's being; aside from his being for other people, a being for the world is thus created under the inspiration of the world. Such is the being of cosmic childhood. (PR 108/92)

Paradoxically, cosmic reveries, which require radical solitude and freedom from the reality function, prepare us to inhabit the finite world. The union of memory and imagination restores idealized aspects of childhood's (already idealized) first impressions. For example: "Poetry gives not so much a nostalgia for youth, which would be vulgar, as a nostalgia for the expressions of youth. It offers us images as we should have imagined them during the 'original impulse' of youth" (PS 33/47). The objective past of childhood, reimagined, remembered in terms of its reveries, becomes an idealized memory, and hence a "future of its living images, the *reverie future* which opens before any rediscovered image" (PR 112/96). This union of memory and imagination can thus compose a new being in the world, transcending time and open to all possibilities.

This lived "doublet" of ideal and real includes a simultaneous amalgam of wish and perception. The "doublet" enriches our perception of the outside world while not entirely removing us from the world. A positive appreciation of what exists out there can begin as a result of reliving what Bachelard calls "reflected" nature, that is, objects that have passed through a mental process:

> The lake, the pond, still waters naturally awaken our cosmic imagination through the beauty of a reflected world. A dreamer, in their proximity, receives a very simple lesson for imagining the world, for doubling the real world with an imagined world. The lake is a master at natural watercolors. The colors of the reflected world are tenderer, softer, more beautifully fanciful than the [more] heavily substantial colors. Already, those colors borne by reflections belong to an idealized universe. The reflections thus invite any dreamer of still waters to idealization. . . . Such is the phenomenological law of poetic reverie. Poetry prolongs the world's beauty, aestheticizes the world. (PR 198/170–71, trans. modified)

Valorization of the world through projected love can lead to imaginative "reciprocity," a phenomenon also known to us as the "pathetic fallacy" of romantic poets, in which nature appears to respond to the poet's emotions. In developing his theory of imaginative will, Bachelard speaks of an endless exchange between vision and the visible: "All that is seen, sees" (WD 30/44, trans. modified).[7] Imaginative reciprocity assumes a view of humankind and nature as dynamically identical in terms of creative will: "When a poet lives his dreams and poetic creations, he realizes this natural unity. It then seems that contemplated nature helps in contemplation, that it contains within itself the means of contemplation . . . [This] is an elementary law of imagination" (WD 27–28/41–42, trans. modified).

From Aesthetic Reciprocity to Ethics

We now stand at the crossroads of psychology, phenomenology, and ethics. The aesthetic reciprocity of self and world reflects an inner integration of the dreamer's faculties, which Bachelard identifies with intrapsychic gender identity. He applies this phenomenology to interpersonal intimacy in the chapter of *The Poetics of Reverie* devoted to C. G. Jung's theory of mental androgyny—the *animus* that represents "male" rationality and the *anima* that represents "female" intuition and reverie (PR 55–95). Bachelard begins with Jung's study of the alchemists who, in their solitude, projected their dreams into substances but without entering the world realistically: "Reverie idealizes both its object and the dreamer at the same time. And when reverie lives within a dialectic of masculine and feminine, the idealization is at once concrete and limitless" (PR 58/49; trans. modified).

This is the crucial turning point. Such integration of male and female aspects of the mind can nurture a loving perception of the world—and not only with aestheticized nature, but also with another person in his or her otherness. Bachelard here proceeds to analyze "the communion of two people in love, [where] the dialectic of *animus* and *anima* appears as a phenomenon of 'psychological projection' " (PR 73/63). A "complete psychology" unites the poetics of reverie and a prosaic life.

Successful idealization can prepare a true loving relationship, according to Bachelard. His phenomenological model explains how authentic human love can develop from reciprocal fantasies: "The man who loves a woman 'projects' upon that woman all the values he venerates in his own *anima*. Similarly, the woman 'projects' upon the man she loves all the values that her own *animus* would like to conquer" (PR 73/63). This type of "criss-crossed [*croisées*]" projections, "when they are well balanced," makes for strong mutual relationships.

> The function of the unreal finds its concrete usefulness in a very coherent idealization, in an idealized life that warms the heart,

> granting real dynamism to life. The masculine ideal projected by the woman's *animus* and the feminine ideal projected by the man's *anima* are bonding energies that can surmount the obstacles of reality. People love each other in complete ideality, each enjoining their partner with the task of realizing the ideality, such as it is dreamed. What hence becomes animated in the secret of solitary reveries is not the shadows, but the glimmers of light that illumine the dawning of a love. (PR 74/63–64, trans. modified)[8]

We are approaching a true loving relationship; but this is not yet a dialogical situation, conscious mutual communication, such as analyzed by Martin Buber.[9] At this point, Bachelard develops a complex chart of mutual projections that end in a quadripolar relationship. Each person is doubled: a real self in the world and an ideal self within the cosmos of reverie.[10]

Of course this double or binary nature is a flawed conceptual category, as it attempts to map out complex personalities. The dialectic, however, as simplistic as it might appear, points to a process by which the unreal can become integrated into our personality. We can apply this mental synthesis—or *amalgam* of ideal and real—to social and intimate relationships, be they with nature, substances, poetic images, or people.

The fulfilled dreamer, then, is happy, and not only within the ontological bubble of his or her inner space. Autonomous imagination enables the dreamer to be "an other than himself," a double of himself who retains, nonetheless, his rationality. Mastery of this splitting is the key:

> The shadow, the double of our being, experiences "the psychology of depths" in its reveries. And so, the being projected by reverie—for our I-dreamer is a projected being—is double as we ourselves are, and is, like ourselves, *animus* and *anima*. Here we are at the knot of all our paradoxes: *the "double" is the double of a double being.* (PR 80/69)

This doubling—or, more realistically, multidimensionality of consciousness—still allows us to differentiate between fantasy, wish, and the real: although they become mixed in the process of valorization. The values attributed to the Other are in practice projected, even though they may also be "real." Most importantly, the negotiations required by a shared life solidify this mixture of ideal and real as "relationship" or authentic "dialogue."

That is one way in which the function of the unreal restores mental health, enabling us to participate more fully in social (or consensus) reality. Bachelard continues:

> Then, in the most solitary reveries, when we call forth vanished beings, when we idealize the persons who are dear to us, when in our readings we are free enough to live as both man and woman, we feel that all of life takes on a double—that the past takes on a double, that all beings become double in their idealization, that the world incorporates all the beauties of our chimeras. Without a chimerical psychology, there is no true psychology, no complete psychology. In reverie, the person is sovereign. In studying the real person, a psychology of observation only encounters an uncrowned being. (PR 80/69)

Bachelard's defense of "illusory" psychology is of course ironic. He uses that polemic device to remind us that so-called "illusion" contains the seeds of a deeper realism. We are responsible for reconciling our needs and dreams with those of the person we seek to love.

The foundation common to Bachelard's ethics and his phenomenology of the solitary dreamer is precisely this multiplicity of dimensions we can share with nature or with other people. The dualistic paradigm, I repeat, is more rhetorical than metaphysical. Bachelard strives to formulate an intimate *mixture*, less neat than a binary paradox, but closer to who we really are:

> It is here that the intermediary play between thought and reverie, between the psychic functions of the real and the unreal, multiplies and crisscrosses to produce the psychological marvels of human imagination. Human being is a being to be imagined [*un être à imaginer*]. For in the end, the function of the unreal works just as well in terms of humankind as it does in terms of the cosmos. What would we ever know about others if we did not imagine them? What psychological refinement don't we feel when we read a novelist who *invents a character*, and all the poets who invent the prestigious enrichments of the human! And it is those overreaches that we live, without daring to admit it, in our taciturn reveries. (PR 81/70; trans. modified)

Such is Bachelard's goal as scientific and poetic thinker, to restore humankind's fullness of being, surpassing ordinary perception, surpassing ourselves—and not by isolating our creative capacities, however, but by mixing them with reality. For Bachelard, Balzac's novel about androgynous beings, *Séraphitâ*, is an ethical model: "The reverie which idealizes the relationships of *animus* and *anima* is then an integral part of real life; reverie is an active force in the destiny of persons who wish to unite their life through a growing love" (PR 88).

Reverie and Reverence

So the self of poetic reverie can encompass the inner cosmos, the world beyond, and other people. We thus return to Bachelard's original dialogue with Martin Buber: care for others is its keynote. Bachelard concludes his essay on Buber with two crucial references to Buber's later essays, which he read in the original German: "Zwiesprache [Dialogue]," published in 1932, nine years after *I and Thou*, and "Die Frage an den Einzelnen [The Question to the Single One]," 1936), Buber's rejection of Kierkegaard's radical individualism in favor of ethical reciprocity.

For Bachelard, poetry is as necessary for human survival as is scientific knowledge. The mature self is a composite of both I and thou, self and things, ideality and objective presence. Healthy persons harmonize both *animus* and *anima*, reason and imagination. By integrating these competing faculties, Bachelard's phenomenology of imagination mediates between the solitary dreamer and the outside world. The result is that we can revere others, and the world, as we exult in our freest dreams. Gaston Bachelard's recap of Martin Buber summarizes his own aspirations as ethical philosopher: "Eye for eye, breath for breath, soul for soul. I see you and understand you; therefore, we are souls" (P 274/14).

Notes

1. Charles Baudelaire, "Windows," in *The Parisian Prowler, Le Spleen de Paris: Petits poèmes en prose*, trans. Edward K. Kaplan (Athens: University of Georgia Press, 1989, 2nd ed., 1997), 93. See my book, *Baudelaire's Prose Poems: The Esthetic, the Ethical, and the Religious* (Athens and London: University of Georgia Press, 1990), esp. chap. 7, "Theoretical Fables of Reality: The Ontological Paradox of Literature," 116–33, and my prefaces to the second edition of *The Parisian Prowler*.

2. Bachelard's commentary was published in French as "Préface à *Je et Tu* de Martin Buber" trans. Geneviève Bianquis (Paris: Aubier Montaigne, 1938),

7–15. My revised English translation of Bachelard's Preface to Buber's *I and Thou* (abbreviated P) appears as appendix A in this volume).

3. The following discussion extends my original paper, "Gaston Bachelard's Philosophy of Imagination: An Introduction," *Philosophy and Phenomenological Research* 33, no. 1 (September 1972): 1–24; hereafter cited as Kaplan.

4. Baudelaire, "Windows" (n. 1 above).

5. For instance, see Bachelard's ERW 13–26, RA 1–11, MR 1–36.

6. See Eugene Minkowski, *Vers une cosmologie: Fragments philosophiques* (1933; Paris: Aubier-Montaigne, 1936). Bachelard's connection with Minkowski deserves further research.

7. See also Kaplan, 9–11.

8. Bachelard here proceeds to diagram a more complex, quadripolar system of projections (PR 74–79).

9. See Buber, *Between Man and Man, Knowledge of Man,* and of course *I and Thou.* See also my study "Martin Buber and the Drama of Otherness: The Dynamics of Love, Art, and Faith," *Judaism: A Quarterly Journal of Jewish Life and Thought* 27, no. 2 (Spring 1978): 196–206.

10. "Here, the reverie of communion is no longer a philosophy of the communication of consciousnesses. It is life in a double, through a double, a life animated in an intimate dialectic of *animus* and *anima.* Doubling [*doubler*] and splitting [*dédoubler*] exchange functions. Doubling our being by idealizing the beloved being, we split our being into its two powers of *animus* and *anima*" (PR 77/67).

Chapter 14

Missing Land: Between Heidegger and Bachelard

Edward S. Casey

This chapter takes its start from two recent concerns of mine. On the one hand the idea of the end of the earth, its very edge, and on the other the importance of "land" as a middle term (and latent phenomenon) between "earth" and "world." The first concern stems from an ancient obsession with discovering the limit of the physical planet we inhabit, its endpoint or ultimate horizon, the second, from a much more recent problem, one found within Heidegger's influential essay,"The Origin of the Work of Art" (1935).[1] My hypothesis is that Bachelard, though not dealing with either of these concerns directly, casts remarkable light upon them and that conversely they help to illuminate his thought in *Earth and Reveries of Will* (1947) and *Earth and Reveries of Repose* (1948), so beautifully brought into English in the translations recently published by the Dallas Institute of Humanities and Culture. My deeper obsession is with a phenomenon that remained surprisingly unthematized in all three sources: land. Why is this so? What kind of blind spot is operative here? It will turn out that we have to do with three distinctive forms of blindness, of which only Bachelard's harbors redemptive resources for poetry, for painting, and for life. How can this be?

Consider the ancient case first of all. The ancient peoples of the Mediterranean—the Greeks, the Phoenicians, the Cretans, the Carthaginians, and others—had their own obsession. This was to find the end of the known earth, the *eschaton* of the *oikoumene*. Perhaps precisely because of the self-enclosed status of the Mediterranean, they were fascinated with going beyond its outer edges; intimations of a greater earth were given in the Caspian Straights, as they led to the Black Sea to the east, and above all to the Pillars of Hercules to the west, as we know from the accounts of Hanno the Carthaginian and others. The pillars beckoned to an unknown world where the ocean, Okeanos, ruled. Okeanos signified the undelimited, and the question it posed to the early navigators and equally to the early poets and philosophers was whether it had any ultimate limit. The existence of the horizon over land and sea alike suggested that some kind of perimeter out there existed, but just as horizons recede with every advance toward them, so these oceanic *eschata* vanished continually from view as sailors headed into the open sea. Pindar, contemplating this daunting prospect, had this sobering thought: "What lies beyond [the Pillars of Hercules] cannot be approached by wise men or unwise. I shall not try, or I would be a fool."[2] No wonder, then, that Hanno the Carthaginian clung so closely to the West African coast in his voyage of the sixth century BCE, very happy to find mountains, and beaches, and very hairy people who inhabited them. Looking east as he sailed south, the land provided the reassuring limit which the voyage otherwise failed to provide when one wheeled around and faced the west, which was limitless. Yet it was the west in its limitless limit that drew out the earliest known sailors, not just from Carthage or Greece, but from Scandinavia and Ireland, indeed from ancient China, and so on.

What were all these people seeking? They were not trying to prove some overriding theory about the extent of space. Rather, the interest was in going beyond land's end, beyond its reassuring limits to an open region whose apparent endlessness struck terror in the hearts of the early explorers, and yet lured them ever outward beyond shores and accustomed limits. The terror was already evident in the fact that, within the Mediterranean itself, sailors preferred to go from one coastal point to another in the ancient manner of the *periplous*, the voyage whose epic expression was the *Odyssey*, and whose actual technique came to be called *costaggiare* by later Portuguese navigators, meaning sailing by hugging the coast. Despite the anxiety occasioned by the trackless sea, there was a palpable push toward finding out where the largest possible body of water, the ocean that surrounds the earth, might come to an end, and how it could do so—as a sharp edge, as a blunt recession, or as a slow fading out? So powerful was this question that it dominated many generations of Mediterranean peoples, and it leads us to ask: Why was this so? Why, if it not only courted danger and disaster, when it was literalized in outer-sea voyages, but also tempted whole peoples to forsake their own countries of origin, indeed their own land, more notably the fearless Vikings, the Mediterraneans, and so on, who were always wishing, like Ulysses, to return home, a phrase that exactly translates the *nostos* root of the word "nostalgia"?

To find an answer we need only consider that every place is a place *on earth*, and that earth in turn, as we feel it under our feet and see it receding in the distance, not only supports us physically and biologically, but conveys to us a distinct sense of a greater spatial whole that exceeds the very place in which we find ourselves at any given moment. To be in place is to know that we are part of a much more extensive place of places, which is that of the earth itself. The earth is at once utterly concrete—so much so that phenomenologically it never seems to move, except in earthquakes—and it is resistant to our efforts to displace or transform it. What would resistance be, asks Bachelard, without its stubbornness, its deep substantiality, its depth—that of matter itself. Not only depth, but breadth is a major access of our primal experience of the earth, which brings with it a sense of outgoing outreach toward the visible horizon; breadth takes us out and beyond, thus even when I stay in place, lingering at home in Athens, I sense that the earth goes wide as well as deep, and I start wondering, how wide? How far can I go on land or sea to get to its final limit? Without going to sea, I begin to experience that primordial wonder, or *thaumazein*, which the Greeks treasured as the beginning of philosophical thought.

But the full sense of this earthly width is to be had outside the walls of the polis, the city, in that unmapped space of the margin in which Plato's *Phaedrus* is set so precariously: "Forgive me, my friends," says Socrates, as he reluctantly leaves the city for a rare conversation that cannot take place in the city, "I am devoted to learning. Landscapes and trees have nothing to teach me. Only the people in the city can do that."[3] In fact, much of great interest is to be found out there in the liminal zone, the margin: the nature of beauty, whose more exact delineation is pursued in this same conversation in this same place outside the city.[4] The perception of the horizon, the character of unbounded space, not to mention the natural world in its teeming multiplicity—all this arises, in short, in the landscape, a concept that has no proper name in Greek. Indeed, there is no coherent notion of "land" in ancient Greek culture and language; there is *place*, *region*, and *unbounded space*, but no *land* proper, a curious and telling omission with enormous consequences, one of which is precisely the passion for finding the edge of the earth at the risk of losing secure footing on the land. One is driven to go at any cost to earth's end, whether in speculation or in actual exploration, and to do so by leaving the land that subtends one's home place and entering the ever-spacious sea beyond the wildness of the boundless. The obsession with land's end comes at the expense of land itself.

A second loss of land occurs in 1935, the date of Heidegger's "Origin of the Work of Art." This is a short, late modern tale, but one just as instructive. But let me first say that I take earth to be what subtends human experience; in Husserl's phrase, it is the basis-body for all more particular bodies that reside in it or on it, whether animate or inanimate. Earth stands under the movements of our bodies, the upsurge of organic matter, and the settling down of stone. For all its vulcanism, its metamorphic shifts and evolutionary drifts, earth is the guarantor of all that we do on it. Its felt immobility puts paltry human motions in their place. It is an ultimate place of places against which we measure the comparative instability and waywardness of whatever we humans and other animals do. Even earthquakes eventually equilibrate. Land is something else again. Not merely is it the crust of the earth, its surface, whether as soil for agriculture, as the basis of landscape, thus something for viewing and painting, or as objectified property for possession as real estate. It is also land as *mediatrix* between earth and world, where I take world to be the communal, historical, and linguistic domain of human speech and action. Heidegger, who dramatized the earth-world contrast in his celebrated essay of 1935, significantly failed to single out land in his insistent emphasis on the polemical relationship between earth and world, their unremitting struggle (PLT 48–49). I have long felt that we cannot leave matters just there, that there is an unacknowledged *Zwischenraum*, a space of the between, between the two epicenters of earth and world, and this is land—the very land that is the inspiration of landscape painting, earthworks, photography of nature, and of much mapping.

Land is a liminal concept. It is both literally liminal—a *limen*, or threshold, between earth and sky in our direct perceptual experience—and liminal in the more expanded sense that it is the arena in which earth turns toward world and thereby gains a face, a *facies* or surface.[5] Land is not a surface in the sense of a mere covering, that is, as sheer topsoil, but rather in the richer sense of that which bears out its own depths. Here "the depths are all the surface" (Wittgenstein), and just as "land brings earth out into visibility" (Gibson) in that layout of surfaces which is the experiential basis of the natural environment, so land allows earth to become imageable in paintings, photographs, or maps and intelligible in the historical deeds and language of a given human life-world. Land turns earth inside out, as it were, putting tellurian contents on display, setting them out in particular places and regions, so as then to become subject to articulation in language and to play a role in the history of those who live on it. The configuration of the local lands in Texas, for instance, not merely expresses the character of the geological forces beneath it, but it also furnishes soil for wheat and other crops, as well as redoubts for ranchers.

That Heidegger misses the crucial *tertium quid*, the third term, or dissolves it into one or both—either earth or world—is not accidental. This critical omission reflects his anti-Hegelian effort to eliminate third terms and to conceive of human culture in terms of a pitched *polemos*, a battle royal; it also reflects his own world-time, the mid-1930s, a time of mounting armed conflict and forced choices, with no compromise allowed, no middle ground, no land that is not *ours* or *theirs*. Understandable perhaps, as a response to the terrors of his time in which he was himself complicitous, Heidegger's bipolar model is nevertheless ill equipped to deal with the subtlety of land, its complex configurations. Here I am not so much rejecting Heidegger's framework of earth and world as letting it stay in place in order to show how at every turn it must be supplemented. What is called for is a much more resolute commitment to the concreteness of experience of the land, which draws earth and world together in one embrace as their deeply common term. This is land, which in effect deconstructs the dyad of earth and world from within; land is a *mediatrix*, but odd and upsetting, and metaphysically untenable.

Land undeniably relates closely both to earth and to world. Earth subtends it from below, world extends it above, but land has its own unique form of being as depth in surface; it is the basis of the places and regions that fill out earthscapes, and it makes possible, directly or indirectly, the worlds that are established in its midst—in farms, cities, cultures, languages, and traditions—thereby creating worldscapes. It is the primal scene of concrescent tellurian forces downward and cosmic directions outward. It is itself always singular; it is always just this land, located in this particular place and nowhere else. We are lucky to have it; no wonder we crave it so much and miss it so mightily when we have lost it. Not just its sheer materiality as soil or property, in the phenomenological fact that land is the inner frame of all outgoing and ongoing perception, a basis for personal as well as public identities, for just where we are, after all, has much to do with just who we are.

From the ancient mariners to Heidegger is a giant step, and one can hardly imagine a more landlocked philosopher than Heidegger, who once wrote an autobiographical essay entitled "Why I Stay in the Provinces," but from Heidegger to Bachelard the distance is much less drastic. In the late

1930s, the same decade when Heidegger wrote "The Origin of the Work of Art," Bachelard was just starting his series of books on the material imagination. Each thinker had a special sensitivity to the elemental character of the poetic imaginary. Each was of peasant stock and grew up in a small rural village far from any metropolitan center. Perhaps precisely because of this deeply ingrained *Bodenständischkeit*, or earthboundness, neither philosopher felt the need to thematize "land" as such in his writings; it was in their blood, part of their habitual body-memory.[6] Was this the basis for the conspicuous absence of land at the very point where one would have most expected it in Heidegger's "Origin" essay and in Bachelard's *Earth and Reveries of Will*? Maybe, but one might suspect that more than oversight, or the taken for granted, is at stake.

Land is a concept that does not fit into familiar Western schemata; it is a maverick notion, what Kant would have called a *reflective concept*, that is to say, an idea that cannot be subsumed under an already existing concept. Exemplary cases of reflective concepts on Kant's own list include the beautiful and the sublime, and it is not accidental that these latter arise in the realm of art, just where land is ostensibly missing from Heidegger's aesthetics, as well as Bachelard's if to a lesser extent. I consider it symptomatic, for instance, that in the common preface to both of his volumes on earth, Bachelard explicitly disavows any recourse to land in the work to come. To quote:

> Before concluding these general remarks, I want to explain an omission for which I will doubtless be reproached in a work devoted to earth. I have left out images of agriculture. Certainly this is not due to any lack of love for the soil; in fact, it seemed to me a betrayal of the orchard and the garden to speak of them only in one short chapter. It would require an entire book to unearth the agriculture of the imagination, the joys of spade and rake. (ERW 11)

Here Bachelard admits that it is his rootedness in the land that leads him to set it aside as a topic requiring special treatment that would exceed the limits of *Earth and Reveries of Will*, his essay on the imagination of forces.[7] An entire book that would unearth the agriculture of the imagination is a book he did not write as such, although many of the transmutational elements of agriculture are woven into his remarks on roots, vineyards, and wine in his *Earth and Reveries of Repose*. In fact, his own stated limitations do not prevent him from occasionally adverting to these and other aspects of land even in the first chapter *of Earth and Reveries of Will* where he talks of the laborer, a poet with hands that knead, who gently works the sluggish elasticity of matter. Surely the paradigm case of such a laborer is the farmer, who can very well be said to work the sluggish elasticity of soil. Indeed, many other passages in this same book betray an uncanny proximity to descriptions of land, even though the term itself, *le sol*, is not used. I pick out at random the following instances, all from the first chapter:

> By means of imagination we human beings convince ourselves that we are responsible for bringing the energies potentially in matter to life . . . we sharpen the mineral hostility of what is hard, and bring the fruited orbs of what is soft to ripeness. (ERW 21)

> When prevented by the ever-renewed resistance of matter from becoming too mechanical, manual labor restores to our bodies, to our energies, to the expressions and even the words we use, their original force. (ERW 22)

> The tactile sensation of digging into matter with one's fingers, discovering its substance beneath form and color, gives one the illusion of touching the very *essence* of matter. (ERW 24)

In each case we can replace matter with land. Land after all is a form of matter, perhaps even the primary form for earthlings. Thus energy's potential can lie as well in land as in matter per se.[8] Both "mineral hostility" and "fruited orbs" belong to the land. The act of being an agriculturalist, a word that signifies cultivating the field or reshaping the land as well as digging into matter with one's fingers and discovering its substance, is experienced at the most primal level in relation to the land.

This is not to mention the entire thematics of energetic dualism of hand and matter in Bachelard's book, which is pervasive in the book as a whole. Is not the first and most abiding form of such dualism that of hand and *land*? And if this is indeed an active dualism quite different from the classic dualism of subject and object, is this not because the land that links them is recalcitrant to this very dualism? A related question concerning "resistance," with which Bachelard opens his entire analysis of earth: Don't we first find the resistance of matter itself in the ground on which we stand

and in the soil we plow and plant; that is, in the land which our active bodies, hands and feet alike, encounter as we cope with being on earth? And is it not the same land that is also simultaneously yielding, thereby forming the basis for what Bachelard later calls ideal earth and matter—a perfect synthesis of yielding and resistance, a marvelous equilibrium of the forces of acceptance and refusal?

More generally, can we not say that land is where will meets earth? If so, land would be every bit as much the missing third term between Bachelard's will and earth as it is between Heidegger's earth and world. At least this is so on a first reading of Bachelard's text, but a more generous reading detects in Bachelard a saving grace not found in Heidegger, or for that matter in those ancient exploration narratives. Even if the explicit language of land—for which there is admittedly no precise French equivalent (the closest cousins being: *sol*, *terre*, *terrain*)—is sparingly used in Bachelard's discourse, there are promising ways by which land becomes a positive presence in its own right, and not merely a *tertium quid* between home-place and open sea, or between polis and *eschaton*, or between earth and world.

I have in mind two ways in particular. First there is Bachelard's intriguing model of the nexus of imagery, energy, and matter: "By experiencing the curious condensation of imagery and energy that characterizes work with matter, we experience for ourselves the synthesis of imagination and will. This synthesis, largely ignored by philosophers, is nonetheless the first synthesis to consider in a dynamology of the human psyche" (ERW 18). If we extend this claim expressly to land, we can begin to think of the latter as a comparable nexus that, far from being sheer soil, is something dynamic and changing and moving, and doing so not only in the natural world outside us, where mass is enlivened, but within, psychically, where habits are dissolved in an onrush of transition. All of this happens slowly, as befits dealing with land, and it results in what Bachelard calls "a dialectical animism," where matter reveals to us our own strengths.

Put in terms of land, this means that the working through of any concerted intervention on the land is in effect an interanimation of psyche and soil, self and other. This is more easily glimpsed in the gentle intentionality of gardening than in the willful and sometimes violent actions of farming. Wherever genuine cultivation of earth takes place, we witness preoccupation with the land, with its potentialities and its vistas, rather than being a matter of labor alone, as Bachelard often tends to hold. Such preoccupying cultivation can be creative work, as we see most notably in the case of earthworks created by Smithson and Heiser, Oppenheim and Stuart. To move to the level of land is to open up the prospect of such concrete creativity, which is the equivalent of poetic possibility in the realm of extension.[9]

A second way by which land is enlivened is found in Bachelard's emphasis on the sublimation of earth in works of art. This had already been a theme in *Air and Dreams: An Essay on the Imagination of Movement*, where Bachelard distinguished between discursive sublimation in search of a beyond and dialectical sublimation in pursuit of the close-by (AD 6). Bachelard discerns two directions of sublimation. In the first, we sublimate upward, toward the beyond, *au-delà*, toward height in the preferred word of *Earth and Reveries of Will*. To sublimate in terms of the close-by, *à coté*, on the other hand, suggests movement into the proximity of one's local place, into the here and now of being on earth. Instead of height, the pertinent dimensions now become depth and breadth: "The contemplation of the landscape whose depth and breadth would seem to call forth dreams of limitlessness gives rise to a sort of panoramic dream state" (ERW 293). Landscape is the face of the land, its visual garment, as it were. If its surface brims with depth, its edge creates breadth, the felt width to which I alluded earlier as being intrinsic to land; thanks to the horizon that at once encircles land and leads it ever further outward, it also invokes the limitless immensity, which Bachelard ascribes specifically to the earth:

> The fundamental image of immensity is terrestrial. The earth is immense, vaster by far than the sky; naturally the sea too forms part of the earth, a simplified earth, and, where quasi-elemental meditation is concerned, one whose primary attribute is its immensity. Earth is an instance of absolute grandeur, at once beyond compare, yet concrete and material. (ERW 292)

So much for any equipoise among members of what Heidegger sometimes calls the twofold: earth and sky. So much, too, for any claim that the sea is vaster than the known earth. Rather than Okeanos as the boundless, it is earth itself that is out of bounds. We need not settle this ancient competition for the most limitless element or regions; for our purposes what matters is that according to a certain notion of sublimation, we do not transcend the earth but return to it, like Antaeus, in its concrete immensity. At its most concrete, such immensity is that of the land around us and under us, which knows no precise limit, least of all that of any property line. As in the perception of any field, we cannot determine the exact edge of land, which is limitless without being colossal, specific without being formal or geometric, finite yet not closed, fitting into the sweep of our look, but not measurable by human means. In short, land gives to us a progressive solidification in the materials offered in the human imagination. It hands back to us what our hands reach out to touch in it—not an absolute grandeur but an intimate immensity that shares the scale of our lived bodies and experienced histories. It gives us a place, a very particular place, on the earth itself. Thanks to his ideas of the energetic nexus and a localizing sublimation, Bachelard allows us to deliteralize land, to free it from the perennial temptation to regard it as something merely functional or cartographic or legal, and thus to see in it possibilities for a redemptive role in poetry and painting, in earthworks and earth mappings, and in our daily lives as well.[10]

Now we are left with a question: Why land? Why, if earth presents us with such an embarrassment of riches, as Bachelard and Heidegger so surely demonstrate, do we need land beyond earth? My answer runs like this: If land is earth turned inside out and made available to us, it is the effective concretization of earth, the arena in which earth comes forward to meet us, as it were, there where we can work and play with it. And if it is true that, in J. J. Gibson's words, the surface is where most of the action is, the land is indeed the surface of the earth, the place where its depths are put on display for labor and work, delectation and delight. Land is also the wherewithal for the intertanglement of the human and the natural. Only in the land is it the case that—as in Merleau-Ponty's words, "everything is cultural in us and everything is natural in us"—that is, everything is historical in us, and everything is wild in us.[11] In contrast, world in Heidegger's sense is only cultural-historical, while earth for him is only wild. We need land not just to bridge the conceptual gap between earth and world, but also to ensure that the antipodes of the cultural and the natural truly connect and interpenetrate. In land alone do these extremes *se touchent*.

This is true as well for the extremities of the ancient world, home and horizon, coast and sea; the diremption of these dyads as oppositional, as Heidegger's preferred pairs of earth–world, earth–sky, fails to take into account the connective tissue of land. This is not the land of "land and sea"—the familiar phrase that keeps land locked into a literal opposition to water—but land as felt and imagined, kneaded and plowed, that is to say, worked through with hands and feet as well as shot through with words and images, those of poetry and painting and maps. Then land can be seen not as the sublimation of raw matter in an ascensional direction, but as something sublime within matter itself. It becomes the *descension of material images*—a phrase from Bachelard (ERW 81)—rather than their rarefication; a matter of concrete reflection instead of abstract determination; and finally, as many things in many modalities rather than one kind of thing in one sort of format. Land circulating polymorphically in our equally wild and cultural lives moves to the level of landscape, deliteralized and at long last worthy of this latter, still powerful, still mysterious notion that is called for insistently when we reflect on the place of land in human experience. To move from earth to land, as I have done in this chapter, is one bold step we need to make in the wake of two and a half millennia of confusion and neglect. To move from land to landscape would be another major step, but I shall leave making the case for that move, mercifully, for another occasion.

Notes

1. Heidegger's use of *earth* and *world* in "The Origin of the Work of Art" designates a binary tension between the emerging/receding forces of nature and the realm of culture. For Heidegger, the constant friction between the two, in which the cultural *world* is grounded or set up upon the *earth*, is generative of a site-specific ontology. See Martin Heidegger, *Poetry, Language, Thought*, trans. Albert Hofstatdter (New York: Harper, 1975), especially 42–49; hereafter cited as PLT.

2. Pindar, "Olympian 3: For Theron of Acragas, Winner of the Chariot Race," in *The Complete Odes*, ed. Anthony Verity (Oxford: Oxford University Press, 2007), 3.45–48.

3. Plato, *Phaedrus*, 230d.

4. *Phaedrus*, 237b–257b. *Phaedrus* 237c–238c addresses the danger of what is, for Socrates, a tyrannical desire for beauty—ἔρως—that is unchecked by reason; 248d defines a philosopher as a "lover of the beautiful"; in 249d, Socrates argues that, although *eros* (desire for the beautiful) is a kind of madness, there is a "best kind"—that which, when viewed or experienced on earth, invokes a memory of the *true* form of beauty derived from the divine. Values such as moderation, reason, self-control become vital to justly maneuvering through the lure of beauty as experienced on earth in helping one to recall the vague hints of beauty's divine *form* behind its instances. (I thank Chatham Lovette for this last line of thought.)

5. See Bachelard's comments on "thresholds" in *Earth and Reveries of Will* (146–47) and in his chapter on the "Dialectics of Inside/Outside" in *The Poetics of Space*, where he approaches thresholds as subtle dynamic phenomena.

6. Inklings of land, nonetheless, could not help but trickle into Bachelard's passing reveries on his beloved Champagne—as in his lines on the region of Champagne where he was born, in *Water and Dreams* (7–8). See also his comments on the power of vineyards to transmute earth into word, in *Earth and Reveries of Repose*

(236–43), or his comments on the metabolic forces at work in Flocon's engravings in "Introduction to the Dynamics of Landscape" (RD 55–70).

7. The original subtitle of *Earth and Reveries of Will* in the first editions in French had been *Essai sur l'imagination des forces* (Paris: Corti, 1947). Reflecting the error of later editions in French, the translation of Bachelard's *Earth and Reveries of Will,* however, carries the subtitle *An Essay on the Imagination of Matter* (a subtitle already assigned to his earlier *Water and Dreams*).

8. See, for instance, Bachelard's discussions on rocky landscapes, in his chapter on "Rock" in *Earth and Reveries of Will* (152–54).

9. See also Bachelard's discussions on Flocon's engraved landscapes in his "Introduction to the Dynamics of Landscape" (RD 55–70)—a graphic case in the field of visual arts.

10. Bachelard devotes an entire chapter to the experience of "intimate immensity" through poetic imagery in *The Poetics of Space* (183–210).

11. Maurice Merleau-Ponty, *The Visible and the Invisible* (Evanston: Northwestern University Press, 1968), 253: "everything is cultural in us (our *Lebenswelt* is "subjective") (our perception is cultural-historical) and everything is natural in us (even the cultural rests on the polymorphism of the wild Being)."

Chapter 15

Environmental Politics in Light of Bachelard's Elemental Poetics

Samuel Talcott

> The art of propaganda consists . . . in being able to awaken the imagination of the public through an appeal to their feelings, in finding the appropriate psychological form that will arrest the attention and appeal to the hearts of the national masses . . . The broad masses of the people are not made up of diplomats or professors of public jurisprudence nor simply of persons who are able to form reasoned judgment in given cases, but a vacillating crowd of human children who are constantly wavering between one idea and another . . . The great majority of a nation is so feminine in its character and outlook that its thought and conduct are ruled by sentiment rather than by sober reasoning.
>
> —Hitler, *Mein Kampf*[1]

> A being deprived of the *function of the unreal* is just as neurotic as those who are deprived of the *reality function*. One could say that a disorder in the function of unreality has repercussions on the reality function. If imagination's essential function of *openness* is deficient, perception itself is blunted.
>
> —Bachelard, *Air and Dreams*[2]

Discussions of the environment today, especially climate change, often turn into heated debate between the representatives of two mutually exclusive sides, each regarding the other as either the very incarnation of stupidity or part of some conspiracy. In such an atmosphere of contestation, and despite the continuing growth of overwhelming scientific consensus, scientific reports are attacked as manipulative distortions by so-called climate skeptics. And those who raise questions about such reports risk being regarded by environmentalists as part of a conspiracy to justify the subjugation of natural resources to the pursuit of profit by energy industries. Though such a climate sustains a polemic without apparent end, it also gives rise to stony silence, in which those opposed refuse to engage each other, no longer able to even begin a discussion of problems and possible responses. Or there is the silence of those who know that the endeavor to speak and write in such an atmosphere leads inevitably towards partisan classification, not public discussion. As a result, many despair that there will ever be a unified political will regarding the climate and environment, or, if there is, it may come too late. This chapter, side-stepping this polemical and leaden atmosphere, has its origins in the thought that the scientific controversy and its solution are not the only possible basis for an environmental politics.[3]

This thought came to me, quite surprisingly, in the course of reading Gaston Bachelard's works on elemental poetics and in the sudden realization that this poetics has profound political implications. On May 2, 1943, a time when censors would have sought to prevent the publication of any signs of the emerging resistance to the German occupation of France, Bachelard signs the final pages of his book on the poetics of air, a seemingly innocuous, apolitical topic. Indeed, if anything, it might seem at first glance to appeal to Nazi ideology, which lauded the purity of mountain air and its healthful effects for the Aryan race. Yet, a careful examination of Bachelard's claims in his *Air and Dreams*, written not long after the Germans occupied the Southern Zone, shows that the virile rationality championed by Hitler in the name of the Aryan race could only be a distortion of the aerial (*aerien*) imagination for Bachelard. His work does not take the form of a direct condemnation, a judgment against Nazism, but rather by exploring the aerial imagination, and describing its myriad manifestations in the experience of poetry, it proposes a new account of the *aerien*—one that, as I will show, leaves room neither for Hitler's notion of "sober reasoning" nor for his denigration of imagination. Instead of a virile, rigidly practical reason that plays on the predictable imagination of the effeminate and childish masses, Bachelard makes not imagination but the imaginary, experienced through the verbal images of poets, central to human life in all its aspects—from perceiving to reasoning—because it keeps the imagination agile and open. Without the imaginary, there might be perception and memory, but no openness, no creative rupture of the perceived and the remembered in the face of the new, in anticipation of the new. Its focus on the experience of poetry, of verbal images, means that his work depends on the careful and critical analysis of his very own encounter with the words of poets. No other words enter this text, except for those of a few others commenting on poetry and its verbal images. Bachelard's work is, therefore, patient and without apparent polemic, yet its political implications, I argue, seem undeniable.

In order to draw this out, I offer a focused reading of *Air and Dreams*, but to set the stage for his poetics of the aerial imagination and better understand it as a political response to Nazism, it is first necessary to consider his work on scientific rationality in the 1930s, 1934 in particular. Furthermore, by focusing the examination on two works, each clearly located in a historical moment, I do not intend to give a static image of his thinking, but a glimpse of the dynamics of his thinking. And such a move also provides insight into the relation between the conceptual discourse of the sciences and the imaginative discourses of the poets as Bachelard—in his attempt to honor both the conceptual and the imaginative—thought it in the critical moment of May 2, 1943. Bachelard's work in that moment, I will suggest in conclusion, offers a different, more productive approach to environmental politics than the popular polemics of the present day.

Bachelard's Epistemology in 1934

Bachelard's 1934 study of new developments in physics, *The New Scientific Spirit*, argues that the discipline has surpassed classical physics through the discovery of "indeterminacy" in its underlying microstructure, effectively rationalizing the indeterminate and the uncertain.[4] The method of classical physics, as formulated by René Descartes and others, had urged an analysis based on the intuition of simple truths that can serve as foundations for knowledge of more complex phenomena. Such a methodology, Bachelard suggests, is essentially contiguous with ordinary ways of experiencing the world, in which we find that the senses convey impressions of things to us. Quotidian experience reveals an apparent world of simple substances, each having its own immutable and irreducible nature. While Cartesian science would seek to get beyond sensory appearances that offer themselves as objectively true, it did so only to discover other, simpler substances that were, in conjunction with our own sense organs, causes of our sensory experience.[5] For Bachelard, though, this science discovers an immutable and irreducible substantial reality beneath appearances because of its very method; with methodological rules designed to resolve appearances into their simplest elemental and conceptual components, it is no wonder that it discovers indivisible corpuscles of matter as the substrate of all phenomena. In reducing the natural world to matter in motion, Descartes hoped to found a physics that would have all the classic hallmarks of knowledge: truth would display the necessity that things be as they are, that things happen as they do. Proceeding quantitatively, physics would then describe the universal, immutable laws of nature that determine all natural phenomena.

Physicists, Bachelard argues, have now recognized such a search for determinate knowledge as an obstacle to the development of science. In the ferment of problems associated with the development of quantum theory, Bachelard finds that physicists are no longer bent on discovering ultimate, immutable substances that determine physical reality, or on acquiring absolute certainty about them. Instead of working analytically towards the simple in order to reconstruct the complex later, the goal—in Bachelard's view—is to provide open-ended synthetic accounts of the complex relations from which apparently simple phenomena arise. There are no irreducible and immutable substances since any given thing is understood to exist through the very *relations* that define it and is subject to modification with the changes of these relations. Thus, scientific research no longer seeks or expects absolute precision, but recognizes "approximate knowledge" as an inescapable aspect of its methods, even if it still expresses these relations through mathematical formulae. Furthermore, this way of working recognizes that research methods and instruments—what Bachelard identifies as "phenomeno-technologies" (NSS x, xiii, xx, 13)[6]—determine the shapes that reality gradually adopts for us in the course of its investigation. Phenomena are not passively accepted in their ordinary appearance, but sciences develop theories about reality and then employ instruments in deliberate attempts to discover or realize corresponding phenomena, which then become the basis for further empirical inquiry and experimentation.[7] Borrowing from the standardized and mass-produced technologies of industrial society, the scientist as scientist puts these goods to use in a novel manner, not for the sake of mastering the world, but for the sake of an open-ended exploration of the unknown, the as yet not rationalized.[8] Phenomeno-technology is integral to scientific activity since it is through this that the mind (*esprit*) can break with the world of ordinary appearances and its power over us. The perceived image of fire, for example, functions as an epistemological obstacle insofar as it exercises a power over human imagination or practical activities. When we watch a fire, we are drawn into reverie by its movement and rhythm.[9] Or, alternatively, fire becomes a technology that can be controlled, at least to an extent, and will be used in the attempt to manage the environment. In failures to control such technology, and facing the following adversity, humans learn about the world and endeavor to address its changing circumstances. But it is only with technologies that allow for the study of chemical combustion that scientific research can be undertaken; and when it is undertaken the original object, fire, is no longer present at all.[10] Objectivity in science is approximated by radical questioning, that is, by the negation of the apparent object of experience at a given time.[11] Thus, particular sciences are born in the establishment of epistemological ruptures,[12] and all subsequent progress in the history of a science takes the form of a radical revision of concepts such that the history of a well-developed science, like physics, is marked by the periodic appearance of discontinuities and ruptures.

In studying the methods of the new physics, Bachelard hoped to provoke a crisis in thought, a philosophical crisis comparable to the one going on in physics (NSS 171).[13] If physicists go to school in the investigation of complex phenomena and thereby revise their accounts of rationality itself, so too philosophers must go to the school of contemporary science in order to revise age-old prejudices about human reason and thinking about science itself. One of the primary lessons concerns the historicity of scientific truths and, thus, of scientific activity. The discontinuous history of science shows that any truth, no matter how firmly established in the present, can find itself dispelled as an error—as what was believed true but since shown to be false or, perhaps better put, relative to a limited context (NSS 172).[14] Sciences constitute themselves and progress by dispelling errors, not by identifying immutable facts or substances. In this, scientific work is an open rationalism that works by processes of verification in which apparent truths are repeatedly tested and verified, or found wanting and disqualified. The scientific value of any truth, therefore, is questionable, making the history of science that of a polarized movement as the contents and methods of a discipline are revised by processes of verification. Recognized errors of science are relegated to the past, while current truths are subjected to the light of the unknown, finding themselves tested at the horizon of the known. As Bachelard writes:

> [Human] history can certainly be an eternal return [*recommencement*] in its passions, its prejudices, in all that arises from immediate impulsions. But there are thoughts that do not return [*qui ne recommencent pas*]; these are thoughts that have

> been rectified, enlarged, completed. They do not return to their limited or faltering terrain [*aire*]. And the scientific mind is essentially a rectification of knowledge, an enlargement of the frame of knowledge. [The new scientific mind] judges its historic past by condemning [*condamnant*] it. Its structure is its awareness of its historical errors. Scientifically, truth is thought as the historical rectification of a persistent error, experience is thought as rectification of common and primary illusion. (NSS 172/177, trans. modified)[15]

Scientific work, thus, is also an active empiricism since it carries out its attempted rationalizations by testing these empirically. This requires, Bachelard claims, an open-ended courage before what may initially appear to be irrational. The experience of the irrational, the "inevitable murkiness of reality" (NSS 150), it turns out, is synonymous with "intellectual torpor" for the scientist who understands "irrationality" to be more a problem in our scientific methods than a feature of the world itself (NSS 155–57, PN 6–7). The physics of the moment could be better approached by modifying and transforming the current methods of investigation for what appears to be inexplicable. As he puts it, the scientist goes home at the end of the day nourished by the thought, "Tomorrow I shall know the truth" (NSS 171). In the course of this pursuit, an adventure in thinking happens, but this is not a thinking that leads to single-minded, proactive applications; rather, it is an adventure nourished by the problems it addresses, by breaking with perceptual or cultural images that govern daily life. Nor does this unending search for truth lead to silence and inaction in the face of failure, potential or real, for scientific work treats the unexpected as a good reason to courageously risk new explanations and new applications. It is, in its very activity, a thorough realization of human liberty, but a liberty maintained through constant vigilance and attentiveness to the ongoing challenges that the world raises to its own claims to knowledge. Philosophers and others who seek closed systems, absolutely exhaustive explanations, Bachelard suggests, would do well to heed these events and embrace the openness of contemporary science as a new value for human life.

Scientific research is inherently technological in this picture, since instruments are used in order to produce phenomena that can be investigated in an attempt to make sense of the apparently simple world of daily experience. But technologies and other practical applications are not the primary fruits of scientific work. Rather, it is in response to the failures of our own techniques and technologies that the scientific endeavor first arises.[16] While the truths produced by scientific research can be appropriated for broader practical purposes—especially by industry—the values and aims of such technologies and science are radically different. If scientific activity is an open rationalism, technology as such can only be understood as a closed rationality, that is, as a system designed to perform a certain function within specific conditions.[17] Should the basic conditions change, the technology will fail. It is in such a context of failure, when things do not make sense or work as they should, that one wants to know the truth of things, making technological failures creative of scientific research. For Bachelard, then, technologies are not primarily well-thought-out applications of a preconceived truth, but tentative and provisional endeavors to satisfy the desires of the living.[18] And when scientific knowledge is deployed in these efforts to master the world, this work is no longer scientific, since it no longer searches for the resistance that the world offers its endeavor, expecting instead obedience.[19] But, insofar as instruments are deployed and developed in order to help test and materialize particular scientific theories, technology serves as a useful tool in the search for truth. In scientific work, for Bachelard, the interplay between theoretical invention and material production forms a kind of open-ended dialectic, in which concepts seek to rationalize the world, inscribing themselves in it and thereby disclosing/inventing new phenomena, and then finding themselves faced again with the seeming irrationality of the given which calls forth a new effort to comprehend the dynamic rationality of the world (NSS 155, 157; PN 7).[20] For Bachelard, this means that science, the free rationality of research, is *the* aesthetics of intelligence (FSM 21/10).[21] Here we have a corrective for naive ideas about science—one that highlights the creativity of its rationality.[22] But it is in his poetics that I propose we can discover an evocative sketch of what I am here calling an elemental politics. I turn now to these.

A Poetics of the Imaginary

Commentators have been puzzled by the apparent split within Bachelard's oeuvre, since, in addition to his epistemological works, he published a series of works devoted to poetry and poetic imagination, at least one book dedicated to each of the four elements. Especially puzzling is the fact that the very epistemological obstacles of scientific works here come to be vaunted by Bachelard as important aspects of poetic imagination—that poetic imagination is itself now cast as an essential aspect of human life. The same images—such as the image of fire—thus appear to be both obstacles to and instances of the flourishing of human spirit. Such a puzzle, to be answered completely, needs to be examined in light of the larger development of Bachelard's thought, his movement from publication in the philosophy of science to his poetics, and back to philosophy of science after a hiatus of ten years.[23] Since the limits of this piece do not allow the necessary space to address such overall development, in what follows I will focus specifically on *Air and Dreams* (1943)—one of Bachelard's early works vaunting the powers of poetic reverie—in order to sketch out both his elemental poetics and a response to this puzzlement.

In his accounts of image and imagination, I will argue, Bachelard provides a key to grasping the complementarity of his two branches of work. As he states, especially in later works, the faculties of mind and soul, understanding and imagining, are not mutually exclusive.[24] While thinking (*la pensée*) can either seek understanding through concepts or engage in reverie by imagining, both functions are ultimately essential to each other. The performance of different functions[25] provides no reason to assert a division into mutually exclusive faculties—after all, I can use my hands at once to communicate and to hold a tool. Nonetheless, as different ways of thinking, science and poetic reverie do each require their own sort of philosophical defense. And so, Bachelard, a defender of the philosophy of the concept in his epistemological works, will dismiss it as inadequate in *Air and Dreams*, embracing instead Bergson's philosophy of movement in his poetics—though not without first revising Bergson's theories. Indeed, Bergson—famous for his appeal to an intuitive approach to reality that would avoid treating the natural world and thought in cinematic terms—is ultimately criticized for remaining too conceptual, for not further pursuing the rich possibilities of his own images and the material imagination. Bergson's images thus often tend to fall into the role of expedient metaphors designed to compensate for the failings of conceptual language, as Perraudin demonstrates in his piece earlier in this volume.[26] Bachelard's poetics moves thinking beyond thought's apprehension via well-defined or quasi-conceptual images, to find what is primary—not the constituted image but the *act of imagining* in the living tension of the moment (AD 256–57/291–92).[27]

The act of imagining is primary, for Bachelard, not because imagination is a power to form images or reproduce copies, but because imagination is fundamentally "the power to deform images furnished by perception; above all it is the power to liberate us from first images, to change images" (AD

1/7, trans. modified). To imagine is to set an image into motion, to transform it, and so free ourselves from it. This applies to images of perception, as well as to images that come to us from art and culture. The familiar flowery images found in much poetry, Bachelard claims, are not a mark of imagining but of an established, imitative imagination that has lost its novelty and inner dynamism (AD 2/9). An image that emerges from the *act of imagining* is never passive, but it evokes absent images and provokes a plethora of aberrant images; it is a veritable "explosion" of images. "The value of an image," he writes, "is measured by the extent of its *imaginary* aura" (AD 1/7). Rather than being a self-contained organ of imagination, the imaginary thus renders human psychic experience open. It marks the very experience of a "breakthrough."[28] In *Air and Dreams* Bachelard examines this "act of imagining" by grasping it in its verbal form, which, in his words, "forms the temporal fabric of spirituality, and is therefore not bounded by reality" (AD 1/8). Note here that it is the poetic "function of the unreal, and not the sciences of realism, that founds an enduring subjectivity or spirit (AD 7/12).[29]

While we act in response to particular perceptions, or particular truths we have grasped, the imaginary opens us up to the possibility of the new. And this makes the poem an aspiration for new images that respond to the essential human need for newness (AD 2/7).[30] Thus, Bachelard's interest in this poetics of the literary image is not in the constituted image, but the image as constitut*ing*, the image as spiritual movement. Indeed, his work now centers on the literary imagination of air, which is "a kind of spiritual mobility of the greatest, liveliest, and most exhilarating kind," in the hopes of drawing up a veritable holograph which traces the movement of each image (AD 2/9). Bachelard even appears to efface himself from his own text—as some commentators have remarked—to allow literary images themselves to take flight through the words of poets.[31] A book inhabited by literary images, he writes, then "suddenly becomes an intimate letter. [Such images] play a role in our life. They vitalize us. . . . Thought expressed by a new image is itself enriched as it enriches language. Being becomes word [*parole*]. The word appears at the psychic summit of being. The word reveals itself as the immediate becoming of the human psyche" (AD 2–3/9, trans. modified). In the poem—either read aloud or under one's breath—the human spirit flourishes.

Given that the poetic word is itself so free from the perceived visual image, Bachelard understands from the outset that the approach to the pure mobility of imagining via poetry can be undertaken in relation to any object. He writes, "Every object contemplated, every great name murmured is the start of a dream, a verse . . . a creative linguistic movement. How many times at the edge of a well, on the stone covered with wild moss and ferns, have I murmured the name of far-off waters, the name of a buried world. How many times has the universe suddenly answered me. . . . Oh my things! How we have spoken!" (AD 5/12, trans. modified).[32] But if we can commune poetically with all objects, in the imaginary, every such immanence must be accompanied by a transcendence, that is, by a dynamic literary image that transports us into infinity. The infinite sea, the unending depths of the earth, an ever-living fire, and the blue of the sky (*bleu de ciel*), each of the four elements has its own infinite, demanding its own sort of dreams and poetic reveries.[33] In the infinite of each element, imagining affirms its purity. Such an infinite is an absolute beyond distinctions of right and wrong, "transgressing the stiffest laws governing human values" (AD 6/13, trans. modified).[34] Imagination begins by deforming perceptual images, purifying them and expanding their reach as far as possible so as to give rise to the imagination of essential elements. But if these pure elements emerge in the sublimation of imagination towards an infinite image, Bachelard is most interested in the kind of dynamism afforded by each of these elements (AD 6–8/13–15).

The case of air is of particular importance for an essay on movement, since the imagination of matter is virtually dispersed by its innate dynamism, even though it could not take place without the very substance of air. Whether wind or breath, air is less of a tangible substance than it is the feeling of movement itself. The force of aerial imagination essentially consists of the power of breath giving wing to the resonant word, more than of the force of winds buffeting and sculpting cold mountaintops. Yet either of these images participates in the imaginary power of climbing, ascension, sublimation (AD 9/17).[35] For it is only by an elemental and dynamic induction that Bachelard suggests our intimate being can be quickened and elevated. "We will discover this [induction]," he writes, "by establishing a correspondence in materiality between things and ourselves" (AD 9/16).[36] From aerial phenomena, then, Bachelard draws lessons about change and substantial mobility—in short, a detailed "physics" of the dynamic imagination focused on countering forces that otherwise would weigh ominously upon us. The intimate aerial pyschology revealed by such physics is hence releasing, lightening, ascensional: "At the very heart of these psychic phenomena a real *verticality* will be experienced" (AD 10/17). And it is in terms of this verticality that the life of soul is lived; all emotions (whether hopes or fears), all the moral forces that carry one toward a future are experienced in terms of such verticality. Hence the first principle of ascensional imagination: "*of all metaphors, metaphors of height, elevation, depth, sinking, and the fall are the axiomatic metaphors par excellence.* Nothing explains them, and they explain everything" (AD 10/18, Bachelard's italics). It is in terms of these very metaphors that we experience our joys and anguishes. As he puts it, "Vertical valorization is so essential, so sure—its superiority is so indisputable—that the mind cannot turn away from it once it has recognized its immediate and direct meaning. It is impossible to express moral values without reference to the vertical axis . . . Every valorization is verticalization" (AD 10–11/18).[37] For Bachelard, then, it is through aerial imagination that we learn the basic places and movements of our affective and moral experience.

We are thus justified—Bachelard writes, broadening his metaphorical horizon—"in characterizing the four elements as the hormones of imagination. They activate groups of images. They help in assimilating inwardly the reality that is dispersed among forms. They bring about the great syntheses capable of giving somewhat regular characteristics to the imaginary. Imaginary air, in particular, is the hormone that allows us to *grow* psychically" (AD 11/19). Bachelard then resolves to treat literary images of air with regard to their possibilities, that is, to the extent they can work upon us, freeing us from habitual images that already govern us. He is not interested in completion, but in the power of different literary images to set us in motion. In such images, Bachelard expects to find, "words that have an immediate future in us, hopeful words that allow us suddenly to discover a novel idea, fresh and vibrant, an idea that is our own special treasure" (AD 12/20, trans. modified). For this reason he also does not seek to provide an exhaustive historical account of aerial images in their many mutations. Instead, he holds onto that which animates the poet, that which remains "faithful to the infinite dreams [songes] of natural elements" (AD 14/22). His method—he admits—expects much from the reader, since a literary image is essentially ambivalent, and can only be experienced dynamically as both dream and thought—that is, simultaneously as "a vision and a view, depicted reality and dreamed movement" (AD 13/21, trans. modified).

If one can do this, then it is possible to recognize that the literary image is not simply a technical production. Rather, the aerial image elicits a certain way of being, a certain attitude and will in us. For Bachelard, such an image that arises in us is itself an agent of the verb to imagine, not its complement (AD 14/22).[38] This means that will and affect have to be understood in their dependence on reverie, on the world's emanating dream of itself. While night-dreams of flight may instinctively stir up aerial images (AD 27–29/37–38), it is in the waking attempt to explore *poetic images* by following their dynamic materiality as air, that Bachelard finds their greatest benefit to us, and a deeper awareness of the breathing word/world. The poem then acts as a kind of silent speech in which written words are inwardly reanimated by the rhythm of respiration.[39]

Nonetheless, scientific understanding and poetic imagining are not necessarily at odds with each other, for Bachelard. Rather, we see now that each activity is inaugurated by a break with the image understood as a "realized object" that is hence taken for granted and reproduced as a matter of habit. The movement of scientific activity is against such images of perception, as is the movement of imagining, but whereas the one forms concepts, the other deforms images by opening them onto other images. Yet, if there is a kind of complementarity here, the dreaming and poetic saying are more elemental insofar as they open up the "unreal" or imaginary coordinates that orient us in the world and that, in fact, orient the world.[40] The value of the imaginary and its connection to the unreal thus implicitly exposes a dual limitation in scientific work. As research, the sciences embrace errors and irregularities, the seemingly irrational, as having an inherent value even if this is a provisional one—to be eventually negated. In this sense, Bachelard sees no end to the scientific endeavor—the horizon for research is never closed thanks to the powers of imagining, which exposes limits in established scientific thought, and sets new questioning into motion. But insofar as this research is conducted by people living in a world, with others, the imaginary implies rather clear limits for scientific activity. As the free, imaginative search for truth, scientific work remains faithful to recognized scientific methods and standards, while conceptualizing phenomena and materializing these conceptions. And when it deforms its own methods, it is insofar as this better enables the search for the guiding scientific value: truth. While human needs and problems may give rise to such a search, once initiated, it proceeds according to criteria generated by its own activity. Though its rationality is, for Bachelard, one of the most creative and free expressions of the imagination in its interplay with the world, this does not mean that every aspect of the human spirit is to be treated scientifically. The conceptual truths of the sciences—acknowledged to be historical and open to rectification—should therefore not be confused with intimate intuitions and elemental experiences of the imaginary and the poetic. I now present some evidence for, and an extension of, this reading through the elemental politics implicit in *Air and Dreams*.

An Elemental Politics

There is much debate going on today about facing harsh realities of (human-generated) climate change, or returning to "the hard facts of reality" and acknowledging that there is no global warming, or that, if there is, it is not a matter that need concern humans since it could be neither caused by us, nor influenced by our actions.[41] On both sides of the polemic we find the same no-nonsense claims to "reason" (without an appeal to feelings) that Bachelard would have encountered in the 1938 French translation of Hitler's *Mein Kampf* (see the opening epigraph to this piece).

My wager here is that Bachelard's own *Air and Dreams*, finished in Dijon on May 2, 1943, lends itself to be read as a subtle yet pointed response to *Mein Kampf*'s account of the imagination and its accompanying politics. For, facing France's uncertain future, Bachelard's book defends the right—indeed the duty—to imagine, and I suggest that this is meant to have a political import despite a complete lack of reference to the occupation of France, National Socialism, or Hitler. The word "Aryan" (Fr. *Aryen*) is mentioned once, but only in passing, and appears only in a quotation from another writer, who is quoting yet another.[42] But this "once" is enough to catch the attention of an English-speaking ear. For reading Bachelard's text, one is struck by the repeated used of *aerien*, which I have been translating as "aerial," but which indeed sounds much like the English word "Aryan." Perhaps this is just a coincidence arising for an English-speaking ear that reads a text written in French. I think not. If we consider the etymology of the word in French, as Bachelard surely would have with his interest in the formation and deformation of words, the relation of his book to its present situation becomes clear. The French *Aryen*, like the English "Aryan," comes from the Indo-European *arya* meaning noble (see OED). Drawing on nineteenth- and twentieth-century anthropological and racial science, Hitler in fact conceived the Aryans as the noble race, and the Jews and others as degenerates threatening this very nobility.[43] But to be noble, following the Latin *nobilis*, is to be noted or high-born.[44] The Aryan, then, claims to come from the mountain heights. Yet etymological connections, Bachelard warns in the first line of his book, are often deceptive and not to be trusted (AD

1/7). Rather, it is in the sound of spoken words—which reveals affinities to the French ear, and even to the relatively untrained foreign ear—that the two words *aryen* and *aerien* appear remarkably similar. We have heard Bachelard's claim, above, that the aerial imagination (*imagination aerienne*) works not through the printed word *per se*, but when brought to life in the poem spoken or silently read through the rhythm of breathing, which vitalizes us by opening us up to the world and orienting us in it. The Aryan appeal to sober reasoning over and against supposedly passive imagination is then a misconception of the very power of "deformation" that is the imaginary—a power that Bachelard comes to grasp as central not only to scientific rationality but to human life as such: bodily and psychic. Bachelard's book therefore calls to be read as a critique of the Aryan claim to nobility as "a human race," a claim that founds a clearly delineated conception of social-political order on supposedly sober reasoning.

I write this not because I want to identify contemporary Nazis, but in order to show the political import of Bachelard's elemental poetics. In the face of an uncertain political situation, in which many felt incapable of opposing the Occupiers, Bachelard—dedicating the book to his daughter—presents an argument for the liberative powers of imagination. Bachelard's approach does not allow one to speculate that such powers would guarantee an actual political liberation from an oppressor. It does, however, identify an elemental sort of politics that can account for where this particular oppressor comes from in spite of itself, in spite of its purported knowledge of its own rights. The Nazi Aryan must be, for Bachelard, an inauthentic aerial imagination, since it is rooted in the material and dynamic imagination of the air while simultaneously denigrating the imagination as such, in the name of sober rationality. In place of National Socialism's high-minded political orthodoxy that regards human biological, social, and political difference as a threat to the health and rationality of the political order, Bachelard argues for the rights of imagination by defending it as a power of deformation or creative mutability. Imagination, as we have seen, is dynamizing and materializing—before all else, a power of form-transgressing becoming. In examining diverse literary images according to their present possibilities, Bachelard seeks to inspire a liberative movement of the human spirit. And having gone to the school of the poets, Bachelard philosophizes by defending the right and duty to imagine in the face of an intellectual regimen that devalues imagination altogether, except insofar as it is a useful tool of social control. But, faced with an atmosphere of contestation about scientific claims and a fragmented political will, what—it will be asked—could poetic reverie do for us today?

It is through the imaginary that subjects and subjectivities are primarily formed, in Bachelard's view. They are not first formed as autonomous individuals capable of choosing rationally in terms of their own self-interest. Such a social-political rationality can only come later for Bachelard, being developed out of an earlier subjectivity defined better in terms of its underlying affects, the shared orientation of emotions by objects, humans, and world. And these shared affects, we remember, come to us through the imaginary experience of the elements.[45] The elements, these hormones of the imagination, orient our range of imaginary experiences (e.g., ascent, descent, breadth, intimacy, rootedness, renewal, etc.) giving them a certain value in our lives. Moreover, it is through imagination that the will first emerges as a power of motion. But this is not a unified sovereign will that emerges, but rather a pluralized will, one that does not rule from a standpoint of complete and totalized authority. Bachelard's "elemental poetics" thus tacitly yields an "elemental politics." By this is meant a politics of the elements, the imagination of the elements taken as the initial source of an open, dynamic pluralism of values and wills. In this, air, water, earth, and fire come to consciousness as forces and substances worthy of respect, as irreducible to manageable resources. Such "elemental" politics would also be meant in the sense of what is most basic. For without the imaginary of these elements, and the possibility of seeking a place within their vital realm, political life would not be possible.

This "elemental politics" does not tell us much about what institutions *should* look like, but it does help us understand minimal conditions of the political so as to disqualify certain forms of political organization or recognize certain collective activities as destroying the possibility of politics. Nor does "elemental experience," by itself, spell out a moral theory, functioning instead as the very condition of such theories insofar as it is the original experience of valorization.

Notes

1. Adolf Hitler, *Mein Kampf*, trans. J. Murphy (New York: Hurst and Blackett, 1939), 148–50. See also the French translation, *Mon combat* (Paris: Nouvelles Editions Latines, 1935).

2. AD 7/14. This translated passage and a few others from Bachelard's *Air and Dreams* and *The New Scientific Spirit* in this chapter have been modified to reflect the author's reading. In such cases, pages first cited correspond to the pub-

lished English translation (AD or NSS, respectively), followed by a slash and page numbers from the original French editions, for comparison.

3. This is not to be read as a dismissal of the value that scientific truth holds in human life. It is rather intended as the assertion of other values, particularly those of imagination, which are *essential* for diverse human endeavors—including science—as Bachelard himself would insist.

4. The following account is drawn from Bachelard's chapter on "Non-Cartesian Epistemology," in Arthur Goldhammer's translation of *Le nouvel esprit scientifique* (1934), *The New Scientific Spirit* (Boston: Beacon, 1984). While I will here focus on this crucial text, Bachelard continued pondering these issues in philosophy of science even after his initial works on the four imaginary elements. See *Le Rationalisme appliqué* (1949), in particular, on the question of "application" in contemporary science.

5. This is really about the early modern distinction between primary and secondary qualities.

6. The French term Bachelard used in his 1934 text, *Le nouvel esprit scientifique,* was *phénoménotechnique*. Goldhammer translated it in 1984 as "phenomeno-technology," rather presciently considering the epistemological impact of the explosion in "technological" development toward the end of the twentieth century and beyond.

7. Even if contemporary physics does appeal to the idea of simplicity, as in the idea of a simple substance or particle, for Bachelard this is now undertaken provisionally, for the sake of better establishing a tentative and complex model of the relations constituting the physical world (NSS 163). The attempt to produce the Higgs Boson Particle is most the striking recent example of this. The particle, theorized in 1964, was first detected on July 4, 2012, through nuclear technologies developed at CERN (European Organization for Nuclear Research), and confirmed on March 13, 2013, though it remains open to question and interpretation. While this appears as an example of the persistent "drive for certainty" in the scientific search for fundamental substances in nature, the "Boson particle" is itself indeterminate and elusive, produced by intense dynamic collisions.

8. In the early *Essai sur la connaissance approchée* (Paris: Vrin, 1927), Bachelard had discussed the way mass-produced, standardized candles and then mass-produced light bulbs served as the standard units of measurement for brightness. See the excerpt and English translation in Gary Gutting's *Continental Philosophy of Science* (Oxford: Blackwell, 2005). This does not mean that the knowledge, techniques, and technologies produced by scientific activity are not valuable as we attempt to deal with concrete human problems. Rather, it means that scientific research, for Bachelard, is not confined in advance by such problems. Moreover, because the sciences are oriented by the search for truth, not utility, any practical application of scientific knowledge involves a kind of experimental risk. The success of such an application cannot be determined in advance, but only in the test of experience.

9. Bachelard writes of his task: "But since, for us, the past represents ignorance just as reverie represents futility, our aim will be as follows: to cure the mind of its happy illusions, to tear it from the narcissism of first evidence, to give it assurances other than mere possession, and powers of conviction other than heated enthusiasm—in short, proofs that are not mere flames! (PF 4–5/16, trans. modified). This shows why Bachelard might worry about inflammatory discourse, about discourse that, shaped by the very verbal image of fire, inflames and prevents human freedom. Scientific discourse, Bachelard is clear, is polemical, and while this forms part of its strength, his work on the elements shows that this is not the only productive approach to experience. See *The Formation of the Scientific Mind* (1938), where Bachelard himself adopts a polemical approach in order to more effectively aid in the overcoming of obstacles to scientific rationalization. It is telling that Bachelard eventually recognizes that such elemental obstacles are also the starting points, thus the impetuses, not only to research but to liberating poetic experience as well.

10. Does this imply the abandonment of sight as ultimate model of knowledge, and with it, perhaps, the notion of form? Perhaps not, given Bachelard's discussion of "theoretical oversights" (NSS 144) and the way this is taken up by Foucault and Althusser. Moreover, phenomeno-technologies do not imply the obliteration of intuition, but simply its deliberate reshaping. See, for example, Michel Foucault's *La Naissance de la clinique* (Paris: Presses Universitaires de France, 1963), or L. Althusser, E. Balibar, R. Establet, P. Macherey, J. Rancière's *Lire le capital* (Paris: Maspero, 1965); also Martin Jay's *Downcast Eyes: The Denigration of Vision in Twentieth-Century French Thought* (Berkeley: University of California Press, 1994).

11. This is precisely the problem with positivist medical science for Canguilhem. Not only do its methods, which deny a qualitative distinction between health and illness, deny the ontological reality of health, but also, in so doing, they imply that health has no value whatsoever. See *The Normal and the Pathological* (1943; New York: Zone Books, 1989). Canguilhem argues there that despite the technical powers of such medicine, it implicitly, and against its own stated aims, undermines both the ontological and axiological realities of health.

12. The legacy of this notion is fairly well established. Consider the works of Foucault, *L'Archéologie du savoir* (Paris: Gallimard, 1969) in particular, and Althusser (ibid.) here.

13. It is hard not to read this as a response to Husserl's discussion of a crisis of European sciences.

14. See also PN 117–18, where Bachelard makes it clear that non-Euclidean geometry includes Euclidean geometry, and that microphysics includes classical physics.

15. Bachelard, though full of praise for the new spirit found in the sciences and the value it might have for us today, is also implicitly critical of these sciences or at least their place in our lives. For they are not social, they do not enter into our lives, they go without human sympathy, and thus they do not affect us. The work he undertakes in *The New Scientific Spirit* is thus not only an endeavor to

extend the values of the new scientific spirit to human life more generally, but also to place the sciences in the context of their inescapable historicity in order to show their very creativity.

16. Georges Canguilhem takes this point up in his writings about the relation between medical practice and knowledge.

17. Bachelard announces this in his early 1927 book, *Essai sur la connaissance approchée*, writing: "Science faces up to the fundamental irrationality of the given. This irrationality ceaselessly provokes science, pushing it to ever-renewed efforts. Industry, on the contrary, seeks to inscribe in matter a rationality that, since it is desired, is clearly recognized. One searches for the rational, the other imposes it" (cited in Gutting, 179). See also Hans-Jörg Rheinberger, "Gaston Bachelard and the Notion of Phenomenotechnique," *Perspectives on Science* 13, no. 3 (Fall 2005): 313–28.

18. Fire for cooking, domesticated grains for a plentiful harvest, genetically modified organisms for the sake of a plentiful harvest and corporate profit, are but a few examples.

19. This does not mean that Bachelard would condemn technological endeavors to master the environment, but that such endeavors have to be understood as tentative and basically blind, leading to unexpected consequences.

20. For presentations of this dialectic, and *phénoménotechnique* in particular, see Rheinberger, as well as Didier Gil, *Autour de Bachelard: esprit et matière, un siècle français de philosophies des sciences* (1867–1962) (Paris: Editions Les Belles Lettres, 2010).

21. Also quoted by Gil, 249.

22. But because scientific work is so focused on the search for truth, it does not develop into a more broadly formative, human value, requiring the endeavor of Bachelard, the epistemologist, to provide what is needed for this to occur, namely, "a little social life, a little human sympathy" (NSS 172). Still, this aesthetics is not one that appeals to the imagination in 1934, nor even in his 1938 *Formation of the Scientific Mind*, where imagination continues to be cast as an obstacle to scientific work. If images can be pedagogically useful, they always require a psychoanalysis, in these texts, if thought is to break free from them. See also NSS 132, where we learn that "imagination takes us no farther than sensation." All the same, one should remember Bachelard's notion of "surrationalism" as this prepares the way for his later exploration of the imaginary (PN 117–18).

23. On this, see Jacques Gagey, *Gaston Bachelard, ou la conversion à l'imaginaire* (Paris: Éditions Marcel Rivière, 1969).

24. On this, see Gil, 181, and his discussion of Bachelard's *Philosophy of No* and *Applied Rationalism* (*Le rationalisme appliqué*). In *Earth and Reveries of Will* Bachelard subsumes all faculties under the transcendental, productive imagination, following Novalis (ERW 3). But he still distinguishes between the functions of mind (*esprit*) and soul (*âme*) in *The Poetics of Space* (1969 ed., xvii–xviii), and elsewhere.

In chapter 4 of *The Poetics of Reverie* he distinguishes between the "thinking cogito" and the "dreaming cogito"—dividing his work into two camps, where he follows distinct paths for the exercise of reason and reverie; nonetheless, these two cannot but cross-fertilize one another.

25. Cf. the "functions" of reality and unreality (*Air and Dreams*) cited in the second epigraph to this piece.

26. See J.-F. Perraudin, "Bachelard's Non-Bergsonism" in this volume. Bachelard's critical "rectifications" were intended to intensify the productive potentials of Bergsonism, not to deny them (AD 256/291). The concluding chapter of Bachelard's *Philosophy of No* sums up the rationale behind his unique dialectical approach (PN 115–23/135–45).

27. See Bachelard's introduction to *Air and Dreams* and its conclusion, part 2, for further elaboration of this point. Also implied in Bachelard's argument is his disagreement with Bergson concerning the ontological priority of the living instant versus duration. This controversy—first raised in Bachelard's *Intuition of the Instant* (1932) and followed up in *The Dialectic of Duration* (1936)—is critically discussed in part 1 of this volume.

28. See Edward S. Casey's opening piece to this volume, "The Difference an Instant Makes: Bachelard's Brilliant Breakthrough."

29. Recall that the sciences are defined by epistemological rupture and radical revision of what counts as a part of science and what is to be rejected as the history of science. In this sense, the subject of science is not enduring but always exposed to periodic rupture of its leading paradigms.

30. In retrospect, Bachelard can now suggest that it is the imaginary that makes scientific research possible as well. As he writes, concluding his book, "The mind [*psychisme*] wishes to unite change and security, as it does in all its operations. It organizes habits of knowledge—concepts—which both serve it and imprison it. So much for security, sad security. But the mind renews its images, and it is through images that change is produced" (AD 265/301, trans. modified). While the context here is a discussion of *literary* language, well-formed *scientific concepts* speak to this same need for security. It is indeed the surrational dialectics set in motion by the power of the imaginary—coined "anagogic reverie [*rêverie anagogique*]" in *The Philosophy of No*—that in turn liberates the scientist from such concepts (PN 32–33/39).

31. As Bachelard put it: "Both at the time of its birth and when it is in full flight, the image within us is the subject of the verb to imagine. It is not its direct object. In human reverie, the world comes to imagine itself" (AD 14/22). Gagey's book treats this theme throughout.

32. Even though Bachelard focuses most of his poetic studies on the four elements, he admits the possibility that this sort of approach is possible for all sorts of objects, with which we join in immanence through the spoken word. Thus, later in his life, he engages in a broader poetics of space, as well as a poetics of reverie, neither of which is tied to the four classical elements.

33. It might be worth examining possible connections with Bataille's novel *Le bleu de ciel.* Bachelard's connection to surrealism as well as the College of Sociology is fairly clear, given his discussions of Roger Caillois.

34. Bachelard's epistemologies and poetics are largely responses to questions posed in Nietzsche's *The Birth of Tragedy* (1871).

35. See AD, chap. 5, on the image of cold mountaintop winds with Nietzsche as model of the ascensional poets.

36. Such "induction" is discussed under the rubrics of μέθεξις and "mental homeopathy" in Eileen Rizo-Patron's chapter "Bachelard's Hermeneutics" in this volume.

37. Falling, being swallowed up by the abyss, does not reach its full extent in the aerial imagination; this rather concerns the earth. "[W]hat does not rise, falls. Man qua man cannot live horizontally" (AD 11/19).

38. See passage cited in n. 31. Because Bachelard's elements are images *of* and *from* the world, his poetics does not raise the question of the role that "transcendental categories" and "intuitions" would play in the Kantian constitution of experience. Thus, Bachelard's "poetics" does not quite follow Kant's Copernican revolution, even if—to an extent—it seems to subscribe to Novalis's "idealism" or "transcendental fantasy" (ERW 3). Bachelard's epistemology also acts more as a "discursive idealism" or "open-Kantianism," which he describes as an ongoing "reconstruction of the self in confrontation with the not-self"—where the rational subject is not sovereign and unchanging, but transcended by something "other" that challenges and recreates it through the dialectical interrelationship between reason and reality (É 92). On this point, see Mary McAllester Jones, *Gaston Bachelard: Subversive Humanist* (Madison: University of Wisconsin Press, 1991), 7.

39. In reverie, Bachelard suggests, will and imagination tend to merge naturally (AD 186/213). But it is in the "will to speak" and in the "act of speaking" that these two radical powers become most manifest in their dynamism and materiality (AD 243–44/276). In poetry, "aerial imagination demands . . . the truths of breath, the very life of speaking air . . . Aerial matter runs through all poetry; it is not materialized time, nor living duration. It has the same concrete value as the air we breathe. A line of poetry is a pneumatic reality. It must submit itself to aerial imagination. It is a creation of the joy of breathing" (AD 242/275, trans. modified).

40. In Bachelard's view, the emanations of the imaginary serve "as a schema for *coherence by mobility*. In fact, the way in which we escape reality gives a clear indication of our inner reality"—for we are oriented and carried along in our reveries "by imaginary elements which have idealistic laws that are just as certain as experimental laws" (AD 7/14). On the "function of unreality," see the second epigraph to this chapter.

41. Those who argue that if climate change is happening, we need not worry because we can expect future technologies to solve any problems would do well to read Bachelard's early discussion of the difference between science and technol-

ogy. See the second section of this chapter. While he certainly does not condemn technological experimentation, he would condemn the denigration of the elemental imaginary, its wildness—a denigration that occurs when elements are treated as "natural resources" that can be completely mastered.

42. Bachelard quotes from the French translation of D. H. Lawrence's *Fantasia of the Unconscious* [*Fantaisie de l'inconscient*], 113). Lawrence in turn quotes from Frazier's *The Golden Bough* [*Le Rameau d'or*] (AD 244/255).

43. On this point see, for instance, Ivan Hannaford, *Race: The History of an Idea in the West* (Baltimore: Johns Hopkins University Press, 1996).

44. *Nobilis* is from the Latin "noted," "high-born," deriving from an Indo-European root shared with the English "know," γνῶσις, knowledge, and γιγνώσκω, "I know" in Greek.

45. As he writes, "The imaginary Climate plays a much more decisive [*déterminant*] role than the real one" (AD 160/184).

Chapter 16

Bachelard's Open Solitude

Madeleine Préclaire

Translated by Eileen Rizo-Patron

Does Bachelard's ontological notion of "well-being"—explored through his extensive phenomenological analyses of reverie and being at home in the world—offer a "hypothesis of life" wise and suitable enough to serve as inaugural principle for a vigilant philosophy of repose?[1] In his final publication, *The Flame of a Candle*, Bachelard claims indeed that a being capable of dreaming well, of "actively participating in his or her reverie, harbors a *truth* of being, a vision of human destiny" (FC 2, emphasis added). To outline the countenance of such being at peace with itself and the world, however, we will first need to examine another dimension upon which Bachelard reflected deeply, and at length. It is this dimension that daringly breaks solitude open, exposing it to the advent of surprising instants and discovering otherness.[2]

Never has the accent of philosophical reflection been placed more emphatically than today on *intersubjectivity*; never before has the importance of dialogue and participation been discussed with as much keenness. And, even if communication seems difficult or almost impossible for some people, this attitude of openness persists as the ideal form of human relations. Was Gaston Bachelard concerned with this intersubjective dimension of existence? While a cursory reading of his works may initially lead us to wonder if that was the case, we could not reply more readily that Bachelard was in fact an authentic guide in this domain. In his otherwise appreciative review of Gaston Bachelard's oeuvre, Pierre Quillet had denied him any concern for the other:

> Why did Bachelard constantly denigrate dialogue, debate, and encounter? . . . Why did he turn his readings into a walled bookcase, the circle of his lamplight into an enclosed world? Even his friendships, why did he turn them into a means of not belonging to his times? In his search for truth, he displayed a complete distrust of others, utter indifference toward the other in the solitude of reverie.[3]

On this point we could not disagree more with Quillet, who even asserted that Bachelard offered a "tragically negative solution" with respect to the problem of communication with the other. Here we would like to show that Bachelard, quite the contrary, continues to speak to us with great insight on this matter. To be sure, Bachelard admitted that his writing at times did not address the subject as explicitly as he would like: "We may be chided for the 'disembodied' way in which we treat the problem of otherness in this brief study. We would of course like to address the great problems of friendship and human rivalry otherwise, and to take part in the animated debates of contemporary anthropological philosophy. But that is not our task in the current work" (RA 64).

Time and again, nonetheless, one discovers throughout his writings a genuine concern for the life of solidarity with others, a profound concern for friendship and the importance of intellectual consensus, particularly in the constructions of science. Yet here, as elsewhere, he insists that nothing is directly given, that everything is to be *realized*—everything is to be built upon the courageous action of each human being.

To understand Bachelard's viewpoint, we need to return to his philosophy of the instant, where he claimed that the instant is isolated, "entire and alone" and that a human being has only this solitude to rely on as immediately available to consciousness. At the precise moment when life calls and challenges him or her anew, a human being stands alone—without communication with other souls. The image that perhaps best translates such solitude is the flame, closely examined in his book *The Flame of a Candle*. A flame is "single," he writes (FC 25/37). And this flame speaks only to the dreamer. It speaks to the solitary consciousness: "*Single flame. I am alone.*"[4]

What is the nature of this cry? Is it an avowal of insurmountable destitution? Is it a cry of resignation or, already—through its recognized *insufficiency*—a longing for another consciousness glimpsed in its absence, or the expression of a wish that would fulfill solitary being? "What is the tone of this appeal for impossible communication?" continues Bachelard (FC

25/38). Even if expressed in the negative, don't we find here an implied faith in the need for human being to communicate with others, if one truly wants to be oneself? If so, solitude becomes the necessary point of departure for any *authentic* encounter. But there is more in the verse recovered by Bachelard, and our candle dreamer soon catches a glimpse of it: "To burn alone, to dream alone—a great symbol, a twofold incomprehensible symbol. On the one hand it indicates the woman who, all afire, must remain alone without saying a word, and on the other the taciturn man who has only solitude to offer" (FC 25/38).

A symbol of hidden love, of undeclared flames. For the being who loves, who could be loved, there is of course solitude, and this cry of the poet who would want to open up a dialogue ends in silence, in a solitary dream. But since reverie emerges from the "feminine" aspect of the soul, the dreamer is soon delivered "to the melancholy of reverie"—and there is acceptance. In *The Poetics of Reverie* he asks, "If we did not have a feminine being tacitly dwelling within us, how would we come to rest within ourselves" (PR 92/81)? Only then can an aperture begin to appear in the hollow darkness of solitary consciousness. Then alone does one begin to open up to another's reveries: "one becomes sensitive to the reveries of others" (FC 26/38). The experience of solitude, of solitary reverie, leads to such an opening through sympathy. In this experience, human being is seized by the future, like the flame that consumes itself in a drama of being-becoming.

Bachelard thus finds positive value in lived solitude. It is the first and necessary step for anyone who wants to engage in the path of communication. For it alone enables the discovery of *deep being*, that which in the midst of the din and stress of the world reserves its secret, but which is therefore the source and springboard of dialogue and sympathy. "I fail to communicate so long as I do not make an effort to transmit my deep sense of being to others."[5] Solitude is, paradoxically, a means for this deliverance. It is recognized by Bachelard as an all-too-often forgotten dimension of being itself.

But it is also necessary to interrupt solitude. And for Bachelard, the philosopher of the instant, breaking out of solitude entails courage. It takes courage to respond or to reach out to human beings and things, so that the "symphony" of instants may be played out and the tragic solipsism of solitude be overcome. It is in the work of his Dijon colleague and friend Gaston Roupnel, author of the philosophical novel *Siloë* (1927), that he finds the way. In *Intuition of the Instant*, he carefully and respectfully gathers up his friend's message, while yet retaining the liberty to harvest from it what is most meaningful to him. In his words, "for instants to yield duration, and for duration to give rise to progress, Love must be inscribed upon the very foundation of Time" (II 51/91). In Roupnel's view, love is the image of the absolute, of the transcendence of God. As he wrote in *Siloë*: "Love! What other word could offer a verbal envelope better adapted from our spiritual nature to the intimate harmony that constitutes the nature of things, to the grand and solemn rhythm that brings the entire Universe to fruition?" (quoted in II 51/90–91).[6]

This is, for Roupnel, the way toward the intimate and mysterious source of Siloam. "May each of us follow his or her own path," Bachelard insisted as he commented on his friend's words. And, in his particular case, it was by striving to discover the *rational* character of Love that he pursued his dream. Bachelard found it necessary to reconcile mind and heart to return to the waters of Siloam, that is, to the truth of the person. Hence, it will behoove us to urge life's moments—be they moments of thought or moments of feeling—to follow this "wavelike motion of thought and reverie." Alas, the heart all too often neglects loving. Then it becomes necessary for us to go in search of lost instants. It becomes necessary for us to recover and consciously resume the "deep rhythms" of creation.

"A loving soul truly experiences the solidarity of instants that are repeated with regularity." Such a soul experiences the constant challenge of presence, for "the instant" is no longer single. Duration becomes a matter of commitment. Conversely, a steady rhythm of instants constitutes an "a priori form of affection" (II 29/50). It is in this form that renewed fidelities will come to be inscribed. "The joy of loving, in its essential newness, can surprise and marvel. But by experiencing its depths," Bachelard adds, "one lives in its simplicity." This is his way of contrasting sentimental fantasy with abiding love. The first never endures long enough to fulfill all the possibilities of being. It is at best a vain attempt, "a rhythm out of breath." Deep love, on the other hand, is "a harmonization of all the possibilities of being, for it is essentially a reference to being, an ideal of temporal harmony where the present is endlessly devoted to preparing a future" (II 52/92).

Here, in the final pages of *Intuition of the Instant*, Bachelard sketches out a veritable philosophy of love—not yet as the phenomenologist we will encounter in *The Poetics of Space* and *The Poetics of Reverie*, but as the rationalist he was at this early stage, and will always remain. To strengthen the heart, he writes, we must discover "general reasons" for loving (II 52/92). Only then can one understand the metaphysical scope of theses that seek the very force of temporal coordination in caring. It is necessary to link love and temporality, morality and temporality. Lived feelings demand time, so they can build us up. By reinforcing passion with morality, Bachelard proposes, one gathers up the richness—the weight and value—of full instants, novel instants that constitute the force of love, of its continuity and duration as they are ceaselessly recreated. "Intimate duration is always a matter of wisdom" (II 54/95). In this effort toward duration, we find engraved a movement towards the truth of being, towards its source—a desire for eternity.

But such wisdom, we repeat, is not given. For when it comes to "reality," there is none other than the reality of the instant. The various groupings of instants—duration, habit, progress—are but temporal, perspectival phenomena lacking in ontological privilege. The interweaving of such groupings is the work of human freedom—an effort one might well neglect, or reject. According to Roupnel, this kind of work calls for rational optimism, "measured and courageous." It is no less than a task, and it is in proposing this vision of love that Bachelard appears the most moralizing. To work toward this fruitful use of instants is, in his view, to "progress" towards the intimacy of being—it is the "way to eternal being through truth and goodness" (II 54/95).

Truth and goodness are here, indeed, the two paths invoked by Bachelard to conquer the instant, to transcend solitude, and to encounter others. The first—the path of science—strives to create continuity, a society, a fraternity of thought, a "*cogitamus.*" Here we find an original intuition, quite uncommon in the philosophical domain, which constitutes one aspect of Bachelard's relevance today. The second path—that of poetry and the imaginary—opens the way to a communion of souls. How could a work that conveys such desire for communication (whether in the scientific or the poetic realm) be considered hostile to the encounter with the other? Rather, we believe it sheds new light upon the mystery of our encounters with otherness—perhaps upon their deepest, most urgent dimensions.

In *Le Rationalisme appliqué* Bachelard speaks explicitly about a "society of thought" in the sciences. In fact, he there replaces the Cartesian *cogito* with a *cogitamus*. A man alone, he says, is in bad company. Nonetheless, it is from such solitude that one must start out, in order to experience the longing for fraternity in thought. It is significant to note that in order to describe this *cogitamus*, Bachelard uses the classical vocabulary of affectivity. Thus, speaking of original experiences that "renew the mind," he will consider them as "events of reason" that call for an attentive attitude, for presence of mind and spirit. What is crucial about such I-thou events is that they are "communicable." The proof of their rationality lies in their interpsychological, intersubjective nature. "Such events help absolve us and others of our respective errors." They are, among I-thou events, those that—as events of reason—can achieve a "triangularity" of consciousnesses (RA 44).

The intersubjectivity of rational thought is built, moreover, not only upon an agreement on foundations, but also upon a "mutual admiration" of the fecundity of rational organization (RA 45). There is no trace of psychologism here. Indeed, far from confusing the heat of conviction and the clarity of demonstration, Bachelard's thesis ceaselessly strives to contextualize and recontextualize the most effective features of current scientific progress. But "the updating of mind calls for a constant and full reorganization of foundations" on the basis of new discoveries, so the harmony of minds forever remains something to be achieved. Hence, "at each mutation of a founding idea or paradigm, solitude stalks the scientist" (RA 49). It is in the openness to *problems posed by the object* to be known that interrationalism can begin, launching a community of researchers onto a series of experiments which will continue as the problem becomes increasingly focused, and the issue refined on the way to its resolution, thanks to the constitution of an "atom of rational communion" (RA 56). The *cogitamus* thus delivers a "veritable fabric of co-existence." It is at the origin of a true "scientific city" that the lineage of a dialogic pedagogy will be found, for "scientists go to each other's schools" (RA 23). "The individual committed to scientific culture is an eternal student. School is the highest model of social life. The most secret wish of a teacher must be to remain a student" (RA 23).

In the world of rationality, Bachelard inscribes the values of intersubjectivity by establishing the play of dual thought. To "possess" is not to know. "In order to clarify knowledge, one must unpack it, unfold it, lay it out, and share it with others," for one can no longer cultivate oneself by oneself. Moreover, if a society of thought can exist, there must also be the possibility of communication at a more irrational, secret level—at the level of affectivity. Rather than providing an existential description of this affective dimension, Bachelard will first of all draw out its conditions, which nestle within the depths of the psyche. Once again, the imagination is actively present, playing its role of reunification.

When Bachelard wants to describe "reverie," in *The Poetics of Reverie*, he refers to two psychological aspects, *animus* and *anima*. Reflecting on the dialectic of these signs of depth, he then considers them as the phenomenon of "psychological projection" in a psychology of the communion of two beings. "The man who loves a woman projects upon that woman all the values that he venerates in his own *anima*. And, in the same way, the woman projects upon the man she loves all the values that her own *animus* would like to conquer" (PR 73/63).

A quadripolar rapport thus emerges between two souls who love each other. And it is from such a dialectical rapport, claims Bachelard, that we must henceforth study the value of all close human relationships. According to the tensions or balance of these relationships, unions forged may become strong or weak, felicitous or disappointing. They measure the ups and downs, the adventures in people's lives, and should not be alien to any psychologist. Through this quadripolar dialectic Bachelard helps us understand that the dramas and joys of communication come from such exchanges and projections. Thus wisdom—for anyone who wants to live happily and at peace with others—would consist, on the one hand, in allowing both masculine and feminine aspects of our being to coexist in our selves and to be expressed, as well as in our ability to recognize others and to be in turn recognized by them. Conversely, it would entail being lucid and realistic when an intersubjective relation is unable to succeed. The unconscious, more than the conscious mind, shapes our human relations. It is good to keep this in mind.

More specifically, Bachelard underlines and elaborates on the importance of images in human communion—a logical conclusion from his account of the dynamic character of imagination (examined earlier in this volume). If "ideas are refined and multiplied in the commerce of minds, images in all their splendor can bring about a very simple communion of souls" (PR 15/13), and that is because they first of all "awaken" in human beings the primordial images that lie latent within the depths of every person's consciousness.

In the specific case of a reader of poems, initial communication takes place with the poet who evokes images. This happens in reading Bachelard as well. Are his writings not veritable anthologies that deliver a feast of poetic imagery? Let us take his account of the vigil before evening fire in Henri Bosco's *Malicroix*. If friendship with fire arises from this reading, such friendship is common to both the artist and the dreamer. The image of fire is a binding force—it creates an accord between various characters. "We communicate with the writer because we are communicating with images preserved in the depths of ourselves" (PR 165/168).

The image can lead to sympathy—to sympathetic reading—not only through this living presence of archetypes, but also through the intimate experience it will awaken within the unconscious mind of the subject. In

Air and Dreams Bachelard offers an example of this oneiric genre, on the basis of a story by Edgar Allan Poe, "A Descent into the Maelström." It is a matter of provoking the reverie of a fall; one must therefore start with impressions of vertigo. From the beginning of the story—before the frightful account—the writer suggests the sense of vertigo that grabs hold of the two interlocutors. In Bachelard's words: "Readers do not begin to read this tale with a lively sympathy . . . until the moment they experience, with the narrator, the *nausea of descent*, that is, until the moment when the unconscious is drawn into an experience of elemental life" (AD 101/118–19).

Terror then awakens in the subject. The narrator has placed his reader in a "situation of terror": "The writer directly induces the nightmare of the fall into the reader's soul" (AD 101/119). This strategy used by a storyteller joins and reinforces the medical-psychological technique of Robert Desoille, which consists in a veritable methodology of guided reverie. We are here not far removed from the phenomenon of telepathy or mind reading, which Desoille approaches prudently towards the end of his book:

> If two minds could live an imaginary ascent together, they might be sensitive enough to exchange images and ideas. It seems that by placing oneself on the axis of the aerial imagination and by accepting the *linear* filiation of images that produces ascensional motion, a double reason for communion becomes possible: mind reading takes place in a state of calm, and it is done along the path to ecstasy gradually moving toward sublimation. (AD 120/139)

For this "telepoetry" to work, however, we must be able to set aside descriptive or utilitarian thinking and believe in reverie, "to grant imagination its place within a philosophy of repose," and to understand that repose is "a meditative *state of reverie* [*songe*]" (AD 124/144).[7]

Need we go further? In a page from *The Poetics of Space*, Bachelard leads us to believe so. There would be a possibility of communication even between two closed beings. In a story he cites by Franz Hellens, *Fantômes vivants*, father and daughter understand each other without telling each other so, without knowing it. When the father wants to offer a gift to his daughter, he hesitates between a silk scarf and a lacquer box. He chooses the latter "because it seems better suited to her reserved nature" (PS 82/86). In this strange narrative the two characters hide the same mystery that prepares a common destiny. It is then easy to see that these two beings communicate by the same symbol—a lacquer box, image of a secretive soul—and to witness the positive joy of the young girl as she opens up her new secret, that is, as she "receives from her father the implicit permission to conceal her mystery" (PS 83/86).

These brief notes that punctuate Bachelard's poetics suffice to show in him a presence to another person recognized as a value—a recognition essential to tracing the full image of well-being, and a value not often explicitly analyzed, yet constantly latent in the background. Bachelard seems to have demonstrated that authentic presence places secret demands on us—demands often ignored—and that it may at times be lived otherwise than in an encounter where the other person is physically present. In his preface to Martin Buber's *I and Thou*, Bachelard writes that we live in a "dormant" world and that it is necessary to "awaken" through a genuine encounter with another person or other persons. "What do flowers and trees matter to me, and fire and stone, if I am without love, without a home? One must be two, or—alas!—at least have been two, in order to understand the blue sky, in order to name a dawn."[8]

There are solitudes filled with company—there is an attention of heart and thought more profound than any superficial gaze. The concerns of scientific progress, much as those of a cultural community discovered in the company of poets or artists around human artworks, can unite individuals perhaps more deeply than any long dissertation on the possibility of communication. Bachelard thought so. "Doubtless, a philosopher could be asked to study this communion of souls in more dramatic contexts or fields, by bringing in human or superhuman values which pass as being more important than poetic values. But do the soul's great experiences gain anything by being proclaimed" (PR 15/13–14)?

Bachelard lived this "experience of soul," and that is what removes him from any critique of aestheticism. At the heart of his work there was an "encounter" with Gaston Roupnel, his colleague from the faculty of Dijon, whose intuitions he would unfold, and with whom he shared a "sympathy of goodness." This resumption of a friend's thought in one's own—a thought one must hence live forth—led him to discover a new path and mode of philosophical research (II 65/137–38).

If we wished to characterize an oeuvre that holds all "systems" at bay, we should speak of a philosophy of openness. Bachelard pried open the overly narrow reason of classical philosophy, and this first aperture allowed him another: he opened up and expanded our understanding of imagination, long held as "folly" rather than as "wisdom." In this way, he allowed us to catch a glimpse of a new kind of human being capable of endless re-creation—a human being capable of solidarity and friendship with others, as well as with nature and things. Solitary dreamer that he was, Bachelard received solitude as a valuable gift which he knew how to live and open up, to reveal that well-being (*bonheur*) is possible for whomever knows how to live the instant, and the poetic act, of rebirth. Years after his death, Jean Lescure would poignantly unfold Bachelard's reflection on this matter:

> If the "cruelest mourning is the consciousness of a future betrayed," this initial revelation of suffering, this irruption of the plundering instant is accompanied by the stubborn evidence of time as purveyor of wonder, surprise, and novelty. That which thrusts me into the jaws of death is also that which offers me a chance to be reborn. For never, not for a single moment, are we but the sum of our past. (II 70)[9]

As we reach the end of Bachelard's work—faced with the question that he himself had posed earlier in his career: "Could human destiny be a poetic destiny?" (DD 22/xi)—we see no response other than a positive one that affirms the open-ended possibility for poetic revival, of humanity's incessant regeneration.

Notes

1. Translator's note: Bachelard first stated the possibility of a "philosophy of repose" in *The Dialectics of Duration* (1936) from the perspective of the hypothesis of temporal discontinuity proposed in his *Intuition of the Instant* (1932). His exploration of "repose" would be resumed from a psychoanalytic perspective in *Earth and Reveries of Repose* (1948), from a phenomenological perspective in his two books on *Poetics* (1958, 1960), and from a spiritual or contemplative perspective in *The Flame of a Candle* (1961).

2. Translator's note: Préclaire's updated essay lends itself to be read retrospectively as a critical reengagement with questions raised in recent continental philosophy with regard to Bachelard's notion of "well-being" vis-à-vis Heidegger's notion of "being-in-the-world." See, for instance, Miles Kennedy's *Home: A Concrete Bachelardian Metaphysics* (Oxford: Peter Lang, 2011).

3. Pierre Quillet, *Bachelard* (Paris: Seghers, 1964), 128.

4. Tristan Tzara, *Où boivent les loups* (*Where Foxes Drink*) (Paris: Éditions des Cahiers Libres, 1932), 15.

5. Georges Gusdorf, *La parole* (Paris: Presses Universitaires de France, 1963), 55 (Rizo-Patron's translation).

6. Gaston Roupnel, *Siloë* (Paris: Stock, 1927), 162. The title of Roupnel's novel alludes to the fountain or pool, Siloam, to which Jesus sends the blind man to wash and be healed in the Gospel according to John (9:7).

7. Bachelard here cites Makhali Phal, who designates "meditative repose" as a basic state of the psyche (*Narayana ou celui qui se meut sur les eaux*, Paris, 1942, passim).

8. Bachelard's preface to Buber's *I and Thou*, trans. Edward K. Kaplan (appendix A in this volume).

9. This text from Jean Lescure's "Introduction à la Poétique de Gaston Bachelard" (1966) appears as an appendix in the 1966 and 1992 French editions of *L'Intuition de l'instant* (Paris: Éditions Stock), 146, as well as in the above-cited English translation.

Appendix A

Preface to Martin Buber's *I and Thou*

GASTON BACHELARD

TRANSLATED BY EDWARD K. KAPLAN

You must encounter Martin Buber to understand, at a glance, *the philosophy of encounter*, that synthesis of event and eternity. Then at once you know that convictions are flames, and that sympathy is the direct knowledge of Persons.

Someone exists in the World, unknown to you, then, suddenly, in a single encounter, before knowing him, you recognize him. A dialogue begins in the night, a dialogue which, through a certain tone, completely involves the persons, "Michel, is that you?" And the voice answers, "Jeanne, is that you?" Neither one needs to answer, "Yes, it is I." For if the questioned person were to transcend the questioning, and forego the infinite grace of the encounter, he would then descend into monologue or confession, into *boasting* or *regretting*, into the dull narrative of wishes and woes. He would say what he was, before saying what he is. He would say what he is, before saying what, through the encounter, he has become. The Instant of the human Person would be quite enfeebled, quite weakened, muffled, entirely deprived of the vector of futurity that sympathy just launched.

Martin Buber's entire philosophy of the *person* must reside in this mutual questioning. That philosophy endows the spoken word with a particular tonality composed of trust and astonishment. That philosophy multiplies, as in a thousand-faceted mirror, the delicious and often elusive nuance that plays within the ambiguity of questioning and exclamation. We really feel that we need a sign midway between *?* and *!* We really feel that from *?* to *!* there is room for an entire psychology that would *tonalize* all spoken words, capable of interpreting silences and sounds, *vivaces* and *lentos*—all the resonances and arpeggios of sympathy.

Can a punctuation phantom be so lively? Yes, if it's the sign of an encounter. Can one instant be so rich, so vivid? Yes, if it's the origin of a friendship, the motivating force of a Person.

Now, the time of persons is infinitely rare and empty, when compared with the time of things. We live asleep in a sleeping World. But when a *thou* murmurs in our ear it becomes a jolt that launches persons: the *I* awakens through the grace of the *thou*. The spiritual potency of two simultaneous consciousnesses, united in the awareness of their encounter, quickly escapes the viscous and continuous causality of things. The encounter creates us: we were nothing—or nothing but things—before being united.

Therefore, the correct structure of Buberism is the realm of vectors, and not the realm of *points* and *centers*. The *I* and *thou* are not separable poles. Formerly, we tried to isolate the magnetism of north and south by smashing magnets. We expected to find two different principles of attraction. But at every break, however sudden or hypocritical the shock, in each broken piece we found the two inseparable poles. Similarly, an introspective method might attempt, through solitude, to shatter some social bonds, imagining that by accepting betrayals with irony or with courage, some day we could see our true selves, face to face with ourselves. It is a useless hope: a broken bond is almost always an idealized bond. As Fichte said, a person is human only among human beings. Loving our neighbor is our intimate destiny. And if certain souls find life in solitary contemplation, it is because they have experienced a greater encounter, that they are the pole of a greater attraction . . .

It is not, then, with the centers *I* and *thou* that we must establish an ontological science of the human being. But, since the human being is relative to what is human, it is rather in the linking of the I-thou, on the I-thou axis itself, that we discover the true attributes of humankind. Therein is a type of reciprocal ontology that transcends the substantiality of the self, one which considers the *thou*, in some way, to be the closest, the most fundamental attribute of the *I*. I am a substance if I am a person. I am a person if I am linked to a person. Detaching myself from my brother, I destroy myself. Losing concern for my brother, I abandon God. Martin Buber's book is thus the basic index of personalism. It makes us grasp being, etymologically, in its fundamental religion.

Thus apprehended in its metapsychological genesis, meditation on the *thou* should cast a vivid light on psychology and ethics.

From the book's beginning, at the very level of language, Martin Buber shows us the two sources of spoken words which are, of course, the two sources of thought: things on the one hand, persons on the other, the *it* and the *thou*. But the thousands of murmuring springs, which flow to us from things, are but tributaries of the central spring, which comes to us from the *thou*. And we will appreciate the importance of Buber's philosophy if we study systematically the nomination of objects through the communion of two subjects. The *it* of the third person can only emerge after the *I* and the *thou* of the first two.

What do flowers and trees matter to me, and fire and stones, if I am without love and without a home! We must be two—or at least, alas! we must have been two—in order to understand the blue sky, to name a sunrise! Infinite things such as sky, forest, and light find their names only in a loving heart. And the breeze of plains, its gentleness and its palpitation, is first of all the echo of a tender sigh. Thus the human soul, enriched by a chosen love, animates great things before little ones. It says "thou" to the universe right after feeling the human exaltation of the *thou*.

And then, in the new light of a young home, things become little, they become familiar and close; suddenly they are part the family. Not so much the family of former times, which crushed the child's spirit under the weight of the *it* of *common* teachings, uniquely and passively common, but rather the chosen family, divinely *encountered* on the path of destiny. The *thou* then gives things another name, and even when it gives them the common name, the old name, an unknown resonance emerges to torment and to renew the syllables: "Michel, is that your pen holder?"—"Jeanne, is that your mirror?"

A *participation* of the person imparts to things such obvious poetic values that the entirety of language is magnified by it. In our time when everything is becoming depersonalized, when the worker no longer signs his work, when humankind, fascinated by cinematographic images, no longer *creates* the human face, no longer invents its own expression, how strangely and how gravely do these Buberian verses resound, so faithfully translated by Miss Bianquis!

Human interests should thus be attached to all objects so that those objects can recover their primal function and words their fullest meaning. The ethical lesson does not differ greatly from the essential psychological one. Our spiritual dispersion into the realm of the *it*, to the detriment of the realm of the *thou*, has gradually invaded the domain of social relations, and has irresistibly made us regard people as means to an end. No matter how high one values *utility*, it remains an egotistical theme that must eventually deform souls. In other words, when we want to live only in the presence of things, evaluating them by the benefits they give us, even if those benefits are as spiritually elevated as aesthetic joys, a hint of egotism removes freshness from colors and replaces the fluffiness of things with varnish.

Egotism and romanticism suffer from the same monologues. We strive in vain to enter the center of things, to capture the mood of a landscape. That animism will lack a confirmation, which only the companionship of a *thou* can impart. And here comes the most precious Buberian category: reciprocity. Such reciprocity is never clearly found on the axis of *I-it*. It truly appears only on the axis where the *I-thou* oscillates and vibrates. Then, indeed, the person encountered cares about me as I care about him; he hopes in me as I hope in him. I create him as a person at the very time that he creates me as a person. As Martin Buber often said, only in dialogue does existence reveal itself as having "another side." The noumenon, which gets lost in the vagueness of an open-ended meditation with regard to things, is suddenly enriched as it is grasped and understood by another mind. The clearest noumenon is thus the meditation of one mind by another mind, for the two souls, in a common glance, are closer, more convergent than the pupils of their eyes!

It is perhaps in his little book *Zwiesprache* (*Dialogue*), which appeared in 1932, nine years after *Ich und Du* (*I and Thou*), that Buber differentiates most clearly the life of monologue from the life of dialogue. A monologue can be long and eloquent, but it expresses less soul than the most naïve dialogue. No matter how stifled the dialogue, how badly stammered, it bears the double mark of the given and the received, or at the very least, as a prelude, the double tonality of the aspiration and inspiration of souls. The ear then becomes *active*, since lending an ear is wanting to respond.

Receiving is readying oneself to give. How can we hear without expressing! How can we express without hearing! Once again, our spiritual substance is within us only if it can go out from us. It cannot go out from us, vaguely, as a scent or a radiance. It must be offered to someone, it must speak to a *thou*. As Martin Buber says, "the most sublime thought is without substance if it is not articulated." And just as we must say *thou* in order to say *we*, so "human community can be built only if individual relations are possible." Eye for eye, breath for breath, soul for soul. I see you and understand you; therefore, we are souls.

Last, the thinking described in *I and Thou* was again supplemented in the book *The Question to the Single One*, begun in 1932, but not published until 1936. It is a treatise on responsibility. The Kierkegaardian category of the "Single One" is probably necessary, but it judges human destiny too

quickly and puts him into a procession. Martin Buber considers to be a false simplification Kierkegaard's principle that the "Single One" has no essential relationship other than his relationship with God. We do not reach God by avoiding the World. Through us, we should offer to God, extend actively to God, the entire Universe.

We are thus responsible for more than ourselves; we are responsible for our neighbor. To say with Kierkegaard that the crowd is corruption is to shirk the duty of substituting what ought to be for what is. It is probably true that the crowd is "the most difficult substance of truth to manage," but it is necessary to "unscramble the mess." "The public thing, the most resistant thing above all, is the essential test of the Single One." We can thus appreciate the immense effort of Buberian thought that attempts, by every means—in books nourished by the most diverse studies, formed by the exegesis of Jewish texts and through meditation on the most recent philosophies—to unite the individual to the universal, the instant to eternity, the encounter to the family, the unique fact to the inviolable Law.

Appendix B

Testimony on Gaston Bachelard[1]

Georges Gusdorf
Translated by Eileen Rizo-Patron

In the following passage, Georges Gusdorf (1912–2000) writes about his return to Paris, and to the Sorbonne, after his captivity in Germany during World War II. Georges Gusdorf had come from a German-Jewish family rooted in Bordeaux. He became a student of Gaston Bachelard, who had also studied at the Sorbonne in earlier days under Léon Brunschvicg.

My return to earth was relatively smooth. As if from one monastery to another, I was transferred from a prisoner's camp to the convent of La Rue d'Ulm. My prescient and generous professor Célestin Bouglé had reserved a small room for me, before he died, on the first floor of a lodge facing a garden, where Louis Althusser (whom I had helped prepare for his *agrégation*) would later in turn reside. I had been given three years to write my dissertation. In the backpack I received as a liberated captive, I carried the fruits of my studious leisure: a large volume on the vicissitudes of self-knowledge, and a shorter study, which could be described as a paschal meditation on sacrifice. Writings to strengthen my spiritual life and allay the boredom of my last few months in captivity—not at all related to the academic standards of my career's technical disciplines, to be sure. From the edge of a table—amid the smoke, the brouhaha, and the agitation of twenty prisoners per room—I had tried to weave out the thread of my thoughts, relying on the camp's meager bibliographical resources.

The first question was if these writings, pilfered from Germany, might pass for a doctoral thesis. But that was not for me to decide; I needed a thesis director. The generation of my professors had all vanished: Brunschvicg was no longer there; and I didn't know anyone else besides Merleau-Ponty, who in 1945 was not teaching at the Sorbonne. I proceeded by elimination, resolving to place my academic destiny in the hands of Gaston Bachelard, whom I had never met before. My choice was based on his openness of spirit, his intellectual generosity, as well as on the picturesque character of a personality exempt from the mental constipation and latent jealousies that often betray deep inferiority feelings among university professors. My own writings did not fall anywhere near Bachelard's field of expertise, and that was an additional reason for my reliance on the open-mindedness and genius that suffused his presence. My faith in him was never disappointed.

Bachelard, unlike Brunschvicg, was not a great bourgeois liberal. There was something plain and down-to-earth about him that irresistibly transported one back to his native Burgundy. His good humor was coupled with intuitive insight and excellent judgment. One could sense his keen interest in people and things, by virtue of a vital sympathy that was constantly on the alert. His intellectual career as an autodidact developed on the basis of his study of the exact sciences, undertaken early on, during the leisure hours of his modest profession as a traveling postman—if I'm not mistaken. But his scientific rationalism, unlike that of Brunschvicg, refrained from such triumphalism, which, betting on the future, presumes to know more than the scientists do themselves. With peasant shrewdness, Bachelard was content to track the progress of physicists, chemists, and mathematicians, endeavoring to explain the philosophical implications of their work and discoveries. His was a militant epistemology that insisted on following the advances of science without presuming to overtake or surpass it, adopting rather an attentive attitude whereby his rationalism was ever-poised to multiply itself, always attuning its theories to the creative spontaneity of spirit. . . .

Much like the giant Antaeus,[2] who would regain his strength by touching the feet of Mother Earth, Gaston Bachelard gave himself the task of maintaining, amid the progress of scientific genius, the ontological ballast of the roots of thought within the subconscious depths of the imaginary, within the primary substance of human life where dream-visions are sown. Party to ensuring the success of analytical rationalism, he celebrated the irreducibility of the poetic in human beings with joy. He relished poetry much as one relishes good wine and pursued his dual career path as a thinker, in all good conscience. When I asked him how the junction worked between his initial epistemological studies and his newly discovered poetic epistemology, he responded with good humor and a smile: "That's a problem for you, not for me. It is up to you to find the solution, if there is one. As for me, I am happy to follow the various slopes of my inquisitive spirit. I am keenly interested in mathematics; and I love poetry. Respect my liberty."

Notes

1. Drawn from "Rétractation 1983," a text added by Georges Gusdorf to his earlier *Mythe et métaphysique: Introduction à la philosophie* (Paris: Flammarion, 1953), 304–6 now available in the public domain: http://classiques.uqac.ca/contemporains/gusdorf_georges/mythe_et_metaphysique/mythe_et_metaphysique.pdf.

2. The French version of this testimony, as printed in *L'Association des amis de Gaston Bachelard bulletin* no. 9 (2007), cites Atlas in this passage. In this case, however, the correct mythological figure is Antaeus. In Greek mythology, Antaeus gained his strength by remaining in contact with the earth, but lost it as soon that contact was denied.

Bibliography

NOTE: This bibliography of Bachelard's works has been arranged chronologically, by date of original French publication, followed by publication data of existing English translations. As noted in the abbreviations list, Bachelard's works are cited throughout this volume in their English translations where possible, using English-title acronyms. Critical studies on Bachelard's works, as well as primary texts by other philosophers and authors cited in this volume are found in the notes following each chapter.

Works by Gaston Bachelard: Primary Sources

[1928] *Essai sur la connaissance approchée* [*Essay on Knowledge by Approximation*]. Paris: Vrin.

[1928] *Étude sur l'évolution d'un problème de physique: la propagation thermique dans les solides* [*A Study on the Evolution of a Physics Problem: Heat Transfer in Solids*]. Paris: Vrin.

[1929] *La Valeur inductive de la relativité* [*The Inductive Value of Relativity*]. Paris: Vrin.

[1932] *Le Pluralisme cohérent de la chimie moderne* [*Coherent Pluralism of Modern Chemistry*]. Paris: Vrin.

[1932] *L'Intuition de l'instant: Essai sur la Siloë de Gaston Roupnel.* Paris: Stock. *Intuition of the Instant.* Translated by Eileen Rizo-Patron. Evanston: Northwestern University Press, 2013.

[1933] *Les Intuitions atomistiques* [*Atomistic Intuitions*]. Paris: Boivin.

[1934] *Le Nouvel esprit scientifique.* Paris: Presses Universitaires de France. *The New Scientific Spirit.* Translated by Arthur Goldhammer, with a foreword by Patrick A. Heelan. Boston: Beacon, 1984.

[1936] *La Dialectique de la durée.* Paris: Boivin. *The Dialectic of Duration.* Translated by Mary McAllester Jones. Manchester, UK: Clinamen Press, 2000. Revised edition published by Rowman & Littlefield International, Ltd. (Maryland, USA, 2016).

[1937] *L'Éxperience de l'espace dans la physique contemporaine* [*The Experience of Space in Contemporary Physics*]. Paris: Alcan.

[1938] *La Formation de l'esprit scientifique*. Paris: Vrin. [Edition used: 1999]. *The Formation of the Scientific Mind*. Translated by Mary McAllester Jones. Manchester, UK: Clinamen, 2002.

[1938] *La Psychanalyse du feu*. Paris: Gallimard. *The Psychoanalysis of Fire*. Translated by Alan C. M. Ross. Boston: Beacon, 1964.

[1938] Préface à Martin Buber, *Je et Tu*. Translated from German by Geneviève Bianquis. Paris: Aubier Montaigne, 1938 (7–15). Preface to Martin Buber's *I and Thou*. Translated by Edward K. Kaplan. In *International Studies in Philosophy* 35, no. 1 (2003): 89–94, and as appendix A in *Adventures in Phenomenology: Gaston Bachelard*. Albany: State University of New York Press, 2017.

[1939] *Lautréamont*. Paris: José Corti. *Lautréamont*. Translated by Robert Scott Duprée. Dallas: Dallas Institute of Humanities and Culture, 1984.

[1940] *La Philosophie du non*. Paris: Presses Universitaires de France. *The Philosophy of No*. Translated by G. C. Waterston. New York: Orion, 1968.

[1942] *L'Eau et les rêves*. Paris: José Corti. *Water and Dreams*. Translated by Edith Farrell. Dallas: Pegasus Foundation, 1983.

[1943] *L'Air et les songes*. Paris: José Corti. *Air and Dreams*. Translated by Edith Farrell and Frederick Farrell. Dallas: Dallas Institute Publications, 1988.

[1947] *La Terre et les rêveries de la volonté*. Paris: José Corti. *Earth and Reveries of Will*. Translated by Kenneth Haltman. Dallas: Dallas Institute Publications, 2002.

[1948] *La Terre et les rêveries du repos*. Paris: José Corti. *Earth and Reveries of Repose*. Translated by Mary McAllester Jones. Dallas: Dallas Institute Publications, 2011.

[1949] *Le Rationalisme appliqué* [*Applied Rationalism*]. Paris: Presses Universitaires de France.

[1951] *L'Activité rationaliste de la physique contemporaine* [*Rationalist Activity of Contemporary Physics*]. Paris: Presses Universitaires de France.

[1953] *Le Matérialisme rationnel* [*Rational Materialism*]. Paris: Presses Universitaires de France.

[1957] *La Poétique de l'espace*. Paris: Presses Universitaires de France. *The Poetics of Space*. Translated by Maria Jolas. Boston: Beacon, 1964. Reissued by Penguin Books (New York, 2014) with a Foreword by Mark Danielewski and a new Introduction by Richard Kearney.

[1960] *La Poétique de la rêverie*. Paris: Presses Universitaires de France. *The Poetics of Reverie*. Translated by Daniel Russell. Boston: Beacon, 1969.

[1961] *La Flamme d'une chandelle*. Paris: Presses Universitaires de France. *The Flame of a Candle*. Translated by Joni Caldwell. Dallas: Dallas Institute Publications, 1988.

[1970] *Études* [*Studies*]. Collection of articles, edited by Georges Canguilhem. Paris: Vrin. "Noumenon and Microphysics." Translated from *Études* (11–24) by Bernard Roy, in *Philosophical Forum* 37 (2006): 75–84.

[1970] *Le Droit de Rêver*. Collection of articles. Paris: Presses Universitaires de France. *The Right to Dream*. Translated by J. A. Underwood. Dallas: Dallas Institute Publications, 1988.

[1972] *L'Engagement rationaliste* [*Rationalist Commitment*]. Collection of articles. Preface by Georges Canguilhem. Paris: Presses Universitaires de France.

[1988] *Fragments d'une poétique du feu*. Edited by Suzanne Bachelard. Paris: Presses Universitaires de France. *Fragments of a Poetics of Fire*. Translated by Kenneth Haltman. Dallas: Dallas Institute Publications, 1990.

Critical Studies on Bachelard: Secondary Sources

See our introduction to this volume for an account of Bachelard critical studies in English to date. We refer readers to Roch C. Smith's excellent annotated bibliography of secondary sources on Bachelard's work in both French and English, in his comprehensive study of Bachelard's work, *Gaston Bachelard: Philosopher of Science and Imagination* (Albany: State University of New York Press, 2016).

Contributors

Edward S. Casey (PhD, Northwestern University) is the author of a number of books, among them: *Imagining: A Phenomenological Study; The Fate of Place; The World at a Glance;* and (forthcoming) *The World on Edge.* He is a recent president of the American Philosophical Association (Eastern division) and is currently distinguished professor at SUNY Stony Brook. His dissertation at Northwestern University was titled "Poetry and Ontology in Heidegger and Bachelard." He has written several essays on Bachelard and teaches the French philosopher's work regularly in his graduate courses.

Edward K. Kaplan (PhD, Columbia University) is Kaiserman Professor in the Humanities Emeritus, Brandeis University, where he has taught courses on French, comparative literature and religious studies since 1978. He has a special interest in the relationship of esthetic, ethical, and religious experience. Kaplan's foundational article on Bachelard appeared in *Philosophy and Phenomenological Research* in 1973; he has also published comparative studies of Bachelard and Martin Buber, Bachelard and Baudelaire.

Richard Kearney (PhD, University of Paris X) holds the Charles B. Seelig Chair of Philosophy at Boston College and has served as a visiting professor at University College Dublin, the University of Paris (Sorbonne), the Australian Catholic University, and the University of Nice. He has written more than twenty books on European philosophy and literature (including two novels and a volume of poetry) and has edited or co-edited fifteen more. He is the author of a noteworthy chapter on Gaston Bachelard in his *Poetics of Imagining: Modern to Post-Modern* (Fordham, 1998) and of a new introduction to the Penguin Classics edition of Bachelard's *The Poetics of Space* (2014).

Glen A. Mazis (PhD, SUNY Binghamton) is professor of philosophy and humanities at Penn State Harrisburg. He specializes in phenomenology, current continental philosophy, and philosophy of art. Mazis has published widely in journals and anthologies about Merleau-Ponty, Heidegger, Sartre, interpersonal perception, embodiment, emptiness, gender issues, and poetics. His four books focus on embodiment, emotion, masculinity, and the relationships among humans, animals, and machines. He is also a poet with more than seventy poems published in literary journals. He is a member of the board of directors of the Merleau-Ponty Circle and of the journal *Environment, Space, Place.*

Mary McAllester Jones (PhD, University of Reading, England) is a renowned lecturer who has published widely on Gaston Bachelard, while serving as Senior Lecturer in French Studies, University of Strathclyde, Glasgow, UK. McAllester Jones is the author of *Gaston Bachelard, Subversive Humanist: Texts and Readings* (Madison: University of Wisconsin Press, 1991) and editor of *The Philosophy and Poetics of Gaston Bachelard* (Washington, DC: University Press of America, 1989), a collection of critical essays to which she also contributed two chapters. She has translated several of Bachelard's major texts: *The Dialectic of Duration* (Manchester: Clinamen, 2000), *The Formation of the Scientific Mind. A Contribution to a Psychoanalysis of Objective Knowledge* (Manchester: Clinamen, 2002), and *Earth and Reveries of Repose: An Essay on Images of Interiority* (Dallas: Dallas Institute of Humanities and Culture, 2011). She also translated one chapter from Bachelard's *L'Intuition de l'instant* for Robin Durie's edited collection on *Time and the Instant. Essays in the Physics and Philosophy of Time* (Manchester: Clinamen, 2000).

David L. Miller (PhD in theology and culture, Drew University) is Watson Ledden Professor Emeritus at Syracuse University. For many years, he was also a faculty member at Pacifica Graduate Institute in both the clinical psychology and mythological studies programs. He is an honorary member of the Inter-Regional Society of Jungian Analysts, the International Association of Analytical Psychology, and the International Society for Psychology as the Discipline of Interiority. Dr. Miller was a member of the Eranos Circle in Switzerland from 1975 until 1988, and he lectured at the Eranos Conferences on nine occasions during that period. He has written six books and more than one hundred articles since 1963. For more information see his website at: https://dlmiller.mysite.syr.edu/.

Jean-François Perraudin studied fine arts before specializing in philosophy at the Sorbonne (1964–1968), where he became acquainted with Bachelard's close friend and disciple Jean Lescure. His graduate thesis was entitled *Le Non-Bergsonisme dans la philosophie de l'imaginaire de Gaston Bachelard.* For decades he taught philosophy at the Lycée Carnot, Dijon, France. Perraudin has published several articles on Bachelard, most notably: "Les Thérapies de Bachelard" (in *Cahier Bachelard* No. 1, Éditions Universitaires de Dijon, 1999), and "Lire Bachelard avec Jean Lescure" (in *Bulletin of the Association des Amis de Gaston Bachelard*, No. 8, 2006). He has also published poetry in several French journals, such as *Strophes, Éditions de L'Grycte, Noah,* and *La Bartavelle.*

Madeleine Préclaire (PhD, University of Montréal) is professor emeritus of philosophy at the Collège Jean de Brébeuf, Montréal, Canada. She had formerly taught philosophy at Lille, Toulouse, and Valenciennes (France). Before her retirement and return to France, she also taught courses at the Theology Department of the University of Montréal. Préclaire is the author of *Une Poétique de l'homme: Essai sur l'imagination d'après l'oeuvre de Gaston Bachelard* (Montréal: Desclée Éditeurs, 1971).

Eileen Rizo-Patron (PhD in comparative literature, SUNY Binghamton) is a research associate and translator at the Center for Philosophy, Interpretation, and Culture, Binghamton University. She translated Gaston Bachelard's *Intuition of the Instant* (Northwestern University Press, 2013). She has also authored articles on Bachelard's philosophy for the journals *Religion and the Arts, Philosophy Today,* and *Continental Philosophy Review.* She is co-editor (with Richard Kearney) of *Traversing the Heart: Journeys of the Interreligious Imagination* (Brill, 2010) and of a three-volume series on José Maria Arguedas, *La Dinámica de los Encuentros Culturales* (Lima: Fondo Editorial PUCP, 2013). Her interests focus on the ethical intersections between hermeneutics and poetics.

Kristupas Sabolius is associate professor of philosophy, Vilnius University, Lithuania, and a Fulbright Scholar alumnus at SUNY Stony Brook. He is the author of *Proteus and the Radical Imaginary* (2015, Bunkier Sztuki, in Polish and English), *The Imaginary* (2013, Vilnius University Press, in Lithuanian), and *Furious Sleep: Imagination and Phenomenology* (2012, Vilnius University Press, in Lithuanian), as well as numerous essays, signalizing the contradictory function of imagination, appearing in all the major theories of Western thought. He is also an active public intellectual and a writer of novels and plays, including *The Gambler*, Lithuania's nomination for the foreign-language category at the 2015 Oscars.

Roch C. Smith (PhD, Emory University) is professor emeritus of French studies at the University of North Carolina, Greensboro, where he served as associate vice chancellor for academic affairs, associate dean of the College of Arts and Sciences, and head of the Department of Romance Languages. He is the author of five books and numerous essays on Gaston Bachelard, Alain Robbe-Grillet's novels, Robbe-Grillet's films, André Malraux, Samuel Beckett, and others. His work has appeared in English, French, and Turkish. His latest book, *Gaston Bachelard, Philosopher of Science and Imagination*, revised and updated, was published by SUNY Press in 2016.

Samuel Talcott (PhD, DePaul University) is associate professor of philosophy at the University of the Sciences in Philadelphia. His research focuses on twentieth-century French philosophy, concerning which he has published on historical epistemology and its place in Michel Foucault's writings. He has wide-ranging interests in ethical and political questions, especially as they emerge now from the intersecting histories of the arts and sciences in modern societies. He is now working on a book that critically elucidates the major works of Georges Canguilhem and Foucault by reading them against each other and in light of the problem of error.

Anton Vydra earned his PhD at Trnava University, Slovakia, where he taught for several years in the faculty of philosophy. He is currently a senior scientific fellow at the Institute of Philosophy, Slovak Academy of Sciences in Bratislava. He specializes in phenomenology, aesthetics, and French philosophy of science (Bachelard and Canguilhem). In 2015 he translated Georges Canguilhem's work *Ideology and Rationality in the History of the Life Sciences* into the Slovak language. He is also the author of four books in Slovak (titles here translated into English): *Gaston Bachelard and the Philosophy of the Gaze* (Filozofická fakulta TU 2012); *Day-dreaming: A Commentary to Bachelard's* The Flame of a Candle (Filozofická fakulta TU, 2012); *Academic Writing: How a Philosophical Text Arises* (Filozofická fakulta TU 2010); *On Creativity and Immortality* (Schola Philosophica, 2007).

Jason M. Wirth (PhD, SUNY Binghamton) is professor of philosophy at Seattle University. Some of his recent books include a monograph on Milan Kundera (*Commiserating with Devastated Things*, Fordham, 2015), *Schelling's Practice of the Wild* (SUNY, 2015), the co-edited volume (with Bret Davis and Brian Schroeder), *Japanese and Continental Philosophy: Conversations with the Kyoto School* (Indiana, 2011), and *The Barbarian Principle: Merleau-Ponty, Schelling, and the Question of Nature* (SUNY, 2013). He is the associate editor and book review editor of the journal *Comparative and Continental Philosophy* (and its attendant book series, published by Northwestern University Press). He is a co-director of three philosophical societies: the Comparative and Continental Philosophy Circle (CCPC), the Pacific Association for the Continental Tradition (PACT), and the North American Schelling Society (NASS).

Name Index

Subject Index